FORGIVENESS AND RECONCILIATION

FORGIVENESS
AND RECONCILIATION

Religion, Public Policy,
& Conflict Transformation

Edited by
Raymond G. Helmick, S.J.,
& Rodney L. Petersen

TEMPLETON FOUNDATION PRESS
PHILADELPHIA & LONDON

Templeton Foundation Press
Five Radnor Corporate Center, Suite 120
100 Matsonford Road
Radnor, Pennsylvania 19087

Library of Congress Cataloging-in-Publication Data

Forgiveness and reconciliation : religion, public policy, and conflict transformation / edited by Raymond G. Helmick and Rodney L. Petersen.
    p. cm.
  Includes bibliographical references and index.
  ISBN 1-890151-49-1 (cloth : alk. paper)
    1.Forgiveness. 2. Forgiveness—Religious aspects.
    3. Reconciliation—Religious aspects.
  I. Helmick, Raymond G. II. Petersen, Rodney Lawrence.

 BJ1476 .F67 2001
 291.2'2—dc21   2001027132
   234.5
Printed in the United States of America

01 02 03 04 05 06   10 9 8 7 6 5 4 3 2 1

Contents

PART IV. *Seeking Forgiveness after Tragedy*

Foreword

Archbishop Desmond M. Tutu

IT PLEASES ME to open this symposium, offered by the Sir John Templeton Foundation, for which I have so much fondness, on Forgiveness and Reconciliation.

People have tended to think of forgiveness as something nebulous, something esoteric, something that was all right for people so inclined, but that tended to happen only between individuals and had really no significance for the body politic.

It's turning out to be different.

We've also been told that, on the whole, the kind of people who would ask for forgiveness would probably be sissies: weak, not amounting to a great deal.

You notice these days that forgiveness, confession, and so on are coming into their own. We've heard the president of the United States publicly confessing to faults and asking for forgiveness. The prime minister of Israel and the German chancellor have gone together to a concentration camp and carried out a kind of ritual of confession and forgiveness. Perceptions are changing. People are beginning to think of forgiveness and reconciliation as spiritual values that have more significance than they had previously recognized for life as it is lived.

We tend to believe that we live in a cynical, hard world, a world that pooh-poohs spiritual values. I said how we thought that it was sissies, the weak ones, who asked for forgiveness. Let me give you a counter example.

In South Africa we had a bit of trouble in the Truth and Reconciliation Commission. Someone accused one of the commissioners of being implicated in a criminal activity. President Mandela, after the commission had tried very hard to deal with the matter internally, appointed a special commission under Judge Richard Goldstone, who had been the prosecutor in a tribunal relating to Bosnia and Kosovo.

Judge Goldstone, aware of its importance for the commission, acted very quickly to deal with the matter. He produced his report, which he handed over to our President Mandela. And the president, being the kind of person he is, knew that the commissioner who had been accused must have been on tenterhooks and very anxious. And so the president got in touch with him to say that in fact the commission had exonerated him.

I then got in touch with the president's secretary and I said, "Do you know what? Tell the president that I'm upset. I am the chairperson of this commission. And if there was anybody who had to be told first what the Goldstone Commission had said, then it was I. Tell him I think he botched on etiquette." Just a few minutes later, Nelson Mandela was on the telephone. And he said, "Mpilo, you're quite right. I'm sorry."

That was exceedingly humbling that he, the head of state and someone who is a colossus, should actually get on the phone so very quickly and apologize to trifling little me. It was a deeply moving thing but I think it demonstrates how it is, that the bigger you are, the easier it gets for you to acknowledge when you have made a mistake.

It isn't the easiest thing to do. People get upset about the fact that someone like P. W. Botha, or whoever, has not apologized. You say to them: "You know, some of the most difficult words I know in any language are 'I'm sorry.'" We find it difficult to say them even in the intimacy of our own bedrooms, as between spouses. You can imagine what it must mean for someone to do so in the full glare of publicity.

I really want just to say to you that I have gone through the crucible of the Truth and Reconciliation Commission and have been devastated by the extent of the evil revealed in that process. As when somebody can say:

"They undressed me. They opened a drawer. And they shoved my breast into the drawer, and they slammed it several times on my nipple, until a white stuff oozed." Or: "We abducted him. We gave him drugged coffee, and we shot him in the head. And we burned his body. And as his body was burning, because it takes so long for a human body to burn, we had a barbecue on the side. Turning two kinds of flesh—cow flesh on one side and human flesh on the other."

I have looked into the abyss of human evil and seen the depth to which we can in fact plumb. But paradoxically one comes away from it exhilarated by the revelation of the goodness of people. You encounter people who, having suffered grievously, should by right have been riddled with bitterness and a lust for revenge and retribution. But they are different.

One of our liberation movements attacked a golf course, and several people were killed, white people. One woman was so badly injured that she had to have open-heart surgery. She returned home and because of her injuries her children had to bathe her, clothe her, feed her. She said to us, "You know, I can't walk through the security checkpoint at the airport because I think there's shrapnel in me, and if I were to walk through, all kinds of bells and alarms would go off."

She came to the commission and she said, "This experience, that has left me in this condition, has enriched my life." Enriched my life! And then she said, "I'd like to meet the perpetrator. I'd like to meet the guy who threw the hand grenade! I'd like to meet him in the spirit of forgiveness, which is wonderful! I'd like to forgive him." But what was mind-boggling was when she added, "I hope he forgives me."

And we went on to have a hearing on something called the Bisho Massacre, when the ANC marched on Bisho, which used to be the capital of one of the homelands. The homeland army had opened fire and killed several people. We wanted to find out what had happened and generally what was afoot at the time.

The hall in which we held the hearing was packed to the rafters with people either injured on that occasion or people who had lost loved ones. The first witness was the head of the Ciskeian Defense Force. It probably wasn't *what* he said so much as *how* he said whatever it was that he said, but the tension in the room rose. I mean it was tangible. You could feel the anger of the people just multiplying. And then we had the next batch of witnesses, four officers, one white and three black.

They came onto the stage, and the white guy became their spokesperson. And he said, "Yes, we gave the orders for the soldiers to open fire." Ho! It was combustible! And then he turned to the audience, this angry audience, seething, and he said, "Please, forgive us. Please accept my colleagues back into the community."

And do you know what that audience, that angry audience, did? It broke out into deafening applause. And afterwards I said, "Please let us keep quiet because we are in the presence of something holy."

We have been incredibly privileged to have been part of a process of seeking to heal a traumatized people. Many times I have said, "Really, the only appropriate response is for us to take off our shoes, because we are standing on holy ground."

And so one comes away from the experience of some of the most gruesome evil, exhilarated at the fact that people can be so good, that people can be filled with such magnanimity, that people can have certain incredible gifts of generosity.

And so, my friends, I thought that after all this I was retiring. And yes, maybe I am retired actually. But I believe that one of our vocations now is to remind people: "Hey! You are made for goodness. You are made for the transcendent. You are those who soar, you are made to reach out to the stars. The sky's the limit!"

Now you may think that, oh, he's just waxing crazy, as we've always thought Tutu to be crazy. But have you noticed something about us?

Who are the people the world thrills about? It's not the militarily powerful. It's not even the most successful economically, though the world goes gaga about a Mother Teresa. Ah, yes!

She was about that size that you could put her in your back pocket and no one would miss her. She wasn't particularly successful, was she? She went around trying to make people be concerned about poverty. She wanted to serve the derelict in Calcutta and elsewhere. And you can't speak of success. I mean, she would have a very tough time remaining in a class that asked, "How about the success of things you have done?"

And yet the world says, "Isn't it wonderful to be alive when there was a Mother Teresa!" Think of the world saying that, this cynical world, this hard world.

You remember Tiananmen Square. There was a minute little student, with a little paper bag, standing in front of a tank and making the tank veer. And then as it changed direction he went and stood in front of it again. Didn't our hearts thrill to know that there are forces that are more potent than the military?

Nelson Mandela isn't exactly the greatest orator in the world. (That's between you and me. Don't let us tell him!) And yet the world is almost about to turn him into an idol. The world worships him. No, let's not use extravagant words. The world admires him. Why? The world admires him because the world says, "This is what we think we ought to be, to be those who embody forgiveness, reconciliation, who embody goodness."

And so friends, God bless you. For you know, God is actually saying, "Yah! I've got into a lot of trouble creating this lot. Sometimes I ask myself actually why I ever did get myself into this." But then God looks at you, and God says, "Aren't they neat? Aren't they something? They justify the risk I took."

We are made for goodness. We are made for love. We are made for friendliness. We are made for togetherness. We are made for all of the beautiful things that you and I know.

We are made to tell the world that there are no outsiders. All, all are welcome: black, white, red, yellow, rich, poor, educated, not educated, male, female, gay, straight, all, all, all. We are meant all, all to belong to this family, this human family, God's family.

Acknowledgments

THIS BOOK GREW out of a conference of public policymakers and theologians who came together in October 1999 for a symposium entitled, "Forgiveness and Reconciliation: Religious Contributions to Conflict Resolution," at the John F. Kennedy School of Government, Harvard University, and sponsored chiefly by the John Templeton Foundation. It is part of the ongoing Campaign for Forgiveness Research stimulated and made possible by the Templeton Foundation.

Many people helped bring this book to completion. Our thanks must go first of all to Sir John Templeton, who generously supported this initiative with funding through the Foundation. John M. Templeton Jr. and Charles L. Harper Jr. proposed the symposium and invited the Boston Theological Institute to lend its name and assistance. Special thanks also goes to the John F. Kennedy School of Government for hosting the symposium.

We also want to thank Thomas J. Massaro, S.J., Weston Jesuit School of Theology, who chaired the first session of the symposium on "The Theology of Forgiveness in Christianity." Professor Massaro is himself an authority on Roman Catholic efforts to promote social justice. Penetrating questions were addressed to the panel and audience by Professor Orlando Patterson, Department of Sociology, Harvard University, whose own recent publication on the consequences of slavery is shaping moral conscience and public policy. Thanks also go to Judith Lewis Herman, MD, of the Harvard Medical School, who chaired the session on "The Role of Religion in Conflict Resolution—Theoretical Issues." She has been a good critic of what some have called the "forgiveness bypass," or failure to deal fully with issues of justice in settings of abuse. Thanks also to discussant Brian Mandell of the John F. Kennedy School of Government for his perceptive comments and questions. Sara Cobb, director of the Program on Negotiation at Harvard Law School, chaired the session on "Interrelationships between Forgiveness and Reconciliation." Questions were posed and analysis offered in this section by discussant Keith G. Allred, also of the John F. Kennedy School of Government. Finally, Monica Toft of the Kennedy School chaired the session entitled, "Applications of Forgiveness to Transitional Societies." Here questions were posed and analysis offered by discussant Pumla Gobodo-Madikizela, Visiting Fellow, Carr Center of Human Rights Policy at the Kennedy School and by B. Stephen Toben, the Hewlett Foundation.

As coeditors, we are grateful to many others who helped make this book possible. Marian Gh. Simion worked tirelessly to prepare the appendix for this volume. His assistance, from an Orthodox perspective on elements pertaining to other aspects of programming related to this work, has been extremely helpful and insightful. Thanks should go to Laura Barrett, managing editor at Templeton Foundation Press, for assistance in developing and editing the chapters of this book. We also wish to acknowledge the tireless work of Pamela M. Bond, special deputy to Charles L. Harper Jr., executive director and senior vice-president of the John Templeton Foundation. Finally, we wish to thank our respective institutions for the support offered in pursuing the work of reconciliation. It is our common hope that those being trained as future leaders for our churches, other faith communities, and the various nonprofit and volunteer agencies frequently served by seminaries, schools of theology, and divinity schools today will learn to model forgiveness and do the work of reconciliation in our communities and world.

Introduction

Raymond Helmick, S.J., and Rodney L. Petersen

R ELIGION, WE HAVE ALL LEARNED, plays sometimes a destructive, sometimes a constructive role in our societies' life and in our conflicts. It is at its best when it speaks of forgiveness and reconciliation, the themes of this book.

Ours is a study in political penitence. Its horizon is not the confessional, but public policy and conflict transformation. The book grows out of a symposium entitled, "Forgiveness and Reconciliation: Religious Contributions to Conflict Resolution," held at the John F. Kennedy School of Government, Harvard University, in October 1999 and sponsored by the Sir John Templeton Foundation. It is a part of the ongoing Campaign for Forgiveness Research stimulated and made possible by the Templeton Foundation. It was our good fortune to be able to begin with Archbishop Desmond Tutu's reflections on his experience in heading the Truth and Reconciliation Commission in the aftermath of South Africa's agony of apartheid.

If ideas like "forgiveness" and "reconciliation" are moving out from the seminary and academy into the world of public policy, there is a need to understand, first, how these terms have been used and defined in the past. In the first section, "The Theology of Forgiveness," the chapter by Rodney L. Petersen explores the terminology, rhetoric, and dialectical nature of forgiveness that shape our perception of the term. This exploration is developed in relation to several concrete experiences of forgiveness in human relations. Forgiveness, we are all learning, is not just about the words we use. It is also about the deep resonance between mind and heart— an existential reality that calls us beyond analysis and technique to the life of immediate relationships. When we are willing to go here life becomes more intense, even dialectical, as we are drawn into different histories of woundedness, growth, and integration.

Miroslav Volf deepens our understanding of the meaning of forgiveness and the ways in which forgiveness is related to categories of reconciliation and justice. He notes the surprising resurgence of religion at the end of the twentieth century but takes issue with those who see in this resurgence a relation to religiously legitimized violence. He contests the claim that Christian faith fosters violence and makes the carefully qualified argument that a more "costly discipleship" rather than less religion is required. By pointing to the critical role played by a variety of institutions and approaches to conflict settlement, Volf lays siege to the idea that religion, and Christianity in particular, is by nature violent through his critique of Maurice Bloch and Regina Schwartz. Christian faith, through its death to self-centered desire and universalist tendencies, provides the space required for harmonious peace. This argument, running in tandem with R. Scott Appleby's "ambivalence of the sacred," finds in Christian faith as deeply practiced the will to embrace the other, making possible forgiveness and meaningful reconciliation.[1] The impetus for such will comes, in Volf's opinion, from a communion of love embedded in the intertrinitarian relations of non-self-enclosed identities that constitute Christian theology.

The internal meaning of this theology is drawn out by Stanley Harakas, who completes our theological analysis of the terms of forgiveness by taking us through the history of Orthodox Church understanding.[2] Harakas writes of the tension between relational and legal approaches to forgiveness and reconciliation. In doing this he outlines important anthropological

1. R. Scott Appleby, *The Ambivalence of the Sacred: Religion, Violence, and Reconciliation* (Lanham, Md.: Rowman and Littlefield, 2000).
2. For an analysis of Orthodox reflection in relation to public policy, see Hildo Bos and Jim Forest, eds., *For the Peace from Above: An Orthodox Resource Book on War, Peace, and Nationalism*, produced by the World Fellowship Syndesmos of Orthodox Youth (Bialystok, Poland: Orthdruk Printing House, 1999).

assumptions in the tradition with respect to human nature. Second, Harakas draws attention to three dimensions of God's forgiveness—transcendent, imminent, and present—as they relate to sacramental understanding and human practice. Finally, he illustrates how the sacramental aspect of forgiveness provides the ontological ground for the possibility of the practice of forgiveness and meaningful reconciliation. It is a theology of forgiveness that gives deep meaning and shared reality to the practice of forgiveness.

Religion is never practiced in a vacuum, and theology, the analytical aspect of religious belief and practice, is best done when engaged with human affairs. The second section of our book picks up such engagement with public policy. Raymond G. Helmick begins by drawing attention to the strange alienation between the Christian churches and their own constituencies, most evident since the end of the Wars of Religion. The alienation exposes the churches easily to cooptation for purposes alien to themselves, as people tend not to trust them to define their own agendas. In what we have called, since that time, "The Modern World," trust has been granted instead to three elements that have shaped modern consciousness: science and its resulting technology, the celebration of reason in the Enlightenment, and political liberalism. But as the devastation and violence of the twentieth century have sapped faith in this secular trinity of values, interest in the wisdom traditions, including the religions, has grown anew, though without lessening the suspicion of religious institutions. Helmick would challenge the faith communities, in the context of the separation of church and state, to put into practice their professed commitment to human rights, justice, and peace. This comes as our societies have moved from a politics of interest to one of identity since the late twentieth century.

Joseph Montville writes from the perspective of one working with this new conception of religion in a world divided by conflicted identities. Having coined the term "track two diplomacy" for those forms of diplomacy that occur apart from or outside regular government, Montville has continued to foster this through the Center for Strategic and International Studies (CSIS) in Washington, D.C.[3] In his chapter Montville begins by

---

3. Vamik D. Volkan, Demetrios A. Julius, and Joseph V. Montville, eds., *The Psychodynamics of International Relationships: Concept and Theories*, vol. 2 (Lexington, Mass.: D. C. Heath, 1991).

noting the intersection of religion and mass psychology and focuses attention on the ways in which the sacred can intensify or mitigate violence. He draws upon the evolutionary analysis of religion by R. Scott Appleby and the role of religion in shaping identity, worked out by Marc Gopin, for his argument.[4] Montville illustrates how several of the world's religious traditions offer ways to foster human rights, justice, and the means for peace-building.[5]

Our next author, Douglas Johnston Jr., picks up this theme in a practical vein and illustrates it through the work of the International Center for Religion and Diplomacy (ICRD) and by way of his own study, coedited with Cynthia Sampson, *Religion: The Missing Dimension of Statecraft.* Recognizing the precarious lives that many people lead in the context of violence, Johnston acknowledges the psychological and social function of religion and tries to harness this for peace building. This argument is further established in recent work by the pioneer advocate for peace studies, Elise Boulding. Similarly, Johnston argues that the positive role of religion is often underreported or ignored. He maintains that the members of faith communities, if trained, might contribute tremendously to conflict transformation. Johnston offers several helpful illustrations in southeast Europe and in central Africa that relate to the constructive work of ICRD.[6]

Donna Hicks picks up a theme evident in the chapters by Helmick and Montville, the important relationship between religion and identity. She outlines the central role identity plays in maintaining and perpetuating interethnic conflict. Existential threats to identity have been described as one of the main sources of intractability in such conflicts by creating a zero-sum view of the relationship with the enemy, where one's very existence seems inextricably linked to the negation of the other. Hicks argues that the current conflict resolution and reconciliation processes have not directly

4. Appleby, *Ambivalence of the Sacred;* Marc Gopin, *Between Eden and Armageddon: The Future of World Religions, Violence, and Peacemaking* (New York: Oxford University Press, 2000).
5. Montville draws attention here to the work of Gopin for Judaism, Carl Evans for Christianity, and to Abdulaziz Sachedina for Islam (*The Islamic Roots of Democratic Pluralism* [New York: Oxford University Press, 2000]).
6. Douglas Johnston and Cynthia Sampson, eds., *Religion: The Missing Dimension of Statecraft* (New York: Oxford University Press, 1994); Elise Boulding, *Cultures of Peace: The Hidden Side of History* (Syracuse, N.Y.: Syracuse University Press, 2000).

addressed the issue of identity. Her chapter attempts to clarify the issue by carefully examining the process of identity development and what happens to that process under conditions of threat and conflict. Finally, she proposes adaptations to the current methodologies that are being used in interethnic conflict resolution that could directly address the issue of identity and examines the possible role of forgiveness in creating the conditions that promote genuine reconciliation through the reconstruction of identity.

Issues of religion and identity, and the chilling way in which they enter into and define conflict, run through this section of our book. Such surveys as that by journalist William Shawcross, *Deliver Us from Evil,* of contemporary war zones illustrates this; moreover, Donald Shriver, crafted pioneering work on the interface between forgiveness as understood in the church/faith communities and the public policy community, both embroiled in the contemporary search for conflict transformation.[7] Shriver argues that the solution to such conflict lies in our capacity to forgive. His chapter in this volume raises pertinent questions about our desire to forgive and to practice forgiveness. The illustrations that he offers take us not only to his larger study but also to the more recent litany of testimony laid out by author Michael Henderson.[8] They also point to the real effect that conflict mediation, the intervention of international norms and activity, can have on diminishing regional conflict as pointed out by Ted Robert Gurr.[9]

The third section of this book draws us to a more particular analysis of the relationship between forgiveness and reconciliation with perspectives

---

7. William Shawcross, *Deliver Us from Evil: Peacemakers, Warlords, and a World of Endless Conflict* (New York: Simon and Schuster, 2000); Donald W. Shriver Jr., *An Ethic for Enemies: Forgiveness in Politics* (New York: Oxford University Press, 1995).

8. Michael Henderson, *Forgiveness: Breaking the Chain of Hate* (Wilsonville, Ore.: Book Partners, 1999). Henderson's work and the stories he shares draw heavily upon and support the work of the Foundation for Moral Re-Armament, Caux, Switzerland. The booklet by Bryan Hamlin, *Forgiveness in International Affairs,* Platform Four (London: Grosvenor Books, 1992), published in association with *For a Change* magazine, illustrates the principles of moral re-armament and forgiveness in international affairs.

9. Ted Robert Gurr, *Peoples Versus States: Minorities at Risk in the New Century* (Washington, D.C.: U.S. Institute of Peace, 2000). In distinction from his 1993 book, *Minorities at Risk: A Global View of Ethnopolitical Conflicts* (Washington, D.C.: U.S. Institute of Peace), which presented a disturbing picture of spreading ethnic violence, this volume documents a more recent decline as states have apparently abandoned earlier strategies. The spread of international norms, rise of political democracy, and the interventionism on the part of international actors may all be factors in the current setting.

that are quite diverse but represent primary voices in the academic and theological community. These include fields of clinical psychology, regional conflict mediation, social science, and global youth ministry.

We begin with clinical and social psychologist Everett Worthington Jr., who also serves as director of the Campaign for Forgiveness and edited the previous volume in this series.[10] Worthington alerts us to important scientific work in forgiveness studies in a chapter that clarifies terminology and proceeds to suggest ways of reducing unforgiveness. In this, his work draws, in part, on the restorative justice thinking of Howard Zehr.[11] In addition to justice, punitive or restorative, Worthington also discusses conflict resolution, and social justice as a means to reduce unforgiveness. The value of such suggestive methodologies is that when Worthington turns to other areas of personal and group conflict, patterns of unforgiveness reduction form pathways toward possible forgiveness in relationships and societal interventions. Along the way we are alerted to a rich and growing field of research.

A social science approach also frames the second chapter in this section, that by John Paul Lederach, but Lederach is clear that in his opinion reconciliation processes do not lend themselves to social technology. Rather, the qualities that lend themselves to the practice of reconciliation tend more toward attitude and character than toward technique. As such, Lederach outlines five qualities of practice that lend themselves to reconciliation, the centrality of relationships, the challenge of accompaniment, a space for reconciliation created by humility, community as the place for reconciliation, and the recognition that time and even barrenness—not unlike wandering in the desert—are places to which one may have to go before reconciliation can be achieved.

The chapter by Ervin Staub and Laurie Anne Pearlman draws together the worlds of social science and experience with its focus on "healing, reconciliation and forgiving after genocide and other collective violence." It asks us to reflect on the effect of collective violence on victims and perpetrators. Having raised initial questions about the need to forgive in order to

10. Everett Worthington Jr., ed., *Dimensions of Forgiveness: Psychological Research and Theological Perspectives* (Philadelphia: Templeton Foundation Press, 1998).
11. Howard Zehr, *Changing Lenses: A New Focus for Crime and Justice* (Scottdale, Pa.: Herald Press, 1995).

find healing, the focus of this chapter is on the conflict in Rwanda and the lessons that are raised for forgiveness and reconciliation from that situation. Qualities that contribute to healing include empowerment, truth, testimony and group ceremony, justice, understanding, exposing, acknowledgment, cooperative work, attention to children, and political responsibility. Other factors are considered as well if healing is to occur among victims and perpetrators.

Rwanda represents for many an open illustration of the effects of collective violence and need for healing. In his chapter, John Dawson lists many of the different areas of social existence that stand in similar need of healing. Dawson's perspective on forgiveness and reconciliation is set within a distinctly Christian narrative, but the illustrations he raises have clear universal applicability. As has been the case in each of the three sections of this book thus far, at least one author in the lot has drawn us to the point of human fallibility, or sin and its corrosive effects in relationships: Stanley Harakas, Donald Shriver, and now Dawson. Dawson's understanding of peacemaking in the twenty-first century finds its agenda in the litter of abuse and violence that has dominated western civilization. He sketches out areas that require healing and offers some powerful examples in the course of such categorization. His chapter will not let the reader alone without first taking stock of one's own willingness to be involved in the work of reconciliation, if not always as precisely defined by Dawson.

The final section of this book, "Seeking Forgiveness after Tragedy," highlights the remarkable work of a number of practitioners currently working with religion, public policy, and conflict transformation.

Writing first in this section is Audrey Chapman. Her chapter investigates the role of truth commissions as a means toward societal forgiveness and reconciliation. Acknowledging the context in which the Truth and Reconciliation Commission (TRC) of South Africa did its work, her conclusion is that such commissions assist a society in coming to terms with its past, without which no new society is easily birthed. In the face of the TRC's acknowledged inadequacies, most appear to have concluded that it moved South Africa in this direction. Toward this conclusion, Chapman presents interpretations of forgiveness as a commitment to a way of life and practice (Jones), a commitment of the will (Suchocki), that which entails liberation from the past (Müller-Fahrenholz), and as applicable to the secular realm and public policy (Shriver). Her requirements for reconciliation include discernment of the truth, open and shared acknowledgment, letting go of the past, justice, a commitment to restored relationships, and the establishment of a new social and political covenant.

Olga Botcharova carries the work of forgiveness through "track two diplomacy," as defined earlier by Montville, into southeast Europe. Having scored the political community's failure to provide leadership in the region, she suggests three factors that block a successful peace: a failure to attend to the need for healing, suggestions for resolution that are foreign to local requirements, and strategies that appeal to ruling hierarchies but not to members of a given society. Botcharova follows other authors in this volume in arguing for the role of a deep diplomacy made possible through religious and other organizations in civil society. She illustrates ways in which this has happened through the Center for Strategic Studies and in the Balkans. In moving toward reconciliation she argues for the central role of forgiveness as graphically displayed in her diagrams.

Author Anthony da Silva takes us to three case studies in India, coming to terms with forgiveness and reconciliation as understood by Gandhi. For purposes of comparison and contrast, *satya* (truth) and *satyagraha* (truth force) and *ahimsa* (nonviolence) are presented and set in relation to reconciliation. Reconciliation through nonviolence is said to have much in common with the four dimensions of forgiveness noted by Shriver: moral judgment, forbearance, empathy, and the restoration of relationships.

With author Geraldine Smyth we are carried back to Europe and face the Northern Ireland Troubles. She writes of the quest for peace in Ireland as it has grown from the stories of loss and bereavement into a vision for the future. Her chapter creates a bond between personal suffering and the public efforts by all parties to find and hold the peace. With a certain irony in relation to all we hear about religion's incitement to conflict, Smith argues that the Christians and their churches have mitigated the violence that could have been through their calls for nonretaliation and forgiveness. Awareness, a willingness to forgive, healing and reconciled relations, and a commitment to new community mark dimensions of her story. Such steps give tears and flesh to the theories outlined elsewhere in this volume.

Andrea Bartoli bears a similar message from Mozambique through his report on the work of peace facilitation through the Community of Sant' Egidio. He argues that a religious contribution made the political discourse flexible and, in the end, helped to implement a successful conclusion to the conflict. Having presented a brief history of the conflict, Bartoli discusses the role of religious actors in the conflict and the willingness of different sides in the conflict to use a multiplicity of channels toward its resolution. The facilitation of communication through the Community of Sant'Egidio was described as a form of "pastoral diplomacy." It permitted a shift in relations from enmity to partnership and cooperation, a normal role for third-party actors in facilitating mediation.

Finally, by turning to the article by Ofelia Ortega, we are drawn to one of the most protracted conflicts in the Western Hemisphere, that between Cuba and the United States. Without dealing with that larger relationship directly, Ortega asks us to wrestle with otherness and difference as essential for the healing and reconstruction of community. The violence that we encounter in a variety of relationships is said to be always shaped by the complex character of a culture. Ortega writes of the difference between a culture of death and a culture of life. Her piece makes helpful reference to such programs of the World Council of Churches as the "Ecumenical Decade—Churches in Solidarity with Women," the "Peace to the City Campaign," and "Decade to Overcome Violence." Each of these has been an effort to marshal the moral conscience of the churches and their adherents to commit themselves to a culture of peace.

Our afterword, by George Ellis, carries us back to the themes seen in our foreword by Archbishop Desmond Tutu. Ellis marks out the concentric circles in which forgiveness runs even in the face of what he terms the pleasure of resentment. He adds further documentation to places where forgiveness has functioned in a remarkable peacemaking fashion. In light of such examples he advocates the systematic study of forgiveness for the role it can play in personal as well as community health. Linked to programs of education and development, forgiveness, and the possible reconciliation that it affords, becomes the way into a future unfettered by cyclical violence.

Ellis's afterword brings us to one of three concluding points to be made in this introduction. First, this book begins, and thus ends, with the continent of Africa and, in a way, with the *kairos* moment in South Africa the day that Nelson Mandela left Robben Island, opening the way to the National Unity and Reconciliation Act of July 16, 1995, and the establishment of the Truth and Reconciliation Commission in South Africa. As we move along into the twenty-first century there is a certain symbolism here. It is to say that the themes tied up in the title of this book, "forgiveness and reconciliation: religion, public policy, and conflict transformation," carry a special meaning as they are allowed to play out with sepulchral or jubilant tonality in this continent that symbolizes so much of human endeavor. It is possible that here we will learn whether our interest in forgiveness is restorative or merely one more road down the path of denial, the "forgiveness bypath" noted by some.

Second, in addition to showing us something about ourselves, this book has carried us through four sections dealing with theology, or the ontology behind our terminology, public policy, psychological and social theory, and social policy implementation. Central to this work of implementation are voluntary associations as they operate freely in civil society. Organizations such as the Mennonite Central Committee, Community of Sant'Egidio, World Vision, and others that might have been included have promoted and made possible this plurality of expression upon which democratic society depends. The community at large is the embracing association within which other associations live, the state being one of these. The state in this perspective is the creature and servant of the community, not its creator. The state is not omnipotent or omnicompetent. In other words, there is a valid place for "track two diplomacy" apart from its utilitarian value, for the state is nurtured by a volunteerism born of a larger vision. From this perspective religious organizations, frequently those that birth other non-governmental associations, have an important part to play in the emerging civil order.[12] Such ideas, grounded earlier in the work of Ernst Troeltsch, have found their way into the twentieth century through John Courtney Murray, Hannah Arendt, and Abraham Heschel.[13]

12. See James Luther Adams, *Voluntary Associations: Sociocultural Analyses and Theological Interpretation*, ed. J. Ronald Engel (Chicago: Exploration Press, 1986).
13. Abraham Heschel, *Moral Grandeur and Spiritual Audacity*, ed. Susannah Heschel (New York: Farrar, Straus and Giroux, 1996), 235–30.

Finally, to come full circle, "there is no future without forgiveness." These words by Desmond Tutu tell us not only something about ourselves and our societies, but also something about history itself. *Forgiveness* is a word that makes for freedom. This is as true in southern Africa and the Balkans as it is in the Western Hemisphere. Forgiveness makes it possible to remember the past without being held hostage to it. Without forgiveness there is no progress, no linear history, only a return to conflict and cycles of conflict. This is a very old lesson.

His brothers came and fell down before him, and said, "Behold we are your servants." But Joseph said to them, "Fear not, for am I in the place of God? As for you, you meant evil against me; but God meant it for good, to bring it about that many people should be kept alive, as they are today. So do not fear; I will provide for you and your little ones." (Gen. 50:18–21)

PART I

The Theology of Forgiveness

CHAPTER I

A Theology of Forgiveness

Terminology, Rhetoric,
& the Dialectic of Interfaith Relationships

Rodney L. Petersen

ACROSS ALL OF THE GRAND WISDOM TRADITIONS run terms that reflect a desire to heal broken relationships and to find ways of acceptance that enable us to live together. In Islam we find great emphasis on the quality of mercy, reflective of the merciful nature of God. Buddhism stresses the importance of compassion. And Judaism, according to Rabbi Harold Kushner, finds that the key to breaking the spell that locks us up in patterns of resentment is forgiveness. The "discoverer" of the role of forgiveness in the realm of human affairs, according to political theorist Hannah Arendt, was Jesus of Nazareth.[1] Whether this is *quite* true, or true in only a particular way given the attention all religions pay to forgiveness at some level, does not detract from the insight it raises as we look back on the most consciously violent of centuries since the "discoverer" alluded to by Arendt.

Many in the public policy community in North America now believe that the term *forgiveness* will be central to working with the political order of the twenty-first century.[2] Joseph Montville and others have made the

---

1. Hannah Arendt, *The Human Condition: A Study of the Central Conditions Facing Modern Man* (Garden City, N.Y.: Doubleday, 1959), 212–13.
2. Douglas Johnston and Cynthia Sampson, eds., *Religion: The Missing Dimension of Statecraft* (New York: Oxford University Press, 1994). The book is a collection of essays on the crucial role of religion in international conflict. It seeks to raise this issue up before the public policy community. In doing this the authors stress the value of track two diplomacy.

practice of forgiveness central to what they define as "track two" diplomacy.[3] Its efficacy, however, as a tool for diplomatic practice, or for a deepening of our understanding of human health, will depend in large measure on how we conceive of the topic in its ontological foundation and the ways in which the possibility of forgiveness can cross confessional, or religious, and conceptual boundaries. Therefore, while the purpose of this chapter is to note the ontological foundation for forgiveness in Christian theology and to understand its terminology and rhetoric within a community of common narrative, that is, the church, the chapter will also sketch the ways by which a dialectic of forgiveness can cross confessional boundaries.

In the history of the church the practice of forgiveness has been clearly tied to penitence, most often privatized as a part of individual religious practice since the early medieval period.[4] Throughout what became recognized as "Christendom," the public significance of forgiveness often languished as more retributive conceptions of justice dominated social theory, power politics, and practice. Forgiveness was often "spiritualized" and removed from the practice of everyday life.[5] While forgiveness might happen between God and an individual penitent, among persons and groups in society only some lesser form of condoning, dismissal, or forgetting appeared possible.[6] The recovery of particular patterns of religious behav-

3. The term *track two diplomacy* was coined by Joseph Montville of the Center for Strategic and International Studies for those forms of diplomacy that occur apart from or outside regular government—track one—channels, specifically the work of religious organizations and other NGOs. See his chapter in *The Psychodynamics of International Relationships: Concept and Theories,* ed. Vamik D. Volkan, Demetrios A. Julius, and Joseph V. Montville, vol. 2 (Lexington, Mass.: D. C. Heath, 1991).

4. One point of departure might be seen in the formulation of Irish penitential handbooks in the sixth century. Another might be a retributive conception of justice pointed to by James C. Russell in *The Germanization of Early Medieval Christianity: A Sociohistorical Approach to Religious Transformation* (New York: Oxford University Press, 1994). I owe this reference to Fr. Raymond Helmick, S.J.

5. Donald W. Shriver Jr., *An Ethic for Enemies: Forgiveness in Politics* (New York: Oxford University Press, 1995). A philosophical interest in forgiveness can be traced to Alasdair MacIntyre's work, *After Virtue* (Notre Dame: University of Notre Dame, 1981), with few precursors. The field is not so bleak when we turn to literature. Themes of forgiveness run through the works of such authors as Fyodor Doestoevsky, Flannery O'Connor, and Toni Morrison, to name a few. Notable individuals like Simone Weil and Dietrich Bonhoeffer stand out as well.

6. Geiko Müller-Fahrenholz, "Distortions in Church History," chap. 2 of *The Art of Forgiveness: Theological Reflections on Healing and Reconciliation* (Geneva: WCC Publications, 1997), 9–16. Shriver writes that from fairly early on, at least by the time of the fourth and

ior and theology in the Protestant reforms caused Christians to rethink the topic. While it has often been said that all of Luther's thoughts "radiate like the rays of the sun from *one* glowing core, namely the gospel of the forgiveness of sins," a juridical and sacrificial view of the atonement continued into the early modern period, as seen in the classic liturgies and theologies of the newly established national churches in the West.[7] Nevertheless, the Protestant Reformation and Roman counter-reforms stimulated simultaneously in the church a recovery of the term *forgiveness* and thoughts about its practice, although this often occurred in more pietistic-oriented circles, apart from the institutional churches.[8]

As we move into the modern period, a division in theological thinking and practice has been evident between those who join forgiveness to justification, with a personal and vertical view of salvation, and those who connect it with justice and the search for reconciliation but in language that often moves from transcendence to a prevailing political rhetoric,[9] a spiritual division lamented by those seeking a more integrated spirituality. Generally the tradition of reflection in systematic theology and ethics is more remarkable for its omission than its treatment of the topic of forgiveness.[10]

<hr />

fifth centuries after Christ, the place of forgiveness in the public square was becoming increasingly problematic. He notes the appearances and disappearances of forgiveness in the political order of the time and of a sacramental captivity of forgiveness into the early modern period (*Ethic for Enemies*, 45–58).

7. Einar Billing, *Our Call* (1909), cited by Martin Marty, "The Ethos of Christian Forgiveness," in *Dimensions of Forgiveness: Psychological Research and Theological Perspectives*, ed. Everett L. Worthington Jr. (Philadelphia: Templeton Foundation Press, 1998), 12; Gustaf Aulén, *Christus Victor: An Historical Study of the Three Main Types of the Idea of the Atonement* (New York: Macmillan, 1969), 1–15. Perspectives outlined by Aulén include (1) a ransom paid to the Devil (Origen), (2) Christ our representative (Athanasius), (3) Christ, the sacrifice to satisfy God's anger (Anselm), (4) Christ's death as exemplary love (Abelard), (5) Christ, the voluntary substitute on our behalf (Luther), (6) Christ, the condemned or the penal theory (Calvin), (7) Christ, our example (Socinus), and further modifications of these positions. Compare in Shriver, *Ethic for Enemies*, 49–58.
8. See George H. Williams, *The Radical Reformation*, Sixteenth Century Essays and Studies 15 (Kirksville, Mo.: Sixteenth Century Journal Publishers, 1992).
9. Notable exceptions exist although our perception of them is often clouded by contemporary religious rhetoric that reflects this same division. Examples include the German Lutheran and Pietist Ludwig von Zinzendorf, Anglican and proto-Methodist John Wesley, North American Quaker John Woolman, British Nonconformist J.M.F. Ludlow, and Anglican Frederick Denison Maurice.
10. Albrecht Ritschl's three-volume work on justification and reconciliation (1870–74), vols. 1 and 3 translated as *The Christian Doctrine of Justification and Reconciliation* (1900), remains the most extensive and instructive. A moving personal treatment is by Wilhelm

Nevertheless, interest in forgiveness is currently growing through the course of political events. In North America it is also arising from reflection and analysis in the health-care sciences. The Christian community is not alone in calling attention to the corporate value and theological foundation of forgiveness for personal and social life in the twenty-first century.[11] Indeed, one might say that the value of forgiveness was implied in the remark by the French minister of culture, André Malraux, who observed that the twenty-first century would be religious or it would not be at all. This might not appear so surprising if we reflect back on the nature of the violence that has pervaded the twentieth century. Forgiveness, long irrelevant to public and foreign policy, of little direct concern in health, and reduced to the confessional in the church, is now an aspect of public policy discourse and psychological analysis. A few points of departure might be named.

The Second World War brought not only history's most evident and documented holocaust but also some of our most contemporary examples of what living a life of forgiveness might look like in such persons as Dietrich Bonhoeffer, Corrie Ten Boom, and Simone Weil. Notable in the field of holocaust studies, Simon Wiesenthal asks what forgiveness would mean for the victim as well as the perpetrator of the crimes in the Nazi concentration camps? Taken from his work detail to the bedside of a dying member of the SS who wanted to confess and obtain absolution from a Jew, Wiesenthal said nothing, betraying neither compassion nor criticism but leaving alone "an uncanny silence in the room."[12] It is in this context that the young

---

Herrmann, *The Communion of the Christian with God,* ed. and with an intro by Robert Voelkel (Philadelphia: Fortress Press, 1971), and by H. R. Mackintosh, *The Christian Experience of Forgiveness* (1927). Further critical treatment was given by Karl Barth, *Church Dogmatics* I/2, II/2, IV/1, and IV/2 (see appropriate sections). A recent and helpful assessment is by L. Gregory Jones, *Embodying Forgiveness: A Theological Analysis* (Grand Rapids: Wm. B. Eerdmans, 1995). Other less systematic treatments exist.

11. Two points of departure might be noted: The Woodstock Colloquium on Forgiveness in Conflict Resolution: Reality and Utility, a series of conferences held from December 1996 to March 1998, and movements and literature associated with Reconciliation Networks of the World. See works by John Dawson, *Healing America's Wounds* (Ventura, Calif.: Regal Books, 1994), and Rudy Pohl and Marny Pohl, *A Matter of the Heart: Healing Canada's Wounds* (Belleville, Ont.: Essence Publishing, 1998).

12. Simon Wiesenthal, *The Sunflower: On the Possibilities and Limits of Forgiveness* (New York: Schocken Books, 1969, and later eds.). The 1997 edition carries a symposium with responses from fifty-three persons of note engaged with the topic.

German theologian Dietrich Bonhoeffer began to lay the groundwork for a theology of forgiveness in forms of what he called "costly grace" (*The Cost of Discipleship*) and in a pattern of spirituality that committed us to healing relationships (*Life Together*).[13] The simple trust and evangelical obedience of Corrie Ten Boom has left an inspiring legacy in popular piety. It is through suffering and forgiveness that Simone Weil found the means to a spiritual unity with God.[14]

A more recent point of departure began the day that Nelson Mandela left Robben Island, opening the way to the National Unity and Reconciliation Act of July 26, 1995, and the establishment of the Truth and Reconciliation Commission in South Africa. Other national tragedies exist in Chili, Argentina, the Middle East, Rwanda, the Balkans, and Chechnya, to name but a few. But the political and religious leadership in South Africa has pointedly raised the issue of public forgiveness as the only way to a constructive future. This is the point made by Anglican Archbishop Desmond Tutu in his assessment of the transition being made in South Africa in *No Future Without Forgiveness*.[15] In a recent book that examines national tragedies, legal scholar Martha Minow balances difficult pairs of responses to horrific violence, remembering and forgetting, judging and forgiving, reconciling and avenging. In her chapter, "Vengeance and Forgiveness," she marks these as ends on a spectrum of human responses to atrocity that call for therapy, politics, cross-communal reconciliation, recognition of cruelty, and lack of closure.[16] Donald Shriver writes of the leftover debris of national

13. Books written while Bonhoeffer was in charge of the Confessing Church seminary at Finken-walde after 1935: *The Cost of Discipleship*, trans. R. H. Fuller (New York: Macmillan, 1963), and *Life Together*, translated and with an introduction by John W. Doberstein (San Francisco: HarperSanFrancisco, 1993). I am following L. Gregory Jones, "The Cost of Forgiveness: Grace, Christian Community and the Politics of Worldly Discipleship," *Union Theological Seminary Quarterly Review* 46 (1992): 149–69. The biographical details of Bonhoeffer's life are best traced in Eberhard Bethge's biography, *Dietrich Bonhoeffer*, trans. E. H. Robertson et al. (London: Collins, 1970).

14. Corrie Ten Boom with John Sherrill and Elizabeth Sherrill, *The Hiding Place* (New York: Bantam Books, 1982); Simone Weil, *Gravity Grace*, introduction by Gustave Thibon and trans. Arthur Wills (New York: Putnam, 1952).

15. Desmond Tutu, *No Future Without Forgiveness* (New York: Doubleday, 1999); see also the case for restorative justice in South Africa made by Charles Villa-Vicencio, in his manuscript, "Restoring Justice: Dealing with the Past Differently," and his fuller study on human rights in international perspective, *A Theology of Reconstruction* (Cambridge: Cambridge University Press, 1992).

16. Martha Minow, *Between Vengeance and Forgiveness: Facing History after Genocide and Mass Violence* (Boston: Beacon Press, 1998).

pasts that continues to clog the relationships of diverse groups of humans around the world that these will never get cleaned up and animosity will never drain away "until forgiveness enters those relationships in some political form."[17] Such debris contributes to the spiraling cycles of conflict analyzed by social scientists.[18]

Brian Frost reminds us that forgiveness in politics, as in personal life, is a process "rather than something to be applied temporarily, like a poultice."[19] This process draws us to another point of departure in forgiveness studies, that which has taken root in the medical and health-care fields. Work among health professionals over the past quarter century has drawn increasing attention to forgiveness as a powerful psychotherapeutic tool. This recognition has often come with respect to trauma studies. Richard Fitzgibbons points to major mechanisms for dealing with anger that affect health and well-being. These draw upon forgiveness, particularly cognitive, emotional, and spiritual levels in the process of healing.[20] Particular studies in interpersonal relations, marriage and the family, and private and social behavior are pointing to the deep connection between personal psychological health, social bonding, and healthy civic life and forgiveness.[21] Learning to forgive one's self, or self-acceptance, and addiction and personal

17. Shriver relects on his own developing perspective: "Slowly, I have arrived at the belief that the concept of forgiveness, so customarily relegated to the realms of religion and personal ethics, belongs to the heart of reflection about how groups of humans can move to repair the damages that they have suffered from their past conflicts with each other. Precisely because it attends at once to moral truth, history and the human benefits that flow from the conquest of enmity, forgiveness is a word for a multi-dimensional process that is eminently political" (Shriver, *Ethic for Enemies*, ix–x).

18. See the analysis and cyclical graphs prepared by Lewis Kriesberg, *Constructive Conflict: From Escalation to Resolution* (New York: Rowman and Littlefield, 1998).

19. Cited in Michael Henderson, *Forgiveness: Breaking the Chain of Hate* (Wilsonville, Ore.: BookPartners, 1999), 4.

20. Richard Fitzgibbons, "Anger and the Healing Power of Forgiveness: A Psychiatrist's View," in *Exploring Forgiveness*, ed. Robert D. Enright and Joanna North (Madison: University of Wisconsin Press, 1998), 63–74. He endorses a definition of forgiveness given by philosopher Joanna North and psychologist Robert Enright who define forgiveness as a matter of *willed* change of heart, the successful result of an active endeavor to replace bad thoughts with good, bitterness and anger with compassion and affection. See North, "Wrongdoing and Forgiveness," *Philosophy* 62 (1987): 499–508.

21. Thomas J. Sheff, *Emotions, the Social Bond, and Human Reality* (Cambridge: Cambridge University Press, 1997). For further information on forgiveness and health, see the Campaign for Forgiveness Research at *www.forgiving.org*; and the International Forgiveness Institute at *www.intl-forgive-inst.org*.

depression, or violent and abusive behavior are seen to be increasingly connected and with social and even public policy consequence.[22]

Still, acceptance of the need for forgiveness is not universal. Psychologist Lewis Smedes writes that people who are inclined to write off forgiveness often do not know what they are rejecting. He outlines what
forgiveness is and is not.[23] Numerous pastoral counselors, like Smedes, have
come to the fore in recent years, mixing the inherited wisdom of Christianity, most often oriented to personal trauma, with developing understanding from the fields of psychology and psychiatry, with some relating
forgiveness to theories of psychological maturation and stages in a process
that intermingles popular psychology with spiritual wisdom.[24] While helpful, such mixing has also been scored for adding to the internalization and
privatization of forgiveness, a criticism that has been raised of Smedes's
work and one that is common for much of the treatment of the topic in the
therapeutic community.[25]

These points of departure in the fields of public policy and health care
draw us to consider forgiveness in Christian theology and practice, its terminology, rhetoric, and dialectic. If we have not talked much about theology proper to this point, it is because the argument of this chapter follows
the logic set forth by the Reformed Swiss theologian John Calvin, that our
knowledge of God and of ourselves often run parallel, that it is difficult to
know one without the other.[26] In other words, if public policy and the

22. Andrew P. Morrison, M.D., *The Culture of Shame* (Northvale, N.J.: Jason Aronson, 1996).
See, similarly, Donald Capps, *The Depleted Self: Sin in a Narcissistic Age* (Minneapolis:
Fortress Press, 1993).

23. Lewis B. Smedes, *The Art of Forgiving: When You Need to Forgive and Don't Know How*
(New York: Ballantine Books, 1996), 55–56; see his earlier *Forgive and Forget: Healing the
Hurts We Don't Deserve* (New York: Harper and Row, 1984), and note its criticism in Jones,
Embodying Forgiveness, 48–53. See also Smedes, "Stations on the Journey from Forgiveness
to Hope," in *Dimensions of Forgiveness,* ed. Worthington, 341–54. Joram Graf Haber works
with similar points of analysis in *Forgiveness: A Philosophical Study* (Lanham, Md.: Rowman and Littlefield, 1991).

24. Another popular example is that of David W. Augsburger, *Helping People Forgive* (Louisville,
Ky.: Westminster/John Knox Press, 1996). James W. Fowler, *The Personal and Public Challenges of Postmodern Life* (Nashville: Abingdon, 1996). See, for example, William A. Menninger, *The Process of Forgiveness* (New York: Continuum, 1998). Menninger lists (1)
claiming the hurt, or the denial stage, (2) guilt, (3) victim, (4) anger, and (5) wholeness. He
draws upon the work of Beverly Flanigan, *Forgiving the Unforgivable: Overcoming the Bitter Legacy of Intimate Wounds* (New York: Macmillan, 1992).

25. Jones, *Embodying Forgiveness,* 47–53.

26. John Calvin, in *Institutes of the Christian Religion,* ed. John T. McNeill, trans. Ford Lewis

health-care sciences are discovering forgiveness, they are also recovering, or perhaps uncovering, a place for theology in contemporary discourse. In an interesting twist of culture, if our own modern period might be said to have begun with Ludwig Feuerbach's Materialist dictum that theologians should become "anthropologians," we are beginning the twenty-first century with a recovery of spiritual sensitivity and the need for theological analysis on many different levels.[27]

For forgiveness and conflict studies the work of cultural anthropologist and literary critic René Girard might be said to unite the fields of psychology and politics and bring us most clearly to the domain of theology.[28] Girard stresses, first, the relationship between desire and imitation, or what he calls "mimetic desire." Desire is self-seeking but socially constructed. One desires something because another possesses it. What another person has shapes the desire of the object to be possessed. The resulting conflict in mimetic desire leads to social conflict.[29] Girard argues that human society finds cohesion in the face of conflict through the "victimage mechanism" whereby a person or group become a scapegoat, blamed for whatever seems to threaten or disrupt the group. As society unites to seize, accuse, and kill the scapegoat, it fails to deal with the deeper social cleavage that results from mimetic desire. The sacrifice of the scapegoat becomes, in Girard's understanding, the origin and description of religion. Biblical religion is unique, argues Girard, in that it does not side with the powerful who benefit from the violence of scapegoating but aligns itself with victims.[30] A point of special interest for Girard is that he finds in Jesus one who refuses to enter the spiral of violence, one who breaks this spiral by yielding to it despite his evident

Battles, Library of Christian Classics 20 (Philadelphia: Westminster Press, 1960), I.1.i. (35): "Nearly all the wisdom we possess, that is to say, true and sound wisdom, consists of two parts: the knowledge of God and of ourselves. But, while joined by many bonds, which one precedes and brings forth the other is not easy to discern. In the first place, no one can look upon himself without immediately turning his thoughts to the contemplation of God, in whom he lives and moves [Acts 17:28]."

27. Note the connections between spirituality and political life in the work of Michael Lerner.

28. René Girard, *The Scapegoat* (Baltimore: Johns Hopkins University Press, 1986), and Girard, *Things Hidden Since the Foundation of the World* (Stanford, Calif.: Stanford University Press, 1987).

29. Fred Smith, "Black on Black Violence: The Intramediation of Desire and the Search for a Scapegoat," *Contagion* 6 (1999): 32–43.

30. Girard, *Things Hidden Since the Foundation of the World,* 154.

guiltlessness, and so through forgiveness opens the way to reconciliation.

While forgiveness is not listed as one of the Ten Commandments, it does underlie biblical religion as argued by Girard. When forgiveness in human relationships is grounded in a deep ontological understanding of life, reconciliation becomes more than conciliation, a hasty peace, a managed process, or even liberation.[31] It is rooted in a costly self-immolation in the heart of being itself. It affects my being and the one with whom I exist in a state of alienation insofar as I will allow it. In fact, the whole thrust of the self-understanding of biblical religion in theory and in its manifest communities grows out of a conception that God is in the world "reconciling it to God's self" (2 Cor. 5:19), which is the very process of forgiveness.

THE TERMS OF FORGIVENESS

What are the terms of forgiveness? I was forced to wrestle with this question while teaching in Geneva, Switzerland. Many of the students in my classes had come from situations of violence and trauma across the globe. They were often locked in patterns of behavior shaped by their pasts, and I encouraged them to begin to listen to their selves and to become more aware of their verbal maps of the future. These maps often included scenarios where the cost of forgiveness appeared too great a sacrifice to make and so many believed themselves to be in situations that offered little hope. There was often a certain unreality: their past was gone, their future was on hold. The topic of forgiveness often came up and I was reminded of the observation made by Hannah Arendt that we were created with the power to remember the past, but left powerless to change it; and that we are created with the power to imagine the future, but left powerless to control it. As she concludes with need for forgiveness as the only effective response to the past, so these students required the faculty of forgiveness and, through it, the same means to open up an effective future.[32]

---

31. Terms used and discarded by Robert J. Schreiter in defining reconciliation, *Reconciliation: Mission and Ministry in a Changing Social Order* (Maryknoll, N.Y.: BTI/Orbis Books, 1997), 5–28.
32. Arendt, *The Human Condition.*

The terms of forgiveness are shaped by our perception of the past and the future and given form in our language. Permit me to share an example from a recent workshop put together by the Boston Theological Institute (BTI) to South Africa and Ghana.

The group of students, faculty, and friends left South Africa for Ghana in order to "process" what they had heard and seen in another African setting. Ghana, a home for "pan-Africanism," was the historical setting for much of the African slave trade. While at the Cape Coast Castles, holding dungeons and shipping points for the newly enslaved, a certain discomfort began to develop between the Euro-Americans and African Americans in our group. This was only to come out fully the next day as we joined the students and staff of the Akrofi-Christeller Memorial Institute (Akuapem). There, gathered for morning devotions, our group was taken aback as Ghanaian students began to confess to their African American brothers and sisters their sorrow for the fact that their ancestors had sold the ancestors of the African Americans into slavery. This began a time of mutual confession, forgiveness, and repentance among all races present. There was not a dry eye in the room as those of European and African background confessed to one another their sorrow for the past, ways it was impacting the present and shaping the future. As we left we were given literature by a young Ghanaian student reminding us that Abraham's third wife had been a woman of African descent, that Moses's wife was of the darker peoples of Midian, and that the first apostolic sending had occurred with dark hands in the majority of those laid on Paul for his first missionary journey into Europe.

Our encounter in Ghana was about perception and language, but we were led to think about the distinctions among terms such as *forgiveness, justification,* and *reconciliation.* For example, while at the Cape Coast it had been easy for some in the group to behave in self-justifying ways, impeding any movement toward forgiveness. Because the process of forgiveness at Akuapem began with a mutual African awareness, the Euro-Americans were drawn into the process and moved from self-justification to seeing their own complicity in a practice that deepened the abuse and human tragedy of a people. They were enabled to express their own sorrow, asking for forgiveness.

Justification, insofar as it relates to an offense against another, can only be set right by that party, not by the perpetrator. Otherwise justification becomes self-justification. This blocks the process of forgiveness and, consequently, the possibility of restored relationships or reconciliation. Given certain assumptions about our personhood, or identity, the offended party might be said to be God when forgiveness and justification are considered from a "vertical" dimension. Understanding justification from a more "horizontal" perspective as stimulated by various forms of liberation theology, the victim—whether poor, marginalized, or subject to active violence—has been more clearly brought into view. To consider the victim as a person is to take the victim's rights seriously and elicit forgiveness as warranted. This perspective has become basic to issues of human rights and peace building on a variety of levels. It is easy for racial divisions in our society to be caught up into patterns of self-justification. When they do, we do not allow for the possibility of forgiveness or reconciliation. Justification reflects the fact of a restored relationship that can only be done by another. Forgiveness expresses the divine or human, wherever warranted, assurance and human acceptance of this fact.

Reconciliation, a restoration or even a transformation toward an intended wholeness that comes with transcendent or human grace, expresses the result of a restored relation in behavior. Forgiveness expresses the acknowledgment and practice of this result. In this sense, *forgiveness* is not so much a middle term as one that includes both justification and reconciliation.[33] It restores and transforms. It cannot be manipulated by either conceptual "poles," justification or reconciliation. The literature we were given in Ghana outlined ideas for different patterns of relationship more conducive to reconciliation than alienation. Reconciliation not only draws upon forgiveness, but also elicits the qualities of truth and justice in the recovery of harmony or peace.[34] It reminds us of Pope Paul VI's exhortation, "If you want peace, work for justice."[35]

33. Marty, "Ethos of Christian Forgiveness," 11; Paul Lehmann, article on "Forgiveness," in *The Westminster Dictionary of Christian Ethics*, ed. James F. Childress and John Macquarrie (Philadelphia: Westminster Press, 1986), 233.
34. See the quaternary developed by John Paul Lederach for seeking reconciliation drawn from Psalm 85, truth, justice, mercy, and peace, in *Building Peace: Sustainable Reconciliation in Divided Societies* (Washington, D.C.: U.S. Institute of Peace Press, 1997).
35. See the foreword to Scott Appleby, *The Ambivalence of the Sacred: Religion, Violence, and Reconciliation* (New York: Rowman and Littlefield, 2000), ix.

From a theological perspective, forgiveness is not only a transactional relation but is grounded in and reflects a deeper need for forgiveness that is presumed in biblical religion. Humanity, created in the image of God, has distorted its personality such that each of us individually and corporately is in need of forgiveness and restoration. Girard pointed to one of the ways in which this is understood. Forgiveness, as conceived in biblical history, law, prophetic insight, and wisdom, indicates three elements that appear taken up in Jesus' teaching, particularly in the Gospels of Luke and John. First, forgiveness is the free and sovereign gift of a loving God as revealed in a relationship best described as a covenant. Second, the chief instrument for the realization of forgiveness is the sacrificial cult that Jesus was understood to personify. Finally, a realization of repentance grows out of the release of forgiveness. In other words, because we have been forgiven, and thereby accepted at a most fundamental level, we can extend forgiveness to others. The focus of this process is the renewal of holiness, or the integrity of the person in all of his or her relationships. In assuming these three mediating movements, Jesus indicated that the covenant was about content, not form; that the cult reflects the implications of the covenant; and that both covenant and cult are effective in light of repentance, which requires recognition of the need for forgiveness in order to find integrity. Many biblical texts illustrate this mediation that makes possible forgiveness. Historian Martin Marty organizes several of these under what he calls "a quatritarian organization of Christian reality," forgiveness as seen through the lens of God as "Abba" (Father), God in Jesus Christ, the Holy Spirit, and in the "ethos" (character) of the believer.[36]

Language, or the terms of forgiveness, also draws us to a larger narrative, the context for the terminology we use to understand the present, the nature of forgiveness, or its reflection of divine mediation. A Christian theology of forgiveness in the face of violence, whether done by another or by me, draws upon a commitment to the idea that peace or goodness, however defined, is ontologically prior to violence. This reaches into our understanding of whether an ultimate goodness can be personified, whether the

36.Marty, "Ethos of Christian Forgiveness," 15–27; see Müller-Fahrenholz, "The Go-Between Factor," in *Art of Forgiveness*, 31–35.

nature of God is really characterized by such goodness.[37] This assumes that the dysfunctional or violent pattern into which we fall is escapable, whether by nurture or a radically altered nature (i.e., conversion), or both.[38] Contrary to voices that would argue differently, the crucial question becomes how we cope with forces of destruction in our own lives and around us.[39] Here the perspectives of such disciplines as sociology, psychology, sociobiology, and anthropology come into play. So also does the insight of spiritual fathers and mothers in a long line that includes prophets and Desert Fathers. Christians have read the larger narrative so as to find in the crucified and risen Christ the paradigmatic solution to the pervasive nature of violence whether conceived of as internal or contextual and external.[40] This forgiveness is not to be construed as degeneration or weakness or a refusal to participate in the struggle for power. Such would be a "cheap grace" and foreign to the larger narrative in which the disciple is called to live, a narrative that demands practices that reflect the epitome of the narrative.[41] Far from being weak or masochistic, this is the power seen in Christ that breaks the cycle of violence. What makes forgiveness more than conflict management or a program for negotiation is that it draws us to the center of what we believe to be the nature of things. Central to the Christian story is the forgiveness that we are asked to give to one another by the resurrected Christ, perhaps best construed as the material foundation of the church: "Peace be with you! As the Father has sent me, I am sending you." "Receive the Holy Spirit. If you forgive anyone his sins, they are forgiven; if you do not forgive them, they are not forgiven" (John 20:21–22). Jesus' declaration to Peter, whether in his person or affirmation of faith, "on this rock I will build my church" (Matt. 16:15–19), might better be seen as its formal and institutional foundation.

37.Jones, *Embodying Forgiveness*, 71–98. See the discussion on characterizing the God that forgives, 101–34.
38.Horace Bushnell and other prominent nineteenth-century American theologians carried on the debate over the place of conversion into or education into the Christian life, a debate that continues to shape American Evangelical Christianity.
39.See John Milbank's argument that Friedrich Nietzsche attempts to reverse Augustine's emphasis on the priority of God's goodness in the created order in *Genealogy of Morals,* in *Theology and Social Theory* (Oxford: Blackwell, 1990), 389.
40.Julia Kristeva, *Black Sun,* trans. Leon Roudiez (New York: Columbia University Press, 1989), 189.
41.Robert Schreiter, *In Water and in Blood: A Spirituality of Solidarity and Hope* (New York: Crossroad, 1988).

When set next to the appropriate clause in the Lord's Prayer the significance is not missed: "Forgive us our debts, as we also have forgiven our
debtors. For if you forgive men when they sin against you, your heavenly
Father will also forgive you. But if you do not forgive men their sins, your
Father will not forgive your sins" (Matt. 6:9–13, 14–15). The power of
implementation is the Holy Spirit, God's power in and to us to make efficacious the reality of God's nature. This is mirrored by the disciple in behavior patterns that include a willing repentance and forgiveness before entering
into worship.

> Therefore, if you are offering your gift at the altar and there remem-
> ber that your brother has something against you, leave your gift
> there in front of the altar. First go and be reconciled to your brother;
> then come and offer your gift. (Matt. 5:23–24)

As we develop the terms of forgiveness for a Christian theology of forgiveness, then, we need to pay attention to several sets of ideas. First, it is important to see how our perceptions shape our understanding of the past and our
perspective on the future. Second, we need to understand the interrelationship of justification, forgiveness, and reconciliation, finding the latter term
embedded in a wider set of qualities that permit human wholeness. Third,
mediation gives efficacy to this triad of justification, forgiveness, and reconciliation. Mediation is exemplified in both the biblical cult and person of
Jesus. It is what gives biblical religion its deep meaning. Finally, forgiveness
makes sense in relation to our premises about the essential goodness or violence of life. The film *Terms of Endearment,* with Shirley MacLaine, Jack
Nicholson and Deborah Winger, reminds us of our "terms of forgiveness."
This is the story of a difficult relationship between a mother and daughter
and the tale of caring yet dysfunctional relations through generations. It is
a story that points to different degrees or types of forgiveness. It reminds us
that inherent to each person is a sense of the value of forgiveness and its
essential place in human relationships, even if only offered in part.[42]

42. Michelle Nelson identifies at least three degrees of forgiveness that build on one another:
    detached forgiveness, a reduction in negative feeling but no reconciliation; limited, adding
    the restoration of partial relationship and a decrease in emotional investment; and full,

THE RHETORIC OF FORGIVENESS

A great deal of rhetoric occurs around the topic of forgiveness. For this reason the term is easily off-putting. If rhetoric is interpreted as the art of speaking or writing effectively, that is, the study of the principles and rules of composition that enable this to happen, we also know how easy it is for good rhetoric to spill over into insincere and grandiloquent language. With forgiveness, so much can be beside the point if the form does not represent the content.

The terms of forgiveness are meant to bring us into relation with one another, not to drive us apart through self-justification or modes of insincerity. The quality of our relationship with our neighbor is assumed in Christian theology to be a mirror of that between us and God, or ultimate reality. Christianity assumes a deep need for neighbor, a need that is symmetrical to our need for God. This is seen in the structure of the Ten Commandments and in their dominical summary (Matt. 22:36–40). Writing about this relationship, the theologian Karl Barth includes the forgiveness of neighbor as a central feature of his material on "The Praise of God." He argues that in Christian theology the neighbor is not the abstract "other" but God in our own image facing us in the other. He adds, "In the biblical sense of the concept my neighbor is not each of my fellow-men as such as such consists of mere individuals. My neighbor is an event, which takes place in the existence of a definite man definitely marked off from all other men. My neighbor is my fellow-man acting toward me as a benefactor." Further, taking up the biblical challenge to "love my neighbor as I love myself," Barth writes that to love my neighbor means accepting the future that is shaped by the reality of my neighbor. We are, in fact, given to one another in order to benefit from each other, to find the restoration that is only possible because of each other, and to find our respective identities through each other.[43]

Barth is clear about drawing us to those aspects of Christian theology that

---

adding a total cessation of negative feelings and restoration and growth in relationship. See Beverly Flanigan, "Forgivers and the Unforgiveable," in *Exploring Forgiveness,* ed. Enright and North, 95–105.

43. Karl Barth, *Church Dogmatics,* ed. G. W. Bromiley and T. F. Torrance, trans. G. T. Thomson and H. Knight (Edinburgh: T&T Clark, 1970), II.2, 18.3. (401ff.), 419–20, 430.

ask me to love my neighbor as I love myself. In this light, we might ask about what it means for us to be people of different races, yet brothers and sisters? Miroslav Volf puts this question forward from his background in southeast Europe: What does it mean to love *cetnik* and *ustashe*? What, might we add, about Afrikaner and Bantu?[44] How about Jew and Palestinian?

While we were in South Africa we were impressed with many of the stories we heard and people we met. One of these was from that of our host in Cape Town, Dr. Russel Botman. This story had its beginning in the 1980s. Russel Botman, dean of the faculty of religion at the University of the Western Cape, invited us to his home where he related his experience of being abducted by security forces. Russel is "Colored." This means he comes from a mixed racial background, often White, Indian, and Black. He had been a young minister in the early 1980s and was involved in the struggle against apartheid, but only as a minister of the gospel. He was awakened in the middle of the night, blankets thrown off the bed, and taken away to a state security office. He was not fingerprinted when taken before the state security officers. He knew that this meant he was destined for swift and silent elimination. Coincidentally, a call came over the dispatcher that an uprising had broken out at a prison in another area of the city. The security forces left him in the hands of the local police and went to the scene of the conflict. Botman said that at this point he began to strike up a conversation with the local police officer. They realized that they knew similar ministers in the Dutch Reformed Church. The officer asked if he knew a certain pastor, Botman said that he did, and would the officer please send his greetings to the pastor. This continued until the return of the security forces. Upon learning that Botman's identity had been revealed to the police, the security forces were furious and Botman was eventually released. This story and other events were told to us with the eyes of four admiring adolescent children focused upon their father.

Russel Botman helped to draft the Belhar Declaration of the Dutch Reformed Mission Church (1982), which labels apartheid not only a sin,

---

44. Miroslav Volf, *Exclusion and Embrace: A Theological Exploration of Identity, Otherness, and Reconciliation (Nashville: Abingdon Press, 1996),* 9; Wilhelm Verwoerd, *My Winds of Change* (Randburg: Ravan Press, 1997).

but also a heresy in the Dutch Reformed Church.[45] Apartheid (which means "apartness") was built on the idea of the irreconcilability of peoples. As such, it contradicts the biblical argument that all humanity is made in the image of God, called to be one in Christ (Gal. 3:28), finding its image of restoration in him (Col. 1:15). The Belhar Declaration is being used to draw all of the Reformed (White, Black and Colored) together, through forgiveness and reconciliation, into a new Uniting Reformed Church where all races are treated with equality.[46] This father, like many mothers in South Africa, has opened the doors of life not only to the children of his family and race, but to all children in South Africa.

The experience in South Africa reminds us that forgiveness often is nurtured by and finds its authenticity in the extent to which we are willing to embrace the kind of "costly grace" articulated by Dietrich Bonhoeffer in the midst of the Nazi terror.[47] Bonhoeffer's case is that Christian forgiveness is modeled on that of Jesus in whose dying and rising we are shown the cost of forgiveness. Forgiveness is not merely a juridical absolution from guilt; it is the medium to lead us to communion and reconciliation. Its proper understanding draws us into a fuller conception of the atonement, embracing all of its various resonance. This view of forgiveness finds its value underrated in strictly therapeutic settings, yet possible in light of the personal transformation it elicits. Bonhoeffer's articulation of "costly grace" and emphasis upon the communal life to which it leads us gives forgiveness its deep authenticity. It might be said that forgiveness is effective to the extent it draws us into communal life characterized by transformative practices with our neighbor.

Such costly forgiveness, made possible through the forgiveness found at the cross, challenges all forms of therapeutic forgiveness.[48] First, costly forgiveness challenges individual autonomy. The Belhar Confession has

---

45. See the discussion in Kader Asmal, Louise Asmal, and Ronald Roberts, *Reconciliation Through Truth* (New York: St. Martin's Press, 1997), 51, 164; also *To Remember and to Heal: Theological and Psychological Reflections on Truth and Reconciliation*, ed. H. Russel Botman and Robin M. Petersen (Cape Town: Human and Rousseau, 1996).
46. Interview with Nico Smith, BTI/BC Films, June 1999.
47. I am following Jones, *Embodying Forgiveness*, 3–33; see Bonhoeffer, *The Cost of Discipleship*.
48. Schreiter, *In Water and in Blood*, 63–73.

called out the church in South African society to identify itself.[49] The church and its members can choose to embrace and be embraced by all people groups in South Africa, or it can draw itself into greater isolation and alienation. Forgiveness either drives us toward community in reconciliation or, left unresolved, allows us to become ever more autonomous and isolated. Forgiveness is the "boundary," to use terms suggested by Volf, between "exclusion and embrace." Second, when we forgive we enlarge our understanding by learning to see the world through the eyes of the other, our neighbor. By entering into the process of forgiveness we begin to appreciate more fully the meaning of personhood, how others and we are made gifted, yet often undermine the very gifts we bring to life. Forgiveness draws us to look for new forms of community heretofore unrealized. This is the triumph and tragedy of the South African experiment. It is why apartheid is not just a sin but also a theological heresy.

Finally, as we enter into new patterns of community through forgiveness, new practices in life are required in line with our new allegiances. These practices grow out of a spirituality of "costly grace." Such grace is pictured in the Passover story in Exodus, reminding us that the creation of a community of people only came through a blood ritual epitomized earlier in the blood of the sacrificial lamb granted Abraham. This theme, pictured in Christian theology in the sacrifice of Jesus, illustrates again the cost of genuine community. As we live with forgiveness we are called to "fill up the sufferings of Christ for the sake of his body, the Church" (Col. 1:24). It is a spirituality of costly grace that enables new forms of reconciliation to grow out of authentic forgiveness.[50] Forgiveness makes for good rhetorical resonance.

THE DIALECTIC OF FORGIVENESS

We might, in the third place, ask about a dialectic of forgiveness. How is this a part of a theology of forgiveness in Christianity? Dialectic has to do with analysis. It is the discussion and reasoning by intra- or interpersonal

49. Asmal, Asmal, and Roberts, *Reconciliation Through Truth*, 164.
50. I am following Schreiter here, *In Water and in Blood*, 83–93.

dialogue that takes place in the course of intellectual investigation. It is often defined as development through thesis, antithesis, and synthesis. Dialectic is often associated with systematic reasoning.

If the terms for a Christian theology of forgiveness are set in the context of the work of the Triune God, that is, set in God's forgiveness in the first instance, not interhuman forgiveness, and that an account of this forgiveness must be worked out in terms of the person and work of Jesus Christ as made efficacious through the work of the Spirit, dialectic drives us to ask about those who define their religion differently.

The de-escalation of conflict can have nothing to do with forgiveness and everything to do with it. When we were filming the material for the documentary, *Prelude to Kosovo,* our group from the BTI was in the city of Zenica where we had been invited to speak with some local Muslim leaders. After identifying initial presentations and ourselves we spent an uneasy hour or more on the front porch of the new Islamic Academy attempting to carry on a dialogue about the nature of the conflict in Bosnia from their perspective. After getting almost nowhere in the conversation for quite some time, a young professor of Sharia (Islamic Law) turned to me and said, "All we really want is for someone to say 'I'm sorry.'" This having been said, statements of apology having been heard, we proceeded into a more fruitful, if still incomplete conversation.

Forgiveness certainly takes place outside of Christian circles. Some will even contend that—given a track record that includes crusades, inquisitions, pogroms, and the pettiness of everyday church life—forgiveness is better understood elsewhere than in the church. Indeed, this chapter began with such parallel or suggestive terminology as *mercy, compassion,* and *acceptance.* That forgiveness is recognized, given, and received by all people is an aspect of our common identity. That it happens through God's grace and the work of the Spirit through Christ as we are drawn into the mystery of the church is a sign of the restoration and reconciliation of all things (Col. 1:15–20).

The Christian understanding of forgiveness is embedded in the larger narrative of the Gospel, in the work of the Triune God seen in the life, death, and resurrection of Jesus of Nazareth. This is understood to be of universal significance. However, when the question comes from a Jewish,

Muslim, Buddhist, or other context, that "all we really want is for someone to say 'I am sorry,'" there is a special poignancy for Christian theology. The notion of "Christian parables," proposed by Karl Barth, is a way of dealing with such an issue.[51] In other words, in seeking to explain why the light of God's forgiveness might appear as clearly or more so without reference to Jesus Christ, Barth turns to the parables of the New Testament, suggesting ways by which human words might nevertheless be true insofar as they correspond to the true Light. Barth uses the image of three concentric circles, an inner circle of Bible and church, another of mixed traditions and backgrounds, and a third of pure secularism. For Barth, and for Christian theology, their common point of reference in Jesus Christ, even if unacknowledged, unites all three.[52] This tactic is not new. It finds its counterpart in such representative theology as Justin's First Apology (c. 155 A.D.) and in the work of C. S. Lewis (1898–1963) or Hans Küng (1928-).[53] In fact, Barth argues that the more Christians embody authentic forgiveness and reconciliation, the more they are likely to find it elsewhere.[54]

The larger narrative of the Gospel draws us into a dialectic or conversation not only with those of other traditions, synchronous forgiveness in real time, but also with those who have come before. At this point the histories of the churches become a vast repository or laboratory in the history of successes and failures at forgiveness. This might be termed a diachronic exercise to accompany a contemporary synchronous understanding of what it means to forgive and is, at heart, what ecumenism is all about. It is in this diachronic dimension that we learn what it has meant to embody our faith such that our words are one with the identity we claim in Christ. Here practices such as baptism, eucharistic fellowship, a penitential life under the discipline of prayer and healing, our understanding of ways in which we

---

51. I am following Jones, *Embodying Forgiveness*, 220 n. 21. See Barth's discussion in *Church Dogmatics* IV/3/1, 38–165.
52. Paul Hiebert's analysis of the term *Christian* draws upon the mathematical categories of bounded sets, fuzzy sets, and centered sets as he seeks to bring clarity to the meaning of the term. Opting for the latter category, he writes that a line of demarcation exists but the focus should be on reaffirming the center and not on maintaining the boundary. See his article, "The Category Christian in the Mission Task," *International Review of Mission* 72 (1983): 421–27, 424.
53. Hans Küng, *Christianity: Essence, History, and Future* (New York: Continuum, 1995), 788–97, with reference to a global ethic.
54. Barth, *Church Dogmatics,* IV/3/1, 122.

express our sexual and procreative identities—all of this speaks to the embodying or rhetorical clarity of our lives. And it is here that the question must be raised as to whether it is possible to live a life of forgiveness and, hence reconciliation, apart from a community dedicated to such virtues. The time-honored answer is that this is the purpose and necessity of the church as community of disciples.

What does it mean to say, "I am sorry?" And what does this mean across the boundaries of competing narratives where antagonists share the same grand story or live in radically different universes of understanding? It cannot mean, "I am glad that I did it, but I am sorry that you feel so emotionally distraught over it."[55] This is not being neighbor to the other. It is not seeing myself in my neighbor or the image of God coming to us in the other. David Steele, working with conflict resolution the Balkans where competing narratives continue to bump up against each other, enumerates four stages of relational expression that need to be worked through before common problems might be faced across racial or ethnic lines: an expression and acknowledgment of grievance, a clear understanding of the identity of the other, the acceptance of the basic needs and concerns of the other, and critical honesty in how we view our history and that of the other.[56] Only having worked through these four steps, Steele argues, were the groups with which he worked able to move to a fifth stage, the creation of alternative approaches.[57] His work and the lessons he has learned illustrate how our identity, often derivative of our religion, can be misused and instrumentalized, not for the ends of forgiveness but for deeper forms of exclusivity and communal resentment.

---

55. W. H. Auden, *For the Time Being: A Christmas Oratorio* (London: Faber and Faber, 1945), 303–4. Herod's reflections after hearing the wise men announce that grace and forgiveness have entered the world: "Every crook will argue: I like committing crime. God likes forgiving them. Really the world is admirably arranged." Cited by Marty in "Ethos of Christian Forgiveness," 13.

56. David Steele, "Conflict Resolution among Religious People in Bosnia and Croatia," delivered at Restorative Justice Conference, Boston, March 1999, 11. This requires the struggle with looking at the past in its entirety; see Minow, *Between Vengeance and Forgiveness.* Guilt is usually not one-sided and each of our societies are driven by myths of racial and ethnic identity. In this the SA renaming of the Day of the Vow (12/16) to the Day of Reconciliation is intriguing and merits reflection in U.S. society with respect to our Thanksgiving Day, i.e., to the extent that it is interpreted in a one-sided way.

57. It is at this stage that I see the value of work by Roger Fischer and various schools of negotiation and conflict management coming into play.

We have not learned the terms of forgiveness until we can see our neigh-bor in the present, not as encumbered by the past or as prejudged in the future. Our rhetoric quickly becomes insincere and grandiloquent language unless nurtured by patterns that promote authenticity. The dialectic of for-giveness involves intercommunal dialogue, synchronic and diachronic reflec-tion, and interreligious reflection. Geiko Müller-Fahrenholz writes, "It is necessary to think about forgiveness not in spite of Auschwitz but because of Auschwitz."[58] It is also important to remember those voices, however small in number, who said "no" to Auschwitz. It is at places like this that our terminology, rhetoric, and dialectic for thinking about forgiveness become seen for what they are. From such a critical perspective, a theology of forgiveness drives us to realize the extent to which our religion, or that which functions as its equivalent, defines our identity whether this be the Confessing Church in Germany or the Uniting Church in South Africa. And, in becoming a part of our self-definition, religion becomes susceptible to being used in an instrumentalized fashion. Something so powerful as that, which shapes community, myth, ritual, and experience, can be easily manip-ulated as individuals or communities begin to experience differentiation, tension, and discover bases for social conflict. This has happened in South Africa. It can be tracked in the Middle East. It happens in the United States.

Finally, insofar as religion moves beyond institutionalization or "eccle-sio-cracy," it drives us to mystery.[59] This is not religious syncretism, nor is it the absence of interest in truth, but it does drive us to reflection on the experience of mystery, the Holy, and deepen our attempt through dialogue to define it. There is a tremendous interest in spirituality today, often up to the point that it becomes institutional in expression. Such reflection includes ways in which we think about myth and belief, how we define these terms and how they interpenetrate. Ritual and religious life become important as ways of patterning understanding. Community functions as the place in which understanding is reinforced through a social construc-tion of reality that includes the possibility of forgiveness. This morphology

58. Müller-Fahrenholz, *Art of Forgiveness.*
59. Term developed by Clarence Goen, "Escclesiocracy without Ecclesiology: Denominational Life in America," *Religion in Life* 48 (1979): 17–31.

of religion calls for an increased attention to the place of interreligious dialogue. This is important for its own sake as well as for social conflict in that when religious factors are drawn into such disputes the potential for violence escalates.

CHAPTER 2

Forgiveness, Reconciliation, & Justice

A Christian Contribution to a
More Peaceful Social Environment

Miroslav Volf

INTRODUCTION

IT IS NOT WHAT THE MAINSTREAM sociologists who followed in the footsteps of Karl Marx, Max Weber, and Emil Durkheim were predicting over the past century or so, but it happened. Instead of slowly withering away or lodging itself quietly into the privacy of worshipers' hearts, religion has emerged as an important player on the national and international scenes. It is too early to tell how permanent this resurgence of religion will be. The processes of secularization may well continue, though not so much in the older sense of the increasing loss of religious observance as in the newer sense of the diminishing influence of religion in contemporary societies. Be the fate of secularization in contemporary societies as it may, presently religion is well and alive on the public scene, so much so that a collection of essays with the title *Religion: The Missing Dimension of Statecraft* can become obligatory reading for diplomats in many countries, Western and non-Western, despite the fact that it bears all the marks of an initial effort to push at the boundaries of a discipline.[1]

In the public perception, the reassertion of religion as a political factor has not been for the good. It seems that the gods have mainly terror on their minds, as the title of Mark Jurgensmeyer's book on the global rise of

1. Douglas Johnston and Cynthia Sampson, eds., *Religion: The Missing Dimension of Statecraft* (New York: Oxford University Press, 1994).

religious violence suggests.[2] In the Western cultural milieu the contemporary coupling of religion and violence feeds most decisively on the memories of the wars that plagued Europe from the 1560s to the 1650s and in which religion was "the burning motivation, the one that inspired fanatical devotion and the most vicious hatred."[3] It was these wars that contributed a great deal to the emergence of secularizing modernity. As Stephen Toulmin has argued in *Cosmopolis,* modernity did not emerge, as is often claimed, simply as a result of its protagonists' endeavor to dispel the darkness of tradition and superstition with the light of philosophical and scientific reason. It is not accidental that Descartes "discovered" the one correct method to acquire knowledge in a time when "over much of the continent, people had a fair chance of having their throats cut and their houses burned down by strangers who merely disliked their religion." A new way of establishing truth "that was independent of, and neutral between, particular religious loyalties" seemed an attractive alternative to war fueled by dogmatic claims.[4] As was the case with their Enlightenment forebears, many of our contemporaries see in religion a pernicious social ill that needs to be treated rather than a medicine from which curative power is expected. The resurgence of religion seems to go hand in hand with the resurgence of religiously legitimized violence. Hence it is necessary to weaken, neutralize, or eliminate religion as a factor in public life.

In this chapter I want to contest the claim that the Christian faith, as one of the major world religions, predominantly fosters violence and assert, instead, that it should be seen as a contributor to a more peaceful social environment. I will not argue that the Christian faith has not been and is not often employed to foster violence. Obviously, such an argument cannot plausibly be made; not only have Christians committed atrocities and other lesser forms of violence, but they have also drawn on religious beliefs to jus-

---

2. Mark Jurgensmeyer, *Terror in the Mind of God: The Global Rise of Religious Violence* (Berkeley: University of California Press, 2000).
3. R. Scott Appleby, *The Ambivalence of the Sacred: Religion, Violence, and Reconciliation* (Lanham, Md.: Rowman and Littlefield, 2000), 2. See Ronald Asch, *The Thirty Years' War: The Holy Roman Empire and Europe, 1618–48* (New York: St. Martin's, 1997).
4. Steven Toulmin, *Cosmopolis: The Hidden Agenda of Modernity* (New York: Free Press, 1990), 17, 70.

tify them.[5] Neither will I argue that the Christian faith has been historically less associated with violence than other major religions; I am not at all sure that this is the case. Rather I contend that, at least when it comes to Christianity, the cure for religiously induced or legitimized violence is not *less* religion but, in a carefully qualified sense, *more* religion. Put differently, the more we reduce Christian faith to vague religiosity or conceive of it as exclusively the private affair of individuals, the worse off we will be; inversely, the more we nurture Christian faith as an ongoing tradition that by its intrinsic content shapes behavior and in its regulative reach touches the public sphere, the better off we will be. "Thick" practice of the Christian faith will help reduce violence and shape a culture of peace.

I will first offer some general remarks on the relation between Christian faith and violence, and then attempt to show that at Christianity's heart, and not just at its margins, lie important resources for creating a culture of peace. Before I proceed, one comment about the focus of my exploration and two disclaimers are in order. I cannot offer here a perspective on the entire complex of issues that relate to the reassertion of religion as a political factor on the national and international scenes. For instance, I leave completely aside such crucial issues as the question of whether there is a shift today toward religiously driven conflicts and, if so, what are the dynamics characteristic of security action on behalf of religion. Instead of looking at religion as an object of securitization, I am exploring normative dimensions of the impact a particular religion—the Christian faith—should have upon the security action taken in defense of *any object* and upon the way in which relations between the parties after such action are negotiated.

And now the disclaimers. First, by concentrating on religious resources I am neither excluding other resources nor suggesting that they are less important. "Shared democracy," "interdependence," and "dense international

---

5. For a survey see Gottfried Maron, "Frieden und Krieg. Ein Blick in die Theologie- und Kirchengeschichte," in *Glaubenskriege in Vergangenheit und Gegenwart,* ed. Peter Herrmann (Göttingen: Vandenhoeck und Ruprecht, 1996), 17–35. See also Karlheinz Deschner, *Kriminalgeschichte des Christentums,* 6 vols. (Reinbeck bei Hamburg: Rohwolt, 1986ff.) and, in response to his work, H. R. Seeliger, ed., *Kriminalizierung des Christentums? Karlheinz Deschner's Kirchengeschichte auf dem Pruefstand* (Freiburg im Breisgau: Herder, 1993).

organization networks," for instance, are crucial, as Bruce Russett has argued, echoing major themes of Kant's essay, "Perpetual Peace."[6] Second, by concentrating on the resources of the Christian faith I am not claiming that other religions are by nature violent or even that Christianity owns the comparative advantage. I merely want to argue, by exploring the religion I know best, that contrary to the opinion of many academics, politicians, and the general public religion can be associated with the very opposite of violence-inducing passions.

CHRISTIAN FAITH AND VIOLENCE

In the past, scholars have argued in a variety of ways that the Christian faith fosters violence. I will concentrate here only on two types of arguments that, in my opinion, go to the heart of the matter. Other arguments, such as the one based on the combination of divine omnipotence, omniscience, and implacable justice—claiming that the omnipotent God, who sees everything, wills the punishment of every transgression—will take care of themselves, if adequate response is given to the two kinds of arguments I address here.

The first type of argument claims that religions are by nature violent, and that the Christian faith, being a religion, is also by nature violent.[7] In his book *Prey into Hunter* Maurice Bloch has, for instance, argued that the "irreducible core of the ritual process" involves "a marked element of

---

6. Bruce Russett, "A Neo-Kantian Perspective: Democracy, Interdependence, and International Organizations in Building Security Communities," in *Security Communities,* ed. Emanuel Adler and Michael Barnett (Cambridge: Cambridge University Press, 1998), 368–94; see also Russett, *Grasping the Democratic Peace: Principles for a Post-Cold War World* (Princeton, N.J.: Princeton University Press, 1993); Immanuel Kant, *Perpetual Peace,* trans. Lewis White Beck (New York: Bobbs-Merrill, 1957).
7. Juergensmeyer's *Terror in the Mind of God* depends on such a belief. One central reason why violence has accompanied religion's renewed political presence, he argues, has to do with "the nature of religious imagination, which always has had the propensity to absolutize and to project images of cosmic war" (242). Of course, cosmic war is waged for the sake of peace, so that precisely as a phenomenon at whose core lies cosmic war "religion has been order restoring and life affirming" (159). But if it is not to be violent, religion cannot be left to itself; it "needs the temper of rationality and fair play that Enlightenment values give to civil society" (243).

violence or . . . of [a] conquest . . . of the here and now by the transcendental."[8] He explains:

> In the first part of the ritual the here and now is simply left behind by the move towards the transcendental. This initial movement represents the transcendental as supremely desirable and the here and now as of no value. The return is different. In the return the transcendental is not left behind but continues to be attached to those who made the initial move in its direction; its value is not negated. Secondly, the return to the here and now is really a conquest of the here and now by the transcendental.[9]

It is this violent return from the transcendental sphere, Bloch continues, that explains "the often-noted fact that religion so easily furnishes an idiom of expansionist violence to people in a whole range of societies, an idiom which, under certain circumstances, becomes a legitimation for actual violence."[10]

Let us assume that Bloch has analyzed the core of the ritual process correctly. The question still remains whether one should look at the core of the ritual process, stripped of the texture as well as of the larger context that a concrete religion gives it, in order to understand the relation of religions to violence. Here is a thought experiment. Imagine that the first part of the ritual—the leaving of the here and now by the move toward the transcendental—is understood by a religion as the death of the self to his or her own self-centered desires and as entry into a transcendental space of harmonious peace. And suppose that the second part of the ritual consists in the conquest of the here and now by the transcendental precisely as understood in this peaceful way. If this is how the formal structure of ritual can be filled in materially, would such a religion serve as "a legitimation of actual violence"? Would not the "conquest," if successful, be precisely the victory of "transcendental" peace over the violence of the here and now?

8. Maurice Bloch, *Prey Into Hunter: The Politics of Religious Experience* (Cambridge: Cambridge University Press, 1992), 4–5.
9. Ibid., 5.
10. Ibid., 6.

As we are aware, such a religion need not be imagined as hypothetically existing. For what I have proposed is precisely how the Christian faith understands itself.[11] Violence is fostered by Christianity in the way Bloch suggests only when its notion of the "transcendental" is stripped of its proper content and then infused with the values of the "here and now" around which the conflict rages. One could object that *any* conquest of the here and now by the transcendental involves violence. But if the noncoercive victory of peace over violence is itself seen as implicated in violence, then one may well wonder whether the notion of violence has been hopelessly muddled.

Other scholars, like Regina Schwartz in her book *The Curse of Cain,* try to explain the Christian faith's complicity in violence by pointing not to the general features of the Christian faith as religion, but to one of its characteristic components. Along with Judaism and Islam, Christianity is a monotheistic religion, and therefore, Schwartz argues, an exclusive religion that divides people into "us," who know the one true God, and "them," who do not. Such monotheistic exclusivity, which imports the category of universal "truth" into the religious sphere, is bound to have a violent legacy, the argument goes.[12] "We," the faithful, have on our side the true God who is against "them," the infidels and renegades.[13]

But is the divine oneness necessarily violent? Is simply *any* notion of divine oneness violent? Does not, for instance, universalism, which is implied by divine oneness, work also *against* the tendency to divide people

---

11. Bloch engages the Christian faith directly, envisaging the possibility of its not underwriting violence. But in his account such a possibility is predicated on a "refusal of the second phase of rebounding violence, that is, a refusal of the conquest of external vitality which is therefore ultimately a refusal to continue with earthly life" (90–91). St. Paul's Christianity, he believes, is an example of such a refusal—or rather, an example of a half-hearted refusal, since Paul also undertook the "prudent organization of a well-organized church firmly embedded in the continuing practical and political world" (94). On my reading, St. Paul's Christianity is not an example of a refusal of the conquest of the here and now, but of the kind of conquest for which nonviolence is constitutive; communities of faith were meant to instantiate precisely this conquest.

12. Jakov Jukic sees the heart of monotheism's exclusivity precisely in the insertion into the religious domain of the question of truth which the belief in one God inescapably raises. To believe in one God means to believe in one *true* God. The claim to truth in religious domain has immediate consequence in the public realm (*Lica i Maske Svetoga: Ogledi iz drustvene religiologije* [Zagreb: Krscanska sadasnjost, 1997]; 242–43).

13. Regina Schwartz, *The Curse of Cain: The Violent Legacy of Monotheism* (Chicago: University of Chicago Press, 1997).

into "us" and "them"? More significantly, would not pressure be exerted against self-enclosed and exclusive identities if the monotheism in question were of a Trinitarian kind?[14] Let me explicate this last rhetorical question.[15] One of the socially most important aspects of the doctrine of the Trinity concerns the conceptualization of identities. To believe that the one God is the Father, the Son, and the Spirit is to believe that the identity of the "Father" cannot be understood apart from the "Son" and the "Spirit." To be the divine "Father" is from the start to have one's identity defined by another and therefore not to be undifferentiated and self-enclosed. More-over, the divine persons as non-self-enclosed identities are understood by Christians to form a perfect communion of love; the persons give them-selves to each other and receive themselves from each other in love. It would be difficult, so it seems to me, to argue that *this* kind of monotheism fos-ters violence. Instead, in Bloch's terminology, it grounds peace here and now in the transcendental peacefulness of the divine being. The argument for the inherent violence of monotheism works only if one reduces the thick religious description of God to naked oneness and then postulates such abstract oneness to be of decisive social significance.

Again, my point is not that the Christian faith has not been used to legit-imize violence, or that there are no elements in the Christian faith on which such misuses build. It is rather that, at its heart, the Christian faith is peace-creating and peace-sustaining, so that those misuses are less likely to hap-pen when people have deep and informed commitments to the faith, commitments with robust cognitive and moral content—at least when these commitments stem from historic Christian beliefs rather than being recast arbitrarily by the leaders of short-lived and oppressive communities. If reli-gious commitments of all cognitive and moral content are stripped out and faith reduced to a cultural resource endowed with a diffuse aura of the sacred, what likely remains is religiously inspired or legitimized violence. Nurture people in the tradition and educate them, and any militants will be militants for peace. As R. Scott Appleby argued recently in his book *The*

14. For a critique of Schwartz along these lines see Miroslav Volf, "Jehovah on Trial," *Chris-tianity Today* (April 27, 1998): 32–35.
15. For the following see Miroslav Volf, "The Trinity Is Our Social Program: The Doctrine of the Trinity and the Shape of Social Engagement," *Modern Theology* 14 (1998): 403–23.

Ambivalence of the Sacred, contrary to the misconception popular in some academic and political circles, religious people play a positive role in the world of human conflicts and contribute to peace not when they "moderate their religion or marginalize their deeply held, vividly symbolized, and often highly particular beliefs" but rather "when they remain *religious* actors."[16]

Religions contribute to violence between parties in conflict in two main ways: (1) by assuring the combatants of the (absolute) rightness of their cause and, correlatively, the (absolute) evil of their enemies,[17] and (2) by sacralizing the communal identity of one party and, correlatively, demonizing others.[18] In hopes of showing that the Christian faith puts pressure on its mature and informed practitioners *not* to act out of persuasion as to the absolute rightness of their cause, I will explore the nexus of issues around the questions of forgiveness, reconciliation, and justice that lie at the heart of what this faith is about. As the example of South Africa, with its Truth and Reconciliation Commission, paradigmatically attests, these issues are particularly relevant to postconflict situations. An argument similar to the one I make here about religion and the absolute rightness of one party in conflict could be made in relation to the sacralization of communal identities, though I will not pursue that here.[19]

In the following I will first discuss and discard two wrongheaded ways to relate forgiveness, reconciliation, and justice and then argue for an alternative.

CHEAP RECONCILIATION

The first wrongheaded way to relate justice to forgiveness and reconciliation can be called "cheap reconciliation." It attained prominence in theo-

---

16. Appleby, *Ambivalence of the Sacred,* 16.
17. So, for instance, Juergensmeyer, *Terror in the Mind of God,* 242.
18. So, for instance, Michael Sells, *The Bridge Betrayed: Religion and Genocide in Bosnia,* Comparative Studies in Religion and Society 11 (Berkeley: University of California Press, 1998).
19. See Miroslav Volf, *Exclusion and Embrace: A Theological Exploration of Identity, Otherness, and Reconciliation* (Nashville: Abingdon Press, 1996).

logical circles through the Kairos Document, written by theologians critical of the South African regime before the dismantling of apartheid. They used the term in analogy to the notion of "cheap grace," which designates the readiness to receive love from God with no sense of obligation toward one's neighbors. Significantly, the term "cheap grace" was coined by Dietrich Bonhoeffer, a theologian who for religious reasons participated in the resistance against the Nazi regime.[20] The drafters of the Kairos Document set the context for understanding what they meant by "cheap reconciliation" as follows:

> In our situation in South Africa today it would be totally unchristian to plead for reconciliation and peace before the present injustices have been removed. Any such plea plays into the hands of the oppressor by trying to persuade those of us who are oppressed to accept our oppression and to become reconciled to the intolerable crimes that are committed against us. That is not Christian reconciliation, it is sin. It is asking us to become accomplices in our own oppression, to become servants of the devil. No reconciliation is possible in South Africa without justice.[21]

As I will argue shortly, I am not persuaded that reconciliation should be pursued only *after* injustices have been removed, but rather believe that the struggle against injustice is part of the more fundamental pursuit of reconciliation. But, putting this matter of the temporal sequencing of justice and reconciliation aside for a moment, the critique of cheap reconciliation that emerges from the text is clear. Cheap reconciliation sets "justice" and "peace" against each other as alternatives. To pursue cheap reconciliation means to give up on the struggle for freedom, to renounce the pursuit of justice, to put up with oppression.

If I am not mistaken, some such meaning of the notion of "reconciliation" predominates in public discourse today. One speaks of "national

---

20. Dietrich Bonhoeffer, *The Cost of Discipleship*, trans. R. H. Fuller (New York: Macmillan, 1963), 45–47, 59.
21. *The Kairos Document: Challenge to the Church. A Theological Comment on the Political Crisis in South Africa* (Grand Rapids, Mich.: Wm. B. Eerdmans, 1986), Art. 3.1.

reconciliation" and expects from it "collective healing" and greater "political unity" or, conversely, fears that behind it lurk organic notions of the
social "body" and the centralization of power. Stripped of its moral content,
reconciliation is contrasted so starkly with "justice" that one has to weigh
the relative values of "justice" and "unity" in order to assess to what extent
the sacrifice of justice can be morally acceptable and politically desirable in
order to achieve political unity.

To advocate cheap reconciliation clearly means to betray those who suffer injustice, deception, and violence. Though the Christian faith has been
all too often employed to advocate such reconciliation—indeed, the Kairos
Document as a critique of "cheap reconciliation" was directed against the
theology of the pro-apartheid churches—such a concept of reconciliation
really amounts to a betrayal of the Christian faith. Almost universally, theologians and church leaders today recognize that the prophetic denuncia-
tion of injustice has a prominent place in the Christian faith. This prophetic
strand cannot be removed without gravely distorting Christianity. The struggle against injustice is inscribed in the very character of the Christian faith.
Hence an adequate notion of reconciliation must include justice as a constitutive element. And yet it is precisely here that watchfulness is needed. For
the imperative of justice, severed from the overarching framework of grace
within which it is properly situated and from the obligation to nonviolence,
underlies much of the Christian faith's misuse by religiously legitimized violence.

In the context of cheap reconciliation, forgiveness is best described as
acting toward the perpetrator "as if their sin were not there."[22] The offense
has happened—or one party thinks that it has happened—but the injured
party treats the offender as if it had not. At the popular level, one is told simply to shrug one's shoulders and say, "Oh, never mind." This "never mind"
exculpates the offender even from "moral reproach."

In *The Genealogy of Morals* Friedrich Nietzsche advocated a version of
"as-if-not" attitude toward transgression. He suggested it in the context of
the opposition between "slave morality" and "noble morality." The first,
which operates along the axis of "good-evil," is reactive in the sense that it

---

22. John Milbank, *Theology and Social Theory: Beyond Secular Reason* (Oxford: Blackwell,
    1990), 411.

is shaped by the situation with respect to which it defines human conduct; the second is purely positive, existing in sovereign disregard of the situation. In the process of making this distinction, Nietzsche advocates an attitude toward transgression untouched by concerns for justice as desert. He writes:

> To be unable to take his enemies, his misfortunes and even his *misdeeds* seriously for long—that is the sign of strong, rounded natures with superabundance of a power which is flexible, formative, healing and can make one forget (a good example from the modern world is Mirabeau, who had no recall for the insult and slights directed at him and who would not forgive, simply because he—forgot). A man like this shakes from him, with one shrug, many worms which would have burrowed into another man; here and here alone is it possible, assuming that this is possible at all on earth—truly to "love your neighbour."[23]

Such sovereign disregard for injuries from others demands extraordinary strength, almost that of an *übermensch*, and a person with sensibilities nurtured by the culture of late modernity may be tempted to reject Nietzsche's proposal simply on that count. This, however, may be less an argument against Nietzsche than against the weakness of the victims of offenses. At least for those who, unlike Nietzsche, think that moral concerns are legitimate, the crucial question is whether the "as-if-not" attitude toward transgression is morally acceptable. The answer is arguably "No." It is morally wrong to treat a murderer "as if" he had not committed the murder—or at least it is wrong to do so until some important things have happened: for example, until the murder has been named as murder and the murderer has distanced himself from the deed. One may also suggest that disregard for justice as desert entails the abdication of responsibility for the transformation of the perpetrator and the world at large. For it is hard to imagine how one could induce offenders to change without, at least implicitly, morally reproaching their deeds.

Significantly, Nietzsche himself never described the "as-if-not" attitude

23. Friedrich Nietzsche, *On the Genealogy of Morals,* trans. Carol Diethe (Cambridge: Cambridge University Press, 1994), 23–24, pt. 1, sec. 10.

as forgiveness. Mirabeau, his example of the "virtuous," *could not forgive* because he had forgotten! Because forgiveness is conceptually tied to justice as desert, Nietzsche had little positive to say about it and tended to replace it with "forgetting."[24] Nietzsche rejected forgiveness precisely because he saw rightly its positive relation to justice. Forgiveness is more than just "the overcoming of anger and resentment."[25] It always entails forgoing a rightful claim against someone who has in some way harmed or offended us. Such forgoing of a rightful claim makes forgiveness unjust and precisely thereby prevents forgiveness from falling outside the concern for justice.

The concern for justice is integral to forgiveness and reconciliation. But what is the precise relation between justice on the one hand and forgiveness and reconciliation on the other?

FIRST JUSTICE, THEN RECONCILIATION

One way of positively relating justice to reconciliation is to suggest that the process of reconciliation can begin only *after* injustice has been removed. This, as noted earlier, seems to be the position of the Kairos Document, which so rightly denounces "cheap reconciliation." But is this "first justice, then reconciliation" stance plausible? There are major problems with it.

First and most fundamentally, "first justice, then reconciliation" is impossible to carry out. All accounts of what is "just" are to some extent relative to a particular person or group and are invariably contested by that

24. See Nietzsche, *Beyond Good and Evil: Prelude to a Philosophy of the Future,* trans. Marion Faber (Oxford: Oxford University Press, 1998), 110, Aphorism 217. In *Human, All Too Human: A Book for Free Spirits* (trans. Marion Faber [Lincoln: University of Nebraska Press, 1996]), Nietzsche argued for the impossibility of forgiveness by tying it to (1) the knowledge of the evil-doer about what he or she is doing and (2) to the right of the offended or of the third party "to accuse and to punish." Since the evildoer can never fully know what he or she is doing and since we do not have the right to accuse and to punish, Nietzsche argued, forgiveness is impossible. So clearly, for Nietzsche, forgiveness presupposes the framework of justice.

25. So Jeffrie G. Murphy, "Forgiveness and Resentment," in *Forgiveness and Mercy,* ed. Jeffrie G. Murphy and Jean Hampton (Cambridge: Cambridge University Press, 1988), 14–34, 24. Pamela Hieronymi's response to a prevalent claim that forgiveness is primarily a matter of manipulating oneself out of resentment is to the point: "Ridding one's self of resentment by taking a specially designed pill, for example, would not count as forgiveness" ("Articulating an Uncompromising Forgiveness," *Philosophy and Phenomenological Research* [forthcoming], 2).

person's or group's rivals. In any conflict with a prolonged history, each party sees itself as the victim and perceives its rival as the perpetrator and has good reasons for reading the situation that way.

Even more significantly, as Nietzsche rightly noted in *Human, All Too Human,* given the nature of human interaction, every pursuit of justice not only rests on partial injustice but also creates new injustices.[26] In an ongoing relationship, as the temporal and spatial contexts of an offense are broadened to give an adequate account of it, it becomes clear that any action we undertake now is inescapably ambiguous, at best partially just and therefore partially unjust. No peace is possible within the overarching framework of strict justice for the simple reason that no strict justice is possible. Hence the demand at the communal or political levels is often not for "justice" but for "as much justice as possible." But the trouble is that, within the overarching framework of strict justice, enough justice never gets done because more justice is always possible than in fact gets done.

Second, even if strict justice were possible, it is questionable whether it would be desirable. Most of us today feel that the legal provisions of the Hebrew Bible, which insist that the punishment be commensurate with the crime, are excessive. "An eye for an eye, a tooth for a tooth" strikes us as too severe. Originally, of course, the provision was meant to restrict the excesses of vengeance. And yet it is precisely the demand for more than equal retribution that is strictly just. If a person's tooth is broken in retribution for that person's breaking mine, we are *not* even for the simple reason that the situation of offense is manifestly not one of exchange. In a situation of exchange, both of us would have disposal over our teeth, and I would give mine under condition that I was given his in return. But in a situation of offense, the consent to the exchange is lacking. By breaking my tooth he has violated me and therefore deserves greater punishment than just the equal breaking of his tooth. Most of us, however, don't think that a world in which corrective justice was pursued even with such strictness as the principle "tooth for a tooth" demands would be a desirable one; and so, even when we demand "justice," we are in fact after something much less

26. Nietzsche, *Human, All Too Human,* 216. For a related but different critique of justice see Jacques Derrida, "Force of Law: The Mystical Foundation of Authority," in *Deconstruction and the Possibility of Justice,* ed. Drucilla Cornell, Michel Rosenfeld, and David Gray Carlson (New York: Routledge, 1992), 24–26.

than strict justice, which is to say that we are ready tacitly to "forgive" part of the offense. We are at least implicitly aware that the normal functioning of human life is impossible without grace.

Third, even if justice could be satisfied, the conflicting parties would continue to be at odds with one another. The enforcement of justice would rectify past wrongs but it would not create communion between victims and perpetrators. Yet some form of communion—some form of positive relationship—needs to be established if the victim and perpetrator are to be fully healed. Consider the fact that personal and group identities are not defined simply from within an individual or a group, apart from relationships with their near and distant neighbors. We are who we are not simply as autonomous and self-constituting entities but essentially also as related and other-determined. I, Miroslav Volf, am who I am not simply because I am distinct from all other individuals but in part also because over the past two years, for instance, I have been shaped by interaction with my son, Nathanael. Similarly, to be a Serb today *is* in part to have Albanians as one's neighbors and Kosovars as a minority within one's borders, to be a citizen of a country that waged wars against Bosnia and Croatia and was bombed by NATO. If we are in part who we are because we are embedded in a nexus of relations that make others part of ourselves, then we cannot be properly healed without our relationships being healed too. The pursuit of justice, even if *per impossibile* fully successful, would satisfy our sense of what is right but would not heal us. It would bring us peace only as the absence of war, but not as the harmonious ordering of differences.

The "first justice, then reconciliation" stance implies that forgiveness should be offered only after the demands of justice have been satisfied. Forgiveness here means no more than the refusal to allow an adequately redressed wrongdoing to continue to qualify negatively one's relationship with the wrongdoer.

Strange as it may seem, forgiveness *after* justice is not much different from forgiveness *outside* justice. Forgiveness outside justice means treating the offender as if he had not committed the offense. Forgiveness after justice means doing the same—only the demand that justice be satisfied before forgiveness can be given is meant to redress the situation so that one can *rightly* treat the wrongdoer as if he had not committed the deed. Whereas in the first case forgiveness is the stance of a heroic individual who is "strong" and "noble" enough to be unconcerned with the offense, in the second case forgiveness is the stance of a strictly moral individual who shows enough integrity so that after the injustice has been redressed he or she refuses to feel and act vindictively. To forgive outside justice is to make no moral demands; to forgive after justice is not to be vindictive. In both cases it is to treat the offender as if he had not committed the offense or as if it were not his.

The first and decisive argument that I brought against the "first justice, then reconciliation" stance applies to this notion of forgiveness, too. If justice is impossible, as I have argued, then forgiveness could never take place. There is another important argument against this notion of forgiveness. If forgiveness were properly given only after strict justice had been established, then one would *not* be going beyond one's duty in offering forgiveness; one would indeed *wrong* the original wrongdoer if one did not offer forgiveness. "The wrong has been fully redressed," an offender could complain if forgiveness were not forthcoming, "and hence you owe me forgiveness." But this is not how we understand forgiveness. It is a *gift* that the wronged gives to the wrongdoer. If we forgive we are considered magnanimous; if we refuse to forgive, we may be insufficiently virtuous—for, as Robert Adams argues, "we ought in general be treated better than we deserve"—but we do not wrong the other.[27]

We need to look for an alternative both to forgiveness and reconciliation outside of justice and to forgiveness and reconciliation after justice. I want to suggest that such an alternative notion of forgiveness and reconciliation is to be found at the heart of the Christian faith—in the narrative of the cross of Christ, which reveals the very character of God. On the cross, God is manifest as the God who, though in no way indifferent toward the distinction between good and evil, nonetheless lets the sun shine on both the good and the evil (cf. Matt. 5:45); as the God of indiscriminate love who died for the ungodly to bring them into the divine communion (cf. Rom. 5:8); as the God who offers grace—not cheap grace, but grace nonetheless—to the vilest evildoer.

27. Robert M. Adams, "Involuntary Sins," *The Philosophical Review* 104 (1985): 24.

WILL TO EMBRACE, ACTUAL EMBRACE

So what is the relationship between reconciliation and justice that is inscribed in the very heart of the Christian faith? Partly to keep things rhetorically simpler, I will substitute the more poetic "embrace" for "peace" as the terminal point of the reconciliation process as I explore this issue in the reminder of my text. The Christian tradition can be plausibly construed to make four central claims about the relation between justice and embrace.

The Primacy of the Will to Embrace

The starting point is the primacy of the will to embrace the other, even the offender. Since the God Christians worship is the God of unconditional and indiscriminate love, the will to embrace the other is the most fundamental obligation of Christians. The claim is radical and, precisely in its radicality, socially significant. The will to give ourselves to others and to welcome them, to readjust our identities to make space for them, is prior to any judgment about others, except that of identifying them in their humanity. The will to embrace precedes any "truth" about others and any reading of their action with respect to justice. This will is absolutely indiscriminate and strictly immutable; it transcends the moral mapping of the social world into "good" and "evil."

The primacy of the will to embrace is sustained negatively by some important insights into the nature of the human predicament. Since the Christian tradition sees all people as marred by evil and since it conceives of evil not just as act but as a power that transcends individual actors, it rejects the construction of the world around exclusive moral polarities— here, on our side, "the just, the pure, the innocent," and there, on the other side, "the unjust, the defiled, the guilty." Such an exclusively polarized world does not exist. If our search for peace is predicated on its existence, in its factual absence we will be prone to make the mistake of refusing to read conflicts in moral terms and thus lazily falling back on either establishing symmetries in guilt or proclaiming all actors as irrational. Instead of conceiving of our search for peace as a struggle on behalf of "the just, the pure, the innocent," we should understand it as an endeavor to transform the world in which justice and injustice, innocence and guilt crisscross and intersect, and we should do so guided by the recognition that the economy of undeserved grace has primacy over the economy of moral desert.

Attending to Justice as a Precondition of Actual Embrace

Notice that I have described the will to embrace as unconditional and indiscriminate, but not the embrace itself. A genuine embrace, an embrace that neither play-acts acceptance nor crushes the other, cannot take place until justice is attended to. Hence the will to embrace includes in itself the will to determine what is just and to name wrong as wrong. The will to embrace includes the will to rectify the wrongs that have been done, and it includes the will to reshape the relationships to correspond to justice. And yet, though an actual embrace requires attending to justice, it does not require the establishment of strict justice. Indeed, the pursuit of embrace is precisely an alternative to constructing social relations around strict justice. It is a way of creating a genuine and deeply human community of harmonious peace in an imperfect world of inescapable injustice.[28] Without the grace of embrace, humane life in our world—in which evil is inescapably committed but our deeds are irreversible—would be impossible.[29]

The Will to Embrace as the Framework of the Search for Justice

To emphasize the will to embrace means more than to advocate learning how to live with inescapable injustice while not giving up on the pursuit of justice. For the will to embrace is also a precondition of (even tenuous) convergences and agreements on what is just in a world of strife. Without the will to embrace, each party will insist on the justness of his or her own cause, and strife will continue. Given the nature of human beings

28. Robert Burt, "Reconciliation with Injustice," in *Transgression, Punishment, Responsibility, Forgiveness: Studies in Culture, Law and the Sacred* (Madison: University of Wisconsin Law School, 1998), 106–22 (*Graven Images* 4 [1998]).
29. On the need for forgiveness against the backdrop of the irreversibility of deeds see Hannah Arendt, *The Human Condition: A Study of the Central Dilemmas Facing Modern Man* (Garden City, N.Y.: Doubleday, 1959), 212–13.

and their interaction, there is too much injustice in an uncompromising struggle for justice.

The will to embrace—love—sheds the light of knowledge by the fire it carries with it. Our eyes need the light of this fire to perceive any justice in the causes and actions of our enemies. Granted, our enemies may prove to be as unjust as they seem, and what they insist is just may in fact be a perversion of justice. But if there is any justice in their causes and actions, only the will to embrace will make us capable of perceiving it, because it will let us see both them and ourselves with their eyes. Similarly, the will to exclude—hatred—blinds by the fire it carries with it. The fire of exclusion directs its light only on the injustice of others; any justness they may have is enveloped in darkness or branded as covert injustice—a merely contrived goodness that makes their evil all the more deadly. Both the "clenched fist" of exclusion and the "open arms" of embrace are epistemic stances; they are the moral conditions of adequate moral perception. The clenched fist hinders the perception of the possible justness of our opponents and thereby reinforces injustice; the open arms help detect any justness that may hide behind what seems to be the manifest injustness of our opponents and thereby reinforce justice. To agree on justice in situations of conflict a person must want more than justice; that person must want embrace.

Embrace as the Horizon of the Struggle for Justice

As in many of our activities, in the struggle for justice much depends on the *telos* of the struggle. Toward what is the struggle oriented? Is it oriented simply toward ensuring that everyone gets what he or she deserves? Or is it oriented toward the larger goal of healing relationships? I think the latter is the case. Hence the embrace should be the *telos* of the struggle for justice. If not, reconciliation will not even be attempted until the "right" side has won. And unless reconciliation is the horizon of the struggle for justice from the outset, it is not clear why reconciliation should even be attempted after the victory of the "right" side has been achieved.

Pulling all four features of the relation between reconciliation and justice together we can say that reconciliation, in its social sense, is an eschatological or "utopian" term with a robust moral content. It describes primarily a process whose goal is not so much the integration of citizens into a political unity as the creation of a community in which each recognizes and is recognized by all and in which all mutually give themselves to each other in love. In this way the concept of reconciliation stands in opposition to any notion of self-enclosed totality predicated on various forms of exclusion. And far from standing in contrast to justice, for such a notion of reconciliation justice is an integral element. Though reconciliation issues *ultimately* in a state "beyond justice," it does so precisely by attending to justice rather than by circumventing it.

And yet, though it is primarily an "utopian" concept, reconciliation nevertheless also describes a way of living in a world of strife—a world of conflict over scarce goods between actors who differ in power. In such a world, the practice of reconciliation does not translate into the imposition of harmony by coercively suppressing strife; this would be mere pacification as an act of power. Rather, it translates into the shaping of cultural sensibilities that help people live in a humane way in the absence of the final harmony.

FORGIVENESS AND
THE PRIMACY OF EMBRACE

First, forgiveness does not stand outside of justice. To the contrary, forgiveness is possible only against the backdrop of a tacit affirmation of justice. Forgiveness always entails blame. Anyone who has been forgiven for what she has *not* done will attest to that. Forgiveness should therefore not be confused with acceptance of the other. Acceptance is a purely positive concept; any notion of negation is foreign to it, except, obviously, that it implies negation of nonacceptance. But negation is constitutive of forgiveness. To offer forgiveness is at the same time to condemn the deed and accuse the doer; to receive forgiveness is at the same time to admit to the deed and accept the blame.[30]

---

30. It is important to note that human forgiveness cannot remove guilt. As Nicolai Hartmann rightly pointed out in his *Ethics*, human forgiveness is "a moral act on the part of him who forgives and solely concerns his conduct toward the guilty." "Forgiveness may very well

Second, forgiveness presupposes that justice—full justice in the strict sense of the term—has not been done. If justice were fully done, forgiveness would not be necessary, except in the limited and inadequate sense of not being vindictive; justice itself would have fully repaid for the wrongdoing. Forgiveness is necessary because strict justice is not done and strictly speaking cannot be done.

Third, forgiveness entails not only the affirmation of the claims of justice but also their transcendence. More precisely, by forgiving we affirm the claims of justice in the very act of not letting them count against the one whom we forgive. By stating that the claims of justice need not be (fully) satisfied, the person who forgives indirectly underscores the fact that what the sense of justice claims to be a wrongdoing is indeed a wrongdoing.

Fourth, since it consists in forgoing the affirmed claims of justice, forgiveness, like any instantiation of grace, involves self-denial and risk. One has let go of something one had a right to, and one is not fully certain whether one's magnanimity will bear fruit either in one's inner peace or in a restored relationship. Yet forgiveness is also laden with promise. Forgiveness is the context in which wrongdoers can come to the recognition of their own injustice. To accuse wrongdoers by simply insisting on strict justice is to drive them down the path of self-justification and denial before others and before themselves. To accuse wrongdoers by offering forgiveness is to invite them to self-knowledge and release. Such an invitation has the potential of leading the wrongdoer to admit guilt and to repent, and thereby healing not only wrongdoers but also those who have been wronged by them.

Fifth, the first step in the process of forgiveness is unconditional. It is not predicated on repentance on the part of the wrongdoer or on her willing-

---

take from the guilt that special *sting of guilt* which inheres in the deserved contempt and hostility of the man who has been wronged; and it may give back to the guilty the outward peace which he had spurned; but it can never remove the moral guilt itself" (Nicolai Hartmann, *Ethics III: Moral Freedom,* trans. Stanton Coit [London: George Allen and Unwin, 1932], 271–72; italics added). Only divine forgiveness actually removes guilt. When human beings forgive they (1) forgo resentment, (2) refuse to press the claims of justice against the other and therefore also (3) bear the cost of the wrongdoing. As a result of human forgiveness, the guilty *is treated* as if he or she were not guilty (to be distinguished from *defining* forgiveness itself as treating the other as if he or she had not committed the offense). But unless forgiven by God, he or she remains guilty, human forgiveness notwithstanding.

ness to redress the wrong committed. Yet full-fledged and completed forgiveness is not unconditional. It is true that repentance—the recognition that the deed committed was evil, coupled with the willingness to mend one's ways—is not so much a prerequisite of forgiveness as, more profoundly, its possible result. Yet repentance is the kind of result of forgiveness whose absence would amount to a refusal to see oneself as guilty and therefore a refusal to receive forgiveness as forgiveness. Hence an unrepentant wrongdoer must in the end remain an unforgiven wrongdoer—the unconditionality of the first step in the process of forgiveness notwithstanding.

Finally, forgiveness is best received if in addition to repentance there takes place some form of restitution. Indeed, one may ask whether the repentance is genuine if the wrongdoer refuses to restore something of what she has taken away by the wrongdoing—provided that she is capable of doing so.

In sum, forgiveness is an element in the process of reconciliation, a process in which the search for justice is an integral and yet subordinate element.

CONCLUSION

In the latter part of this chapter I sought to explicate the social significance of the foundational act of the Christian faith—the death of Christ. This step from the narrative of what God has done for humanity on the cross of Christ to the account of what human beings ought to do in relation to one another has often been left unmade in the history of Christianity. The logic of God's action, it was sometimes argued, was applicable to the inner world of human souls plagued by guilt and shame; their outer relationships in family, economy, and state ought to be governed by another, more worldly logic. At least in Protestantism, this disjunction between the inner and outer was one important reason why the Christian faith could be misused to legitimize violence.[31] Emptied of their social import, religious

---

31. See, for instance, Paul Tillich, *Against the Third Reich: Paul Tillich's Wartime Addresses to Nazi Germany* (Louisville, Ky.: Westminster/John Knox, 1998).

symbols nonetheless floated loosely in the social world and could be harnessed to purposes at odds with their proper content. Significantly, this disjunction is never to be found in the New Testament; instead, the central
religious narratives and rituals shape all aspects of early Christian lives.
Arguably, the central Christian rituals, baptism and eucharist, enact the
narrative of divine action precisely as the pattern for the lives of believers.

It may well be the case, someone may respond, that the Christian faith
at its heart fosters peace rather than violence. But in what ways can it do
so in concrete social and political settings? First, the narrative of divine
action can motivate and shape the behavior of individual actors in conflict
situations. Depending on their position, such individual actors can be significant and even decisive for the future of conflicts.[32] Second, this narrative
can shape broader cultural habits and expectations that make peaceful solutions possible. It takes a particular cultural soil for the seed of peace to bear
fruit. Of course, the narratival portrayal of the divine redemptive action
cannot be simply mirrored in human interaction, be that on the individual,
the communal, or the political planes. Instead, one has to aim at culturally
and situationally appropriate practical analogies as near or distant echoes
of the divine redemptive action that lies at the heart of the Christian faith.
Finally, the narrative of divine action as it applies to human interaction can
help shape social institutions. One way to think about how this may be the
case is to recall the concluding words of Anthony Giddens's book *Modernity and Self-Identity*. After noting the emergence in high modernity of what
he calls "life politics" (as distinct from "emancipatory politics") which
demands a remoralization of social life, he writes:

> How can we remoralize social life without falling prey to prejudices?
> The more we return to existential issues, the more we find moral
> disagreements; how can these be reconciled? If there are no trans-
> historical moral principles, how can humanity cope with clashes of
> "true believers" without violence? Responding to such problems will
> surely require a major reconstruction of emancipatory politics as
> well as the pursuit of the life-political endeavors.[33]

32. See Johnston and Sampson, eds., *Religion*, 317ff.
33. Anthony Giddens, *Modernity and Self-Identity: Self and Society in the Late Modern Age*
(Stanford, Calif.: Stanford University Press, 1991), 231.

The narrative of the God of unconditional love who reconciles humanity without condoning injustice, along with this narrative's intended patterning in the lives of human beings and communities, contains, I suggest,
at least some resources for such a reconstruction of politics.

CHAPTER 3

Forgiveness & Reconciliation

An Orthodox Perspective

Stanley S. Harakas

THE MORAL PARADOX

ONE OF THE EARLIEST CONTROVERSIES in the history of the Church was the issue regarding the possibility of the forgiveness of sins committed by Christians after baptism. One of the tragedies of the controversy was that the issue found the very question of forgiveness a cause of separation and schism. Some emphasized the sufficiency of forgiveness in baptism, denying any subsequent reconciliation. Others argued for deliberate sinning on the part of Christians so that "grace would abound." In light of these extremes, the Church has always dealt with such doctrinal problems by sampling the extreme aspects of a given issue and then adopting its own formulation, which includes both affirmations in dynamic relationship.[1]

This chapter will approach the discussion of the forgiveness of sin by means of a model that will serve, I hope, to bring what I have labeled extreme positions into a dynamic tension, for which I will use the traditional names of *mystery* and *paradox*. In the first part I will outline the Orthodox Church's understanding of sin in the framework of a model of dynamic mystery or dynamic paradox. Second, I will place the drama of divine reconciliation in the same framework. Both of these treatments will serve as preliminaries to

1. T. G. Goman and Ronald S. Lowra, "The Development of Orthodoxy: An Historical Model," *Greek Orthodox Theological Review* 15 (1970): 187–206.

provide an understanding of forgiveness in dynamic terms in other contexts.

This chapter uses a model of dynamic mystery or dynamic paradox for its treatment of the question of the sacramental dimensions of forgiveness. It is based in the classic affirmations of the Church in its early christological and trinitarian affirmations and is most clearly seen in the doctrinal *horoi*, the faith-oriented decisions of the first four Ecumenical Councils, though the model is evident in all councils up to and including the seventh. In defending and defining the content of its faith, the Church has insisted on the priority of its experience and the continued witness of its Founder and his disciples. It is on the basis of the *kerygma*, the Scriptures, and the living experience of its own tradition that the Church has constructed its understanding of its truth.

Such revelatory experience was augmented through reason to enable the Church to develop its faith into intelligible statements. For instance, it affirmed at Chalcedon that Jesus was "perfect in His humanity . . . a true human being . . . of the same essence as we according to His humanity." Parallel to this, the same process of definition took place with regard to the divinity of Christ. Thus, the dogmatic decree of Chalcedon defined that revelatory experience in terms of Jesus' being "perfect in His divinity . . . truly God . . . of the same essence of the Father."[2]

For the purposes of the development of our model the results were two. One was that doctrinal definition formulated in rational terms the content of the Church's revelatory experience in separate affirmations: Jesus Christ's full divinity and full humanity. The other was that the conceptualization of the revelatory did not extend to synthesizing the two truths. The result was a paradox or mystery with which the Church was content to live, defined as an antinomy by the Russian Orthodox theologian Sergius Bulgakov. Antinomies recognize the truth of two contradictory, but ontologically necessary assertions. He wrote:

All fundamental dogmatic definitions are of this nature. [The] paradoxes of faith are inevitable, not because the divine reality is self-

---

2. From the dogmatic decision of the Fourth Ecumenical Council, "Ioannes Karmires, Ta Dogmatika kai Symbolika Mnemeia tes Orthodoxou Katholikes Ekklesias" ("The Dogmatic and Symbolic Monuments of the Orthodox Catholic Church"), Athens, 1952, 1:165.

contradictory, but because when we "objectify" it all our judgments are in some measure falsified. There should always be a sense of tension between the two opposite sides of our paradoxes, driving us back to their source in our actual religious experience.[3]

The failure to do this has always resulted in the collapsing of one or the other aspect of the full Christian experience into its opposite, a failure to convey the full meaning of the Christian revelatory experience. This is the model in accordance with which I would like to draw a theology of forgiveness, especially in the Sacrament of Holy Confession. There is need to emphasize all sides of the Christian experience of forgiveness and reconciliation, to keep them in a dynamic tension and not to succumb to the temptation of subsuming all experiences under the rubric of one. On the basis of this approach this chapter will draw some general guidance for all those seeking to promote forgiveness and reconciliation in other circumstances and venues.

THE PARADOXES OF SIN

The Christian experience of the event and condition of sin has led to a multitude of attempts to define it. In the Old Testament the Hebrew word *hattat* and the Septuagint word *hamartia* carry the same connotation of missing the mark. Other Hebrew words for sin indicate "straying from the right path," "distortion," "rebellion," as well as "evildoing." In the New Testament the idea of the nonfulfillment of the will of God is the bedrock of the idea of sin. "Thy will be done on earth" is a characteristic phrase.[4] Other images of sin have been used by both Scripture and the Fathers of the Church. The Fourth Gospel characterizes it as darkness and death, as does

---

3. See my article, "Sergius Bulgakov and His Teaching," *Greek Orthodox Theological Review* 7 (1961–62): esp. 104. A similar conclusion is arrived at by means of studies in linguistic analysis and theological statements by Michael Foster in his article, "Contemporary British Philosophy and Christian Belief," *Cross Currents* 10, no. 4 (Fall 1960).

4. J. J. Von Allmen, ed., *A Companion to the Bible* (New York: Oxford University Press, 1958), 405–10, and Panagiotes Demetropoulos, "*Amartia* [Sin]," *Threskeutike kai Ethike Egkyklopaideia* (*Encyclopedia of Religion and Ethics*) (Athens: Martinos Publications, 1963), 2:250–55.

Eastern Christian liturgical piety. Clement of Alexandria saw it as a perverse form of irrationality.[5] Chrysostom saw it as ingratitude and insult,[6] an idea picked up later by Anselm and emphasized in a feudal society that was in a particular position to appreciate it thus defined.[7] Other expressions with which the Christian experience has sought to define sin are transgression, disobedience, unlawful act, failure, a defective act, impiety, a debt or trespass, an injustice, and inequity.[8]

Nearly all of these descriptions can be reduced to two fundamental approaches, one relational and the other legal in character. On the one hand are those expressions or concepts that see sin essentially as the breaking of the relationship of love between man and God and also between human beings and their fellows. On the other there are those expressions that suggest that the essential nature of sin is the disobedience of the law of God. While the Roman legal tradition of the West emphasized sin as violation of God's law, the Eastern patristic tradition tended to see the character of sin in the reality that humanity was not sharing in and responding to the action, activity, and energy of God on humanity's behalf. Irenaeus writes that "the glory of God is a living man; and the life of man consists in beholding God."[9] But "separation from God is [spiritual] death," in the words of one of St. Irenaeus' commentators.[10] An Eastern Christian theologian, Constantine Callinicos, writing in 1909, expressed the idea characteristically in the following passage:

> If religion is defined and is the innermost bond of man with God, and if sin is nothing other than the opposing force which seeks to destroy that bond with satanic passion and to snatch the child from the arms of its Creator, then Christianity . . . must needs present itself in no other light than as an enemy of this opposing power and as a restorer of the broken bond.[11]

5. Paidagogos, *Ante-Nicene Fathers,* II, 1.210.
6. "Homilies on Matthew," LXL,1. in *Ante-Nicene Fathers,* 10.376–77.
7. Etienne Gilson, *Reason and Revelation in the Middle Ages* (New York: Scribner's, 1938).
8. Constantine Callinicos, *E Amartia Kata ten Christianken Antilepsin (Sin According to the Christian Understanding),* 2nd ed. (Athens, 1958), 31.
9. *Against Heresies,* Bk. IV.20.7, see also bk. IV.20.5 and bk. V.12.2. *Ante-Nicene Fathers,* II.49, 538.
10. John Romanides, *To Propatorikon Amartema (Original Sin)* (Athens, 1956), 118, 119.
11. Callinicos, *E Amartia,* 16.

I do not believe that it is necessary to extensively document the legal understanding of sin, which became common practice not only in Roman Catholic catechetical instruction, but also in the Protestant, sectarian, and perfectionist traditions. The point is that there is always the danger and the temptation of allowing the one to be swallowed up by the other. In the past, in Western Christian traditions the idea of "sin as disobedience to law" was dominant. Today there is a movement in the other direction, seeing sin rather in relational terms with little regard for traditional normative moral rules. One of the beginnings of this movement in the mid-twentieth century is seen in Joseph Fletcher. His definition of love as the only intrinsic good, his exclusion of law as a norm, his understanding of justice merely as love distributed, and his admitted relativism are the collapse of the one pole of the traditional understanding of sin into the other. It is thus possible in his situationist ethic to pronounce, in certain cases, right and good, those acts that by the historic scriptural and patristic tradition are characterized as sinful.[12]

"Mainline" Protestantism and liberal Roman Catholicism have moved heavily into this approach. Little attention is accorded to ancient Christian norms regarding the sinfulness in personal relations such as abortion, premarital sex, marital fidelity, homosexuality, and even honesty, in some cases, when it harms one's interests. In their place, the operative criteria are acceptance, inclusiveness, and tolerance for what Alan Wolfe calls "The Pursuit of Autonomy." He writes: "Paradoxically, [contemporary] Americans have a specific distaste for the theological doctrine that has informed our national morality from the beginning: Puritanism. The Puritans believed in an inherent human depravity that could be countered only by God's willingness to extend, even arbitrarily, his grace."[13] Thus, the sins of concern are not so much the violations of the Decalogue and the rules governing personal morality, but a failure to accept others, violations of inclusiveness, and intolerance. They are the failures in relationships, which also happen to coincide with the values of civil religion in a pluralistic democratic environment.

Certainly Wolfe overstates his case by claiming that all Americans have rejected the Puritan rule-based type of ethos required to control human sin.

---

12. Joseph Fletcher, *Situation Ethics: The New Morality* (Philadelphia: Westminster Press, 1966).
13. *New York Times*, Sunday, May 7, 2000, sec. 6, 53.

A significant portion of Americans are Evangelical or Fundamentalist Protestants and ecclesially oriented Roman Catholics with a strong sense of human sin as the violation of God-given rules of human behavior. Wolfe does, nevertheless, describe the liberal Protestantism of most university theology departments (both Protestant and Roman Catholic) and many liberal Protestant seminaries. Critics of the abandonment of foundation-based normative ethics responded to Fletcher and continue to critique liberal Protestant relationalist ethics.[14]

In contrast to a return to rule-based ethics, the only type of response to receive a hearing by those who have adopted the liberal Protestant approach has been an ethic based on character and virtue, most clearly articulated by Stanley Hauerwas.[15] He accomplishes this by abandoning the effort to speak for the whole of American society and to find recourse for the moral community in a specifically Christian community focus. Others have also moved in this direction, including some Orthodox writers.[16] Nevertheless, the dominant mindset is captured in the title of Shane O'Neill's recent book,

14. An early collection of responses is to be found in Harvey Cox's *The Situation Ethics Debate* (Philadelphia: Westminster Press, 1968). Other writings of the time were Robert L. Cunningham, *Situationism and the New Morality* (New York: Appleton-Century-Crofts, 1970); Gordon Kainer, *Faith, Hope, and Clarity: A Look at Situation Ethics and Biblical Ethics* (Mountain View, Calif.: Pacific Press Publication Association, 1977); Erwin W. Lutzer, *The Morality Gap: An Evangelical Response to Situation Ethics* (Chicago: Moody Press, 1972); Fritz Ridenour, *It All Depends: A Comparison of Situation Ethics and the Playboy Philosophy with What the Bible Teaches about Morality* (Glendale, Calif.: G/L Regal Books, 1969).

15. Stanley Hauerwas, *Character and the Christian Life: A Study in Theological Ethics* (San Antonio: Trinity University Press, 1975). Hauerwas, *Vision and Virtue: Essays in Christian Ethical Reflection* (Notre Dame, Ind.: Fides Publishers, 1974); Hauerwas with Charles Pinches, *Christians among the Virtues: Theological Conversations with Ancient and Modern Ethics* (Notre Dame, Ind.: University of Notre Dame Press, 1997). In Hauerwas's book written with William H. Millimon, *The Truth about God: The Ten Commandments in Christian Life* (Nashville: Abingdon Press, 1999), the authors interpret the Decalogue as not applicable to all societies, including that of pluralistic America, but as applicable only within the Christian church. For the authors, they are not timeless ethical principles that are applicable to all Americans."

16. Vigen Guroian, *Incarnate Love: Essays in Orthodox Ethics* (Notre Dame, Ind.: University of Notre Dame Press, 1987); Guroian, *Ethics after Christendom: Toward an Ecclesial Ethic*; H. Tristram Engelhardt, *The Foundations of Bioethics*, 2nd ed. (New York: Oxford University Press, 1986). Forthcoming is Engelhardt's *Foundations of Christian Bioethics*. These authors subscribe to a course of disengagement with the larger society in the pattern espoused by Hauerwas.

Impartiality in Context: Grounding Justice in a Pluralist World.[17]

Faithfulness to our model requires that the two affirmations, sin as broken relationship and sin as disobedience to God's law and will, must be affirmed together. The first attests to the experience of sin in the Christian community as a personal separation from the source of light and life and strength and power. As separation from God it is *meonic,* that is, it is the absence connection with the Ultimate Reality. St. John of Damascus says regarding meonic evil, "evil, then, is nothing else than the absence of the good, just as darkness is the absence of light."[18] Yet, if the breaking of the relationship permits Christians to see sin as meonic, as not having the characteristic of true reality, the view of sin as disobedience to the will and law of God points to the empirically concrete content of sin experienced as rebelliousness, passion, hatred, and positive evil acts of destruction. To collapse the law aspect of sin into the relational aspect of sin as liberal Protestants and liberal Roman Catholics tend to do is to lose the Christian experience of the concrete personal dimension of sin. This same danger is attendant to all meonic concepts of evil. That is why the Eastern Church has always felt the need for correctives in dealing with this issue. On the other hand, to collapse the relational aspect of sin into the law aspect of sin is to depersonalize and make rigidly legalistic a living human experience. The answer, then, according to our model is to do neither. Rather, it is to maintain a place for sin as the violation of God's will while keeping alive the sense of sin as the breaking of relationships and separation from the sources of life itself.

It is not necessary to maintain an absolute one-to-one parity between the two. The relational aspect of our understanding of sin, as a denial of God's love and the denial of love as the primary root of human evil, can be maintained without denying the character of sin as concrete disobedience to the law of God. In summary, Maximos the Confessor, the seventh-century vigorous opponent of Monotheleticism (the doctrine that Christ had only a divine will), writes:

17. Shane O'Neill, *Impartiality in Context: Grounding Justice in a Pluralist World* (Albany: State University of New York Press, 1997).
18. *Exact Exposition of the Orthodox Faith,* PG, XCIV, 973A. See Vasilios Antoniades' quite vigorous attack on meonic concepts in his *Encheiridion Kata Christon Ethikes (Handbook of Ethics According to Christ)* (Constantinople: Fazilet Press, 1927), 1:190–93.

Just as it is the characteristic of disobedience to sin, so it is the characteristic of obedience to act virtuously. And just as disobedience is accompanied by the violation of the commandment and separation from the giver of the command, so it is that obedience consists of the fulfillment of commandments and unity with the giver of the command. Thus, he who keeps, through obedience, the command has done the right and has kept unsundered the loving unity between himself and the giver of the command.[19]

THE DYNAMIC MYSTERY OF RECONCILIATION: THE MULTIPLE DIMENSIONS OF GOD'S FORGIVENESS

We now turn our attention to several aspects of the Sacrament of Holy Confession as an act of grace from God toward humanity. Here, in accordance with our model, I will point to certain affirmations that have the tendency to absorb each other in Christian thought as it seeks to comprehend the various dimensions of the divine act of reconciliation, especially in its sacramental dimension. For this purpose we may analyze the act of divine forgiveness into its transcendent, imminent, and present dimensions.

The transcendent dimension of forgiveness is to be seen in the figure of God the Father. Five passages in the New Testament use the term *katallage* (reconciliation) in its theological sense. All five use the word with God as the subject and God as the "sole initiator of this movement of reconciliation, which is unaffected by the attitude of His Creatures. It is He who has decided upon this action and who unceasingly fulfills it: `All this is from God' (2 Cor. 5:18)," says Bouttier.[20] One of the classic Christian terms that expresses this gracious man-directed love of God is *philanthropy*. God's *philanthropia* is one pole of a twofold affirmation about God's attitude toward humanity. The well-known study of Demetrios Constantelos may

---

19. Maximos the Confessor, *Peri Theologias: Deutera Ekatontas,* in *Philokalia ton Neptikon Pateron* (Athens, 1960), 2:70.
20. In *A Companion to the Bible,* 352. The five passages are Rom. 5:10–11; 1 1:15; 2 Cor. 5:18–20; Eph. 2:16; and Col. 1:20, 22.

serve as a focus of this emphasis for our purpose here. In the third chapter of his book, *Byzantine Philanthropy and Social Welfare,* he traces the biblical and patristic tradition that emphasizes the mercy, love, forgiving, agapeic attitude of God, which seeks humanity's justification, redemption, salvation, and sanctification.[21]

If then, the one pole of the attitude of God toward humanity in the plan of reconciliation is "philanthropic," what is the other? The second pole is found in the role of God as Creator and it finds itself expressed in various concepts, all of which serve to point to a stable and structured expectation of God's action in human society. We can discern a common direction in such varied positions as the emphasis on the positive will of God for human beings (a characteristic emphasis of Eastern Orthodox thinking),[22] or natural law (a characteristic emphasis of Roman Catholic thought),[23] or the orders of creation (a characteristic of Reformation thinking).[24] The common affirmation to be found in these positions is that God has also established, for the sake of humanity, a kind of "nature of things," an order and a pattern, expressing God's will, to which human beings are required to conform: in terms of our model, a second pole, that of order and righteousness. The pole of God's philanthropy and that of God's righteous expectation will remain in a dynamic tension or paradox.

The collapse of one into the other is also the betrayal of these truths. The overemphasis on the pole of order and patterned expectation has always led to an attempt to freeze the status quo and to appeal to Divinity in order to maintain political conservatism. When the forgiving, merciful, and philanthropic concern of God is collapsed into the appeal to order, religion truly becomes an "opiate of the people." A classic example in the West, but of course not by any stretch of the imagination the only one, was Martin Luther's social conservatism. When seen in the framework of the Eastern Orthodox sacramental approach to sin, as we shall see, the tendency to

21. Demetrios Constantelos, *Byzantine Philanthropy and Social Welfare* (New Rochelle, N.Y.: A. D. Caratzas, 1991). See also Constantelos, *Poverty, Society, and Philanthropy in the Late Mediaeval Greek World* (New Rochelle, N.Y.: A. D. Caratzas, 1992).
22. See Romanides, *To Propatorikon Hamartema* (*Original Sin*) and Vladimir Lossky, *The Mystical Theology of the Eastern Church* (Cambridge: Cambridge University Press, 1973).
23. Thomas Aquinas, *Summa Theologica,* bk. III, questions 90–95, especially question 94.
24. Ernst Troeltsch, *The Social Teachings of the Christian Churches,* trans. Olive Wyon (Chicago: University of Chicago Press, 1931), vol. 2.

emphasize the pole of order and righteousness led to the creation of a vast
portion of Canon Law and shaped a whole literature of "Penitentials," that
is, handbooks of casuistic guidance based primarily on the retributive conception of penance.[25] An emphasis on order all but wiped out the emphasis
on *philanthropia*. The other possibility is equally real. An emphasis on philanthropy, or concerns with relationship, can diminish claims of order, pattern, and the nature of things. Alan Wolfe cites the cultural philosopher
Allan Bloom concerning the unwillingness of Americans to understand people as sinful.

> Americans are simply too nice to see Satan everywhere around them.
> The niceness of Americans can drive thoughtful people to distraction.
> Allan Bloom . . . believed that the willingness of his students to see
> good in everyone rendered them "spiritually unclad, unconnected,
> isolated, with no inherited or unconditional connection with any-
> thing or anyone."[26]

Significantly, Wolfe adds, drawing upon Bloom, it works out that on
balance the primary values worth fighting for are the values that affirm that
every stance, any moral opinion, all views are acceptable, so long as someone holds them. The major sin, it would appear, is holding to the view that
this stance is not correct and is therefore uncharitable, rigid, judgmental,
and unfriendly. There is disinterestedness in what the traditional moral law
or what the established patterns of life might be. The "philanthropy pole"
swallows them all.

This says much about contemporary organized Christian religious thinking. Church historian Martin Marty cites author Craig M. Gay with apparent approval when Gay speaks of "the suspicion that the church is really not
fundamentally different from other humanly-constructed organizations."[27]

---

25. John T. McNeill, *A History of the Cure of Souls* (New York, 1951), chaps. 6 and 7.
26. Alan Bloom, *The Closing of the American Mind: How Higher Education Has Failed Democracy and Impoverished the Souls of Today's Students* (New York: Simon and Schuster, 1987).
27. Martin E. Marty, "McDonaldization." Web magazine *Sightings* e-published by the Martin
Marty Center at the University of Chicago Divinity School, *midway@.uchicago.edu*. See
also an older study with similar conclusions, Robert Wuthnow and Charles Y. Glock, "The
Shifting Focus of Faith: A Survey Report," *Psychology Today* (November 1974): 131–36.

The classic expression of this view is *antinomianism*. It tended to downgrade or eliminate most sacramental aspects of the forgiveness of sin. The Sacrament of Confession of Sins was readily substituted by a general confession that presumes mercy of God without concern for personal responsibility to the moral order. The struggle for politically guaranteed acceptance of almost all behaviors overwhelms many traditionally held moral norms. Instead, in accordance with our model, the course to follow is neither to collapse philanthropy into order nor order into philanthropy. It is to maintain a dynamic tension of paradox between the two poles, without resolving the tension.

There are also two poles in the significance of the redemptive work of Jesus Christ that effect the sacramental approach to forgiveness. These need to be kept in the dynamic tension if the truth in each is not to be lost. We might call this the immanent dimension of forgiveness. It centers not on the Father but on the Incarnate Son, the person of Jesus Christ. One aspect of the pole is the sufficiency of the saving work of Christ. On the basis of the great Pauline witness, the Reformation emphasized salvation by faith alone in the redemptive work of Christ. This truth lays the full weight of salvation, redemption, and forgiveness in the "grace" or work of Christ. This emphasizes the fact that God has acted, that human beings can only accept or reject this redemptive work. It refers to the "power of God for salvation to everyone who has faith" (Rom. 1:16, 9:16).

The primacy of God's grace contrasts with the role of human freedom to choose, to "work out" salvation, in the face of imperfection, to develop the spiritual life for the realization of that salvation in the life of the individual and the community. Thus the same Paul in Ephesians (4:15) declares that "we are to grow up in every way into Him who is the head, into Christ" and He prays for the Colossians that they "may be filled with the knowledge of His will" and that they may "lead a life worthy of the Lord bearing fruit in every good work and increasing in the knowledge of God" (1:9, 10). For our purposes, then, we may label the other pole "growth," emphasizing the contribution of each to his or her own salvation, the uneven and faltering efforts to increase "in the grace and knowledge of our Lord and Savior Jesus Christ" to use the phrase found in 1 Peter 3:18. The exclusive emphasis on the second pole is Pelagianism. The exclusive emphasis on the first is a purely forensic understanding of redemption. When applied to the question of repentance and forgiveness, the necessity of grace on the one hand and the requirement of growth implying frequent failure and reorientation on the other find many interesting applications.

James G. Emerson Jr. provides us with a useful view of this dynamic paradox.[28] The emphasis on "grace" he calls a concern with the "context" of forgiveness. Here we relate directly with the Savior through a mystical identification in the divine life. Faith, worship, mysticism, sacramental life form its focus. The other pole emphasizes our role in growing toward an unrealizable perfection. It concerns itself with the specific means by which forgiveness may be made concrete. Its categories are obedience/disobedience, forgiveness/reconciliation, and growth/increase in godliness. This Emerson calls an emphasis on the "instrumentation" of forgiveness. An example of the Church's divided attitude comes from the second century. Tertullian, for whom serious or "deadly" sins following baptism were unforgivable, is frequently contrasted with the author of *The Shepherd of Hermas,* for whom forgiveness and the acceptance of the sinner after baptism was more generous. By the end of the Novatian Schism a century later, all sins were considered forgivable, with the exception of the blasphemy against the Holy Spirit (Mark 3:28).[29]

However, the issue still holds an ambiguity for which our terms *grace* and *growth* may stand as symbols. In the forgiveness granted sacramentally, did repentance and the tears and the alms and the years of abstinence from Holy Communion required by the canons that accompanied the development of the Sacrament of Confession effectually displace the consciousness of the saving grace of God in Jesus Christ? The Reformation may be seen in this light. The extreme emphasis on the "growth" pole in medieval penitential practice seemed to the Reformers to be a denial of the grace of God in practice. As a result, Luther rejected penances and individual contribution to growth through works of any kind.

Yet a truth was denied in both positions. Effective and practical denial of the free gift of grace on the one hand seemed to be the legacy of the medieval penitential tradition. But what is minimized (but not eliminated,

28. James G. Emerson Jr., *The Dynamics of Forgiveness* (Philadelphia: Westminster Press, 1964).
29. Williston Walker and Robert T. Handy, *A History of the Christian Church,* rev. ed. (New York: Scribner's, 1959), 91–93.

of course) in the Reformation approach is the serious concern with the struggle of the Christian to be again, in the words of St. Paul, "transformed by the renewal of [his] mind, that [he] may prove what is the will of God, what is good and acceptable and perfect" (Rom. 12:2). When growth is collapsed into grace, then concrete acts of forgiveness, the spiritual struggle, and moral transfiguration are lacking, and with them the need for sacramental forgiveness. But when grace is collapsed into growth, humanity's own efforts at self-salvation dominate people's concerns. Is it any wonder in today's age, when the pole of grace is rejected by a technologically sophisticated society, that even ostensible Christian church members seek "do-it-yourself" salvation on their own terms? Redemption and salvation are sought in self-development, drugs, music, politics, national identity, and, for some, university degrees.

It need not be this way. In accordance with our model, a synergy of both grace and growth is a distinct possibility. A classic expression that serves beautifully to define the dynamics of the imminent dimension of forgiveness through the Son of God, Jesus Christ, is found in 1 Corinthians 3:9, in which St. Paul writes "we are coworkers with God."[30]

All of this takes place within the living presence of the Pentecostal experience. The redemptive work of Jesus is realized, increases, and bears fruit in the Holy Spirit. The Lutheran theologian Gustaf Aulén summarized it beautifully when he said that

> through Jesus' work the power of evil is broken; that is to say, not that sin and death no longer exist, but that, the devil having been once and for all conquered by Christ, His triumph is in principle universal, and His redemptive work can go forward everywhere, through the Spirit who unites men with God and "deifies" them.[31]

This mention of the Spirit leads to another duality of poles in the context of what we might call the present dimension of reconciliation "for the

---

30. *Ypomnema eis tas Epistolas tes Kaines Diathekes. Epistolai: Pros Romaious—Pros Korinthious* (Commentary on the Epistles of the New Testament. Epistles: To Romans—To Corinthians), 2nd ed. (Athens: Zoe Publications, 1956), 260.
31. Gustaf Aulén, *Christus Victor* (New York, 1951), 59.

Spirit helps us in our weakness" (Rom. 8:26) and is the source of Christian living (Romans 8; 1 Corinthians 2, 12; and Galatians 5). That duality refers to the locus or place of forgiveness or, to use Emerson's phrase, its "instrumentation." Where does forgiveness take place? What are the channels of the mediation of forgiveness? In accordance with our model one pole will obviously be the Sacrament of Holy Confession in which the very concrete and specific manner of the Christian expresses repentance and receives assurances of the forgiveness of sins through absolution.

There is a long history of scholarly and polemical effort to discredit this sacrament as an authentic expression of the Christian teaching. Yet, the empowering words of the apostolic absolution of sins found in Matthew 16:19, 18:18, and John 20:23 seem to have been rapidly followed in Church practice with the formal confession of sins before bishops and later, priests. Evidence from Ignatius of Antioch (*Epistle to the Philadelphians* VIII, 1), Tertullian (*De Paenitentia,* chap. 9, and *De Pudicitia,* chap. 18), Origen (*Second Homily on Leviticus, Homily XVII on Luke,* and *Homily V, 3 on Leviticus*), Cyprian (*De Lapsis,* 16 and 29, and *Epistles* IX.1, XI.2) as well as many other early writers support both its antiquity and authenticity.[32]

Whatever the theological case, historically the Sacrament of Reconciliation has been a continuing factor in the spiritual life of the Church and the locus for forgiveness of sins in its life. While in Eastern and Oriental Orthodox tradition and in Roman Catholic practice it has a full sacramental status, in some of the Protestant traditions such as the Lutheran and Episcopal churches it has existed and has been practiced as a pastoral rite. More informally, prayer for forgiveness of sins confessed is present in many other church traditions.

However, the forgiving action of the Holy Spirit appears not to be limited to sacramental and pastoral practice. Forgiveness has numerous less defined dimensions, which form the other pole of reconciliation, the Christian life as a whole. "The Spirit blows where it will" (John 3:8). The Church has always seen forgiveness as available to believers within the total frame-

32. Epiphanios Theodoropoulos in *"To Mystyerion tes Exomologeseos"* ("The Sacrament of Repentance"), in *Threskeutike kai Ethike Enkyklopaideia* (*Encyclopedia of Religion and Ethics*), vol. 8 (1959–66).

work of the Church's life. For the early Church, prayer, fasting, and, most important, almsgiving as expressions of repentance and remorse were held to be effective means of forgiveness of sins. Almsgiving seems to be one of the criteria for entrance into the Kingdom in Jesus' teaching (Matt. 25:35–46 and 6:24).[33] Almsgiving as an important aspect of Christian life rapidly increased in importance in the early years of the church.[34]

One of the most interesting aspects of almsgiving is that the receiver of the alms may or may not be a fellow believer. As Galatians says even more broadly, "as we have opportunity, let us do good to all men, and especially to those who are of the household of faith" (6:10). Forgiveness is a good work that is an essential characteristic of Christian living, since the Lord's Prayer indicates that our own forgiveness is a condition of our willingness to forgive others (Matt. 6:12). In commenting on this passage Chrysostom challenges believers to assume a stance of forgiveness toward others who have injured them for the sake of their own forgiveness by God.[35]

For Chrysostom, "to have a human soul" necessarily implies a readiness for forgiveness. Though the sense of "justice abused" often makes forgiveness difficult, the thrust of this position is that granting forgiveness to others is the only way to foster the opposite pole of growth. It can open possibilities otherwise unattainable. For example, asking for and giving forgiveness is necessary in ecumenical dialogue, where memories of injustice and experienced abuse are often nurtured in the process of cultivating self-identity. An example comes from the recent practice of the Ecumenical Patriarchate of Constantinople and the See of Rome to send representatives to the annual thronal celebrations of the other Church. Roman Catholic representatives go to Istanbul on November 30 annually for the observance of the Feast of St. Andrew, the patron saint of the Ecumenical Patriarchate. On June 29 Orthodox representatives go to Rome for the feast day of St. Peter. In the observance in the year 2000, it was reported that John Paul II asked God's mercy for anything Catholics had done in the past 1,000 years which harmed relations with Orthodox, that Catholics and Orthodox must work

33. See Cecil John Cadoux, *The Early Church and the World* (Edinburgh, 1955), 198–99, 285ff.
34. Emerson, *Dynamics of Forgiveness,* 123.
35. *On Matthew, Homily xix. Nicene and Post-Nicene Fathers,* ed. Philip Schaff (Peabody, Mass.: Hedrickson Publishers, 1994), 10:136. Translation altered to reflect contemporary English usage.

to "write a new history in a spirit of brotherly love, respect and cooperation."[36]

The attitude and tone of such "seeking and granting forgiveness" in this
ecclesial setting can obviously be expanded to numerous other fields of
human relations. The conclusion would be that no growth in relationships
and in having "a human soul" in such relationships can take place without
forgiveness for "the importance of a purification of memories makes itself
felt at every turn." Whether it involves Orthodox and Roman Catholics,
Protestants and Roman Catholics in Northern Ireland, victims of the Nazi
Holocaust, Turkish and Greek Cypriots, racial relations, and alienated
minorities in every society, the concept of giving and accepting forgiveness
has application to social conflict wherever it is found.

The other sacraments present themselves also as arenas of forgiveness
and reconciliation. The Eucharist, for example, is presented as offering forgiveness with the repetition of the words of institution ("this is my blood
of the covenant, which is poured out for many for the forgiveness of sins,"
Matt. 26:28). Further, the whole liturgical action is the making real of the
Kingdom of God, a Kingdom of forgiveness and reconciliation. This point
admirably developed in reference to the Orthodox Divine Liturgy by the late
Father Alexander Schmemann.[37]

The frequent appeals for mercy and forgiveness in all forms of the
Eucharist, so readily subsumed in the simple formula, "Lord have mercy,"
show clearly that the Eucharist is also a locus of forgiveness as a work of
the Holy Spirit. The words of institution of the healing Sacrament of Unc-
tion express the same point. A survey of sacramental practice in the Church
generally will show the same anticipation of forgiveness.[38]

In addition, common worship carries the same presupposition of appeal
for and expectation of forgiveness. In the rich and varied tradition of the
Eastern Orthodox Church it is to be found everywhere, from the "church-
ing" of a mother and her baby on the fortieth day after birth through the

36. Cindy Wooden, "Pope Asks God's Pardon for Times Catholics Hurt Orthodox," Catholic
News Service, Vatican City, June 30, 2000.
37. Father Alexander Schmemann, *Introduction to Liturgical Theology*, trans. Ashleigh E.
Moorhouse (Crestwood, N.Y.: St. Vladimir's Press), 1986. See also Emerson, *Dynamics of
Forgiveness*, 94–95.
38. Evelyn Underhill, *Worship* (New York: Harper Brothers, 1937), esp. chap. 1.

blessings of inanimate objects, to prayers for healing, to the funeral service. This is perhaps nowhere more profoundly registered than in the Eastern Orthodox Church's doxology. Rationally one would expect a doxology to be an act of pure adoration of God. Yet of its twenty distinct stanzas (not counting the exact repetitions) nine stanzas are appeals for mercy or for forgiveness of sins or for aid to keep from sinning. Finally, it ought to be pointed out that a large portion of Church discipline, that is, Canon Law, functions on the presupposition that it deals within the whole framework of the forgiveness of sins and the reconciliation of the sinner to the body of Christ.[39]

Thus there are two poles where the Holy Spirit makes the present dimension of forgiveness real: concretely and specifically in the Sacrament of Holy Confession, and in a more diffused manner in the whole of life. The temptation here, in accordance with our model, is to collapse the one into the other. The tendency of historical theological definition in the history of Christian thought seems to have sought to downgrade the general Christian experience of forgiveness while insisting on the absolute exclusiveness and necessity of the Sacrament of Holy Confession for forgiveness of sins. Such an attitude was promulgated by the Council of Trent.[40] A similar attitude was expressed within Orthodoxy by the Orthodox theologian side Christos Androutsos.[41] In both cases the pole representing the experience of the life of the Church as a community of reconciliation is collapsed into the pole representing the specific sacramental tradition.

On the other hand, the denial of the Sacrament of Holy Confession in Protestantism generally has meant that forgiveness of sins has become a highly subjective experience. In sectarian expressions it fueled the drive for the creation of a strict, literalist, and legalistic understanding of Christianity, a fact delineated by Ernst Troeltsch so clearly in his *Social Teachings of the Christian Churches.*[42] In mainline Protestantism it seems to have led to

---

39. *Hiera Synopsis kai Akolouthia ton Pathon* (*Concise Prayerbook and Service of the Holy Passion*) (Athens: Saliveros Publications, Athens, 1966), 10, 11, stanzas: 5, 6, 9, 11, 13, 16, 17, 19, 28. For an English translation without the stanzas, see *Daily Prayers for Orthodox Christians: The Synekdemos*, ed. N. Michael Vaporis (Brookline, Mass.: Holy Cross Orthodox Press, 1986), 42–44.
40. McNeill, *History of the Cure of Souls,* 289.
41. Christos Androutsos, *Dogmatike tes Orthodoxou Anatolikes Ekklesias* (*Dogmatics of the Eastern Orthodox Church*), 2nd reprint ed. (Athens, 1956), 387.
42. Troeltsch, *Social Teachings of the Christian Church,* 2:4.

a secularization of much of the reconciling function of the Church. The alliance of psychology with religion in some of its practitioners leads to a deterioration of the element of gracious forgiveness and the relativizing of the reconciling, forgiving, and redemptive function of the Church.[43]

The errors on both sides can be avoided if the two poles are kept in dynamic tension. The sacramental aspect should be retained as the focus for the sharpest expression of forgiveness and as a necessary clear and direct focus on forgiveness. On the other hand, the Christian life as a whole both in its corporate and personal dimensions is the more diffused realization of one of the ever-present requirements in all aspects of life—the specifically religious, as well as the ordinary aspects of life.

This threefold dimensioned dynamic of reconciliation, expressed by reference to the Trinity, also points to the need to keep each of these three multiple dimensions in a creative and dynamic relationship: first, the tension of philanthropy and ultimate moral order; second, the tension of grace and growth; and third, the tension of sacramental forgiveness and life as a whole should not be resolved in favor of any one of the three. It is necessary that in the very exercise of forgiveness and reconciliation, all three of these dynamic mysteries should be kept in balance and effectively expressed. Subsuming all of the other dimensions to one will of necessity cause distortion and a falsified view of forgiveness, redemption, and reconciliation.

THE DYNAMIC MYSTERY
OF FORGIVENESS REALIZED

The purpose of this section is to reflect on some aspects of sacramental forgiveness and reconciliation as a possible model for forgiveness and reconciliation in other contexts. The *Heilsgeschichte*, which serves as the background of the Sacrament of Forgiveness as understood in the Eastern Christian patristic theological perspective, provides a stance from which

43. This is my main criticism of Emerson's work, which is an heroic attempt to keep the Church in the process of forgiveness and reconciliation. Yet the weak ecclesiology underlying the book opens the door to understandings of forgiveness and "wholeness" which in the end deny the necessity of divine forgiveness and see it a simple psychological process. See chapter 2, and especially the conclusion.

subsequent sacramental perspectives flow. Because the theological context is so important, it deserves a thorough description.

The Eastern Orthodox theological approach first emphasizes the complete unknowability of the *essence* of God, while pointing to the activities or *energies* of God as they relate to the world. Thus, the absolute character of God is unknown, but God's energies, that is, His relatedness to the world, which He has created, are in part known. As we know them, in a real, yet far from absolute sense, we know God.

God created the world freely and without constraint. There are no preexisting ideal patterns or absolutes according to which God created the world. This is just one possible world brought into being positively and concretely by the *autexousion* (self-determining will) of God.[44] So humanity is created in the image and likeness of God. In the thinking of the Eastern Church Fathers, the "image" refers to the given divine-like attributes of human nature, such as intellect, creativity, freedom, moral sense, and personal existence in community. The "likeness" was understood by the Fathers as the potential to fulfill and complete the human purpose and *telos* so that human beings can approach God-likeness. But human existence historically has shown that in exercising self-determination we chose, rather, not to realize our potential. Human existence is a story of rebellion against the Creator. The consequence is the loss of the God-like potential and that the "image" of God in human beings is marred and weakened. But it is not destroyed completely. "The natural precepts which he had from the beginning implanted in mankind" are the basic and necessary presuppositions of social and therefore individual life.[45] This natural law is a moral law, seen also in the Decalogue or as summarized in the Sermon on the Mount, basic to all human beings in society, and it is to be understood as a positive, intrinsic factor of our human nature, a part of the divine image in us, distorted as that image might be.[46]

This affirmation of an elementary norm for social living in the natural law provides a basic assumption about all human existence and, therefore,

44. Irenaeus, *Against Heresies*, II.1.4 and II.3.2, and II.30.9, bk. II.3.2 and bk. II.
45. Ibid., IV.15.1.
46. Romans 2:12, 14–15. See my article, "The Natural Law Teaching of the Eastern Orthodox Church," *Greek Orthodox Theological Review* 9 (1963–64): 215–24; reprinted in Martin Marty and Dean Pearlman, eds., in *New Theology*, no. 2 (1965), 122–33.

is a commonly shared ethic of all humanity. Its principles are found in every religious tradition with Scriptures, and they are commonly supported by legal traditions in various cultures. The message it conveys is that human society is empirically flawed. In the effort to understand the context of forgiveness and reconciliation, this theological presupposition means that, on the one hand, there is a common and shared sense of human existence, including a sense of right and wrong and a moral deposit in persons and societies that exists and to which appeals can be made. In essence, this perspective affirms that forgiveness and reconciliation can come about only if there is a shared moral sense at some level. In a situation of pure moral relativity there would be no reason to ask for forgiveness, no need to grant it.

Human beings can react and respond with self-determination with this basic moral equipment, either living in harmony with it or rebelling against it. Among those who lived in accordance with it are the personages known by the founders as the "righteous ancients" of the Old Testament and even some from among the Gentiles. In spite of these exceptions, human beings, personally and as societies, constantly fall short of God-likeness. This is another way of saying that we sin toward God and one another. We violate justice continuously in myriads of ways personally and socially. Or, put slightly differently, we are constantly offending others and distorting human relations among us. Human beings are continuously in need of redemption, forgiveness, and restoration.

Given the human track record, there is a message in this for those who would seek to overcome our unremitting history of abuse, injustice, coercion, violence, exploitation, and inequity, on any level and in any venue. The need for forgiveness is permanent and perpetual in human relationships. Consequently, it is difficult to overcome remembrance of injustice, to forgive others and to achieve reconciliation.

From the faith stance of the Christian Church, the possibility for human forgiveness is rooted in Christ's saving work. Christ's redemptive work restores to humanity the "likeness," that is, the potential to fulfill our *telos* to become God-like, to become "perfect as our Father in heaven is perfect." And this means nothing less than becoming completely, fully, and totally human. The Church holds that without the work of Christ this is impossible. In this sense all men and women are in reality less-than-human, less than what they can be and ought to be, and thus all are in need of redemption. The prototype of the kind of human being we ought to be is Christ; the prototype of what society should be is the eschatological Kingdom of God. Christians only partially realize that goal and never fully realize it. This ought to convey a sobering message to all who seek to cultivate in conflicted human relations attitudes of forgiveness and steps that lead to reconciliation.

It is important to note that in the Orthodox sacramental approach to sin and forgiveness, what is and what ought to be are on a continuum. The minimum for human social and individual existence is the natural law as we have defined it; the maximum is the fullest realization of the Christ-like image in our individual and social existence, that is, sainthood for the individual and the Kingdom of God for society. The Church in the moral sense exists as the arena where the Holy Spirit forgives, supports, and strengthens Christians in their struggle for growth into the image of God. This places us at a point of tension between anarchical disorder on the one side and eschatological perfection on the other. It requires of each person to realize as much as possible the image of God in his or her own life and in the society in which that person lives (in the Church community especially).

For those interested in fostering processes of forgiveness and reconciliation in economic, political, racial, ethnic, religious, and cultural conflicts, there is also a never-ending struggle to cultivate styles of living and institutions that support them, that contribute to reconciliation and open paths to understanding and forgiveness. Conversely, the types of attitudes and styles of living that hamper human reconciliation and raise barriers to forgiveness must be battled against.

In the Church's understanding of sacramental forgiveness and the struggle for growth there is rejoicing in progress. But there is always also the recognition that we continually fall short and so there is always the liturgical petition "Lord have mercy" and the Jesus Prayer ("Lord Jesus Christ have mercy upon me a sinner"), and, more concretely, the Sacrament of Forgiveness.[47] The pattern in this sacramental understanding of forgiveness readily transfers itself to many varied and socially disparate situations.

---

47. Peter of Damascus, *Prooimion* (*Preface*) in *Philokalia*, III.7.13–24.

Reconciliation and forgiveness are ongoing processes. They can give new beginnings to strained and fractured relationships, but the very distorted and fragile pattern of all human relationships will not stay "restored" for long without a long-term—in fact, perpetual—struggle to reach working patterns of cooperative and constructive relationships. Nonecclesial settings may not want to speak of sin, but that is what all those struggling for reconciliation encounter at every step of the process. It would be foolish to assume otherwise. Christians will argue that the solutions can never be considered established without the grace of God. In any case, the human side of the equation requires persistence and long-term commitment to the goal of mutual forgiveness and reconciliation. In part, this comes about because it is very difficult to forgive and equally difficult to acknowledge wrongdoing so as to ask for forgiveness.

What message is in this sacramental stance for those who seek to foster reconciliation outside of ecclesial existence? Those who seek to foster reconciliation must understand that they are dealing with deep, ingrained, and complex memories, identities, hurts, and suffering. Often these memories become so dominant that they provide powerful reasons for maintaining divisions and antipathies long after they have taken place. Taking lives of their own, they color emotions, attitudes, and judgments. I am a first-generation Greek American. The bitterness of four hundred years of second-class citizenship of my people under Ottoman rule is etched into my psyche. I remember stories told by my father, rejoicing at the expulsion of Turkish armed forces from his home island of Samos in the Aegean Sea. A few years ago, I was seeking to purchase a home. A real estate dealer showed me a home owned by Turkish Americans, decorated to reflect their homeland. I, who thought I was immune to prejudice, found myself agitated and unwilling to consider the home for purchase! The depth of division and antagonisms should never be underestimated.

In the Church's sacramental perspective, the relationship with God can be restored, and the potential for freedom to grow can be reestablished only if the sin is "forgiven." Forgiveness does not erase the past act. What it does is remove accountable guilt for the behavior and erase the consequences of separation and limitation upon the potential of growth. Thus, in the words of one student of Christian forgiveness, "As a living experience, forgiveness is needed and is relevant to the condition of man. Without it man cannot live. Without it he cannot grow."[48] As such, forgiveness in the early Fathers of the Church was oftentimes referred to as freedom.[49]

Sacramentally how is this freedom regained and how is the broken relationship restored? Certainly there is no claim by the repentant sinner on the basis of right or privilege before God, so that forgiveness can be demanded. We approach the throne of God because God is *philanthropos* and His stable love makes it possible for us to presume the possibility of release from the burden of guilt for the violation of divine norms, and responsibility for the separation from God. But how does one approach the throne of mercy upon which one has no real claim? There must be first a sense of the sin committed and cognizance of it. There must follow of necessity a true sorrow and shame for having transgressed against the will of God, for having insulted divine generosity, and for having slipped back from the freedom of opportunity to grow toward the fulfillment of one's human *telos* into servitude to the powers of evil. Together with this contrition there should be desire to regain and reestablish the lost relationship and to move forward in freedom in the process of growth toward the fulfillment of the image of God. Where sin has occurred through the violation of God's will regarding our neighbor, reconciliation and restitution are prerequisites, not for forgiveness but for approaching the throne of mercy. To do less would be evidence of a lack of the sincere desire to restore the relationship with God and to begin again the road to growth.[50]

Thus, from this point of view, repentance is not a personal or private atonement for sins committed; it is not in any sense an emotional "payment" for the guilt of the sin. It simply is the only way by which we may dare to call again at the throne of mercy. Just as a man who insults his benefactor can approach him again only as a suppliant, so the sinner can make possible forgiveness and restoration of the broken relationship and reobtain

---

48. Emerson, *Dynamics of Forgiveness,* 73.
49. "[T]he Eastern church leaders seemed to concentrate on a different word for the experience of forgiveness than the word itself. This was the word freedom!" Ibid.
50. This treatment is based on Mesoloras's fivefold analysis of repentance in his *Symbolike tes Orthodoxou Anatolikes Ekklesias: Ta Symbolika Biblia (Eastern Orthodox Symbolics: The Symbolic Books)* (Athens, 1904), 4:302. See also Frank Gavin, *Some Aspects of Contemporary Greek Orthodox Thought* (Milwaukee: Morehouse, 1923), 355–70.

the freedom for growth by way of an evident and clear change of direction or change of mind. It is in the light of this fact that the New Testament Greek word for repentance is *metanoia,* which means a change of mind. The change that permits the possibility of forgiveness and restoration of the relationship is the change from an attitude of egocentrism and rebellion involving a rejection of God's will to one that recognizes the claim of that will and the benefits of obedience to it.

God, unlike ourselves, waits patiently for our repentance. Human beings are not so eager to find solutions for long-lasting and long-nurtured hurts. Can people, drawing on their own resources, actually find ways to overcome them? There are some remarkable cases when self-interest may seem to have provided the bases for forgiveness and reconciliation. The restoration of relationships between Japan and the United States after World War II might provide such a model. But ethnic, cultural, and religious strife and personal/social hurts on all levels continue to abound unresolved, unrepented for, without desire for reconciliation.

From a sacramental perspective it is required for the confession of sins to be oral. There are several reasons for this. The psychological need for expression of repentance to make it real and fulfill its essential nature is an insight supported by much contemporary psychological theory. One theologian put it categorically several years ago in the following words: "one might say that where there is no desire for [oral] confession it is the result and manifestation of the absence of true penitence."[51] But further, the aspect of "growth" requires that the person repenting also receive guidance, comfort, advice, suggestions for correction, and direction. Without oral confession such would not be possible. Even in nondirectional counseling such oral confession is a requirement. This will have serious bearing on the nature of imposed penances, a topic we will return to shortly. Further, oral confession in the earliest history of the sacrament was an act done before the whole body of the Church. Despite the drawbacks of such a practice, it points to the need for the penitent to be reconciled to the body of the faithful, the Church. Confession to the priest as a representative of the Church not only gives assurance of forgiveness in a concrete way, it also assures

---

51. Constantine Dyobouniotes, *Ta Mysteria* (Athens, 1912), 133. Quoted in Gavin, *Some Aspects of Contemporary Greek Orthodox Thought,* 361.

the repentant person of his continued membership and solidarity in the Body of Christ.[52]

This sacramental understanding and practice provide a strong message for those who would seek to cultivate reconciliation through forgiveness in other venues. An essential dimension of the process that can foster reconciliation and forgiveness in any kind of venue is that sorrow for past acts of harm inflicted on others be articulated. It must be said, it must be said with genuine contrition, and it must be said in a manner that can be actually heard and understood by the aggrieved party. Forgiveness, in these nonsacramental cases, can be offered only by the aggrieved parties, but it requires that somehow they are willing to put aside long-held memories of unjust treatment, to let them go, and to risk new ways of relating. In this sense, they "give absolution." When, as is the case usually, both sides bear burdens of unjust treatment of others, there is a kind of "mutual absolution" that has to take place for reconciliation to occur.

From the sacramental perspective the Church seeks to establish through compassion, care, understanding, and identity with the penitent a climate that fosters repentance and openness to forgiveness and reconciliation.[53] But what of the content of the confession itself? Since the repentance of the penitent is the *sine qua non* of the act, the details of the confessed sins are not the primary critera. Enough should be said, however, so that the spiritual father is capable of understanding the condition of the penitent, but there is no need to have every detail, every instance, every aspect of the sin ferreted out. The 102nd Canon of the Fifth-Sixth Ecumenical Council in Trullo very wisely compares the work of the father confessor with that of the physician, whose task it is to find out enough about the patient so to heal him, maintaining the middle road between simple generalities and too detailed specifics for, as it says, "the sickness of sin is not simple but varied and multiformed."[54] The persons involved should recognize and acknowl-

---

52. Canon 28 of Nikephoros the Confessor takes this into consideration when it cautions confessors not to prohibit Church attendance as penance to those who have sinned secretly, so that others may not "lord over them."

53. See PG, LXXXVIII, 1890–1901 and Morinus, *De Disciplina in Administratione Sacramenti Poenitentiae* (Antwerp, 1682), 77–117. For a thorough analysis of this service see Constantine Callinicos, *Metanoia (Repentance)*, 2nd ed. (Athens, 1958).

54. Canon 102, in Hamilka Alivizatos, *Oi Ieroi Kanones (The Holy Canons)*, 2nd ed. (Athens, 1949), 116–17.

edge the injustice and the pain caused, but should move beyond them as soon as it is emotionally and rationally possible. Wherever this takes place, with the help of the facilitator, trust-building steps toward forgiveness and reconciliation become possible.

Sacramentally, what is the nature of the absolution offered? The absolution restores the relationship between God and sinner, it empowers the penitent to continue to grow in the image and likeness of God; that is, it does not remove the history and the fact of the sin, it removes the effects and consequences of the sin. St. Athanasius says, "He who repents ceases from sinning, but he still has the marks of the wounds."[55] The penitent becomes a new creature again that makes possible his obedience to the will of God and his growth in the divine image. It is the pronouncement of the confessor, which actualizes this: "Whose sins ye forgive, they are forgiven, whose sins ye retain, they are retained." Yet the pronouncement of that forgiveness ought to point to the philanthropy and mercy of God rather than the power of forgiveness granted to God's agent.[56]

Finally, what is the nature of any penances that the confessor may choose to require of the forgiven penitent? On the one hand they cannot be acts of atonement, satisfaction, so to speak for the sins committed since the purpose of the sacrament is to mediate the forgiving grace of God, to restore the relationship, to provide new freedom for growth. Rather, the penances may serve two purposes. The first is to impress upon the penitent the reality of the forgiveness. This is solely remedial and medicinal and not vindictive and punitive (for) "The Blood of Jesus . . . cleanses us from all sin (1 John 1:7) . . . nor is there any condemnation to them which are in Christ Jesus (Rom. 8:1)."[57]

Such penances need not be imposed if the confessor deems it unnecessary, for they are not an essential aspect of the Sacrament of Holy Confession. The second purpose of the imposition of penances relates to the

---

55. *Epistle to Serapion*, 4, 13. PG, XXVL, 656.
56. "Behold, he says to the penitent, through the will of the philanthropic God, who wishes the salvation of all, having come in repentance and having confessed all, you are released from your previous evil works," is a characteristic prayer of the service of Patriarch John the Faster mentioned above.
57. Emerson, *Dynamics of Forgiveness*, 122–23. See also Canon 102 of the Fifth/Sixth Ecumenical Council and others.

penitent's need for guidance, assistance, and direction. Penances should be imposed on the basis of the specific condition and needs for the improvement and growth of the penitent. They should be designed and imposed with the specific intent of helping him or her to grow in the Spirit into the image and likeness of God.

Here again, the application to extrasacramental situations calling for forgiveness and reconciliation is quite plain. Sometimes, justice requires some form of restitution for harms inflicted. Other times, a facilitator may suggest some changes that are educational or symbolic, that will convince the other party that the expression of sorrow and repentance is genuine, but it should not be presented as a punishment. Thus, American society consistently disapproves of the use of coarse epithets that tend to denote disrespect of minorities. Suggesting such symbolic changes in relationships between aggrieved parties, when they are accepted, can foster willingness to put the past away and look toward a different future in relationships.

The whole sacramental approach to forgiveness and reconciliation in the Eastern Orthodox tradition thus is a case study in maintaining all of these dimensions in a constant interrelated tension, every element in a fruitful and productive paradoxical relationship with every other aspect of forgiveness. Those who would facilitate forgiveness and reconciliation in other situations will also sense the inner dynamic and potential constructive tensions in any given venue.[58]

CONCLUSION

In accordance to our model, then, we have sought to delineate the outlines of the Sacrament of Reconciliation so that no one aspect of the dynamic elements involved is lost and reduced into one of the other aspects. God's philanthropy and the moral order and evangelical way of life; the all-sufficient redemptive grace as well as the implication of fall and restoration in the process of growth; the instrumentation of forgiveness in both the Sacrament and in the whole life of the Church: are all kept in a dynamic ten-

---

58. Gavin, *Some Aspects of Contemporary Greek Orthodox Thought*, 367–68.

sion. Together they help to describe but not to resolve the mystery of how sin as violation of the moral law and the evangelical way of life, as separation from God and as the arrest of the realization of the human goal to be fully and truly human, is overcome sacramentally. The sacrament, variously known by the names of Repentance, Forgiveness, Healing, Reconciliation, Restoration, Penance, and Holy Confession, we have tried to show, can also serve as a model for attitudes and modalities for those in other venues who seek to foster forgiveness and reconciliation.

PART II

Forgiveness and Public Policy

CHAPTER 4

Does Religion Fuel or Heal in Conflicts?

Raymond G. Helmick, S.J.

S OME YEARS AGO, while preparing a conference on the Middle East, I mentioned to the late Israeli general and peace activist Yehoshafat Harkabi that I planned to include a panel on the role of religion in the search for peace. Harkabi reacted in horror, asking, "Why would you do that? I would have thought the role entirely negative." This seemed a bit heavy-handed to me, and I responded to it practically as a joke, saying we had these and these and these speakers, Jewish, Christian, and Muslim, and they would address the positive elements in the role. Harkabi was unflinching: "You are going to take religion to the beauty parlor," he answered, and of course I then introduced the panel, at the conference, with that story.

A caution is required at the very beginning of any discussion of religion as a resource or as a problem for the resolution of conflicts. It is not that religion has too often proven a negative factor, though that is true and we will have to discuss it; rather, one ought not look to religion for purposes other than its own.

A religious faith is in itself an all-encompassing outlook on life, on the world and its meaning. It generates its own agenda and, reluctant though we may be, we must allow it to do that. Outsiders who try to utilize religion for their own purposes may have good or bad agendas of their own.

Even those of us who regard ourselves as insiders to a faith community may yield to the temptation of using religion for an extraneous purpose. People who look to religion as a help in resolving conflicts always feel they have the best motives anyone might think of. But it is always an abuse of religious faith to make it an instrument for something else.

I state this so sharply at the beginning out of a realization of how hard a saying it is. We all have difficulty in trusting religious institutions to set their own agendas because they have behaved so badly in the past. Ethnic nationalism is a primary case in point. In the former Yugoslavia ethnic identities have been so tied to religion that *Serb* and *Orthodox* are practically interchangeable terms in people's consciousness, *Croat* and *Catholic* become equally the badges under which Muslims are persecuted, excluded, "ethnically cleansed." In those countries, where Serb, Croat, and Bosnian Muslim are all from the same Slavic stock, there is hardly any other content to ethnicity than religious difference.

In Ireland, ever since the Protestant Reformation, religion has not been basically about religion. Rather, Catholic and Protestant identities have been loyalty tests, right down to the present, for Irish Nationalism or loyalty to the English/British crown. We often have to remind ourselves that the Anglo-Irish conflict predates the Protestant Reformation by some four hundred years. Everyone in this picture, until then, was Catholic. But as soon as a religious difference became available, it was utilized immediately for the purpose of identifying political allegiance. Religion—Jewish, Christian, and Muslim—invades every corner of the Middle East conflict, with dire results.

South Africa has seen its parallels. The practice and conceptualization of apartheid were basically invented in church. Religious doctrine, judged by its opponents to have been heresy, served then as its rationalization: church as locus of superiority assumptions. And we Americans, with our history of "Manifest Destiny" delusions, take our place in the line.

Religion has in this way acquired a strangely sinister reputation among those who work for the resolution or transformation of conflicts. The assumption, conventional by now, is that religious faith commitment, or the sense of identification with a faith community, fosters division, hatred, and violence.

This impression arises from a badly checkered history. European Western "Christendom" and its American and other once-colonial appendages have witnessed a widespread popular alienation from the institutional churches. I date this phenomenon to the religious wars of the seventeenth century, which left the battered peoples of Europe with the conviction that their churches had failed them.

Several times I have remarked to Muslim friends that the Islamic community, on the whole, has experienced no comparable alienation from its faith or its institutions. The response often given me is that they hope such alienation will not result from the ways Islam is being used, instrumentally, for political purposes or as a means of expressing anger in our own time. Many Western Ashkenazi Jews seem to have acquired a similar alienation from religious authority and institutions as if by contagion from their European Christian neighbors. This manifests itself not only in Europe and America, but also in Jewish secularism in the state of Israel, to the great puzzlement of Sephardic Israelis, who have experienced no such alienation.

But from the time of Europe's religious wars, after a bloody century not rivaled until our twentieth century, professed agnosticism or atheism became commonplace in Christian lands in a way seldom seen before. Institutional religious authority found itself suspect, in the eyes of the intellectual mainstream of society, of promoting only its own private power interests, not the faith agenda of a believing community. There had been reasons enough before to complain of corruption in the Christian Church. Medieval demands for reform in head and members had led eventually to the Reformation itself. But this sense of broken faith on the part of the institutions centered now on the cult of violence.

That massive breach of confidence in religion and its leadership coincided with the opening of what we have called "The Modern Age." That term calls for definition. I see three principal building blocks in what we regarded as modernity. First was the scientific revolution, beginning with Copernicus and Galileo and spreading to all areas of study of the material universe, which has given Western civilization its exponential technological growth. Then came, as a second component, the philosophical Enlightenment of the seventeenth and eighteenth centuries, the cult of reason. The third element was the political liberalism, which led, through the period of "Enlightened Despots," to the English, American, French, and Russian revolutions and the development of representative government.

For true believers in The Modern Age, these three things gave the answers to all the questions. Religious faith began to look like a curious atavism, a throwback to outmoded superstitions. European theologies, with all their differences and rivalries, became of one kind, in that the central question for all of them became: "How can you believe these things in The Modern Age?" The liberation theologies of more recent decades have recognized that this shift to a near-exclusive preoccupation with apologetics led to an impoverishment of faith. They have identified it as adolescent theology, and in its place they make the central question of theology how our faith relates us to the poor or the oppressed, or more generally whether our faith is truly something to be lived, in action.

This amounts to a major theological transformation in our own time, but it is not only the theologians who have changed. The devastating cruelty and violence of the twentieth century have finally taught the intellectual mainstream, so long alienated from religion, that the three holy icons of The Modern Age—science, rational enlightenment and liberal politics—have not in fact answered all the questions.

People mean different things when they speak of "Post-Modernism," but one phenomenon to which the term can be applied is the way serious people now look to the wisdom traditions, including often the whole spectrum of traditional faiths, to supply what modernism has failed to provide. They are as suspicious as ever of the institutions—I surely join them in that. But this turning, at least with curiosity and often with hope, to the traditional sources of faith creates a new situation in which we should look again at the relation between religion and violence. We should see what poisons have been in the mix—let's not pretend they have not been there—and ask how we might get to the healing and reconciling role that we would expect of religion.

There are, of course, some other potential reasons for this tarnishing of the religious record in areas of conflict. Besides this extrinsic cause, the instrumental use of religion, there may be intrinsic stimuli to the rejection and exclusion of others, and the licensing of violence against them: concepts of divine revelation or election that establish sharp separation between the recipients of God's word, or the elect, and the reprobate or unbelievers.

Or great harm may be done by concepts of an angry, vengeful God, in whose service we may visit wrath upon our enemies.

Any of these phenomena, as I read it, truly contradicts the reconciliation tenets of faith, which are a common theme across a broad range of confessional positions. And if here I speak primarily of Christian faith, it is because that is mine and is most familiar to me. I am conscious that some other faiths too lay great emphasis on reconciliation.

In Christian experience a great watershed occurred with the legalization of the Christian Church under Constantine. If we read our way into the dialogue that today begins to take place between Christians and Muslims we soon hear about one great difference that is supposed to exist between us: that for Christians church and state are separate while for Muslims religious and civil society are one. I have never believed that this dichotomy has been as clear or as absolute in actual historic experience as that observation indicates. But it is true that in its beginnings the Islamic faith community, gathered about the Prophet Mohammed first in Medina and then in Mecca, did simultaneously govern civil society. The Christian community in contrast was, for its first three centuries, an outsider group, barely if at all tolerated by the Roman imperial state, alien and marginalized within its culture.

For as long as and to the extent that that was true, the Christian community had neither power in nor responsibility for the state. The Christians were not all, as they are sometimes presented, the poor and enslaved, fringe people in Roman society. Prominent people, even some members of the senatorial class and imperial family, came into Christianity from early on. But it was not until the opening years of the fourth century that the weight of the Christian community was such that the power class of the empire felt they had need of it.[1]

Constantine changed the game, which made a tremendous difference in what it meant to be a Christian. Where before it had been risk, something one undertook only out of deep conviction and that involved everything in one's life, now it was the smart thing to do, one of the conditions of worldly advancement. The emperor needed the bishops and the community they could vouch for. The bishops understood that they had attained their posi-

---

1. A helpful treatment of the whole context can be found in Timothy David Barnes, *The New Empire of Diocletian and Constantine* (Cambridge: Harvard University Press, 1982).

tion of privilege for reasons other than the advancement of Christian faith but chose nonetheless to give unqualified adulation to the emperor. They treated him and his intervention on their behalf as the direct act of God, while giving him the assent and moral support he sought from them. It was politic.[2]

We can describe this as the Constantinian order in the Church. Church and state were to be two parallel bodies, reflective of one another: the state commanding the obedience of the subjects, the Church supporting its demands and providing the moral context within which the state would act. The administrative structures of the Roman state, such as dioceses and vicariates, were exactly duplicated in the Church, and remain even now. The role of the Church was to be the paradigm to the state. For more than a thousand years, this *paradigmatic role of the Church,* the Constantinian pattern, remained the norm, and in some odd places we find vestiges of it even today.

Some may see this as particularly a problem of the Orthodox churches of Eastern Europe, which by consistent tradition have organized themselves as national churches. I raised this a few years ago with an Orthodox theologian for whom I have great admiration, Professor Petros Vasiliadis of the Ecumenical Institute at the University of Thessaloniki. In the Balkan conflict, I felt, national governments had striven hard to commandeer the loyalties of their populations to the church as an instrument for their war purposes.

Professor Vasiliadis's response was interesting. He said he preferred the Orthodox eccesiological model, with its theology of the local church, to the centralized Roman one. The central authority apparatus had its advantages, when quick leadership response was needed in an emergency. But otherwise there was more opportunity for respectfully consultative government, collegiality to use the Roman term, in the Eastern model.[3] I could

---

2. The obsequious treatment of Constantine by the bishops of his time shows clearly in *The Ecclesiastical History* by his contemporary and servant, Eusebius, Bishop of Caesarea, of which the most current translation is by C. F. Cruse, new updated ed. (Peabody, Mass.: Hendrickson Publishers, 1998).

3. One of the best recent treatments of this subject is by Terence L. Nichols, *That All May Be One: Hierarchy and Participation in the Church,* a Michael Glazier Book (Collegeville, Minn.: Liturgical Press, 1997).

not do otherwise than agree with him. The model of the local church, however, as place of the Spirit's leading, is not the church of a nation. It is the congregation, the assembly of believers who meet in one place. They are in carefully cultivated communion, granted, with others elsewhere, but nonetheless they are the *locus* of the Spirit's activity where they are. That is the model of the Pauline and other early churches.

But let's not deceive ourselves that only Eastern Orthodoxy is afflicted with this determination of the state or other organized forces to co-opt the church for purposes foreign to its mission. All governments have caught on to the fact that churches are the custodians of the Just War theory. When the war begins, every government appeals at once to the church to get up in the cheering section and proclaim that "God is on our side." We never belong there. Our role as proclaimers of *shalom* demands of us that we be searching actively for alternatives to violence. But we have all seen churches fall right into the trap and preach national exclusivism and God's wrath, as if they were qualified to declare it, upon the enemy.

The Constantinian model eventually failed to sustain itself as the struggles between church and empire in Europe eventuated in defeat for the church and the stripping away, by Napoleon's time, of those powers that paralleled the state.

But however much the Constantinian order may have compromised the very faith of the Church throughout its long course, the bishops and other authorities who had grown so used to it saw its demise as a sad event, the deprivation of their accustomed institutional position. They instituted a rear-guard action to preserve as much of the old order as they could. If the Church could no longer parallel all the powers of the state, they would preserve and institutionalize those they could, most especially their control of marriage, of education and of the caring services of society (hospitals, charity, and so on). As a substitute for the no-longer-feasible paradigmatic role, we can describe this as a *pragmatic role of the Church.*

It was heavily contested by the power of the state and always exercised with regret for the paradigmatic role that had been lost. Both Church and state authorities saw it as second-best. We can see it in what Germans call *Kultur politik,* the administration of these cultural areas of family, school, and welfare, with Church and state competing for control. Especially the nineteenth-century *Kulturkampf* was a concerted effort of the Bismarckian state to wrest control of these functions from the churches, particularly from the Catholic Church,[4] but we can see it as well in Nazi campaigns against the churches, in the repressive antichurch activities of the Communist states, and even in a good deal of current American policy of creating obstacles to Church control over schools or hospitals.

What substitute remains to us if these two long-traditional models for the Church's role in society, paradigmatic and pragmatic, have both so utterly failed? If, again, we look to the original experience of Christian community in the early centuries, we will not find it useful or historically true to pretend we live in a time other than our own, when Christians were without a recognized role or responsibility in society. But we can usefully look to the way in which their faith convictions as such, the living out of their faith rather than institutionalized power, determined the role of Christian community in society. If our emphasis as Church were consistently on the building up of active faith commitment, that is, basically catechetical, we could expect the presence of a Christian community to influence, in organic and pervasive ways, the free corporate decisions of the society. A useful descriptive term for such a manner of Church activity in society's concern is the mathematical figure of the *parabola,* the plane curve generated by a point moving so that its distance from a fixed point is equal to its distance from a fixed line, the curve widening out between parallel lines without ever touching them. Thus our third model of the Church's activity in society is the *parabolic role of the Church.*[5]

There is no way to claim that such a procedure is accomplished fact in the Church of our own time, only a rather far-out aspiration. That there is a hankering still for the full Constantinian paradigmatic model can be seen in a couple of extraordinarily instructive episodes of recent history.

---

4. For a recent treatment see Ronald J. Ross, *The Failure of Bismarck's Kulturkampf: Catholicism and State Power in Imperial Germany, 1871–1887* (Washington, D.C.: Catholic University of America Press, 1998).
5. These terms for the roles of Church in society—*paradigmatic* for the Constantinian model, *pragmatic* for the familiar fall-back position, *parabolic* for the more faithful model recommended here—are not my own but come from a teacher I felt privileged to hear, Argentinian Methodist professor Jose Miguez-Bonino, when I was in graduate studies at Union Theological Seminary in the late 1960s. Miguez-Bonino uses them extensively in his many works, but I have reflected on them over so many years as to have made my own use of them.

Since the publication in the 1960s of Rolf Hochhuth's play, *Der Stellvertreter* (*The Deputy,* or *The Vicar* [*of Christ*]), the complaint has frequently been made that Pope Pius XII, during World War II, failed to act decisively enough against the Nazi Holocaust of the Jews. Much has been said and written for and against this charge, but we can properly ask: where were the Catholics of Germany that they needed to be ordered by the pope to resist the Holocaust? Was their faith not internalized enough to lead them to this without a papal order?

During the Vietnam War Catholics had a large role in the antiwar movement in the United States, and many of them complained that the Catholic bishops of the United States did not plainly condemn the war as unjust and prohibit participation in it or payment of taxes that would be spent in prosecuting it. Had the bishops done that, they might have ended the war. Simultaneously they would have brought down to ruin the democratic structure of the United States with its separation of Church and state. Given the dire consequences of any such action, we can again ask: where were the consciences of U.S. Catholics that they could not reject a war they saw as unjust without the bishops commanding them to do so?[6]

I have gone through these three models of the Church's sense of its role in the world, paradigmatic, pragmatic, and parabolic, in order to introduce some intelligibility into a dreadful part of our history: how the churches have lent themselves so easily and regularly to co-optation. The parabolic model, at this stage in our history, is simply a hope.

6. Another fascinating instance of the enduring Constantinian concept of church-state interdependence is chronicled in David Steele's lucid account of the church role in the 1989–90 transition in East Germany: "At the Front Lines of the Revolution: East Germany's Churches Give Sanctuary and Succor to the Purveyors of Change," in *Religion: The Missing Dimension of Statecraft,* ed. Douglas Johnston and Cynthia Sampson (New York: Oxford University Press, 1994), 199–52. The Evangelische Kirche in Germany had already experienced Nazi efforts to control it as a state church and established the Confessing Church as an antidote. Faced with Communist determination to make the Church an instrument for its own purposes, the German Protestants crafted a repertory of fine distinctions ranging from the church *within* socialism to a church *for* socialism, to a concept of church as guardian office or voice of conscience against abuse of power by the state, to a church for others that would focus on support for disenfranchised individuals, and a critical solidarity of church with state. This latter was still unacceptable to the state, because it seemed to imply that socialism could somehow be improved (123, 145–46 nn. 24 and 25. Fascinating, too, in this regard is Steele's concluding discussion of the relation of Church, as spiritual force and institutional structure, both to the East German state authority and to the largely unchurched public that demanded a revolutionary change of regime (139–43).

In the Northern Ireland situation, with which I have worked intensively ever since 1972, it became evident to me that many of the people, most with experience of violence and prison, who were the creators of the peace process were thoroughly alienated from their religious roots. They were disillusioned; they felt their churches, as institutions, had failed to do their part or help to heal the conflict. Nonetheless, they themselves operated out of the principles of reconciliation and readiness to forgive injury that were, or should have been, at the very heart of the religious faith and commitment of their churches. They had the substance, even if their church institutions did not. We expect that commitment to reconciliation to characterize any of the faith communities. They seem to be strong in theory, weak in practice of that quality.

I speak from within a community of Christian faith, which has great importance to me. I have seen the working of several other faith communities, understood something of their theological positions and the concrete practice of their commitments. I won't try to speak for them on this subject of reconciliation but commend, to those of you who live in those other traditions, to examine teaching and practice in this matter of reconciliation within them and explain it to the rest of us.[7]

Within my Christian context, nothing has greater theoretical priority. The Christian Gospel accounts abound in summonses to reconciliation, perhaps nowhere more imperatively than in Matthew 5:23–24: "If you are offering your gift at the altar, and there remember that your brother has something against you, leave your gift there before the altar and go; first be reconciled with your brother, and then come and offer your gift." Ritual practice can wait and has no importance comparable to that of reconciliation.

---

7. As one who, on this subject, can only read what is written by my betters, I would commend these fairly recent books: David R. Smock, *Religious Perspectives on War: Christian, Muslim, and Jewish Attitudes Toward Force after the Gulf War* (Washington, D.C.: U.S. Institute of Peace, 1992); Mordechai Nisan, *Identity and Civilization: Essays on Judaism, Christianity, and Islam* (University Press of America, 1999); and Ralph H. Salmi, Cesar Adib Majul, and George K. Tanham, *Islam and Conflict Resolution: Theories and Practices* (University Press of America, 1998); Marc Gopin, *Between Eden and Armageddon: The Future of World Religions, Violence, and Peacemaking* (New York: Oxford University Press, 2000); and Abdulaziz Sachedina, *The Islamic Roots of Democratic Pluralism* (New York: Oxford University Press, 2000).

So much for theory. In practice, Christian history has shown us a lot of concern with justice, consistently retributive justice. We hear far less of reconciliation or the practice of forgiveness that the Gospels so much urge. But a peculiar thing happened to the practice of reconciliation in Christian history. It disappeared into the confessional and became exclusively forgiveness of sin by God.[8] In this way it was privatized, made exclusively a matter between me and Jesus. Reconciliation with the brother, the sister, the neighbor tended to be lost in the shuffle.

Especially the public character of reconciliation and forgiveness, the reestablishment of wholeness in the relations between nations and peoples, failed to become a focus in the life of the faith community. Concepts of retribution and compulsion reigned supreme in all those public areas.

We may think of that disappearance into the confessional as a peculiarly Catholic phenomenon. But indeed, just over these last years I have found myself in a lengthy correspondence with a good friend in Northern Ireland, a leading Protestant clergyman, who contended that the only reconciliation taught or recognized in Christian Scripture is that between God and man. He would acknowledge no possibility or need for reconciliation between human persons. I found myself asking him: did he even read that book? I don't want to cast the blame on him, but the experience told me that Protestants had assimilated some of the bad habits of medieval and current Catholicism.

This is an internal question of practice within the Christian faith community, of interest to all of us within that circle, and surely an instance of serious discrepancy between faith and historic practice. The other faith communities may have a more or a less consistent experience in this area.

Look to the major successes in the healing of conflicts that we have seen in recent years. Sometimes our hopes, once raised, seem to be dashed, but there are in fact genuine accomplishments to record. An important one was the Oslo Declaration of Principles that brought the first real prospect of resolving the Israeli-Palestinian dispute. The principal representatives of these two peoples who, for at least forty-five years, had refused to recognize

---

8. Donald W. Shriver Jr. commented very perceptively on this, as he called it, "Sacramental Captivity of Forgiveness," in his book, *An Ethic for Enemies: Forgiveness in Politics* (New York: Oxford University Press, 1995), 49–52.

one another's legitimacy as peoples, formally and publicly did exactly that. Hesitations there were, reservations within that acceptance, some of which gradually warmed. Rejectionist factions rose on the fringes of both communities. There were disappointments on both sides that the accord contained so little specific agreement.

Yet the mutual recognition, the acceptance by each people of the other, had profound implications. I would regard them as having basis within the faith convictions of each community, the reverence for the other, for the stranger, that each faith inculcated, even for those to whom that faith was only a cultural recollection.

We may have the impression, after the troubles of more recent years, that a determined effort was made to retract that recognition of the other people's legitimacy. If so, the good news is that it proved impossible. Such a solemn recognition, once granted, could not be rescinded, and the seeds of peace once planted have survived to be watered once again.

Something similar happened in the Northern Ireland conflict, leading to the twin ceasefires of IRA and Loyalist militants in 1994. In this case those who had taken the most active part in the violence of the previous quarter century were among the first to accept that their society could only be healed by accommodation of one another. The essential meaning of the ceasefires was recognition by the militants of either side that the other tradition must have their respect, that they must become the guarantors of one another's difference. As either side has aspired to the establishment of constitutional arrangements that would validate their own communal identity, they have found it could be done only by agreement with the other. In Northern Ireland, the mainstream politicians, those who always prided themselves on their rejection of violence, though sometimes calling for extremes of state repression against the dissidents of their society, had far more trouble understanding these developments than those who had been in the throes of the conflict. Even when the ceasefires themselves broke down out of a feeling of intransigence, the breach could not be maintained after the basic recognitions that had been granted.

This tells us, I believe, much about what religion can bring about for the resolution of conflict. I have already mentioned the alienation from religious institutions that characterized many of the people who brought about these enormous changes in attitude in Northern Ireland, yet the roots of their action still lie deep in their traditions of faith, even when they have adjudged their churches, or their religious leadership, lacking precisely in that faith.

Many of us have a very particular interest in the theme of restorative justice, as much a social as a religious issue. It has its importance within the legal system or in any striving for international peace, in the resolution or transformation of conflicts. In our country this has become an important concern among a broad range of lawyers and judges, who have seen the purely retributive system characteristic of our practice of justice as poisoning our society with a cult of vengeance.

The concept needs grounding in the wisdom traditions, something we may seek in the various faith communities. Without that, the work undertaken will likely amount to no more than tinkering with the legal system and will fall short of the profound transformation it could make in our society.

Dr. Rodney Petersen and I, in the Boston Theological Institute,[9] brought groups of theology graduate students to see the work of peacemaking in Northern Ireland, in the former Yugoslavia, South Africa, and most recently in Jerusalem over these last few years. We came close to organizing a conference in Boston that would have been simply among theologians on the theme of reconciliation. But then we got to talking with lawyers, and the congruence of our reconciliation theme with the concern of the legal community for restorative justice so impressed us that our conference took that direction. I believe that it is in the informing of the justice enterprise with the best strivings of the wisdom traditions, even where they have fallen short of their own teachings in practice, that we will best succeed in fostering a more humane society.

Let me turn then, in conclusion, to a consideration of the law. I will tell of an experience that deeply impressed me. Working with the conflicted peoples of Lebanon, as far back as 1983, I found that people in the various confessional communities all tended to express their anxieties about one

9. This is a consortium of nine theological schools in the Boston area: Andover Newton Theological School, Boston College Department of Theology, Boston University School of Theology, Episcopal Divinity School, Gordon-Conwell Theological Seminary, Harvard University Divinity School, Holy Cross Greek Orthodox School of Theology, Saint John's Seminary, and Weston Jesuit School of Theology.

another in terms of the law. Christians and Muslims alike feared that the other would try to cheat them of their true identity and bring them into subjection to themselves by means of the law. Christians felt that if Muslims ever came to power in Lebanon they would introduce Islamic Law and transform the country into an Islamic Republic, leaving them as second-class citizens. Muslims believed that they themselves had already been reduced to second-class citizenship by the introduction of European concepts of law during the French Mandate period.

The actual system of law in Lebanon was basically Code Napoleon from that French period, modified by some positive legislation and some remnants of Ottoman law. But the areas of family law, involving among other things marriage, divorce and inheritance, were governed instead by *Statutes Personelles,* the particular law traditions of each of the confessional communities. As there was no organic link between these particular traditions and the rest of the corpus of public law, their relation mirrored the fragility of Lebanese society.

The particular traditions were, of course, much broader than this area of family law and were profoundly an expression of the culture of the respective communities, deeply rooted, of course, in religious faith. But those parts of them that were inoperative lay fallow in the culture like the parts of an iceberg that are concealed beneath the surface. Concealed so, present but unexamined, they contributed little more to the culture than prejudice and stereotype.

My interest in this Lebanese case was in equality of citizenship and the way each of the traditions, without losing its integrity, could relate to this. I contended that the original formative insights of each of the traditions of law contained great treasures that could be restorative of relations within the whole composite society. My proposal of a program of legal anthropology was that each of the traditions should delve deeply into its own culture of law to find those root insights and illuminate them for people of the other traditions.

I was especially conscious of the way the root traditions of Islam validate the legitimacy of the religious faith of the other Peoples of the Book, and make it a special task of the Muslim community, the *umma,* to preserve the freedom of the other faith communities. The traditional implementation of this profound insight was constricted by the relatively primitive political technology of that early time. As a result, Christians living among Muslims, as in Lebanon, remained wary of the *dhimmi* status, the condition of "protected peoples," by which they were free to maintain their religious faith but were expected to leave all responsibility for the public affairs of the society to Muslims. Deep search into the roots of the tradition, I felt, could bring these creative originative insights fully into the life of a contemporary political culture.

In this way, all the varied confessional traditions of Lebanon could develop a corpus of civil law, coherent but respectful of differences, admitting distinctions of law where necessary in the traditions of the various communities. They could allow appeal to the disparate traditions in such a way that they would acquire standing and a home in Lebanese law, bringing all these strands into an organic relation. The corpus of Lebanese law could then become a true expression of Lebanese society in its unity and its pluralism.

Now law can easily become just a collection of rules and can be treated with a kind of legal positivism that sees only prescriptions and no context— spiritual, cultural, or other. I actually understand this in terms of something much more, of placing the origins of these particular cultures of law in the spiritual contexts that gave rise to them. It is when law functions in that kind of context that it can build and restore relations.

This was of course a particular case, with the limits of a particular case. It had evident relation to the rest of the Arab world and at the time attracted attention in several Arab countries. I believe it has a wider relevance to the healing of relations that will be the making of our peace in other parts of our world. If, from our varied religious heritages, peace and not affliction is to result, we will have to look to such practical effects of them as these in our lives to draw the fruits of reconciliation from them. I would reckon in each of these instances that the good influence of religion has sprung directly from its own premises of faith. But we can too easily sour the impact of religion if we use it as an instrument for purposes otherwise conceived.

CHAPTER 5

Religion and Peacemaking

Joseph V. Montville

T HE SUBJECT OF RELIGION in political conflict is vast, and it is not possible to do justice to it in these few pages. Fortunately, scholars, political analysts, and policymakers can refer to two extraordinary new studies, Marc Gopin's *Between Eden and Armageddon: The Future of World Religions, Violence, and Peacemaking,* and R. Scott Appleby's *The Ambivalence of the Sacred,* for comprehensive treatments of both the destructive and constructive roles religion can play in the lives of ordinary people and nations.[1] Rather, this chapter will focus on the

1. Marc Gopin, *Between Eden and Armageddon: The Future of World Religions, Violence, and Peacemaking* (New York: Oxford University Press, 2000), and R. Scott Appleby, *The Ambivalence of the Sacred: Religion, Violence, and Reconciliation* (Lanham, Md.: Rowman and Littlefield, 2000). In 1991, Daedalus devoted an entire issue to *Religion and Politics* (Summer) launching a new examination of the subject. But it could be said that *Religion: The Missing Dimension of Statecraft,* ed. Douglas Johnston and Cynthia Sampson (New York: Oxford University Press, 1994), restored the subject of religion in politics and diplomacy to broad scholarly and policymaking respectability after perhaps two hundred years of deliberate neglect. Edward Luttwak's trenchant essay in the collection, "The Missing Dimension," describes the origins of the Enlightenment conceit of dismissing the significance of religion in public affairs that in retrospect was one of the most anti-intellectual of the modern West's intellectual biases. The interest in *Religion: The Missing Dimension of Statecraft* at the policy level of the United States and several other democratic governments, may reflect the fact that the book was a project of the Center for Strategic and International Studies (CSIS), a centrist public policy research institution in Washington, D.C. The author of this chapter was a member of the steering group for the project and later joined CSIS to establish its preventive diplomacy program.

complicated but discrete intersection of religion and mass psychology, and the way sacred beliefs can be used to intensify violence and warfare or mitigate against violence and serve the cause of reconciliation and peace between groups and nations in conflict.

In proposing his concept of "the ambivalence of the sacred," Appleby makes a critical contribution to the understanding of the way religion reinforces the human psychological construct, where we are all capable of love and creativity but also hatred and destructiveness. He cites the work of German theologian and philosopher Rudolph Otto (1869–1937), who described the concept of "the holy" as exclusive to the sphere of religion, indeed, the *sine qua non* of religion. Yet "the holy" or "the sacred" (the terms can be used interchangeably) is neither "good" nor "evil" per se. It is the fundamental essence of reality. Its power is undifferentiated. It can create and it can destroy. Quoting Otto, the sacred "may burst in sudden eruption, up from the depths of the soul with spasms or convulsions, or lead to intoxicated frenzy, to transport and to ecstasy. It has wild and demonic forms and can sink to an almost grisly horror and shuddering."[2]

As humankind evolved, we began to substitute salvation religions for the more primordial magical rituals to appease a frightening, willful, and destructive God-power. People came to identify the sacred with the enhancement of life as well as a threat. Thus religion emerged as a dichotomy. "The devout," according to Appleby, "spoke of God as alternatively wrathful and merciful, vengeful and forgiving."[3]

The great world religions vary widely in their substantive differences, but as Appleby says,

> one can trace a moral trajectory challenging adherents to greater acts of compassion, forgiveness, and reconciliation. The competing voices of revenge and retaliation that continue to claim the status of authentic religious expression are gradually rendered as "demonic."[4]

---

2. Appleby, *Ambivalence of the Sacred*, 28.
3. Ibid., 31.
4. Ibid.

This sets the stage for the examination of secular, psychological man, especially in the wake of humanity's most murderous century, to see how it might be possible to have a parallel trajectory of life-enhancing ascendancy over the demonic in the affairs of nations, with, perhaps, important help from religion.

PSYCHOLOGICAL MAN

It starts with the reality that while humankind is one species, we act as though we are divided into endless species. This is the phenomenon of "pseudospeciation" defined by Erik Erikson, one of the greatest of the twentieth century's psychologists and students of the individual in society. We appear on the scene divided into identity groups, whether tribes or nations, religious or linguistic groups, castes, classes, and even ideological groups. These groups "provide their members with a firm sense of distinct and superior identity—and immortality. This demands, however, that each group must invent for itself a place and a moment in the very center of the universe where and when an especially provident deity caused it to be created superior to all others, the mere mortals."[5] In simpler terms, the world is divided between us and everyone else. "We" are superior—we need to believe this to feel safe—and other tribes and nations are inferior and real or potential enemies.

There is a complementary analytical perspective in the physiology of psychological development. Psychiatrist Charles Pinderhughes has studied what he calls "the drive to dichotomize" in human beings, defined as seeing others as safe or dangerous, good or bad. He believes that even young animals and birds are physiologically imprinted or "wired" in their brain's limbic system to distinguish between threatening or safe "other" birds and animals. In the case of forms of life below primates, this phenomenon could be called an autonomous survival mechanism.[6]

5. Erik H. Erikson *Gandhi's Truth: On the Origin of Militant Non-Violence* (New York: W. W. Norton, 1969), 431.
6. Charles A. Pinderhughes, "Differential Bonding: Toward a Psychophysiological Theory of Stereotyping," *American Journal of Psychiatry* 136, no. 1 (1979): 33–37.

The development of the human brain and mind is infinitely more complex. The baby learns to divide the world into aspects that are comforting and those that are frightening. A good mother or mother surrogate helps the child to overcome the negative feelings associated with hunger and pain, loneliness and vulnerability. But frustrations are inevitable, and as the child develops its capacity for anger and hostility grows. Another developmental psychiatrist, John Mack, has written:

> In the representational phase [of psychological development] the dichotomization of experience becomes elaborated through language into familiar paired opposites, such as tall and short, strong and weak, good and evil, dark and light. Thus notions of good and evil, me and not me, self and other, our people and them, God and the Devil, become powerful organizing representations in the realm of human relationships, and serve as the perceptual foundation for the organization of the internal and external worlds and constitute the psychological foundation upon which social organization takes place.[7]

Up until about the age of two, a child's sense of "ethnicity" is based on family contexts. There are familiar clothes, foods and smells, songs, dances, religious rituals, or sports. These are value-neutral in terms of relationships with other people outside the family or extended family setting. Beyond two, the child starts picking up signals from family and other group members that some people out there are not like his people. Maybe they do not wash very much and tend to smell bad. They might be tricky, not to be trusted. In other words, the construct of the inferior or dangerous other enters the growing child's consciousness. The dichotomous us and them begin to be rooted. This, in turn, lays the basis for nationalist identification. People need to feel that they belong somewhere. The ethnic group or nation is the basic political unit of identity, and nationalism is the manifestation of the sense of collective identity. It presumes membership in a specific group defined by overlapping shared characteristics like religion, language, common history, laws, social institutions, and customs.

7. John E. Mack, "Nationalism and the Self," *Psychohistory Review* (Spring 1979): 2 (2–3), 47–69.

Nationalism as defined here is neither good nor bad, but normal. Indeed, psychotherapists have found that patients who have no sense of belonging to some identifiable group show symptoms of schizophrenia. Extreme nationalism is another story. It is a state of collective mind that is filled with rage alternating with despair, and it can create an environment that can lead to political violence and war.

Extreme nationalism is a result of painful, traumatic experiences in history or in recent times, or both, with each reinforcing the sense of loss, which has not been mourned.[8] Extreme nationalism is usually nourished by a powerful sense of injustice on the part of the victimized nation or identity group, and a feeling that the outside world does not care about the injustice it has suffered. The historic wounds are felt as assaults on the self-concept and therefore ultimate safety and security of the victim group. Its very existence could be threatened. Such assaults generate an automatic instinct toward counteraggression or revenge.[9] The situation is also psychologically intolerable because one of the principal characteristics of victimhood is the fear that the aggressor is only waiting for a chance to commit another act of violence. Thus the group, tribe, or nation is in a more or less permanent state of vengeful rage and fear of further attacks. If the victimized side is too weak to fight back by traditional means, it may resort to terrorism as an instrument of revenge.

We are working our way back to the intersection of psychology, religion, political violence, and eventual peacemaking as we approach the critically important phenomenon of dehumanization. This occurs when one group or nation prepares its people for repression of or aggression against another group, leading quite possibly to all-out war and even genocide. Dehumanization is a group psychological process that combines unconscious denial

---

8. Incomplete mourning is characteristic of historic wounds incurred in political conflict over time. Mourning cannot be completed unless and until the perpetrators of the losses acknowledge their wrongdoing and ask forgiveness of their victims. This process is explained at some length in Joseph V. Montville, "Complicated Mourning and Mobilization for Nationalism," in *Social Pathology in Comparative Perspective: The Nature and Psychology of Civil Society,* ed. Jerome Braun (Westport, Conn.: Praeger, 1995), 159–74.

9. See Gregory Rochlin, M.D., *Man's Aggression: The Defense of the Self* (Boston: Gambit, 1973), for a clinical description of the automatic aggressive reaction in human beings to an act of aggression.

and repression of truth, depersonalization and compartmentalization of moral reasoning.

One of the best-known examples of the latter is found in Robert J. Lifton's *The Nazi Doctors,* based on extensive interviews with German physicians who worked in the death camps, support staff for the most meticulously organized genocide in recorded history.[10] The doctors found ways to wall their minds off from the moral demands of their Hippocratic oath to "serve all humankind and above all do no harm." As this writer put it in another essay, the Nazi doctors' "consciences appeared to be separated into the half that accepted systematic murder and the other half that enjoyed a quiet evening at home with wife, children and dog."[11]

An understanding of the dehumanization process is key to developing a practical strategy wherein the universal, human values of the great world religions come front and center in the struggle to reverse the destructive effects of dehumanization. In *Sanctions for Evil,* a very important study of the way societies prepare the way for destructive behavior, Nevitt Sanford and Craig Comstock write that dehumanization

> protects the individual from the guilt and shame he would otherwise feel from primitive or antisocial attitudes, impulses, and actions that he directs—or allows others to direct—toward those he manages to perceive in these categories: if they are subhumans they have not yet reached full human status on the evolutionary ladder and, therefore, do not merit being treated as humans; if they are bad humans, their maltreatment is justified since their defects in human qualities are their own fault.[12]

Some examples of the dehumanization process at work include nineteenth- and early twentieth-century English political cartoons depicting Irish

---

10. Robert J. Lifton, *The Nazi Doctors: Medical Killing and the Psychology of Genocide* (New York: Basic Books, 1986).

11. Joseph V. Montville, "The Pathology and Prevention of Genocide," in *The Psychodynamics of International Relationships: Concept and Theories,* ed. Vamik D. Volkan, Demetrios A. Julius, and Joseph V. Montville, vol. 2 (Lexington, Mass.: D. C. Heath, 1991), 124.

12. Nevitt Sanford and Craig Comstock, *Sanctions for Evil* (San Francisco: Jossey Bass, 1973), 105–6.

Catholics as knuckle-dragging primates with large heads and protruding jaws and teeth, very similar to caricatures in journals and magazines in the United States of African Americans during the same time period. During World War II the U.S. government distributed color posters to cities and towns throughout the country depicting Japanese soldiers as monkeys in trees. Arab publications had a tradition of representing Jews as hooked nosed, money-mad conspirators who steal Gentile children to kill for blood sacrifices. In fairness to the Arabs, the anti-Semitic imagery was created by European Christians in the nineteenth century and widely disseminated in the twentieth. Palestinian Islamic terrorists have had no compunction about bombing defenseless Israeli men, women, and children. The humanity and innocence of the victims was no factor in the decision to kill.

In the wars of former Yugoslavia there have been vicious stereotypes of Orthodox Serbs—"Asiatic barbarians"—by Catholic Croatians, who in turn have been collectively called Nazis by Serbs. Both "Christian" peoples, Serbs and Croats, have been ruthless in degrading and dehumanizing Muslim Bosniaks with the former justifying genocidal acts, as in Srbrenica, as revenge for Ottoman Turkish rule. "Orthodox" Russian leaders have had no compunction about bombing Muslim Chechens who belong to a category of Caucasian and Central Asian Muslims whom Russians traditionally dismiss as "black asses." During the 1975–79 reign of terror by the Khmer Rouge in Cambodia Pol Pot committed "auto-genocide" of educated Khmers whose ethnic and religious roots he shared, but his killers made a special effort to wipe out entirely the Chams, Khmers who were Muslims.

This is not an exhaustive list of dehumanizing tragedies. The bad news is that throughout history dehumanization and its resultant brutality have been predictable and "normal" as tribes and nations set out to conquer or confront stresses in their lives. Identification of enemies, the seeking out of scapegoats, is a regular feature of intergroup relations in times of stress. To illustrate the process, there is the story of a social scientist who put two dogs on an electric grid with the current turned off. At first the dogs simply stood together in a normal, "social" manner. Then the scientist started to turn up the current and the dogs became obviously distressed. At a high point in the voltage, one dog attacked the other. It is clear from what is known that neither dog had done anything else to provoke the other. Both were innocent. Both were also increasingly distressed, feeling that they were in real danger. They also sensed that they had no control over their circumstances. There was nothing they could do to stop the pain. The situation was, indeed, out of control. Either of the dogs could have taken the initiative to attack the other. The instinct to attack came from a powerful urge to restore the sense of control by identifying whatever was available as the source of distress and attacking it to make it stop.[13]

The foregoing makes it easier to understand the brutal repression and mass murder of Jews during the fourteenth-century outbreak of Black Plague in Europe. The disease first appeared in Constantinople in 1334 and moved westward through the Crimea to Europe where it raged from 1348 to 1349. It was a bacterial infection transmitted to human beings by fleas from infected rats causing delirium, black hemorrhages, swollen, suppurated lymph nodes, fever, and blood poisoning. Victims died within three or four days of infection. There is a mordant irony in that the disease, scientifically the bubonic plague, was brought to Europe via rats and returning Crusaders. Millions of Europeans died. As Avner Faulk describes the situation, the people:

> lived in constant fear, terrified of touching one another, deeply suspicious of everything and everybody. They searched for explanations and could not find any. This led to paranoia. Amid all the sufferings and upheavals, the Jews became the scapegoats. The special ferocity of Christian hatred of the Jews was due to their terrible fear of the plague, which they could neither understand nor prevent. The medieval Christians attributed it to the hated Jews and to the devil, which in their minds were one and the same.[14]

Jews were rounded up and burned to death in the German-Swiss cantons of Aargau, Bern, Basel, Zurich, and in the Rhineland towns of Worms,

13. The writer heard this experiment described at a scientific meeting of the International Society of Political Psychology more than twenty years ago. One assumes that with contemporary standards barring cruelty to animals, such an experiment is no longer permissable.
14. Avner Faulk, *A Psychoanalytic History of the Jews* (London: Associated University Presses, 1996), 494.

Mainz, and Cologne. On February 14, 1349, the entire community of Jews in Strassburg, 2,000 people, were locked up in a wooden building in the Jewish cemetery and burned alive. Today, plague is easily treated with penicillin. (There was a brief outbreak in India in 1994.)

Medical miracles would be of little comfort to the Jews of twentieth-century Europe, however. The setting was very dangerous. After World War I Germany endured enormous stress, having lost the war and been burdened with the humiliation of the Versailles treaty. There was enormous economic stress and destructive hyperinflation. The large refugee flows into Germany from Eastern Europe and Russia included many Jews. The situation seemed to be out of control.

In the Munich archives there is a memorandum of a conversation in 1922 with Adolf Hitler, who reportedly went into a rage at hearing the word "Jew." He said:

> As soon as I have power, I shall have gallows after gallows erected. For example, in Munich, in the Marianplatz, the Jews will be hanged one after the other and they will stay hanging until they stink. They will stay hanging as long as hygienically possible, and as soon as they are untied, then the next group will follow and we'll continue until the last Jew in Munich is destroyed. Exactly the same procedure will be followed in other cities until Germany is cleansed, purified of the last Jew.[15]

A haunting *déjà vu* in the destructive dichotomy between Christian and Jews from the fourteenth to the twentieth century.

These are extreme cases. Six million Jews killed in Europe in the last century is extreme. The Cambodian killing fields and the genocide of Tutsis by Hutus in Rwanda are extreme. Ethnic cleansing in former Yugoslavia is extreme. But this fact should not discourage humankind from trying to find a way to end the dehumanizing acts that lead to violence and genocide. First we must recognize that more "normal," less extreme dehumanization occurs in almost all countries. Communities or nations will always react to

---

15. Quoted in Montville, "Pathology and Prevention of Genocide," 137.

generalized anxiety and stress by regressing into more primitive group psychological defenses. Group paranoia is not hard to generate. The search for scapegoats is common. The witchhunt in Salem, Massachusetts, in the seventeenth century was an early American example. Its twentieth century counterpart could be seen in anti-immigrant passion exemplified by the trial and execution of Sacco and Vanzetti in the early 1920s or the Communist witchhunt spearheaded by Senator Joseph McCarthy in the late 1940s and early '50s.

But even less dramatic cases of "hypergroupism," with its anxiety and scapegoating, are common in places we would not think to look. As the psychoanalytic anthropologist Howard Stein has written:

> The doctrine in behalf of which the expulsion, eradication, and extermination are done can be virtually anything: religious, political, racial, even organizational. The root from which all group ideologies derive is group psychology itself, specifically group panics that lead, via regression, to totalistic images of the social universe and the need to engage in cleansing the group of all badness. In workplace organizations in the United States—corporations, industries, hospitals, universities under the chronic dread of mass firings . . ., downsizing, reengineering, restructuring, deskilling, outsourcing, managers and workers alike strain to tell ally from foe, and speak of one another as potential "Gooks."[16]

Human beings constantly deal with *The Need to Have Enemies and Allies,* as Vamik Volkan entitled his insightful study.[17] In most cases we adapt to stresses, get through the day, and perhaps sublimate aggression through sports. In extreme cases we might "go postal," as when an individual goes to his place of work and kills supervisors and fellow workers, or when students kill their schoolmates. In cases of group psychology we have seen the range of modest to extreme up to genocide. For the purposes of this chapter on religion and peacemaking, the focus must be on the dehumanization process.

16. Howard F. Stein, "Hypernationalism and Xenophobia: A Thirty Year Retrospective," *Mind and Human Interaction* 10, no. 2 (1999): 126.
17. Vamik D. Volkan, *The Need to Have Enemies and Allies: From Clinical Practice to International Relationships* (Northvale, N.J.: Jason Aronson, 1988).

Insult, degradation, and dehumanization are the early warning indicators in groups and nations that one part of a community is getting ready psychologically to kill another. Religious values have a very significant role to play in highlighting and then reversing this destructive group process. But first religions have to examine their own tendencies to marginalize, dehumanize, and justify the killing of the "other," to yield to the demonic in the sacred.

RELIGIOUS MAN

Increasingly strong voices in the three Abrahamic faiths focus on the dignity and rights of the individual as central to all religion. The fundamental importance of human rights in this perspective is not merely the sentiment of liberal do-gooders. Protection of the rights of all human beings of all races and religions is seen as the foundation stone for any conception of peace and justice. Thus, there is a direct correlation between the state of human rights and domestic, regional and international security. One need not be a moralist to see this empirical fact.

Christianity

From a Christian perspective, Father Theodore Hesburgh, president emeritus of Notre Dame University, has written that the central point in Pope John XXIII's encyclical, *Pacem in Terris,* is that all social systems based on peace and justice must be built on the concept of the human person and human rights. Further:

> There will be no peace where there is no justice and no justice where human persons do not have these basic human rights. Too often these human rights are demanded for one's own religious or ethnic group but not for the human person, whatever his group or location. It is their search for justice that inspires the exemplary religious leaders to guarantee people, whatever their nationality, religion, or ethnic background, an opportunity to pursue these fundamental

human rights. Indeed, the significant religious leaders of our time see the pursuit of justice as a sacred obligation.[18]

This theme dominated a special address Pope John Paul II made to the UN General Assembly, October 5, 1995. He said:

> In the context of the community of nations, the church's message is simple yet absolutely crucial for the survival of humanity and the world: The human person must be the true focus of all social, political and economic activity. This truth, when effectively put into practice, will point the way to healing the divisions between the rich and the poor, to overcoming the inequality between the strong and the weak, to reconciling man with himself and with God. *For men and women are made in the image and likeness of God.* So people may never be regarded as mere objects, nor may they be sacrificed for political, economic or social gain. We must never allow them to be manipulated or enslaved by ideologies or technology. Their God-given dignity and worth as human beings forbid this. [emphasis added]

Carl Evans, chair of the religion department at the University of South Carolina, extends the human-centered theme in a paper called, "The Scriptural Basis for Peace among Islam, Judaism, and Christianity."[19] He starts with a recognition that Scripture often serves to create conflict and division among groups. As an example, he cites the doctrine of the supercession of Judaism by Christianity, at least in certain interpretations of the New Testament. Thus the appeal to Scripture per se is no guarantee that peace and harmony will result. A basic problem is the presuppositions that various all-too-human interpreters bring to Scripture.

Another problem arises from the fact that Scripture itself is a collection of many pieces of writing by many authors at different periods of time. The writings are naturally shaped by the authors' personal experience with the Divine and the world. Thus, when one reads Scripture one should remem-

---

18. Foreword to Appleby, *Ambivalence of the Sacred*, x.
19. Presented at a symposium at Coker College, Hartsville, S.C., April 5, 2000.

ber that the writer of a given passage *claims* that God said whatever is recorded. Thus the encounter with God is necessarily indirect. Evans says, "God is reflected in Scripture, yes, but just as importantly God is beyond Scripture as the living, sovereign deity of the universe." The challenge, then, is to discern the presence of God within and beyond Scripture, and this is much harder than just citing Scripture. One must work to determine the core values in Scripture. Evans offers fruit of his efforts.

The *first* core value is that we all live in God's world. Muslims, Christians, and Jews answer to the same God. The world is His, not ours, and His authority is not there to affirm our sectarian biases but for us to become attuned to the presence of God in all of life. The *second* core value is the recognition that human beings are created in the image of God. "Human beings have been given sacred worth as their birthright and are therefore deserving of dignity and respect in all relationships." All of the world's great religions teach this truth, "and yet, we often act as if we never knew it." The *third* core value is the recognition that our faith requires us to cross the boundary lines that normally divide us from each other. The *fourth* and final core value is the recognition that justice is required for human flourishing and peace. There is no peace without justice.

The moral compulsion to inclusion of "all God's children" is clear and inescapable. It is usually a struggle for ordinary people—and often clergy—to accept. Indeed, it takes a good deal of work. It took the hideousness of the Holocaust to persuade most, if not all, Christians that they were wrong to condemn the Jews as a people whose religion had been superseded, a people who should have had the decency just to disappear. Pope John Paul II symbolically put an end to this pathological Christian/Jewish dichotomy when he recognized the legitimacy of God's covenant with the Jewish people. The next logical step would be for the Vatican to recognize the legitimacy of God's covenant with the Muslim people. While considering the matter, the papal advisers in Rome might examine the introspection of a Jesuit peacemaker. Father Raymond Helmick shares his thinking in a paper entitled, "How Can a Catholic Respond, in Faith, to the Faith of Muslims?" prepared for a meeting with Christian and Muslim divinity students from the former Yugoslavia in Caux, Switzerland, in February 2000.

As I pondered [this question] I recognized that God, who reveals himself, can require of me that I remain faithful to his revelation as it is transmitted to me through Christian tradition. Equally clearly, I have to admit that I cannot own God. I cannot demand of him that he act or reveal himself only as I know him through the tradition I have received. He remains free. He can reveal himself as he chooses.

I do not have the experience of knowing God through the tradition of the Muslim faith. But as I see the piety and the life of faith of the Muslim community—imperfect, of course, like my own—I find myself bound, even in faithfulness to God as he reveals himself in my own tradition, to recognize him at work in the faith of Muslims. This constitutes, I believe, no derogation of my Christian faith, but actually springs from it.

This is a wonderfully simple, and quite moving, statement of faith and it reveals a special problem for exclusivist doctrines in any religious system. Does any religion have a right to tell God whom he may embrace and whom he may not? Is it not his choice to love and save Hindus and Buddhists and animists—people with a Book and people without a book?

Judaism

The Jewish people have not had the doctrinal problem of dealing with the New Testament and the Koran. They have had enough of their sacred Scripture, Torah, and Talmud, to keep them busy with study and interpretation. Their greatest challenge has been to physically survive Christian instincts to eradicate them from the earth. Coexistence with Muslims has, in fact, been a much easier road for the Jews, since the Koran accommodates them as People of the Book. Indeed, Jews and Muslims together created an extraordinary level civilization in medieval Spain under Muslim sovereignty from the eighth to the fourteenth century. And Jews do have scriptural sanction for embracing the gentile other. It has just been difficult to get them to focus on the embrace during pogroms and in the extermination camps.

In *Between Eden and Armageddon: The Future of World Religions,*

Violence, and Peacemaking, Marc Gopin offers an extraordinarily introspective, wise, and simply brilliant analysis of the complexities and promise of religion in peacemaking. He is especially skilled in the art of conflict resolution and what it can contribute to the effective engagement of religious values in peacemaking for Jews, Christians, and Muslims. For the present, we can only deal briefly with Gopin's treatment of the place of the stranger, the Gentile, the other, among Jews. Gopin describes his introduction of the *ger,* the stranger, in biblical law, to an audience of enthralled Catholics and Protestants in Belfast. The *ger* is different from the Jewish minority but

> he must be included in Jewish celebrations, cared for, and even loved. He is the quintessential outsider, which is a litmus test of the ethical conduct of the majority group. In fact, it is the loving care of strangers that is stated by the Bible as the essential lesson of the Jewish enslavement in Egypt. Furthermore the religious law is meant to counteract the natural tendency of an abused group to pass that abuse onto others.[20]

Gopin writes that the gratitude of his Northern Ireland audience seemed to reflect his emphasis that the embrace of the *ger* did not require the Jews to surrender any of their identity as Jews. Indeed, the embrace strengthened the quality of their Jewishness. In Northern Ireland, where the sense of religious identity has been hardened in centuries, as well as recent decades, of Protestant/Catholic strife, the reassurance that one can value the other without sacrificing identity seemed to be warmly welcomed.

In dealing with the compassionate pole of the dichotomous religious/ psychological Jew (and Christian), Gopin does not avoid the destructive pole of the "sacred." As we contemplate the role of religion in peacemaking we need to confront the scriptural God both in the Hebrew Bible and Revelation, chapter 16, in the New Testament. For the "Day of the Lord," Hebrew prophecies describe the most horrible punishments of death and destruction awaiting the "enemies of the Lord" or "infidels." Armageddon

---

20. Gopin, *Between Eden and Armageddon,* 7.

in both Testaments anticipates a cosmic battle between good and evil, "between those who follow God and those who are less than human, `the beast,' who will be utterly destroyed in the most horrible way imaginable." Note that psychological early warning terms, the use of "beast" and other epithets to describe enemies, is classic dehumanization.

Gopin notes one way of interpreting God's biblical retribution, citing a rabbinic discussion in Exodus 15:3: "The Lord is a man of war, the Lord is his name." In this discussion the Lord is acknowledged as, indeed, a man of war. He fought the Egyptians. But in His name, the Lord has compassion on his creatures. He hears the prayers of everyone who inhabits the world. Gopin explains that God's full name serves to circumscribe the definition of God as a man of war. "God punishes violently the guilty while *simultaneously* hearing the prayers of all creatures, serving their need and having compassion upon them. The terms [used] indicate a specific rabbinic intention to emphasize that God's compassion is universal, not just for Jews, even as he punishes Egypt."[21]

There is a poignant account of the teachings of Samuel David Luzzato (1800–1865), an Italian Orthodox Jewish theologian whose central scholarly and ethical theme was the Italian moral sense of *compassione* or the Jewish moral sense of *hemleh*. This sentiment extended to all God's creatures, even the nonhuman. He wrote:

> The compassion that Judaism commends is universal. It is extended, like God's, to all of His creatures. No race is excluded from the Law, because all human beings, according to Judaism's teaching, are brothers, are children of the same Father, and are created in the image of God.[22]

The poignancy comes from the fact that post-Holocaust translations by Orthodox scholars of Luzzato substitute "all Jews" for "all human beings" in the phrase above. The misrepresentation reflects, in Gopin's view, the pessimism and defensiveness of the Orthodox in particular, who were the targets of vicious repression and pogroms by Eastern European Christians

21. Ibid., 68.
22. Ibid., 91.

and who suffered indescribable losses in the Holocaust. It is little wonder that the all-embracing, "all God's children" theme has been hard to sell in the modern period.

Islam

The Muslim dilemma in embracing the other is not unlike that of the Jews. The guidance in the Koran is explicit even though there are apparent contradictions over the issue, again, of the supercession of Islam over Judaism and Christianity. This and several other issues of Koranic values supporting the idea of democratic pluralism in Islam are examined in the impressive new study by Abdulaziz Sachedina in *The Islamic Roots of Democratic Pluralism.*[23]

Sachedina, a professor of religious studies at the University of Virginia, maintains that the cornerstone of the creative narrative in the Koran is the principle of diversity. The Koran suggests that the variety in humankind is one of the riches in God's world. The guiding verse is:

> O humankind, we have created you male and female, and appointed you races and tribes, that you may know one another. Surely the noblest among you in the sight of God is the most godfearing of you. God is All-knowing, All-Aware. (K. 49:14)

Thus the principle that God is the God of all creation and one who recognizes and embraces all His children is clearly established. Another key verse rejects the idea of exclusivism in Islam, offering salvation to, at least, the other people of the Book:

> Surely they that believe, and those of Jewry, and the Christians, and those Sabaeans, who so believe in God and the Last Day, and works righteousness—their wage awaits them with their Lord, and no fear shall be on them, neither shall they sorrow. (K 2:62)

---

23. Abdulaziz Sachedina, *The Islamic Roots of Democratic Pluralism* (New York: Oxford University Press, 2000).

Sachedina notes that the Koran is remarkably inclusive toward the peoples of the Book. He says,

> The unique characteristic of Islam is its conviction that belief in the oneness of God unites the Muslim community with all humanity because God is the creator of all humans, irrespective of their religious traditions. The Koran declares that on the Day of Judgement all human beings will be judged, irrespective of sectarian affiliation, about their moral performance as citizens of the world community.[24]

But Sachedina acknowledges that the liberalism of these verses caused discomfort for jurists who were trying to support expansionist political claims to exclusive chosenness of the Muslims. And there is a verse to support this position. "Whosoever desires another religion than Islam, it shall not be accepted of him; in the next world he shall be among the losers" (K. 3:85).

Regardless of the contradictions, the preciousness of the individual and the embrace by God of all of his children is the dominant theme of the Koran. Indeed, it is the essence of monotheism. Thus Sachedina's reading of the Koran reveals a set of "core values" similar to those identified by the Christian, Carl Evans, who also contends that the three Abrahamic faiths embrace and are embraced by the one God they share.

WORKING CONCLUSIONS

A short essay on a huge subject can at best suggest some working conclusions and guidelines for the integration of religious values in the work of peacebuilding. It is, of course, not enough to highlight the universality of God's embrace of all human beings as though a presentation of the facts will all of a sudden arrest the hatred of ethnic Albanians in Kosovo for Serbs, and vice versa, or undermine the suspicion among Jews in Israel that Arabs

---

24. Ibid.

are simply treacherous assassins, only waiting for the chance to put a knife into the back of a Jew.

But there are ways that the embracing universal values of Scripture can be integrated into ongoing dialogue among adversaries in unofficial "track two diplomacy" and injected into the more public discourse in conflicted relationships, not unlike Gopin's session with Catholics and Protestants in Northern Ireland. And beyond efforts at cognitive and moral persuasion, the international community can increase its pressure on regimes and groups that commit human rights violations or threaten to do so. Reinforced by our understanding of the pro-human ethics of the great religions, advocates of the defense of human rights, including the often diffident leading democratic governments, can be more militant. It is unacceptable that the international community should ever again agonize for years over the right thing to do when massive human rights violations are taking place as they did in Bosnia, in the last decade.

Religious leaders have a special collective responsibility to sound the alarm quickly whenever any of God's children are threatened. If governments will move only because of the pain of public opinion their hesitance generates, let there be pain. As Ted Robert Gurr writes in *Foreign Affairs*, there is an "invisible hand" at work in the world that explains the quantitative decline in ethnic violence. More antagonists are negotiating, usually with the help of third parties. Regional and international organizations are intervening earlier to prevent political violence. The shame of Rwanda and Bosnia have been gradually replaced by the "last resort" UN/NATO military campaign in Kosovo and the rapid deployment of international forces to East Timor in 1999. Further, most of the recent wars of self-determination fighting, while beginning with demand for independence have settled for increased autonomy. As Gurr writes:

> The principle that serious ethnic disputes [the ones that result in the most brutal human rights violation] should be settled by negotiation is backed up actively by most major powers, the U.N., and some regional organizations. These entities mix diplomacy, mediation, sweeteners, and threats to encourage accommodation. Preventive diplomacy is widely popular—not only because early engagement

can be cheaper than belated crisis management but because it is the preferred instrument of the new regime.[25]

The environment for doing the right thing in protecting the preciousness of human life is improving. But the instincts of political leaders to avoid brave or painful choices is a constant counterweight, as is the aspect of human psychology that from time to time relishes the destruction of other people or is, almost as bad, indifferent to it, as one sees in so many of the tragedies in Africa.

And in the Middle East, where Jews, Muslims, and some Christians battle over who will guarantee the peace of Jerusalem, every human, ethical, and spiritual resource is needed for the task. It is perhaps more important there than anywhere else in the world that the preciousness and dignity of human life God embraces in the Torah, the New Testament, and the Koran be put first in the peacemaking by the peacemakers.

25. Ted Robert Gurr, "Ethnic Warfare on the Wane," *Foreign Affairs* (May/June 2000): 58.

CHAPTER 6

Religion and Foreign Policy

Douglas M. Johnston Jr.

I WAS TAKEN ABACK while walking under the stars in Williams-burg, Virginia, several months ago, when I suddenly realized that my all-too-brief existence on this planet encompassed more than a quarter of our republic's existence. This thought, while sobering in and of itself, caused me to marvel at how much has changed since the nation's birth and how breathtaking the pace of change has become of late.

At the same time, I puzzled over the all-but-total absence of progress in our ability to resolve differences with one another through peaceful means. To the extent that advancing one's interests while avoiding conflict can be considered a *sine qua non* of diplomatic exchange, this then translates to an indictment of "traditional" diplomacy. This failure stands in stark contrast to our skyrocketing ability to inflict harm. Indeed, as the global competition of armaments has yielded increasingly effective weaponry, the byproduct has been the most brutal century in human history.

Yes, we live in an age of turmoil, and much of it is religious-based—Kashmir, Algeria, East Timor, Ireland, Sudan; the list goes on. Whether religion is the root cause of a particular conflict or merely a mobilizing vehicle for nationalist or ethnic passions, it is central to much of the strife currently taking place around the globe. Equally sobering, the level of discontent is likely to grow worse over time as (1) economic globalization produces profound confrontations with traditional values, often embedded in religion, (2) secular governments in hard-pressed areas fail to meet the legitimate expectations of their populations, (3) an increasing fraction of the world's population is left behind by rapid technological change, and (4) the economic gap continues to widen between the "haves and have nots." On this latter note, with the global population now officially at six billion, it is officially estimated that the richest 20 percent of humanity consumes 86 percent of all goods and services, while the poorest 20 percent consumes only 1.3 percent.[1]

As people increasingly turn to religion in such situations, Western governments are ill-equipped to deal with the consequences. Missteps in handling situations from the Iranian revolution of 1979, to the later intervention in Lebanon, to the breakup of Yugoslavia and beyond suggest that traditional diplomacy's neglect of religious factors has rendered the West ineffective both in dealing with religious differences and in combating demagogues who adeptly manipulate religious labels to their own purposes.

U.S. diplomats are a product of the nation-state model of international relations, with its attendant emphasis on maximizing power and all-but-total neglect of religion and its dynamics. A rather glaring example of Western indifference to religious imperatives was the recent NATO decision to bomb Serbia on Orthodox Easter. It was totally unnecessary from a military point of view (one could have bombed twice as much the day before and/or the day after), and it is the kind of decision that will never be forgotten. Serbs were quick to point out that the only others to have bombed them on this holy day were the Germans in World War II.

Adding to the problem is the fact that religious institutions have on more than a few occasions strayed from their original purpose and become an integral part of the problem. Rather than alleviating human suffering, they have exacerbated it. This rather widespread perversion of intent suggests an urgent need for religions to revisit their roots in contributing to neighborly concern and the betterment of humanity.

The divisive influence of religion has long been recognized. Its more helpful aspects have not. In the West this is largely the result of over two hundred years of post-Enlightenment prejudice. As alluded to earlier, Hans

1. U.N. Population Fund, as reported in "Up Front" section of *Business Week* (October 25, 1999), 7.

Morgenthau's nation-state model, which has served as the paradigm for international relations since the late 1940s, attaches virtually no significance to religion as a factor in the policymaker's calculus. Indeed, in the United States the rigorous constitutional separation of church and state so relegates religion to the realm of the personal that most Americans are uncomfortable discussing their religious convictions in any sort of professional context.

To address this oversight, a study was initiated in 1985 by the Center for Strategic and International Studies (CSIS) in Washington, D.C., which resulted in a book entitled *Religion: The Missing Dimension of Statecraft.*[2] Published in August 1994, this book examines the positive role that religious or spiritual factors can play in actually preventing or resolving conflict while advancing the larger goals of reconciliation and social well-being. Already in its tenth printing and second foreign-language translation, the book has been the subject of favorable reviews in numerous journals and periodicals including *Foreign Affairs*, the *New York Times*, the *Washington Post*, and the *Financial Times of London*. More recently, it was selected by *SAPIO* (Japan's equivalent of *Time* magazine) as one of the eight most important books to read in preparing for the twenty-first century.

Beyond the endorsements and the reviews, well over one hundred presentations on the subject matter of the book have been made to various groups around the world, including the U.S. Department of State, the London Diplomatic Academy, the Japanese Foreign Ministry, the Vatican, Oxford faculty, Harvard University, and the Royal Institute of International Affairs. Many of these have been tough-minded audiences. Without exception, the reaction has been positive. In addition, a growing number of colleges and universities around the world are incorporating the book into their graduate or undergraduate curriculums, including Columbia, the Complutensian University of Madrid, the Fletcher School of Law and Diplomacy, Georgetown, Harvard, Johns Hopkins, Notre Dame, Oxford, Princeton, Stanford, and Yale. The same holds true for seminaries as well. Perhaps even more important, it is now required reading at the U.S. Foreign Service Institute.

2. Douglas Johnston and Cynthia Sampson, eds., *Religion: The Missing Dimension of Statecraft* (New York: Oxford University Press, 1994).

MAJOR FINDINGS

The book includes a series of case studies that demonstrate how religious or spiritual factors have contributed to a positive outcome in different conflict situations around the world. From these case studies, principles were derived that are already proving helpful to policymakers, diplomats, and religious leaders. Among the major findings to evolve from the study, two particularly stand out: (1) religious contributions to peacemaking have been underappreciated, if not totally ignored, by foreign policy practitioners and (2) there are substantial underutilized assets within religious communities which, if properly trained, could be applied to peacemaking.

Politicians and policymakers often fail to recognize the role that religious peacemakers can play in building trust and facilitating understanding and reconciliation. As a result, opportunities are lost in which the joint application of religious and political assets could lead to a peaceful resolution of differences rather than a resort to violence. With their past fixation on economic determinism and/or ideological confrontation, U.S. foreign policy practitioners, for example, have tended to miss the mark when dealing with situations in which the imperatives of religion blend inextricably with those of politics and economics. This, in turn, has led to incorrect foreign policy choices in such places as Iran, Lebanon, the former Yugoslavia, and even Vietnam.[3] Policymakers simply have not fully understood the religious dynamics that were taking place.

In an environment of increasing disorder, the world can no longer afford to overlook the significant contribution that religious and spiritual factors can bring to resolving conflict. Not only do the theologies of each of the major world religions contain some version of the Golden Rule, but they also incorporate specific moral warrants for peacemaking.[4] Although the development and articulation of the latter have been inadequate, there is a pressing need to apply religious principles and instruments based on these warrants to the practical work of conflict resolution.

3. Edward Luttwak, "The Missing Dimension," in *Religion,* ed. Johnston and Sampson, 11.
4. Huston Smith, *The Religions of Man* (New York: Harper and Row, 1958), 3, 10; Harvey Cox, Arvind Sharma, Masao Abe, Abdulaziz Sachedina, Harjot Oberoi, and Moshe Idel, "World Religions and Conflict Resolution," in *Religion,* ed. Johnston and Sampson, 266–71.

A MODEL FOR THE FUTURE

One example of how religion and diplomacy can reinforce one another to mutual advantage can be found in the successful collaboration between the lay Catholic Community of Sant'Egidio and official diplomats in resolving the brutal civil war in Mozambique that ended in 1994. The final breakthrough to peace evolved from the community's recognition that it would have to do something to resolve the conflict if the humanitarian assistance it was providing was to have any useful effect. Accordingly, they set out to win the trust of both sides, taking initiatives that governments would never consider: escorting individual guerrillas to their first dental appointments, buying them their first eyeglasses. In short, through winning trust on a personal level they were able to rehumanize the situation and persuade the two sides to come together to negotiate their differences.

Early in the talks these religious peacemakers foresaw that they would not have the wherewithal to monitor a ceasefire agreement or to guarantee fair multiparty elections. Accordingly, they invited diplomats from Italy, the United States, Portugal, France, and the United Nations to attend the ninth round of talks as official observers. In the tenth round they officially passed the baton and these diplomats brought the resources of their respective nation-states (and the UN) to bear in overseeing the signing of the peace agreement, the monitoring of the ceasefire, and the holding of fair elections. Today there is peace in Mozambique with a democratically elected government and an economy on the rebound, all because official diplomacy was able to build upon the trust developed by a religious third party.

WALKING THE TALK

Capitalizing on the momentum generated by *Religion: The Missing Dimension of Statecraft* and out of a desire to operationalize certain of the concepts set forth in the book, a Preventive Diplomacy Program was established at the Center for Strategic and International Studies in 1995. At the heart of this program a conflict-resolution team was formed, having an international makeup. (We didn't want the problem of "here come the

Americans trying to tell us what to do again.") So although the team is headed by an American, it includes people from Russia, Poland, and the Netherlands. Olga Botcharova, a member of this team, has conducted path-breaking analysis on the psychology by which victims of aggression become aggressors themselves and on determining where in the course of that cycle one might intervene to set things on a track that leads to forgiveness and reconciliation. She shares these insights in this volume (see chap. 14), insights that get to the very heart of our common concern.

More than a year prior to the Dayton Accords, the team began conducting conflict-resolution training workshops for religious clergy and laity (usually teachers, journalists, and others who could leverage what they learned) from all of the ethnic groups and religious faiths in Bosnia, Croatia, and Serbia. Although the team went in harm's way on more than one occasion, there was no notion that what the team was doing would affect the then-existing hostilities. After all, there had been joint pronouncements by the leaders of the three major religious faiths condemning the ethnic cleansing and calling for a halt to the hostilities, all to no avail. In this instance, as in so many others, religion was effectively co-opted by the forces of nationalism and used as a convenient mobilizing vehicle and badge of identity. Accordingly, it had little, if any, influence over the political process. The hope of the workshops was to plant the seeds for longer-term reconciliation—a tall order in light of the excessive intermarriage that existed before the conflict erupted. Indeed, it is both remarkable and highly distressing that it proved so easy for political leaders to manipulate populations to the point where neighbor was pitted against neighbor and worse.

The workshops are conducted at three levels. In the first level, there is no attempt to convey peacemaking skills. Instead, the team seeks to help the participants overcome their sense of victimhood. This has proven surprisingly effective, largely because of a "storytelling" technique that is used early in the process. In this phase, a participant will tell the group about the atrocities that have befallen him or her at the hands of another participant's ethnic group. Others then follow suit. The stories are too tragic to bear repeating, but after a while a deep empathy develops as people begin to feel one another's pain and to view the problem through a side of the prism other than their own. A degree of bonding begins to take hold.

At the end of the first workshop in Osijek, Croatia, the group of twenty-six participants, on their own volition, came up with sixteen different initiatives they wanted to pursue on an ecumenical basis. These ranged from influencing their political leaders in positive directions to developing multifaith newsletters for their communities to undertaking cooperative measures in the schools, and a lot in between. Happily, action has been and is being taken on a number of these initiatives—not all, but enough to label the overall effort an unqualified success.

In the second-level workshops, the team conveys the conflict-mediation skills. I, for one, was quite surprised at the euphoric reaction of the participants to this phase. At last they felt equipped to be peacemakers, which is, after all, why they made the effort to attend, often incurring no small degree of risk in doing so. Lest I mislead you, though, in every one of these sessions, there have been one or more participants who have already been serving as peacemakers priests, for example, who put their lives on the line to prevent ethnic cleansing between adjacent municipalities, real heroes whose courage has served to inspire others. They are the ones who lived to talk about it. Others who made similar attempts did not.

In the third-level workshops, graduates of earlier workshops in all three countries are taken to a neutral location in Hungary. There the team attempts to build community across republic lines and to deal with the systematic problems of their respective social systems that contribute to ethnic animosity.

Barring the unforeseen, by next year the team will have achieved its goal of establishing in each country an indigenous, religious-based peacemaking capability firmly anchored in an NGO.

A NEED FOR NEW TOOLS

One of the reasons the concepts of *Religion: The Missing Dimension of Statecraft* have been so well received is because many observers are concluding that the time for unconventional approaches is at hand. They see religious reconciliation coupled with official diplomacy as offering a greater potential for dealing with today's problems of communal conflict, particularly those involving ethnic and religious dimensions.

In response to this awareness, a new International Center for Religion and Diplomacy (ICRD) was formed with the mission of promoting increased understanding and collaboration between policymakers and diplomats on the one hand and religious leaders—both clergy and laity—in addressing differences between people, communities, and nation-states. It will do this by:

+ Serving as a bridge between politics and religion in support of peace-making;
+ Deploying multiskilled, interreligious action teams to address actual or incipient conflicts;
+ Training religious clergy and laity for the tasks of peacemaking; and
+ Providing feedback to theologians and clergy concerning interpretations of their teachings that are contributing to strife and misunderstanding.

Through aggressive outreach and the use of advanced computer and telecommunications technology, the ICRD will build an operational network of peacemakers and partnering institutions that is global in reach and that encompasses all of the major religions. It is from this network that the multiskilled, interreligious action teams are drawn.

FUTURE APPLICATIONS

The center's first undertaking has been the highly complex and difficult situation in Sudan, where the Islamic north and the Christian/Animist south have been engaged in hostilities for eighteen years and where certain factions in the South have been simultaneously warring with one another for local dominance. Capitalizing on relationships of trust already established through religious channels, I was invited to Khartoum to meet with government officials, opposition leaders, and private-sector executives to explore the possibilities for improved dialogue and understanding between the North and the South and between Sudan and the United States. Ordinarily, this would be the normal grist of the foreign-policy establishment. With the U.S. bombing of the El Shifa pharmaceutical factory in Khartoum, however, the relationship between our two countries is currently in a state of paralysis. This standoff comes at a time when the horrific losses of that conflict (second only to World War II in recent times) demand urgent action to halt the bloodshed and secure a lasting peace.

Adding to the difficulty is the fact that certain circles within the United States are demonizing the North because of government-sponsored atrocities taking place in the South. The atrocities are real, and critics have every right to be incensed. Similar brutalities, albeit lesser in scale, are also being committed by the South. But regardless of which side has done what or how much, the key question—the strategic question—is how best to end the hostilities and lay the groundwork for a lasting peace.

Before going to Khartoum I did a great deal of homework on events in the South—reading numerous reports by NGOs and journalists, speaking at length with people who had recently been there and observed first-hand the abuses that are taking place, and observing BBC footage on the plight of the natives in the Nuba Mountains. As for the North, I had assumed before my trip that Sudan was being used by the Speaker of its Parliament, Hasan al-Turabi, as the spearhead for the spread of militant Islam across North Africa and beyond. After several days on the ground, however (including a lengthy session with Dr. Turabi), I acquired a somewhat different impression. While there can be no doubt about Turabi's intent to expand Islam, he appears to be developing and promoting an Islamic model that is more progressive than is commonly recognized—one that will have greater appeal to prospective adherents than its harder-line counterparts.

As one example of the above, approximately twenty seats in Sudan's Parliament are set aside for women. They can hold more if they win the vote (which they often do), but they are guaranteed at least this minimum number, thus ensuring an ongoing voice in the councils of government. No woman that I saw was wearing a veil, and there are more women than men in the universities (although this may result in part from war-related attrition in the ranks of the males). Even most surprising, there are women *and Christians* occupying high-level ministerial posts in the government. It is remarkable how quickly the simplified stereotypes begin to break down when subjected to closer scrutiny. The same holds true in the "Christian and Animist" South as well, where three of the six Sudanese People's Liberation Army (SPLA) military commanders are Muslims.

Although I was one of the first Americans to visit Khartoum in the wake of the El Shifa bombing, I was well received everywhere I went, even in impromptu settings. Out of my many meetings, including an entire evening with thirty opposition leaders, a three-hour exchange with policymakers and scholars at Sudan's Center for Strategic Studies, and interviews with various television and print media, it became very clear that Sudan wants a meaningful dialogue with the United States. However justified our own government's suspicions of Sudanese intent may be, it is my personal view that engaging in such a dialogue will provide us much greater leverage in our expressed desire to bring a halt to the conflict and sanity to the region.

In the course of the above interactions, the government of Sudan has been encouraged to seize the high ground in moving toward peace through enactment of a unilateral, comprehensive ceasefire (as a precursor to negotiating terms for an internationally supervised referendum on self-determination for the South). As of this writing, such a ceasefire is in effect and, for the moment, appears to be holding. I have met with Sudan's foreign minister in New York and suggested that he indicate his government's willingness to extend the ceasefire indefinitely under international supervision (a new twist) and, in this context, to make available to the South a major share of its new oil revenues for alleviating hunger and building infrastructure. He agreed and subsequently announced it to the UN Security Council and General Assembly the following day.[5] We'll see where it goes.

Perhaps of even greater significance is the government's agreement for the International Center for Religion and Diplomacy to organize a meeting of prominent Sudanese and international religious leaders in Khartoum under the joint sponsorship of the ICRD, the Sudan International Friendship Council, and the Sudan Council of Churches. The purpose of the meeting will be to discuss issues of religious freedom in the Sudan and to make related recommendations to the government and the Sudanese People's Liberation Movement (SPLM). Because Dr. Abdul Rahim Ali, a highly respected Islamic scholar and chairman of the Consultative Council of the ruling party, and Foreign Minister Mustafa Ismail (who formerly chaired

5. Mustafa Ismail, "Statecraft Before the 54th Session of the General Assembly," Sudan Permanent Mission to the United Nations, New York, September 30, 1999, 4.

Sudan's Inter-Religious Council) have agreed to participate, any agreement reached on the central religious questions to be addressed (such as what steps Islamic governments can take to alleviate the second-class status of non-Muslims in a Sharia context) is likely to have broader applicability to similar situations elsewhere in the world. I should point out that this meeting will complement, but in no way substitute for, the official mediating process of the Inter-Governmental Authority on Development (IGAD), the subregional intergovernmental organization dedicated to East African cooperation. Rather, the intent is to take religion off the table so that the IGAD, which is ill-equipped to deal with religious matters, can achieve closure on the remaining fronts.

Because a catalyst for the current conflict was religious in nature, that is, the North seeking to impose Islamic law on the entire country, the planned meeting of religious leaders will be dealing directly with the heart of the problem. With sincerity of purpose (facilitated by the earlier mentioned relationships of trust), open-minded dialogue, a strong commitment to succeed, and a healthy dose of divine intervention, the difficult issues can be surmounted, forgiveness and reconciliation can take root, and a lasting peace achieved in which the full potential of this troubled but well-endowed country can at last be realized.

CONCLUSION

In a world of ethnic strife and high-technology weaponry, old concepts of security based on a competition of armaments will no longer suffice. Increasingly, security will be a function of the strength and durability of national, supernational, and particularly subnational relationships. This suggests a need to move toward new mechanisms for international relations, such as the ICRD, that extend beyond the state-centric focus of the power-politics model and which recognize the contributions of nongovernmental organizations (NGOs) and, in some instances, even those of individuals. When dealing with communal conflicts, it becomes necessary to move beyond the normal methods and channels of diplomacy in order to uncover and deal with the deeper sources of conflict, rebuild relationships, and make the necessary concessionary adjustments wherever possible.[6] In this context, reconciliation born of spiritual conviction can play a critical role in inspiring the parties in conflict to break the cycle of revenge that typically characterizes such disputes.

6. Douglas Johnston, "Looking Ahead: Toward a New Paradigm," in *Religion,* ed. Johnston and Sampson, 333.

CHAPTER 7

The Role of Identity Reconstruction in Promoting Reconciliation

Donna Hicks

The crisis consists precisely in the fact the old is dying and the new cannot be born; in this interregnum a great variety of morbid symptoms appear. —Antonio Gramsi

IN PROTRACTED ETHNIC CONFLICTS, threats to identity have been described as one of the explanations for why conflicting parties seem unable to come to a negotiated end to the conflict, even when there appears to be a way in which the interest of both sides can be accommodated. According to Herbert Kelman, threats to identity create a zero-sum view of the conflict, where one's very existence seems inextricably linked to the negation of the other.[1] An acknowledgment of the identity of the other is perceived as an act of self-destruction, as recognizing the experiences of the other fundamentally brings into question one's own interpretation of history, the conflict, and of the responsibility one holds for the past, present, and future shared realities.

In this chapter I would like to explore the obstacles and resistances to delinking those aspects of identity that pose the greatest threat to parties in conflict, then examine ways in which the mutually destructive elements might be reconstructed so that both parties could begin the process of reconciliation, which might enable former enemies to coexist without fear of annihilation. Kelman has described this process of reconstruction as "negotiating

1. Herbert Kelman, "Social Psychological Dimensions of International Conflict," in *Peacemaking in International Conflict,* ed. W. I. Zartman and L. J. Rasmussen (Washington, D.C.: U.S. Institute of Peace, 1997).

identity," where both sides engage in a reciprocal process of examining those aspects of one's identity that do not threaten its core and that, if let go, could significantly allay some of the fundamental threats that the destructive aspects trigger in the other.[2]

In order to better understand what identity negotiation involves, both in terms of the process that is required to bring about the necessary changes in identity and the resistances and challenges to such change, I will anchor this analysis within a theory of human development that describes the "normal" process of identity formation. By "normal" I mean the learning process one engages in when living under conditions that support growth and development. The Piagetian model of social-cognitive development will be the foundation of the conceptual framework, with some additional refinements.[3] By gaining insight into the conditions and circumstances that promote constructive learning about the self and other, we can then examine what happens to the process of identity formation under circumstances of conflict, when one experiences an existential threat.

After describing the developmental framework, this analysis will focus on the specific aspects of identity that are open for negotiation in conflict relationships and what the implications are for the type of process that is needed to promote successful reconciliation. Finally, a variety of processes will be explored to include adaptations to the interactive problem-solving model of intergroup conflict resolution developed by John Burton and later refined by Kelman (1992), as well as an examination of the limits and strengths of the role of forgiveness in promoting reconciliation.[4]

At the outset, I would like to make explicit the following assumptions about identity and its development.

✦ There are two aspects of identity, the "I" and the "Me."[5] The "I" is

2. Herbert Kelman, "The Role of Social Identity in Conflict Resolution: Experiences from Israeli-Palestinian Problem-Solving Workshops," paper presented at the Twelfth Conference of the International Association for Conflict Management in San Sebastian-Donostia, Spain, on June 22, 1999.

3. Donna Hicks, "Beyond Egocentrism: A Question of Certainty," diss., University of Wisconsin, Madison, 1991.

4. John Burton, Conflict: Human Needs Theory (London: Macmillan Press, 1991); and Herbert Kelman, "Informal Mediation by the Scholar/Practitioner," in Mediation in International Relations: Multiple Approaches to Conflict Management, ed. J. Bercovitch and J. Rubin (New York: St. Martin's Press, 1992), 64–96.

5. G. H. Mead, Mind, Self, and Society (Chicago: University of Chicago Press, 1934).

the core identity, that which one cannot change such as the fact that I am a woman, North American, and so on. The second aspect is that part of the self that is socially constructed, the part that evolves as a consequence of our interaction with the world. This is the "Me," that which I will call the constructed identity. I will be focusing my remarks on the "constructed" aspect of identity.

✦ The process of identity development requires social interaction. One's understanding of others and the world is dependent on engaging with them and it. One has to be in relationship with others and the world in order to learn and develop. Development occurs in the context of relationship. The unit of analysis of the development of one's understanding of the self and the world is the relationship, not the individual.[6]

✦ Identity development is a process. In other words, there is not an endpoint one arrives at, but instead it is a lifelong process.[7] If one is open to learning, identity is in constant evolution.

PIAGET'S VIEW OF DEVELOPMENT

It is important to make clear at the outset that Jean Piaget, who has often been (mis)labeled a child psychologist, was not interested in child development per se. His primary concern was how individuals come to understand their relationship with the world and their interactions with it, and on what basis they arrive at conclusions about others and the events of the world. His observations of children, and the progression of their understanding of the world from one in which the egocentric child is the center of the universe to an adult "objective" view, where one can tolerate multiple perspectives and can see oneself in relation to others, provided the data he needed to develop a theory of knowledge that tracked the progression of the construction of reality from the simple to the complex, and that defined growth and development as a consequence of one's active engagement with

6. See Jean Piaget, *Genetic Epistemology* (New York: Columbia University Press, 1970), for further discussion of the issue.
7. R. Kegan, *In Over Our Heads* (Cambridge: Harvard University Press, 1994).

others and the world.[8] In his view, one does not come to know the world by passively observing it and watching it unfold. One's understanding of the self and others emerges as a consequence of interaction, which provides the context for the development of internal structures that serve as both a repository for the acquired knowledge and a way of maintaining a sense of inner equilibrium so that one can function in the world. In fact, in Piaget's view, "development" can be described as a process of "increasing equilibrium" between the organism and the environment,[9] that is, an increase in the individual's capacity to integrate a more complex understanding of and relationship to the world without becoming destabilized. More will be said about the details of the equilibration process below.

We gain an understanding of ourselves and the world through the medium of interaction. We construct our understanding and learn about ourselves and the world by engaging with it. We construct our own reality, our own interpretations of how the world works, and end up with a set of beliefs about the self, others, and the world. The construction of reality and the beliefs that result from the process of "making sense" of the world change with development. There are qualitative shifts in the way we make meaning as we proceed through the lifespan, with implications at every stage for how much we can integrate from the outside world into our internal repository of knowledge without becoming psychologically destabilized. Within this internal repository of knowledge is a collection of beliefs about the self (what I am calling the constructed aspect of identity), others, and the world that one develops as a consequence of one's continued interactions with the world. These beliefs serve two purposes: They provide us with a set of *expectations* about the world that enables us to function without being completely overwhelmed with the barrage of stimuli that confronts us at every moment. Second, beliefs create a sense of inner coherence and *stability*. They allow us to gain control over the anxiety-producing effects of uncertainty in our world, uncertainty that would otherwise overwhelm us. The beliefs provide a (temporary) resting place until such time that we experience the limits of their usefulness; then they become a desta-

8. R. Kitchener, *Piaget's Theory of Knowledge: Genetic Epistemology and Scientific Reason* (New Haven: Yale University Press, 1986).
9. Jean Piaget, *The Construction of Reality in the Child* (New York: Ballantine, 1937).

bilizing force themselves, and we need to reexamine them and open ourselves up to new learning.

I will next describe in more detail the mechanisms that allow for learning in Piaget's view, along with some of my own refinements of the theory that are useful when considering how conflict affects this "normal" process of the development of our understanding of ourselves and the world.

DEVELOPMENT AS A PROCESS OF INCREASING EQUILIBRIUM BETWEEN SELF AND THE ENVIRONMENT

According to Piaget, a major challenge to the process of development is being able to maintain an inner sense of balance (equilibrium) while integrating new information from the outside world. As one develops a more complex understanding of the self and the world, one's capacity to tolerate challenges to one's existing worldview increases. It is, however a delicate balance. There are limits to the amount of anxiety one can tolerate when trying to take in new information that challenges one's existing understanding of the world. Too much change too fast can create tremendous upheaval, the felt experience of which is extremely uncomfortable, setting off what appears to be a reflexive reaction to protect the threatened views of the self and the world. It is important to point out that the instability triggered by an overload of the learning process is more than just a "cognitive" overload. The psychological "disintegration" is felt at an emotional level as well, producing, in extreme cases, debilitating fear, rage, and anxiety when one perceives a threat to one's integrity, at either or both the physical and psychological levels.[10]

The development process that Piaget describes of increasing one's capacity to take in more complex information about the world without being thrown out of balance is the process of *adaptation*. This is a dialectical process where the individual is engaged in *assimilating* the environment

10. Donna Hicks et al., "Addressing Inter-group Conflict by Integrating and Realigning Identity: An Arab-Israeli Workshop," in *Group Process and Political Dynamics,* ed. Mark Ettin (Madison, Conn.: International Universities Press, 1996).

into one's existing cognitive structure, while at the same time *accommo-dating* to the new information from the environment by changing the exist-ing cognitive structure. The end result of this process is not only a new way of looking at the self and the world, but also achievement of a more sophis-ticated balance between the self and its environment. The "assimilative" aspect of adaptation builds an *internally coherent structure,* a repository of what we think we know, part of which contains views of the self in relation to the world. This becomes our "constructed self." The process of "accom-modating" requires an externally focused mechanism that allows us to take in information from the outside world, that which becomes the content of our understanding. The end product of simultaneous interaction of assim-ilation and accommodation is learning. One without the other, that is, only taking in information into the existing structure is not learning, nor is only being open to outside information. Both must be happening at the same time to produce a shift in one's worldview. For example, an individual who perhaps listens to the perspective of the other (a perspective that may chal-lenge one's own view), but does not make the change in one's internal struc-ture or belief, is only Assimilating." No learning is taking place. In Piaget's terms the individual is behaving egocentrically because he is not open to being changed by the new information. On the other hand, a person who is constantly changing her point of view every time she encounters new information and is not developing an internal structure (self) in which to put the information is not learning either, because she is simply parroting the ideas that she has taken in from the outside. Woody Allen's character Zelig from the movie, *Zelig,* is the perfect example of one who only accommo-dates. He takes on the ideas and personality of every new person he encoun-ters. There is no inner coherence, no internal sense of self. This person could be labeled an "aliuscentric," or one is completely "other-"centered.[11]

Under nonthreatening conditions, we constantly make adjustments to our self by integrating new information from the outside which we gain by interacting with others. We constantly refine and expand the self and our beliefs about others and the world with new experiences. Even though the process of identity development is ongoing and ever-changing, in order to

---

11. Hicks, "Beyond Egocentrism."

be able to function in the world we need some *stability* and *certainty* about what to expect in the world, but this comes with a price. As a part of the self-structure we develop beliefs about how the world works, that is, beliefs about our self (both positive and negative evaluations) and beliefs about others and the world. This is necessary so that we can function in the world. Our beliefs underlie our expectations about others and the world. Again, these beliefs are always open to change when one is living under the conditions that promote learning and development.

When we are in a learning mode, under the best case situation, we can live with or tolerate some uncertainty about our beliefs, accepting that with new experiences our beliefs may be open to change, or that they may have been "wrong" to begin with. This is a very important aspect of development, that is, the extent to which one accepts the possibility that one's worldview, images of self and other, are incomplete and subject to change.

In addition, we may have beliefs that are unsettled in our own mind, beliefs around which we experience some *ambivalence*. Accepting ambivalence means that we can tolerate having mixed feelings about ourselves and the world, that we can exist even with competing beliefs that appear to contradict each other. For example, under most circumstances we all have mixed feelings about ourselves. We are aware that there are aspects of the self that we are comfortable with and others that we are not. The same is true for the other. We rarely, if we are honest, have a simplistic view of anything. Under conditions that promote growth and development, we can accept the fact that we are constantly living with ambivalence and uncertainty.

One could consider the extent to which one can tolerate uncertainty and ambivalence to be a measure of egocentrism: the more one steadfastly holds onto beliefs, especially when there may be disconfirming evidence, the more *egocentric* (embedded in one's own perspective) is one's understanding of the world. Conversely, the more one is open to changing one's beliefs (accepting uncertainty and ambivalence) about others and the world when there is new information to adjust to, the more *sociocentric* (capable of tolerating multiple perspectives) one becomes.

I would like to elaborate on the concept of *certainty*. As mentioned earlier, in order to function in the world we need to develop a set of beliefs about our self, others, and the world. Along with the beliefs that we establish comes a degree of certainty about those beliefs. In other words, we seem to have a very strong compulsion to want our understanding of the world to be "right." There seems to be a very strong desire to be "right" and a very strong aversion to being "wrong." This is an interesting phenomenon. There are probably functional, self-preserving aspects to it, but I really do not fully grasp the importance, from a developmental point of view, of feeling the strong need to be right. It creates so much resistance to change and development. It seems to threaten development rather than promote it.

EXPERIENCING THE LIMITS OF OUR CAPACITY TO BE OPEN TO LEARNING

As I mentioned earlier, there are, even under "normal" circumstances, limits to how much new learning we can tolerate. Too much too fast can destabilize us, creating the felt experience of psychological disintegration. Our capacity to take in more and more complex information and the resultant shift in our inner sense of equilibrium change with development. I will not go into this now, but Piaget tracks the qualitative shifts in understanding that take place as we develop over the lifespan (internal structural changes). The more we move through the stages of cognitive development, the more sophisticated we become at integrating information about others and the world. As we develop these more sophisticated capacities, we grow out of our egocentrism, or our beliefs that we are the center of the universe (which characterizes a childlike view of the world) and that our take on the world is the "right" one. With development, we become increasingly aware of the extent to which we must include others in our understanding of the world and develop a "sociocentric" view of the relationship between the self and the world. With this more complex worldview, one is much more reticent to be invested in being "right," realizing the limits of one's capacity to make such a claim in a world where uncertainty dominates reality.

We know we are at the limits of what we can take in because we feel it or experience it as overload. In other words, we begin to "disintegrate" psychologically. Depending on what the nature of the information is that overloads the learning mechanisms, it is experienced as fear, anxiety, anger, exhaustion, a general breakdown in our ability to function. We become psychologically "destabilized," and an automatic, self-preserving homeostatic process shuts down the learning channels. When I say "shuts down the channels," I mean those mechanisms that allow for the changes and refinement of the self-structures and the mechanism that allows in the new information that is used to refine the self-structures. These two dialectic processes (assimilation/accommodation) shut down. The self-structure is therefore no longer open to refinement and expansion, and the capacity to take in information about others and the world is also frozen, as are the existing beliefs about the self, others, and the world. In this sense, the frozen beliefs act as a stabilizing mechanism, one that moves us from a felt experience of disintegration to one where we are psychologically integrated and balanced again. As a consequence of the shutdown, beliefs become rigid and extremely resistant to change, complexity is lost, certainty of our assessment of what is "right" rises, and the feeling of ambivalence about what we "know" is lost—all in the service of self-protection.

IDENTITY DEVELOPMENT UNDER CONDITIONS OF CONFLICT

With the learning/development framework as backdrop, I would now like to examine what happens to the process of identity development under conditions of conflict, that is, when one experiences an existential threat.

Given the assumption that identity development occurs in the context of relationship, when the nature of the interaction between two people or groups becomes threatening, the process of identity formation shuts down. One feels destabilized by the threatening event, creating fear, anger, anxiety, and an impulse toward self-preservation and, as often seems to be the case, directing the anger and hostility toward the threatening other. An impulse (self-preserving/other-annihilating) for revenge and violence toward the threatening other is activated, a reaction that appears to protect us from physical annihilation. The felt experience of being psychologically diminished and the consequent feelings of humiliation that accompany it fuel the need for revenge and violence, perhaps as strongly as if it were a physical threat. This simultaneous impulse toward self-protection and other-annihilation seems to be automatic. In order to right oneself and to return to a state of equilibrium so that we can function, the self-preserving mechanism that I described above is activated, closing down the free flow of information between self and other, information that would normally allow for the refinement of our set of beliefs about our self, others, and the world, in essence, closing down the opportunity for growth and development, all in the service of survival. As a consequence of the traumatic and threatening event, one forms a negative image of the other, which becomes frozen into one's belief system. Any refinements in the beliefs about the other are formed in the absence of interaction. Input from the other is often not available. There is no opportunity for the other to challenge or change the negative images. This is when enemy images and other destructive social psychological processes develop.[12] Because the mechanism that allows in new information is closed down, even new and disconfirming information about the other is not allowed in. The images of the other are frozen in time. The process of identity formaton is also frozen, keeping in mind always that this is a self-protective mechanism. It allows one to function in the world and not experience the psychological disintegration that the traumatic event triggers. The closing down of the learning process is a survival mechanism.

Along with the frozen beliefs, the degree of certainty about one's beliefs also solidifies and becomes rigid. Both sides feel that their take on what happened is "right." They become entrenched in a battle over whose view is more accurate. Not only does one feel that his point of view is the correct one, one also feels extreme certainty about who is responsible and how to rectify the situation. The conclusions that one reaches about how to resolve the conflict are formed in the absence of any interaction with or input from the other. The other's point of view is expelled from the process of forming an outcome to the conflict. The desired outcomes to the conflict are seen in zero-sum terms, because each side has expelled the other and the experiences of the other from one's assessment of what is "right." The need

12. See Kelman, "Role of Social Identity in Conflict Resolution," for an extensive review of social psychological process that underlie conflict dynamics.

to be right seems to intensify as a part of the destructive dynamics of identity threats.

Along with the rigidity of one's need to be "right" about the other and the events surrounding the conflict is the need to place blame for what happened. It is rarely the case that one looks inward for one's own contribution to the failed interaction. There appears, again, to be a reflexive reaction to put all the responsibility onto the aggressive and evil other, protecting one's righteous self-image. The deflection of responsibility is a direct consequence of the powerful reaction to protect oneself from further trauma.

What also naturally occurs is a breakdown in social interaction. Both parties retreat from one another, creating physical and psychological distance between them. The distance further exacerbates the frozen images of the other, as there is absolutely no chance for hearing disconfirming information by listening to each other's view of the conflict. The communication void becomes filled with negativity and hostility, giving rise to the development of a number of cognitive distortions about the other, further limiting the chance for new learning.[13]

Our observations as facilitators of dialogues between communities in conflict have given us ample data that supports the above speculations regarding the role of identity in perpetuating and maintaining intercommunal conflict. In Sri Lanka, where the majority Sinhalese and minority Tamil peoples have been engaged in a violent conflict for more than seventeen years, the protection of identity plays a significant role in the conflict. Both sides feel that their identity is profoundly threatened by the position or desired outcome of the other side, creating what feels to both sides as an existential threat. The Sinhalese demand for a unified, Buddhist state that protects and maintains the integrity of their unique Sinhalese-Buddhist identity completely negates the Tamil Tiger's desire for a separate state, which would protect them from further persecution and marginalization as a minority people. Similarly, the Tamil demands for separation negates the Sinhalese demand for unity. These "zero-sum" positions make it impossible

13. Kelman, "Social Psychological Dimensions of International Conflict"; R. Holt and B. Silverstein, "On the Psychology of Enemy Images: Introduction and Overview," *Journal of Social Issues* 45, no. 2 (1989): 1–11; and B. Silverstein and C. Flamenbaum, "Biases in the Perceptions and Cognition of the Actions of Enemies," in *Journal of Social Issues* 45, no. 2 (1989).

to arrive at an outcome to the conflict that satisfies the needs and interests of both sides.

The threat to the identity of both sides triggers what I have described above as a self-protective reaction to hold onto their beliefs about the self and remaining highly resistant to change. Out of fear of annihilation, both sides have retreated from one another, creating the absence of interaction or isolation from each other that keeps parties open to learning and a possible unfreezing of their views of themselves and the other. They cling to their beliefs about what is "right," making it highly unlikely that they will let go of the "death grip" regarding their positions on how to end the conflict. The history of threatening and traumatizing each other has eroded any possibility of opening the learning process, therefore making it impossible to create the trust that is necessary to move the intractable process of reconciliation forward.

One must keep in mind that underlying a breakdown in trust is a history of trauma and humiliation. In the Sri Lanka conflict, both sides have experienced considerable trauma and humiliation. During the British colonial period, the Tamil minority was "favored" by the British in the sense that they were taught English and, therefore, had greater access to education and job opportunities.[14] The Sinhalese felt marginalized and discriminated by this "favoritism," creating the kind of revenge cycles that one sees being played out in the current conflict. The Buddhist clergy was also marginalized and humiliated during the colonial period, according to their accounts, and lost their power and authority in the Buddhist community. One could argue that it is why they are so adamant today about preserving the Buddhist integrity of the state of Sri Lanka. Such losses of dignity can remain alive within an identity group for centuries. Vamik Volkan has described the power of such trauma and humiliation in maintaining enemy attitudes toward the hated other. He has described how the trauma is transmitted for generations until and unless the parties engage in a healing process that acknowledges and grieves the lost integrity.[15]

For the Tamils, the history of discrimination and marginalization by the

14. David Little, *Sri Lanka: The Invention of Enmity* (Washington, D.C.: U.S. Institute of Peace Press, 1994).
15. Vamik Volkan, "On Chosen Trauma," *Mind and Human Interaction* 3, no. 13 (1991).

majority Sinhalese created very deep traumas. One faction of the Tamil community, the Liberation Tigers of Tamil Eelam, has claimed the need for a separate state in order to protect the Tamil people from persecution. Although other Tamil groups do not support the desire for a separate state, the other "moderate" Tamils would nevertheless agree that their identity has been profoundly threatened over the years and that changes in the political structure are necessary to protect themselves from further threat and persecution.

The important point to be made from this illustration is the extent to which threats to one's identity can interrupt the normal flow of interaction between groups, creating a hard-wired "revenge" reaction that gets triggered in the service of survival. In so doing, beliefs about self and other become frozen in time, resistant to the "normal" social interchange that produces the free flow of information from one's environment, causing an interruption of the normal flow of identity development.

WHAT ARE WE "NEGOTIATING"?

In this developmental framework it is clear that what happens under conditions of traumatic threat is a breakdown in the free flow of information between self and other, or an arrest of the learning process, or the co-construction of identities. I have made the point that when one experiences a traumatic, threatening event that disrupts one's inner stability, the mechanisms that allow for learning close down. There is an automatic shutdown of the mechanism that preserves us from further threat or injury. From this developmental perspective, one could argue that the threats experienced by parties in conflict are experienced not only as threats to one's identity, or our collection of beliefs about who we are, but more broadly a threat to the way we maintain our inner sense of coherence and stability. In so doing, the threat not only challenges the beliefs we hold about ourselves (our identity), but how we arrive at those beliefs, and how we ultimately use those beliefs as stabilizing mechanisms that allow us to function in the world. Furthermore, it challenges our evaluation of the "rightness" of those beliefs. Taken together, the threat becomes a *threat to one's integrity*, as the sum total of our understanding of the self and the world and that which gives us the psychological equilibrium or the felt experience of stability that allows us to navigate through the world with all its uncertainty. The biggest threat of all is to imagine letting go of those beliefs that have stabilized one for a long time. They fear both the other and reexperiencing of the feeling of disintegration caused by the threatening other. Anyone who has been traumatized by a threatening other knows that there is no way he or she would want to reexperience the trauma. The self-protective mechanisms within us are very powerful and prevent us from reliving the injury.

In summary, what is happening under conditions of traumatic threat is a felt experience of psychological disintegration (anger, fear, anxiety); the degree to which this is felt depends on the severity of the threat. The self-protective mechanism is triggered automatically, shutting down the mechanisms that allow the kind of interaction between self and other that promotes new learning. Beliefs about the self and the other become frozen. These "frozen beliefs"(images of self and other) act as stabilizing forces that firmly anchor oneself so that one does not revert back to the terrifying threat. The learning process, that process that opens oneself and the other to new experiences with the other, is indefinitely frozen. The context for growth and development (the relationship) becomes poisoned by the simultaneous destructive impulses of self-protection and other annihilation.

Assuming that the threat that is experienced is a threat to one's integrity, that is, a threat to how one is psychologically held together, what holds us together or stabilizes us back to a sense of equilibrium are our frozen beliefs about oneself and the other (one's identity). What we are actually negotiating is not only identity, but our integrity, that which keeps us stable in the world, that inner coherence and stability that keeps us functioning. We are, more broadly speaking, negotiating our integrity.

What we end up negotiating are the conditions under which one would be willing to open oneself up to new information, information that could change not only one's existing beliefs about the other but of oneself as well. The result of this reopening process is that the experience of the other is reintroduced into one's existing worldview without feelings of destabilization.

IMPLICATIONS FOR PROCESS

What kind of process could create the conditions that would enable parties to "negotiate their integrity"? What would be required of the participants? What would be the components of the process?

The process issues addressed in this chapter are limited to the work of reconciliation, where the goal is to create the conditions that allow former enemies to coexist without the fear of domination and annihilation.[16] The political implications of coming to terms with domination are not of concern here. It is assumed that a different forum convened at the official level (Track One) will address the political aspects of equalizing the relationship between the two groups.

A basic assumption of this unofficial or Track Two approach is that participants would have to agree at the outset that conflict is a relational phenomenon and is a result of failed interaction. Therefore, reflection on both the causes and the potential resolution of the conflict involves an interactive process where the issue of responsibility is explored. This in no way negates the fact that one side may have been more responsible than the other for causing the conflict in that an asymmetry of power often characterizes the relationship where one group is dominating the other to the extent that it's basic human rights are being violated.[17] What it does imply, however, is that both sides have a role in reconstructing the relationship, and in so doing, reconstructing their identities.

What does it require to reconstruct the relationship from one that is characterized by dominance and subjugation to one that is respectful of human dignity? I would like to make a distinction between the role of the low power group and the role of the high power group as the issue of responsibility is not the same for both.

It is necessary for the high power group to come to terms with the

16. See David Crocker for a nuanced examination of the meaning of reconciliation. He describes the process as ranging from thinner to thicker forms where parties agree not to kill one another, to a more comprehensive form where the issues of the past have been at least partially addressed and their shared future without violence appears likely. In "Reckoning with Past Wrongs: A Normative Framework," *Ethics and International Affairs* 13 (1999): 43–64.

17. N. Rouhana and S. Korper, "Dealing with Power Asymmetry: Dilemmas of Intervention in Asymmetrical Intergroup Conflict," *Negotiation Journal* 12 (1996): 315–28.

consequences of maintaining a dominance relationship, insofar as they have denied the low power group their human dignity and rights as a people. They need to accept that, as a result of their domination, they caused immeasurable suffering and humiliation for the low power group. What makes this so difficult is the exposure one feels in accepting the not-so-righteous aspects of one's group identity, that part of the human psyche that is capable of traumatizing the other and thereby denying the other its human dignity.

For the low power group, their role is as difficult, if not more so. If there is any way to reconstruct the relationship to promote reconciliation and co-existence, the low power group will have to let go of their "victim" identity, which would require them to relinquish the moral advantage that has been the source of their power for the duration of the conflict. In so doing they would have to come to terms with—that is to say, let go of—the understandable hostility and need for revenge that they feel toward the group that has caused their suffering for so many years. Some believe that this is too much to ask of the victimized group. Is it even humanly possible to rehumanize the other that has dehumanized you? Perhaps this is the core of the issue. A necessary condition for reconciliation is the restoration of humanity: restoring human dignity to both the victim and the victimizer.

What kind of process would promote the restoration of humanity for both sides? Once again, the structural changes that are necessary and that guarantee the rights of the low power group are not the concern of this chapter. Those political changes are necessary but not sufficient to bring about reconciliation. The psychological shift that enables parties to unfreeze those aspects of their identity—the beliefs that make it possible for them to maintain their inner stability and coherence at the cost of creating an exis-tential threat for the other—is the locus of concern here. The question is, what sort of process could create the conditions for such a shift?

Desmond Tutu has argued that forgiveness is the only way to restore the dignity to a relationship that has been violated by conflict.[18] The low power group would have to forgive the high power group and the high power group would have to forgive itself. Although it may very well be true that

18. Desmond Tutu, *No Future Without Forgiveness* (New York: Doubleday, 1999).

forgiveness not only helps free the victimizer of and shame and the burden of wrongdoing, but can also liberate the victim,[19] the problem is that it cannot be forced. We can no more force a group that is in denial of the effects of its domination and subjugation to face its denial (to examine the not-so-righteous aspects of its identity) than legislate the low power group to let go of its understandable rage and to forgive its oppressor (give up its victim identity). I would argue that it is unethical to push forgiveness onto anyone who is not ready. Martha Minow has pointed out that victims need to feel the anger associated with a violation of their dignity, as it enables them to maintain a sense of self-esteem after the assault.[20]

Even if we all agreed that forgiveness could be the mechanism that would enable the reconstruction of identity—a critical component to the process of reconciliation—we are faced with what feels like a moral dilemma. We have insight into the mechanism that could promote the shift but are aware that it is not something that any third party could require of participants. Engaging in a process of forgiveness is a personal choice and must remain in that realm, whether we are talking about forgiving someone for violating one's dignity or forgiving oneself for robbing others of their dignity. The best one could hope for is to create the conditions that would give rise to forgiveness.

Susan Dwyer has argued that forgiveness is not a necessary component in the reconciliation process.[21] Her conceptualization of reconciliation—what it takes for two parties to arrive at an "equilibrium," or shared interpretation of seemingly incompatible versions of reality—focuses primarily on the level of meaning-making. She argues that human beings create narratives around events, the purpose of which is to provide coherence and stability in one's understanding of the self, others, and the world. In essence, Dwyer argues that when outside forces threaten one's identity, it creates a disruption in one's worldview, particularly one's notion of self and other, creating, ultimately, a breakdown in one's narrative. The task of reconciliation,

19. R. D. Enright, S. Freedman, and J. Rique, "The Psychology of Interpersonal Forgiveness," in *Exploring Forgiveness*, ed. R. Enright and J. North (Madison: University of Wisconsin Press, 1999).

20. Martha Minow, *Between Vengeance and Forgiveness* (New York: Doubleday Press, 1999).

21. Susan Dwyer, "Reconciliation for Realists," *Ethics and International Affairs* 13 (1999): 81–98.

therefore, is to create the conditions so that the two former enemies could develop a "mutually tolerable" interpretation of events. It is an epistemological exercise to the extent that the process involves at least a partial co-construction of meaning, restoring the necessary equilibrium that could enable them to leave the past and envision the possibility of a shared future. Dwyer suggests that tension will always surround this process, and the goal is not to eliminate those tensions. Rather, the goal is to try to incorporate the source of those tensions—the trauma, the humiliation, the violations of one's dignity—into a new way of holding them in one's identity such that it does not cause psychological disintegration for either party.

One can see that Dwyer's conceptualization of the goal of reconciliation is consistent with what we know about identity development and the ideas put forth in this essay. She may be partly correct in describing the process as epistemological in nature except that reconstructing a shared interpretation of events fails to address the "felt experience," what happens at the human level, when one has sustained an assault to one's integrity. When one's narrative has been challenged by a traumatic assault it cannot be rectified by simply engaging in an epistemological exercise of reconstructing the narrative. The injuries endured by the victim require more than a cognitive reconstruction of events, although such a reconstruction is certainly the desired outcome. The process needs to include a component that addresses the emotional trauma victims have sustained. This aspect of the process requires more than just a cognitive exercise. What this aspect of the process looks like is still in question, although much has been written about what it takes to promote healing of victims of politically motivated violence.[22]

To summarize, the process cannot be limited to negotiating a new construction or co-construction of events that took place. That is the desired endpoint, but other emotional demands required to get to a truly "mutually tolerable" interpretation of events requires a much deeper process that addresses the needs for healing and recovery of the assault to one's dignity. Addressing and acknowledging the emotional component *allows* the parties to reconstruct events. One cannot be expected to give up an aspect of one's identity without addressing the conditions that gave rise to it in the first

---

22. See Liza Chambers's review of the literature on trauma and healing and the stages of such a process.

place. The experience of humiliation and suffering that a low power group has experienced must be addressed before being able to "let go" of it in support of a new "mutually tolerable" interpretation of what happened. Similarly, the high power group needs to integrate emotionally that aspect of their identity that enabled them to perpetrate acts of violence upon the other.

Given the delicate nature of the work being proposed, it is recommended that the first phase of the process be done within the communities, before they are brought together for the face-to-face "interactive" phase. What it takes for both groups to "unfreeze" their identities is difficult enough to do without the presence of the other side. Only after the critical task of self-examination should the parties be brought together for the "reconstruction" phase of reconciliation.

For the high power group, exposing oneself to the not-so-righteous aspects of one's identity can be extremely difficult and embarrassing. The first phase is to break one's denial that one is capable of inflicting injury upon the other. This would require the safest of environments, with the support of a nonjudgmental third party, who could create the conditions for such self-analysis. Perpetrators would have to engage in a slow process of exposure before they could be able to expose themselves to those whom they have injured. Exposing too much too soon can be psychologically devastating.

A safe environment would have to be created by the third party in order for the low power group to articulate what happened to them and to have it acknowledged by the other that what happened to them was wrong and that no human being should have to suffer the way they did. They would be taken through their process with the hope that both the telling of their story and the acknowledgment by the third party that what happened to them was wrong could prepare them for facing the high power group in a face-to-face interaction.

As one can see, the role of the third party is not one of impartiality. In fact, the third party should be prepared to acknowledge the suffering and violations of dignity of the low power group. The defining characteristic of the third party work with the high power group would require a nonjudgmental and compassionate approach so that the group would be able to expose themselves without fear of being humiliated. The hope with the high power group is that the environment created by the third party would be safe enough that they would be willing to examine the darker side of their identity and, in so doing, could begin to accept responsibility for their actions.

It is far beyond the scope of this chapter to propose a detailed description of these processes. My point in introducing the issue of process is to help us think more clearly about the role identity plays in the reconciliation and to differentiate the goals of the process for the two groups. What it takes for a low power group to let go of the aspects of their identity that make reconciliation difficult is different from what the challenges that the high power group faces. Finally, it is proposed that the individual group work would enhance the possibility of being able to reconstruct the narratives of both sides so that a "mutually tolerable" interpretation of the past could be achieved, paving the way for the development of a shared future in the context of a relationship that permits both groups' identities to develop and flourish.

One last point that I would like to make explicit regarding the process of reconciliation—a point that is implied in the above analysis—is that, in my view, a disproportionate emphasis has been placed, in the discourse on reconciliation, on the role of the victim in promoting reconciliation and, in particular, on the role of forgiveness. As the above analysis of process indicates, the task of reconstructing identities (narratives) and ultimately the relationship between two parties involves shared responsibility. It is uncommon to read about processes that support perpetrators through the process of coming to terms with the aspect of their identities that allows them to commit acts of violence upon the other. It is my view that practitioners are putting an undue burden on the low power group by suggesting that "there is no future without forgiveness." I would like to balance the scales by suggesting that we focus more attention on what it takes to break the denial of high power groups so that they can come to terms with what they have done in a way that protects their human dignity. It is our challenge, as practitioners, to understand the needs of the perpetrator and to develop process that would enable them to take responsibility for their actions and still maintain their psychological integrity.

It may be true that "there is no future without forgiveness" but what kind of future will it be if forgiveness is not accompanied by responsibility? Are we doing the high power group any favors by enabling them to stay in a state of denial about who they are and what they have done? The restoration of humanity requires an identity shift on both sides of the divide. By emphasizing one process over the other, we are perpetuating the continuation of the asymmetrical relationship and undermining the very idea that the resolution of these deep-rooted identity conflicts requires an unfreezing of *both* identities and the existential threats that are released in the process. The acknowledgment of wrongdoing (and the concomitant shift in identity that it requires) could make it profoundly easier for victims to let go of their anger and need for revenge, creating the conditions that could promote a shift in their identity and the relationship. This could enable both parties to move out of the past, into the present, and onto imagining a future not only absent of existential threat but filled with possibility and the freedom to develop and flourish.

CHAPTER 8

What Is Forgiveness in a Secular Political Form?

Donald W. Shriver Jr.

INTRODUCTORY QUESTIONS ABOUT THE NATURE OF FORGIVENESS

TOWARD THE END OF KEN BURNS'S powerful documentary PBS series, *The West,* a contemporary native American, a Lakota, speaks as follows:

> After my five-year vision quest, I was tempted to go out and shoot every white man. . . . I thought about Sand Creek and Wounded Knee, and I got angrier and angrier. . . . I wanted to grab a gun and start shooting. Then, I thought, my ancestors might honor me . . . but then I saw the beauty of the moon and the morningstar, and I knew that the only way I could live was to forgive. . . . I work on that now every day. If one doesn't work on forgiveness, one will die on the road some day. [Wounded Knee] isn't history. It is still with us. We deal with it every day.

This moving statement confirms to me an agenda list of issues surrounding the place of forgiveness in human affairs.

1. What is the place of religion in defining, denying, or affirming the importance of forgiveness?

In the Lakota's confession, a religious experience, the classic "vision quest," leaves him with feelings of vengeance that give way finally to forgiveness. Religion can fuel vengeance and its alternative, forgiveness.

2. Ought forgiveness to be defined as a personal act, whose meaning
    gets worked out inside individual consciousness?

Much writing about forgiveness has assumed that its natural place, if it
has a place, is inside the human person. The Lakota came to the conclusion
that survival for him depended upon forgiveness, but he concluded that in
an implicit context, that down the road of vengeful murder would lie his
own murder by others. Vengeance certainly implied for him a social threat.
Start killing your neighbors, and they will start to kill you. It is one of the
most "natural" things in human experience. But it is also natural for
humans to want to live. Forgiveness has something to do with that basic
desire, common to most members of our species. One might tag this as the
prudential element in forgiveness.

3. Why all this history? Why is it that for this Native American the
    Massacre of Wounded Knee, over one hundred years ago, is as yes-
    terday?

I am no psychiatrist, but Sigmund Freud said that the unconscious has
no sense of time. The trauma you suffered as a child can be as yesterday,
powerfully conditioning your today. But in this case, the yesterday was
something that happened to your ancestors that exists today not only in
intergenerational memory but in the modern life situation of Native Americans: For them as for most of us in one or another way, William Faulkner's
truth still applies: "The past is not dead and gone, it isn't even past."

4. Among many another implicit issues in this eloquent confession, is
    this final one: For both individual and social survival, what does
    forgiveness do that nothing else can do?

The answer, only superficially paradoxical, is: it forgets the past by
remembering it, and it lets the past become past by adopting a hope of not
repeating it.

Søren Kierkegaard, no stranger to paradox, put it this way:

Forgetting is the shears with which you cut away what you cannot
use, doing it under the supreme direction of memory. Forgetting
and remembering are thus identical arts, and the artistic achievement of this identity is the Archimedean point from which one lifts

the whole world. When we say that we *consign* something to oblivion, we suggest simultaneously that it is to be forgotten and yet also remembered.

One item in that quotation interests me especially as a pragmatic American: "use." In other words, one might ask, "use" for what purpose? That is the real fulcrum question for the ethics of forgiveness. I would answer that in another wry quotation from Faulkner: "Thank God men have done learned how to forget quick what they ain't brave enough to try to cure." What does forgiveness try to cure? Not only the acids of vengeance eating away at internal personal peace, but the undoubted interhuman alienation that is the lasting result of traumatic wrong. Forgiveness in human affairs has purpose, not only the purpose of healing wounds internal to the person but wounds external in social relations.

In this connection we have to say that historical western Jewish-Christian traditions have deposited in our general cultural inheritance three misleading impressions about forgiveness: To the Jewish tradition we owe the great moral-religious assertion that God our creator pays more attention to our sins than do we. From the Garden of Eden right through to Jeremiah and Second Isaiah, the God of Israel weeps over Israel's sins and determines to do something about those sins. The trouble here is that "doing something" about human sin seems to be God's unique business; in the Hebrew Bible God is mostly the exclusive custodian of the forgiveness of sins. Christians, in turn, have perpetuated this serious religious claim with an addition that has also precipitated a misleading impression in our culture: "Forgive us our debts as we forgive our debtors." The prayer comes habitually to Christian lips down two millennia, and through this horizontal-vertical juncture of forgiveness brings forgiveness to earth, so to speak, but keeps it mostly inside the religious community of the church. "Good," one might believe, as far as it goes. But a rising tide of evidence, down through the centuries, suggests that it has not gone far enough.

Forgiveness needs to have a place in the culture by which societies train their members to become citizens. Hannah Arendt, whom all of us interested in this subject will quote sooner or later, writing as a refugee from the Holocaust, claimed forgiveness as an indispensable dynamic in genuine social change, claiming, with Robert Frost, also mostly a secularist, that "to be social is to be forgiving."

But there is a third bit of misleading thinking that intrudes here. This is around a truth on which religious and secular people are apt to agree: some sort of morality is necessary for human society, and forgiveness seems to bypass, erode, or otherwise treat too lightly violations of law, morals, and human good. On this point, well-educated Jews and Christians should simply reply that forgiveness is serious moral business precisely because it takes both moral wrong and the healing of wrong-infested human relationship with *simultaneous* seriousness. That makes forgiveness one specification of what Sir Geoffrey Vickers, British civil servant, called a "multi-valued choice." So long as moral judgment or just vengeance remains the preoccupation of a human injured by another human, a single value sits in the driver's seat. But suppose one is freighted with the burden of wanting the wrong fully acknowledged as part of a restoration of mutual relation between the wrongdoers and the wronged? That is the moral-intellectual-practical burden that a potential forgiver will mean to undertake.

FORGIVENESS IN A SECULAR POLITICAL FORM

This introductory analysis suggests a definition of forgiveness that, as it happens, I first crafted studying a lot of books in the schools and libraries in Cambridge, Massachusetts, decades ago. I have found it to be a studied, useful definition, compounded of four elements: moral judgment, forbearance from revenge, empathy for wrongdoers, and a hope for renewal of the fractured relationship.

The secularists who entertain moral suspicion are on good ground when they observe that in some Christians forgiveness pops up, like the option-of-choice on a computer screen, too quickly as advice to victims. If one has ever been a victim the option is not likely to get chosen quickly. Pragmatic Americans may find it hard to understand this. Consider the example of the white suburban resident from the Chicago area who commented to a reporter from the *New York Times* in 1992, "It's up to [black people] to paddle their own canoe. Don't always think about the fact that they were slaves." One reason that white and black Americans are still in a state of considerable alienation is right here: Not to have your history understood, remembered, and treated seriously is to have your historic pain undervalued. It is to ask that forgetting substitute for remembering, and to substitute the insulting motto "Forgive and forget" for the humane "Remember and forgive."

If the Truth and Reconciliation Commission (TRC) in South Africa has proven nothing else, it has demonstrated to the world the indispensable function of public remembering for taking the first healing steps toward a social bond fractured by atrocities such as apartheid. The rehearsal of thousands of painful stories has infused the public records and the emerging new political culture of South Africa with Soren Kierkegaard's "identical arts" of remembering and forgetting. As the TRC hearings have so movingly demonstrated, there are two radically different reasons for remembering the past: to get long-delayed revenge, or to achieve hoped-for reconciliation. The latter does not forget the past, but it puts the past in the past by credible commitment not to repeat it.

Such credibility, for the public reality of forgiveness, requires an element that goes beyond moral judgment and the refusal of vengeance. It is the element of empathy for victims and perpetrators. When George Herbert Mead said that democracy depends on the ability of voters to take into account the interests of others when they step into the voting booth, he was underscoring the importance of empathy for the very existence of society. Empathy must be carefully distinguished from sympathy. In his monumental study, *The Nazi Doctors* (1987), Robert Lifton asks the painful question: What enabled these German members of his own medical profession to conduct those lethal experiments on fellow human beings in the death camps? He labels his psychological conclusion "doubling," that is, a process by which humans insulate one side of their lives from the other side. This is illustrated in the familiar and horrifying image of the death-camp official who murders people in his or her daily work and who goes home in the evening for happy times with spouse and children. Such people learn to treat certain classes of human neighbors as no longer human. The Nazis called them "life unworthy of life," and in the lingo of the camps they were often called *Stücke,* pieces, things.

Honest psychiatrist that he is, at the end of his study, with its dozens of interviews with surviving camp doctors, Lifton asks: Do they compose for me my own temptation of doubling? Must I not try to extend to them an empathy that they systematically denied to the victims of their corrupted medical practice? It is hard enough, one must say, to empathize with the victims of colossal wrong in ancient and contemporary history, for most of us live by the pleasure principle, and it is not pleasant to listen to the stories of other people's suffering. But once that barrier is cleared and emotions are opened even a little to the horror of those stories, it is doubly hard to clear the other barrier: empathy for the perpetrators.

Perhaps the most threatening aspect of the invitation to enter into this latter empathy is what it does to one's own self-concept. That is the threat that Harvard University's now famous professor Daniel Goldhagen manages to resist in his book, *Hitler's Willing Executioners*. The conclusion of that book is that in their "eliminationism anti-Semitism" German culture and Germans of the Nazi era were unique. Modern democratic Germans, like modern democratic Americans, are rid of that disease and are mostly inoculated against it. That is a comforting conclusion, but it flies in the face of many a historian's review of the book and in the face of Robert Lifton's sober conclusion to his own study of the Nazi doctors.

A CONCLUDING CONTRIBUTION

These remarks are an entry point from one of the oldest and most important contributions of religion, especially the Jewish and the Christian, to the significance of forgiveness in human society. Reinhold Niebuhr used to say that the one truth of this tradition that most assuredly has empirical confirmation is the truth of human fallibility, or what the tradition calls "sin": As the text of Scripture puts it: "All have sinned and come short of the glory of God" (Rom. 3:23). If they have not in fact come short in this or that situation, they are in fact vulnerable to such coming-short. And that surely was what Robert Frost meant when he said, "To be social is to be forgiving." For "if we started counting each other out for the least sin, we'd soon have no one left to live with."

That we can yet live with each other, in spite of all our historical prece-dents of killing each other, is the undergirding hope of those who put their feet on the road to forgiveness. In the mid-1980s, Desmond Tutu said, "In South Africa it is impossible to be optimistic. Therefore it is necessary to hope." It is necessary, yes, if we are to substitute for our politics of death a politics of life.

PART III

Forgiveness & Reconciliation

Unforgiveness, Forgiveness, and Reconciliation and Their Implications for Societal Interventions

Everett L. Worthington Jr.

IN 1987, NEAR BELFAST, sixty-three people were wounded and eleven killed when an IRA bomb exploded amid a gathering of Protestants. Among the dead was Marie Wilson, the twenty-year-old daughter of Gordon Wilson. Her last words as she held her dad's hand beneath the rubble were, "Daddy, I love you very much." From his hospital bed Wilson said, "I have lost my daughter, but I bear no grudge. Bitter talk is not going to bring Marie Wilson back to life. I shall pray, tonight and every night, that God will forgive them."[1]

After his physical healing, Gordon Wilson met with the IRA, forgave them, and asked them to lay down their weapons. "I know you have lost loved ones, just like me," he said. According to P. Yancey, Protestant extremists who planned a bombing in retaliation decided against vengeance because the mercy and love extended by Wilson would make any retributive act politically disastrous for them. "Virulent evil (racism, ethnic hatred) spreads through society like an airborne disease; one cough infects a whole busload," writes Yancey. "The cure, like a vaccine, must be applied one person at a time."[2] But the cure of forgiveness generously bestowed, as by Wilson, can result in ripples of social benefit. Even if each case of forgiveness

1. M. Noll, "Belfast: Tense with Peace," *Books and Culture* (November/December 1995): 12.
2. P. Yancey, *What's So Amazing about Grace?* (Grand Rapids, Mich.: Zondervan, 1996), 117.

does not produce much good, it can at least inhibit hatred and violence.

I will address the interrelationship between forgiveness and reconciliation within the context of international or societal relations. I am a psychologist who does basic research in forgiveness and reconciliation, especially between couples. I also study interventions to promote forgiveness and reconciliation with individuals (alone and with groups) and with couples. I confess, I do not systematically study forgiveness and reconciliation from a societal or public policy point of view.

Winston Churchill is said to have been reading a book of quotes during his youth. Encountering two quotes—which espoused opposing content but with equal force—he was dismayed. How could both be valid? At that moment, his glance fell upon a beautiful black butterfly. Its wings flapped, changing the direction the light struck the butterfly's wings. It suddenly looked blue. In an epiphany, Churchill realized that truth often depends on the angle at which one sees an event.[3] One strength of what I will say is precisely that I am approaching societal and international relations with an outsider's perspective—not as a specialist in international or societal relations, but as a psychologist.

Let me discuss the way I understand unforgiveness, forgiveness, conflict resolution, and reconciliation based upon my research with individuals and couples. I do not claim that these are the correct ways to understand such concepts. In science our charge is to be clear, not necessarily "correct," about definitions. We then let data whisper (and sometimes shout) feedback to correct our definitions.

DEFINITIONS

Unforgiveness

Forgiveness is not merely what people do to reduce unforgiveness. Unforgiveness is a cold, emotional complex consisting of resentment, bitterness, hatred, hostility, residual anger, and fear. Those emotions motivate people to avoid or reduce unforgiveness.

3. A. J. Mapp Jr., *Three Golden Ages: Discovering the Creative Secrets of Renaissance Florence, Elizabeth England, and America's Founding* (Lanham, Md.: Madison Books, 1998).

A model of unforgiveness is inherent in the definition.[4] A transgression occurs and is perceived as a mixture of hurt and offense. To the extent the transgression is perceived as hurt, the person responds with a hot emotion of fear. To the extent the transgression is perceived as an offense, the person responds with a hot emotion of anger. Posttransgression fear and anger are not unforgiveness. Unforgiveness occurs when people ruminate about the transgression, their reactions to it, the transgressor's motives, the consequences, and potential responses. Rumination *can* produce the cold emotions of resentment, bitterness, hatred, hostility, residual anger, and residual fear, which together make up unforgiveness.

People do not like to feel unforgiveness. While the anger and the revenge motive can energize and empower them, generally people try to reduce or eliminate unforgiveness as quickly as they can. If possible, they avoid unforgiveness entirely by forgiving (or dealing with it in other ways) before rumination becomes active. They deal with unforgiveness in many ways, which I have summarized in Table 9.1 and will discuss below.

Forgiveness

Forgiveness is a juxtaposition or superposition of a strong positive emotion over the cold emotions of unforgiveness in such a way that the unforgiveness is contaminated and overwhelmed by the more positive emotions. Alternatively, forgiveness is the emotional replacement of hot anger and fear by those positive emotions.

The positive emotions can be empathy for the perpetrator, compassion, agape love, or even romantic love. Other positive emotions, such as humility over one's own culpability and past transgressions and gratitude for one's own experiences of forgiveness, might intermix to contaminate the cold emotions of unforgiveness or replace the hot emotions of anger and fear.

I am not talking about mere *feelings* when I say that unforgiveness and forgiveness are emotions. Emotions involve feelings (i.e., our ways of label-

---

4. Everett L. Worthington Jr. and N. G. Wade, "The Social Psychology of Unforgiveness and Forgiveness and Implications for Clinical Practice," *Journal of Social and Clinical Psychology* (2000).

TABLE 9.1. REDUCING UNFORGIVENESS THROUGH SOCIETAL AND INTRAPERSONAL MECHANISMS

SOCIAL, SOCIETAL, AND INTERACTIONAL LEVEL	INTRAPERSONAL LEVEL
Justice (Punitive or Restorative)	**Psychological (i.e., unconscious motivational)**
Retaliation or revenge (vigilante justice)	Denial
Civil or legal justice (restitution; punitive damages)	Projection (blame)
Personal restitution	**Forgetting (i.e., cognitive passive)**
Esteem-lowering acts by perpetrators	Passing Time
Soft account	Interfering or distracting events
Admission of wrong	Loses importance relative to other events
Apology (expression of sincere regret and contrition)	**Telling a Different Story about the Event (i.e., cognitive active)**
Repentance	Reframing events, motives of perpetrators, or consequences of events
Asking for forgiveness	Justifying the perpetrator's acts
Public ceremonial confession, apology, or restitution	Excusing the perpetrator's acts
Acknowledging divine justice	Condoning the perpetrator's acts
Belief in karma (unremitting justice)	**Telling a Different Story about the Nature of People (i.e., cognitive active)**
Conflict Resolution	Existence is *Maya*.
Mutual cessation of hostilities	The common personhood of humans
Mutual concessions (compromise)	*Mbutu*
Negotiating agreement	**Letting go (i.e., decisional or behavioral)**
Social Justice	Forbearing or accepting (similar to legally pardoning)
Agreed-upon norms	**Forgiving (i.e., emotional)**
Fair laws	Emotional replacement or juxtaposition using empathy, compassion, humility, gratitude for one's own forgiveness, agape love, romantic love, humor, or sense of noble purpose
Just social structures	

ing emotions).[5] Emotions also involve thoughts, memories, associations, neurochemicals within the brain, brain pathways within various brain structures, hormones in the bloodstream, "gut feelings," facial musculature and gross body musculature, and acts of emotional expression.[6]

A. R. Damasio has argued that people have at least two types of emotional experiences.[7] One type is *primary*. The person's visual systems are activated through real-life experiences and observations or through visual imagery. All of the neural and bodily circuitry are triggered by primary emotional experiences. The other type of emotional experience occurs when people have "as-if" experiences. Those experiences are more cognitive, verbal, and reasoned than are primary experiences. It is as if the primary emotion is experienced. The beliefs, reasoning, or logic trigger the same neural and bodily circuitry; however, the intensity is less.

Obviously, superimposing, juxtaposing, or experiencing emotions such as empathy, compassion, or love while thinking about or remembering a transgression that stimulates (or threatens to stimulate) the emotions of unforgiveness sets up a competition within the body. Emotions are *embodied* experiences. If a person recalls a transgression but his or her mental system (memories, thoughts, and associations), internal systems (neurochemicals, hormones, and "gut feelings"), and external systems (facial expressions, posture, and actions) are compatible with compassion rather than hatred, blessing rather than cursing, and understanding rather than demoralizing, then the person will likely conclude that he or she has forgiven the transgressor. The person simply cannot experience two widely different emotional states in his or her body at the same time. One emotional state

---

5. A. R. Damasio, *The Feeling of What Happens: Body and Emotion in the Making of Consciousness* (New York: Harcourt Brace, 1999); and see his earlier *Descartes' Error: Emotion, Reason, and the Human Brain* (New York: Avon Books, 1994).

6. R. S. Lazarus, *Stress and Emotion: A New Synthesis* (New York: Springer, 1999); Damasio, *The Feeling of What Happens*; J. LeDoux, *The Emotional Brain: The Mysterious Underpinnings of Emotional Life* (New York: Simon and Schuster, 1996); R. M. Sapolsky, "Hormonal Correlates of Personality and Social Contexts: From Non-Human to Human Primates," in *Hormones, Health, and Behavior: A Socio-ecological and Lifespan Perspective*, ed. C. Panter-Brick and C. M. Worthman (Cambridge: Cambridge University Press, 1999), 18–46; Sapolsky, *Why Zebras Don't Get Ulcers: A Guide to Stress, Stress-Related Diseases, and Coping* (New York: W. H. Freeman, 1994); R. Plutchik, *The Psychology and Biology of Emotion* (New York: HarperCollins, 1994).

7. Damasio, *The Feeling of What Happens*.

will dominate. One will attach itself to the stimuli associated with the remembered transgression.

Conflict Resolution

Conflict resolution is the way people or societies resolve differences. Those differences are often loaded with emotion and embedded in personal and societal histories. Conflict resolution involves skills of communication and negotiation. Successful conflict resolution answers previously unanswered questions. It also deactivates power struggles, which are not disagreements over issues but over who has the say about the issues.

Couples, families, or public officials can learn to resolve conflicts, but that does not eliminate problems. Nor does it heal wounds incurred during conflict. People must still deal with the aftermath of conflict—the hurts and offenses that have produced unforgiveness and ruptured trust.

Reconciliation

Reconciliation is the restoration of trust in a relationship where trust has been violated, sometimes repeatedly.[8] Reconciliation involves not just *forgiveness* but also many other ways of reducing *unforgiveness*.

REDUCING UNFORGIVENESS

There are many ways to reduce unforgiveness that do not involve forgiveness (see Table 9.1 above). I divided those into two classes. First are those employed at the social, interactional, or societal level. The second are employed at the intrapersonal (or within-person) level. Forgiveness, as emotional replacement or emotional juxtaposition, is necessarily intrapersonal.

---

8. Everett L. Worthington and D. T. Drinkard, "Promoting Reconciliation Through Psychoeducational and Therapeutic Interventions," *Journal of Social and Clinical Psychology* (2000).

Reducing Unforgiveness at the Societal Level

At the societal level, three subclasses of acts help reduce unforgiveness: People can pursue punitive or restorative justice; they can engage in successful conflict resolution; they can work for social justice.

The first main way to reduce unforgiveness is the reestablishment of a sense of justice. Justice is necessary when the scales of justice have been put out of balance by an injustice (e.g., a crime, a wrong, or transgression). Justice may be restored by means of either punitive or restorative methods. In Table 9.1 I list seven ways people attempt to rebalance the scales of justice after a transgression has occurred.

Retaliation or revenge is perhaps the most primitive means of attempting to rebalance the scales of justice.[9] Retaliation is a quick hot response; revenge is retaliation served cold. In both, a person inflicts a harm for a harm. Successfully executing retaliation or revenge will often reduce a person's unforgiveness because the scales seem to be balanced and the urge to retaliate further is mitigated. (Of course, the recipient of retaliation or revenge seldom feels that the scales are balanced, which leads to further exchanges of retaliation or revenge.)

Second, civil or legal justice involves a presumably neutral third party who awards restitution or punitive damages. Civil or legal justice attempts to rebalance the scales of justice. Through a due process, people submit their case to a socially approved trier of fact. The trier of fact decides on a fair judgment, which supposedly rebalances the scales of justice. To the extent that the parties involved in the legal proceedings accept the judgment as fair, they might experience reduced unforgiveness. Less formal judicial processes, such as mediation and restorative justice, are increasingly being allowed as an alternative to formal court decisions.[10]

Third, individuals might make personal restitution in an attempt to rebalance the scales of justice. An offender might offer to engage in a costly act (such as working to restore a victim's loss) or remunerate an injured party with money or material goods. That rebalancing will, to the degree

9. Howard Zehr, *Changing Lenses: A New Focus for Crime and Justice* (Scottdale, Pa.: Herald Press, 1995).
10. Ibid.

that it is perceived as equitable, reduce unforgiveness in the person transgressed against.

Fourth, the perpetrator might engage in esteem-lowering acts. Such acts are those that apologize for wrongdoing and admit wrongdoing without justification or excuse.[11] Repentance (expressing sincere remorse and regret and showing by action that one does not intend to harm or offend again), making unambiguous efforts to work pro-socially instead of to work against the person harmed, or asking for forgiveness are three esteem-lowering acts.[12] A person who perpetrated a harm thereby lowers his or her public or social esteem and therefore incurs a voluntary cost that is thought, in some ways, to rebalance the scales. Again, to the extent that such an act is perceived by the victim as *fairly* balancing those scales, unforgiveness is reduced.

Fifth, public ceremonial acts of repentance, apology, confession, and publicly asking for forgiveness are also symbolic ways to rebalance justice that has been put out of sorts by public events of wrongdoing. These acts by leaders of a country or group are similar to esteem-lowering acts by individuals. Such public acts differ from acts by individuals in that the people offering public ceremonial acts of confession and apology are not usually the same people who committed the transgressions, just as the people who are being apologized to are not usually the same people who were directly hurt by the transgression. Because atrocious transgressions are remembered, often for centuries, ceremonial apology can facilitate healing if done sensitively.

Sixth, people can also reduce their unforgiveness by acknowledging divine justice. Acknowledgment of divine justice can be done in humility by stating one's sincere belief that God will ultimately judge wrongdoing, not the victim. The victim thus abrogates judgment. Acknowledgment of divine justice can also be done in a spirit of revenge. A victim can relinquish judgment to God with the stated expectation that God will ultimately render severe punishment for a wrong that a perpetrator inflicted. In either case, the victim will likely feel less unforgiveness.

11. J. J. Exline and R. F. Baumeister, "Expressing Forgiveness and Repentance: Benefits and Barriers," and E. Mullet and M. Girard, "Developmental and Cognitive Points of View on Forgiveness," in *Forgiveness: Theory, Research, and Practice*, ed. M. C. McCullough, K. I. Pargament, and C. E. Thoresen (New York: Guilford, 2000), 133–55, 111–32.
12. Zehr, *Changing Lenses*.

Seventh (and finally), in Eastern religions a belief in *karma* can be activated.[13] Karma is belief in immutable justice that suggests that all wrongs will ultimately be balanced in the end. If a person's belief in karma is activated, the person can give up a sense of unforgiveness.

In each of these seven ways, people reduce their unforgiveness by seeking justice. The primary psychological effect of justice is to reduce unforgiveness, not to promote forgiveness.

The second societal subclass by which people reduce unforgiveness is through engaging in successful conflict resolution. When a conflict has existed for a substantial period, emotions of fear, anxiety, and distress can color a person or society's worldview, focusing attention on the negative. If hostilities are brought to an end through a truce or an agreement, people experience an immediate sense of relief. Some of their unforgiveness may be mitigated.

Generally, after hostilities have ceased, the parties may be more willing to compromise. A compromise involves giving up some favored point, making a concession when it seems to be of equal value to a concession made by the other side. By making and getting a concession, the person or society feels more positive toward the other side and thereby reduces some of the unforgiveness felt toward the other side.

Finally, beyond compromise, individuals or elements in society might negotiate agreement in which principles govern their joint solution to problems.[14] Negotiated agreement of a "win-win" solution can reduce the negative emotions that make up unforgiveness.

The third societal subclass for reducing unforgiveness involves working for social justice. Whereas punitive or restorative justice seeks to deal after-the-fact with transgressions, social justice involves establishing conditions in which transgressions are less likely to occur in the future. This might involve establishing agreed-upon norms for behavior toward an offending group, reforming a justice system to incorporate fair laws, or establishing just social structures.

13. M. S. Rye, K. I. Pargament, M. A. Ali, G. L. Beck, E. N. Dorff, C. Hallisey, V. Narayanan, and J. G. Williams, "Religious Perspectives on Forgiveness," in *Forgiveness,* ed. McCullough, Pargament, and Thoresen, 17–40.
14. Roger Fisher and William Ury, *Getting to Yes: Negotiating Agreement Without Giving In* (New York: Penguin Books, 1981).

Working for social justice can prevent future transgressions, or at least make them less likely—rendering future experiences of unforgiveness less likely. Moreover, working for social justice can reduce one's current feelings of unforgiveness because one diverts the energy aimed at the negative emotions of unforgiveness into a sublimated positive energy for social good.

At the societal level, I have identified at least a dozen ways to reduce unforgiveness. Each might successfully reduce unforgiveness. None directly involves forgiveness.

Reducing Unforgiveness at the Intrapersonal Level

Six subclasses of ways people reduce unforgiveness can occur at the intrapersonal level. I will spend a little time on each of the ways.

The first intrapersonal method of reducing unforgiveness is psychological reduction of unforgiveness. People might *deny* their unforgiveness; they therefore reduce unforgiveness by blocking it from consciousness. They might *project* their unforgiveness onto another person ("I'm not unforgiving. She is.") and thereby reduce their own unforgiveness. Or they might try to *undo* their unforgiveness and judgmental motivations by doing something nice for the oppressor. (Undoing, of course, is concurrently both a societal and an intrapersonal way to reduce forgiveness.) In each of those ways, unforgiveness is reduced by unconscious motivational processes.

Second, people can simply forget offenses or hurts. The passing of time erodes memories. Because most current events are more important to people than are most past events, many past transgressions will simply be forgotten, especially if the transgressions were relatively minor, the consequences were not enduring, or the transgressor does not have to be faced regularly. On the other hand, very important transgressions with lasting consequences are often not only not forgotten but are magnified in importance as a person elaborates on the meaning of those events.

Third, people can reduce their unforgiveness by telling a different story about the transgression. That is, people can *reframe* the nature of the event, the motives of the perpetrators, or the consequences of the events in such a way that the transgression does not seem as important, thereby reducing unforgiveness. A victim might *justify* a perpetrator's acts and believe the perpetrator was correct in his or her acts, which reduces unforgiveness of the perpetrator. Or a victim might *excuse* the perpetrator's acts. A victim thus comes to believe that there were good reasons for the perpetrator's behavior and consequently feels less unforgiveness.

Fourth, people can reduce their unforgiveness by telling a different story about the nature of people. They might do so by activating a belief in the fundamental interconnectedness of humans. This might occur within an Eastern religious system in which existence is seen as *Maya* and all of existence is united.[15] Or this might be seen within Christian religion as a sense of common personhood of humans. Or this might be seen within African philosophical traditions as a sense of *Mbutu,* which describes a fundamental unity of people in community.

Fifth, people can reduce unforgiveness by *forbearing* or accepting the hurt. The legal equivalent to this is to grant a pardon. Unforgiveness will be reduced, but not because forgiveness has taken place. Rather, unforgiveness is reduced because the victim simply decides to turn loose of the demands of the law or the demands for justice and fairness.

Finally, forgiving is a way of reducing unforgiveness. With forgiveness, there is more to the story than simply reducing unforgiveness. New emotions of love, compassion, empathy, humility, and gratitude are *also* experienced toward the perpetrator, replacing hot emotions of anger and fear or contaminating cold emotions of unforgiveness.

INTERRELATIONSHIPS AMONG THE METHODS OF REDUCING UNFORGIVENESS

I have presented many ways that people reduce unforgiveness. I have carefully distinguished them from forgiving. However, we should recall what I mentioned earlier—these methods are not completely separate from forgiving. When people see justice done, resolve conflicts, work for social justice, engage in psychological means of self-protection, forget old events,

15. Rye et al., "Religious Perspectives on Forgiveness," 17–40.

tell a different story about the transgression or about the nature of people, or let go of old hurts, they cannot only reduce their negative feelings but can simultaneously experience more positive emotions toward the transgressor. This is an implication of Damasio's "as-if" emotions.[16] Therefore, some forgiveness will almost always happen as unforgiveness is reduced, regardless of a person's method of reducing unforgiveness. Still, it is useful to make a distinction between (1) the reduction of unforgiveness that occurs through various means and is not aimed at forgiving (although some forgiveness might creep in) and (2) forgiveness that is aimed at, focused on, and intentionally sought, which also incidentally reduces unforgiveness.

RESEARCH ON PROMOTING FORGIVENESS AND RECONCILIATION

In our laboratory and clinic, we have developed a method of promoting forgiveness experiences in individuals who say they desire to forgive but have been unable to do so despite their best efforts. I call the method the "Pyramid Model to REACH Forgiveness."[17] REACH is an acrostic for the five steps in the model. The method rests on recalling a specific actual or symbolic hurt (R = Recall), helping people empathize (E) with those who hurt them. They then recall their own guilty harms of others that have been forgiven. They attempt to re-experience gratitude at their receipt of forgiveness. They might give an altruistic (A) gift of forgiveness. By stimulating understanding, empathy, guilt and gratitude, usually over six to nine hours of concentrated reflection, people can often forgive. If they experience the granting of forgiveness, they commit aloud (C) to forgive and develop ways to hold onto (H) their forgiveness in times of doubt.

We have produced reliable forgiveness with briefer groups. In a recent article involving several studies, we presented two dose-effect graphs, similar to dose-effect curves with drugs, that show how empathy-based inter-

16. Damasio, *The Feeling of What Happens.*
17. Everett L. Worthington Jr., "The Pyramid Model of Forgiveness: Some Interdisciplinary Speculations about Unforgiveness and the Promotion of Forgiveness," in *Dimensions of Forgiveness: Psychological Research and Theological Perspectives,* ed. E. L. Worthington Jr. (Philadelphia: Templeton Foundation Press, 1998), 107–37.

ventions in groups can lead to forgiveness.[18] The most recent graph includes research from three other labs as well as our six studies (see fig. 9.1). The correlation coefficient between amount of time people spent trying to forgive a transgressor and the amount of forgiveness was .73. We thus believe that concentrated time spent empathizing with a transgressor (a new, more positive emotion) will lead people to replace unforgiveness with forgiveness.

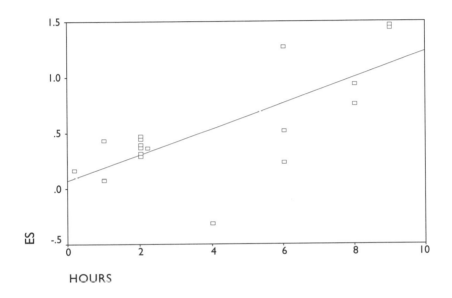

Figure 9.1. Dose-effect curve for group interventions to promote forgiveness. Hours of intervention are plotted against mean effect size (ES) (preintervention minus postintervention divided by mean standard deviation). Reprinted from Everett L. Worthington Jr., T. A. Kurusu, W. Collins, J. W. Berry, J. S. Ripley, and S. B. Baier, "Forgiving Usually Takes Time: A Lesson Learned by Studying Interventions to Promote Forgiveness," *Journal of Psychology and Theology* (2000).

18. Everett L. Worthington Jr., T. A. Kurusu, W. Collins, J. W. Berry, J. S. Ripley, and S. B. Baier, "Forgiving Usually Takes Time: A Lesson Learned by Studying Interventions to Promote Forgiveness," *Journal of Psychology and Theology* (2000).

THE STEP UP TO A HIGHER LEVEL
OF SOCIAL COMPLEXITY IS PERILOUS

When we moved to another level of social complexity—trying to use the Pyramid Model to REACH Forgiveness with couples—we failed dismally.[19] We learned quickly that a couple together in the room at the same time will talk about the transgression (and other transgressions) and will have two different perspectives.[20]

We had to embed the Pyramid Model to REACH Forgiveness as one part of a six-part model of reconciliation, which we called FREE (Forgiveness and Reconciliation through Experiencing Empathy).[21] As is obvious from its name, FREE is centered in promoting empathy between partners. Because the development of forgiveness was not in the control of a single person, though, proportionately more time was needed in coaching partners in how to interact. FREE taught six steps: (1) decide whether, when, and how to reconcile, (2) coach people in how to talk gently about transgressions, (3) teach people the Pyramid Model to REACH Forgiveness, (4) help people take observable steps to repair damage to the relationship, (5) help people not expect perfection from the partner and deal productively with their own and their partner's failures, and (6) encourage partners to build love through action.[22]

Our experience with couples suggests two lessons. First, what we learn at one level of application (the individual experience of forgiving) is not fully generalizable to a higher social level of organization (couples). In short, couples do not reduce to the sum of two individuals. (I am sure that this is not news to anyone when stated as an abstract principle, but it was not an obvious lesson to learn in our intervention research.) Second, promoting reconciliation must focus not on forgiveness but on how members can inter-

19. J. S. Ripley, "The Effects of Marital Social Values on Outcomes of Forgiveness: Couples Enrichment Psychoeducational Groups, or Communication Couples Enrichment Psychoeducational Groups," doctoral diss., Virginia Commonwealth University, 1998.
20. See Worthington and Wade, "Social Psychology of Unforgiveness and Forgiveness and Implications for Clinical Practice."
21. Worthington, "Pyramid Model of Forgiveness," 107–37; Worthington and Drinkard, "Promoting Reconciliation Through Psychoeducational and Therapeutic Interventions."
22. Worthington and Drinkard, "Promoting Reconciliation Through Psychoeducational and Therapeutic Interventions."

act in ways that promote peace, mutually reinforcing interactions, and therefore empathy. From the empathy, forgiveness can flow if people are helped and motivated to forgive (using interventions such as the Pyramid Model to REACH Forgiveness).

What I would love to do is to generalize lessons learned in our research to the societal level. The important implication of our research on individuals and couples, though, is that generalization of lessons about promoting forgiveness in individuals and couples, when applied at the societal level, might be expected to result in some surprises. If we examine crucial differences among individuals, couples, and societies, we might anticipate some of those surprises. With the perils of generalizing from our work with individuals and couples in mind, I want to offer six guidelines that might inform societal interventions to promote reconciliation and forgiveness.

GUIDELINES FOR PROMOTING RECONCILIATION AND FORGIVENESS IN SOCIETIES

Use Multiple Methods

First, there are hundreds, thousands, or perhaps millions of points of view in societies. Individuals (who have *one* point of view) can reduce or eliminate unforgiveness using any one of several methods (such as psychological defenses, justice, forbearance, restitution, social justice). In fact, people tend to develop favorites. One person might prefer forgiving; another, forbearing; still another, seeking revenge. Couples can work out *one* agreement to yield reconciliation.

However, societies must use multiple methods to help members reduce unforgiveness and to reconcile because different individuals and different groups of people will find different methods more palatable. It is impossible for everyone in a society to agree on anything. Therefore, social policymakers who wish to promote forgiveness and reconciliation must give people legitimate choices. Social policies should not put all of their eggs in a single basket. Societies that do not promote *many* ways of dealing with unforgiveness will leave a substantial minority of members unforgiving.

Tackle Issues with a Broad Strategy of Reconciliation

Every issue involving unforgiveness cannot be addressed separately. Ethnic and religious boundaries create different worldviews, priorities, and language systems. Those must be overcome if forgiveness and reconciliation are to occur. On the basis of my experience with marital interventions, let me suggest that couples who seek counseling have many unresolved issues and past hurts. Partners were raised in different families, often with different worldviews, priorities, and language systems. Their stable values *never* change much. Fundamental value differences are behind many hurtful incidents, transgressions, and offenses. Because differences are more fundamental than with isolated issues, compromises on separate issues rarely help. Instead, the wise counselor *uses* specific issues to teach strategies of (a) communicating and resolving conflict based on restoring love and unity, and (b) dealing with past hurts and offenses to repair damage and restore intimacy.

Let me offer a second guideline to social policymakers. Similar to marital counseling, a society cannot be pulled into an unending series of compromises on specific issues under the mistaken assumption that enough compromises will mean that peace will ensue. While some compromises are necessary, the focus must be on a broad strategy of reconciling. The South African experiment has shown that focusing society on a broad strategy of reconciliation, rather than trying to "fix" isolated issues, can work to some degree. Compromise occurs within the framework of a larger issue (reconciliation).

Employ Heroes and Stories to Shape History

History figures more prominently in societies than in marriages. Historical records of hurts and offenses between countries, religions, and ethnic groups can go back thousands of years. (Few couples can draw on such a legacy of harms and inequities to justify their unforgiveness—though I have heard Adam and Eve blamed by some determined couples.)

History involves a *story*. Stories tend to be about salient events, heroes, and martyrs. If societal policymakers recognize the power of the cultural story of history, they can help people tell different stories. Healing stories have heroes who courageously pursued reconciliation (like Nelson Mandela or Desmond Tutu), martyrs who died to bring people together (like Martin Luther King Jr.), or salient reconciliation events (such as a significant restitution by a German company that might have benefited from Jewish slave labor or reconciliation walks). Not only will positive stories help promote reconciliation, they can also lead to intrapersonal experiences of forgiveness (see Table 9.1 above).

Be Sensitive to the Serious Consequences of Advocating Forgiveness

Considerations of power, control of resources, and safety create more sweeping consequences at the societal level than at individual or couple levels. When a society is plagued by ethnic conflict, the deaths of thousands can rest on whether forgiveness can be promoted. The costs of, consequences of, and barriers to advocating societal forgiveness must be carefully weighed.[23] Any government that suggests that the disenfranchised or oppressed members of society simply forgive will be perceived as self-serving.

Use Mass Media to Focus on Goals

Marital counselors help both partners pursue common goals. Many conflicts can be moderated if partners are helped to pursue superordinate goals.[24] To motivate partners to adopt similar goals that are consistent with a broad strategy of reconciliation, communication from the counselor is necessary.

The same is true in helping members of societies adopt common goals. However, we obviously cannot get every person in a country into a counselor's office at the same time, as one can with a couple. Thus communication cannot be as direct or as focused in a society as in couples counseling.

23. Exline and Baumeister, "Expressing Forgiveness and Repentance," 133–55; and Mullet and Girard, "Developmental and Cognitive Points of View on Forgiveness," 111–32.
24. M. Sherif, *In Common Predicament: Social Psychology of Intergroup Conflict and Cooperation* (Boston: Houghton-Mifflin, 1966).

Nor should it be. Because people are different, many communicative efforts are needed. Substantially varied mass media initiatives are needed to reach multiple sectors of society.

Engage Media Cooperation
to Moderate the "Hothead Factor"

The "hothead factor" is at work in societies. No matter what a government does to promote reconciliation, there will always be hotheads who aim to keep people apart by violent and hateful acts. Of course, there are also cooler heads and passionate promoters of peace.

What will national media pay the most attention to? Usually the negative. People pay more attention to the negative than the positive because it is to the benefit of their survival to do so.[25] J. M. Gottman, a marital researcher, and developmental psychologists B. Hart and T. R. Risley have shown that five or six times the number of positive events are needed to compensate for a single negative event.[26] In troubled relationships, according to H. Markman, a divorce-prevention psychologist, the ratio must be 10 to 1 or higher to reverse the tide.[27]

In societies a large amount of attention to the positive is needed to overcome the negative acts making up the hothead factor. Witness the media attention to the Truth and Reconciliation Commission (TRC) in South Africa or the peace negotiations in Northern Ireland. Positive media attention helped promote peace, forgiveness, and reconciliation among many whom might not have ever considered it. Therefore, social policymakers should work closely with media to present news and features on the positive aspects of reconciliation to balance the negative attention caused by the hothead factor.

25. R. F. Baumeister, E. Bratslavsky, and C. Finkenaur, "Bad Is Stronger than Good," manuscript, Case Western Reserve University, 2000.
26. J. M. Gottman, *The Marriage Clinic: A Scientifically Based Marital Therapy* (New York: W. W. Norton, 1999); Gottman, J. Coan, S. Carrere, and C. Swanson, "Predicting Marital Happiness and Stability from Newlywed Interactions," *Journal of Marriage and the Family* 60 (1998): 5–22; B. Hart and T. R. Risley, *Meaningful Differences: In the Everyday Experience of Young American Children* (Baltimore: Paul Brookes Publishing, 1995).
27. H. Markman, S. Stanley, and S. L. Blumberg, *Fighting for Your Marriage: Positive Steps for Preventing Divorce and Preserving a Lasting Love* (San Francisco: Jossey-Bass, 1994).

OBJECTIVES OF SOCIETAL INTERVENTIONS

Social policymakers must target interventions to promote forgiveness and reconciliation at the societal level. Let us consider the general objectives of interventions.

I will grossly classify people within a society into those who contribute to reconciliation (typically a minority), those who contribute to violence, destructiveness, and social disintegration (also typically a minority), and those who consistently contribute to neither. The number and importance of contributions people make tend to increase as they age, until they are beyond retirement age or physical limitations set in. At that point, contributions decline. This is depicted in figure 9.2, which plots contribution versus age.

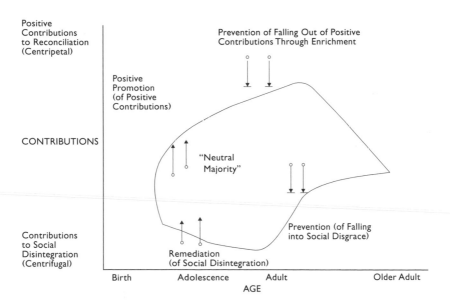

Figure 9.2. Hypothetical graph of contributions toward reconciliation or social disintegration versus age.

The majority of people are concentrated inside of the elliptical area; these constitute the "neutral majority," those contributing little either for or against reconciliation. Above the ellipse are the members of society who are contributing to reconciliation. Their effect is centripetal. Below the ellipse are the members of society who are working (wittingly or not) toward the disintegration of society. Their effect is centrifugal.

The shape is only roughly elliptical because most contributions to reconciliation in society occur in adults in their middle years and beyond. On the other hand, most contributions toward social disintegration (e.g., crime) occur when people are adolescents and young adults.

From a social-policy perspective, social policymakers should aim social interventions to promote forgiveness and reconciliation at four targets. (1) How can policymakers and social architects shore up the promoters of reconciliation and prevent them from falling into the "neutral majority"? These are called prevention through enrichment interventions. (2) How can policymakers support the "neutral majority" and prevent them from becoming a centrifugal force in society? These are called prevention interventions. (3) How can policymakers promote reconciliation among the "neutral majority," stimulating them to centripetal acts? These are called positive promotion interventions. (4) How can policymakers remediate and convert the violent minority, turning more of them into members of the "neutral majority"? These are called remediation interventions.

Efforts at each of the four tasks are necessarily different according to the age group of the target: children, adolescents, young adults, middle adults, older adults, and aged adults. To overgeneralize, remediation might be concentrated mostly at adolescents and young adults, whose actions are often the most centrifugal. The same ages are also good targets for positive promotion. Middle, older, and aged adults are high priority for prevention-through-enrichment and prevention interventions.

SUMMARY

I have approached the arena of social policy as an "outsider," whose specialty is promoting forgiveness in individuals and forgiveness and reconciliation in couples. While our body of knowledge about what forgiveness and reconciliation are and how to promote them is growing, it can be generalized only tentatively to societal interventions. My main points are few.

+ There are many ways to reduce unforgiveness. Promoting forgiveness, through stimulating empathy for the transgressor, is only one of those ways. Forgiveness is nonetheless important because it builds goodwill (in addition to reducing ill will), whereas reducing unforgiveness concentrates primarily on reducing ill will.

+ Societies require use of multiple interventions to reduce unforgiveness because of the number of people involved, each of whom might deal with unforgiveness in different ways.

+ Reconciliation is better promoted if social policymakers adopt a strategy of promoting reconciliation and use mass media to promote widespread adoption of that strategy. The focus on reconciliation as the principal target is essential; forgiveness will emerge more readily if reconciliation is achieved.

+ Social policy needs to be aimed at (1) preventing violence and conflict, (2) maintaining efforts at reconciliation, (3) promoting new involvement in reconciliation, and (4) remediating problems in social disintegration.

+ Social interventions need to be age-specific, broad-based, and clear in their objectives.

If societies think broadly, using some of the guidelines I have suggested, a multiple layered war might be waged against the centrifugal forces that threaten to disintegrate society. Policymakers can set priorities for target issues (such as preventing violence in the schools, promoting ethnic reconciliation within businesses), ages (youth, the elderly), and settings. Social scientists can help understand the issues that contribute to social disintegration. Intervention specialists can then design interventions to promote reconciliation and prevent further disintegration. Scientists can provide evidence of the effectiveness (or lack of effectiveness) of social interventions. Policy analysts can aggregate data and feed back the digested data to policymakers.

The twentieth century was an "age of anxiety" ushered in by the nuclear bomb. Our technology of mass destruction became widely available throughout the world, creating even more anxiety about the future. With the spread throughout the world of free-market enterprise, many of the anxieties have (rightly or wrongly) abated. Despite the perseverance of local tensions, ethnic cleansing, and local political coups, many signs of reconciliation have been increasingly evident in the last decade. Today, I believe we are—at the beginning of the new century—on the threshold of an age of reconciliation.

CHAPTER 10

Five Qualities of Practice in Support of Reconciliation Processes

John Paul Lederach

INTRODUCTION

IN MY EARLY COLLEGE DAYS in the 1970s I searched high and low for a degree program that would provide me preparation and a B.A. degree in conflict and peace studies. At the time those programs could be counted on one hand and probably needed only three fingers. Today they abound. Most focus on conflict resolution, many with an emphasis on the practical skills of mediation. On the far cutting edge of those programs courses are now offered in reconciliation. As a discipline, conflict resolution is still considered in its infancy, soft on the edges, and according to the more accepted fields of academic endeavor still struggling to find the legs of legitimacy. If we were to follow this metaphor, the study, practice, and theory of reconciliation are barely in the stage of conception.

It is a paradox of sorts that human concern for and interest in reconciliation is as old as the hills and at the same in a preinfancy stage. I have been a student, practitioner, researcher, and teacher in the fields of conflict transformation and peacebuilding for twenty-five years. And I come from a faith tradition, the Mennonites, widely known as one of the historic peace churches. So I might be expected to argue that we are further along in our understanding of reconciliation than mainstream academia would wish to acknowledge. I will not. My experiences suggest that while our understandings are rich and varied, they are minuscule compared to the complexities posed by the search for sustainable and authentic reconciliation between people. Several important reasons stand out.

First, much of what we know of reconciliation has been conceptualized from within particular religious frameworks. Whether those criteria and approaches can be generalized into broader social and political processes remains an intriguing, hotly debated question.

Second, much of what has been proposed as the approach for enhancing and building reconciliation emerges first and foremost as individual and interpersonal processes. Whether personal and interpersonal processes can be built, shaped, molded, and ritualized into programs relevant to large intergroup conflicts has yet to be minimally understood, much less harnessed toward predictable outcomes.

Third, in my estimation, unlike other areas of conflict resolution more narrowly defined, reconciliation processes do not lend themselves to reductionist techniques. It seems to me that too much of the current search into reconciliation appears to be oriented toward finding the Holy Grail of social technology that unleashes its power and therefore is overly dependent on technique. My experience suggests that such a technology is neither desirable nor dependable.

So I take a step back, away from the search for the Holy Grail, away from technique, and away from prescription. What I would like to suggest here is a preinfancy view that raises a simple question posed to my personal experience in working as a third party in peacebuilding initiatives: What qualities of process appear to have been pivotal in supporting the practice of reconciliation in settings of deep-rooted and violent contexts? *Qualities* of practice point us less in the direction of technique and more toward attitude and character. *Pivotal* suggests a core, a center around which other things may spin. *Practice* says this is likely to be a long, hard inductive road of discovery. With this in mind I would like to suggest five qualities of process and practice I feel provide support for the complex challenge of seeking authentic reconciliation.

RECONCILIATION
AS RELATIONSHIP-CENTRIC

In my estimation the starting point for understanding and supporting reconciliation processes is a reorientation toward the centrality of relationships. It is in the ebb and flow, the quality interdependence of relationships that we find the birthplace and home of reconciliation. This is quite different than a focus on "issues," the shaping of substantive agreements, or cognitive and rational analytic-based approaches to conflict resolution. In these latter approaches attention is placed on the external, often symptomatic expressions of how the relationship is negotiated. But they often remain just that, external and symptomatic. To enter reconciliation processes is to enter the domain of the internal world, the inner understandings, fears and hopes, perceptions and interpretations of the relationship itself.

Relationship, however, is an odd concept but one increasingly important to the theoretical evolution of science. The cutting edges of quantum and chaos theory, the views of systemic and ecosystemic understandings in biology, the sociological study of social capital or family systems theory in psychology all begin and end with relationship. Yet in each, relationship is the invisible, the assumed connection, that which lies between things. And it is the invisible connection that makes energy, movement, compounds, matter, and meaning.

When I suggest, therefore, that we take up a relationship-centric approach to reconciliation I am pointing us toward the centrality of the invisible. In more concrete terms, I am suggesting that we not use the lens and techniques of conflict resolution oriented toward the visible—issues, agreements, words, and representations of feelings and interests—as the goal and objective of our process but rather as the window into the process. From this lens, reconciliation looks through—at times goes through—what is visible and penetrates the deeper processes of perceptions, understandings, and interpretations of the purpose and meaning of a relationship, how it was constructed and will be reconstructed.

If reconciliation is indeed relationship-centric, then the defining quality of practice is the building of trust. In my experiences with processes of peacebuilding, where relational reconciliation became an important component, third parties were central, but not because they were professional and distant from the people involved. Rather consistently, the deepest experiences of reconciliation came when teams of people supported the process, people who as individuals were seen as close to one side or the other but who as a team themselves had built transparency and trust. It shifts the emphasis away from conceiving the mediator as an outside person, and reconceptualizing mediator as a quality of space created by people close to the conflict but who fill it with a greater level of trust because they are known. If we were to use a bridge metaphor, this approach would say, "You do not build a bridge starting in the middle. You start with a strong foundation on each shore, build toward the middle. When it is solid, others can walk across it."

I have seen this in numerous places. The work of the religious conciliators in Nicaragua, a team of East Coast indigenous and Managua-based leaders, is a good example. Mostly untold is the story of former paramilitary leaders who quietly set about the process of building direct relationships with their counterparts in the opposing community, but who then served as a transformative bridge in cross-community work, even in the brokering of ceasefires and the lifting of revenge killings. Trust is the window into relationship. But in settings of violence, trust is destroyed from all sides and is only rebuilt slowly, over time. It requires transparency, the testing of authenticity over time, and the commitment to stay with it. But most important, in deep-rooted conflicts, trust requires connection to context, a sense from those involved that their experience is truly understood and valued.

RECONCILIATION AS ACCOMPANIMENT

For some time I have found it useful to conceptualize reconciliation as a multifaceted relational journey, one fraught with paradoxes and vulnerability. While we often think of reconciliation as the coming together of people, that only captures a small piece of the process. If we think much more broadly in terms of relationships that have experienced division and separation, then the journey is cycles and deep paradoxes.

In workshops I often use the Old Testament story of Jacob and Esau to describe the journey and the deep questions about reconciliation. In the story a family is divided when one brother deceives the other. They separate in fear and rage. Nearly thirty years transpire before the younger, deceiving brother begins a difficult journey back toward the eldest. They eventually meet and embrace, yet in the end move down separate valleys.

As a guiding story, their journey includes and even requires *movement away*—from conflict and the enemy, the great sources of pain—a *turn back* toward this very same source of anxiety, and *encounters* along the way with oneself, with one's enemy, and with God.

In the retelling of the story I lift out what I consider to be some of the greatest and most perplexing questions posed to any process of reconciliation and to those of us who wish to support reconciliation. When and in what manner is it appropriate to raise and face the injustice? Is there space in reconciliation for moving away from conflict and the other? What makes possible the turn and how does one know it is authentic? How does one create genuine and deep encounters with self, other, and God? Does reconciliation mean we live happily together forever after?

The story suggests that reconciliation is both a place, as in destination, and a journey. It provides a horizon, within sight yet beyond reach. To take up such a journey, by any rational assessment, is ludicrous. But most important, it is a journey that can only be taken up by those involved. We cannot do it for them. We cannot obligate them to do it. I tell my students we get "should-ed" a lot in life. In reconciliation "shoulds" (as in "you should do this or that") and authenticity are contradictory and mutually exclusive social energies. Yet at the same time people invariably seek and feel the need for the presence of support in the journey.

In the biblical account Jacob's journey back toward his brother and enemy, Esau, begins with a voice in the night that says, "Return to your land. I will be with you." While we may debate the source of such voices, I actually find the second phrase to be the most revealing, for it suggests a quality of practice. From my lenses of faith this was the voice of God. And unlike other stories in the Scripture God does not say, "Go, I will prepare the way for you." The phrase used in the launching of Jacob's turn and return to his brother was, "I will be with you." This is the paradoxical challenge of accompaniment as a quality of practice. Accompaniment, to spin out the concept, is built on two Latin words that would translate as "with" (*com*) and "bread" (*pan*). Interestingly, this is a table and eating metaphor. We share bread. We share a common table.

The emphasis of accompaniment is placed on presence, shared common humanity, and a sense of "along-sideness." But it is decidedly not leadership, taking over, or running protection, or is it pushing and forcing. In this story of reconciliation even God chooses accompaniment over mandates, protection, or leadership. In my estimation the greatest quality of practice and contribution of third parties to processes of reconciliation is not their communication or negotiation skill base, or their capacity for process design. It is their discipline and authenticity of commitment to be alongside the people in their journey, whether they are moving away from or toward encounters with self, other, and God.

RECONCILIATION AND HUMILITY

I believe humility and reconciliation are connected. In my view, humility is principally about understanding one's place and one's humanity. Among the greatest of all mandates common to the three Abrahamic religious traditions was the simple phrase of the prophet: Do justice, love mercy, and walk humbly with your God. We are first struck by the extraordinary paradox that an interpersonal and social space could be created where justice and mercy are pursued together. This, as I will explore below, creates a quality of space we can truly refer to as *reconciliation*. However, the greater challenge of the Prophet is to create such a space with humility, not pride or presumption.

There are probably lots of ways to understand humility. From the lenses of conflict transformation and peacebuilding experience I have approached my growing understanding of the centrality of humility in reference to Truth and Truth-seeking.

The opposite of humility is arrogance. Arrogance generally characterizes an attitude of superiority. But it is not superiority that is most frightening. Rather, it is the condition of believing that full knowledge and Truth have been achieved, owned and managed. Arrogance is displayed when I act as if and, more important, actually believe I have nothing more to learn.

Over the years of working across many different international settings I have been struck with how easily our field of conflict resolution, our believing that we have good things to share, has been perceived as arrogant in so many places. We move into exceedingly complex situations with short-term initiatives and connections to small pieces of the overall puzzle. Yet we often act as if our contribution will provide an answer to the complexity of the challenge of the needed change processes. This may be doubly true of reconciliation initiatives, where the purpose is to go well beyond the short-term solution to a particular problem.

Humility, as a quality of practice in support of reconciliation, would suggest something quite different. First, humility is constantly bound up with Truth. It is Truth-seeking as a continuous, life-long adventure and Truth-engagement as a relational discipline requiring self-examination and the building of safe space for others to do the same. In practice, particularly in settings of violent divisions, humility would start with a context focus seeking to gauge and envision the setting from within. It wants to know how people in a given setting understand and create meaning, and view their needs, cultural resources, and challenges. Rather than assuming a prede-termined answer, humility would suggest a need to learn and accompany the building of process that is both rooted and responsive to the context and people.

If humility as a practice suggests anything to our current efforts at under-standing reconciliation processes it would be in the form of a caution. The complexity of authentic reconciliation emerges from the capacity of people to build an appropriate process, created and owned by them, rather than the rote application of preconceived processes. Humility requires the sharing of one's self and ideas, but not the imposition of them. It requires the engage-ment with and understanding of another's journey without being caught in its swirl. But most of all, humility suggests a lifelong commitment to learn-ing and an ever-regenerated spirit of creativity.

RECONCILIATION:
RESTORING THE FABRIC OF COMMUNITY

Reconciliation is typically talked about and understood as a highly personal and interpersonal process. From experience my belief is increasingly pushed toward the idea that healing of torn relationships can only be fully comprehended in the context of community processes, though the root of the challenge posed for us today is perhaps better formulated as a dilemma: How do we engage in processes of healing that are simultaneously relevant and practical for individuals and communities? Communities, whether local or seen in broader national terms, are the contexts in which divisions and violence are played out in contemporary conflict. The healing therefore requires processes at both levels. The challenge lies in the fact that not all individuals, or even significant portions of the broader community, are at the same pace along the journey, or, as may well be the case in many places, even on the same journey. However, in both instances, interpersonal and community, the core of creating a healing social space requires engagement with the themes mentioned above: Truth, justice, and mercy.

"Truth and mercy have met together, Justice and Peace have kissed," the Psalmist once wrote. I have often written and even developed whole training exercises around this verse and the social energies of the voices the Psalmist incarnated. Sister Truth, in the context of conflict, is about remembering, what to remember and how to remember. Sister Truth casts her eyes toward the past. Brother Justice is about what can be done now to rebalance a broken relationship. Brother Justice asks what can make the wrong right and what can restore the balance in the relationship that has been damaged. Brother Justice cast his eyes toward the present. Brother Mercy and Sister Peace ask how will we coexist, how will we start anew, how can we rebuild with each other? They cast their eyes toward the future.

If it seems odd that I make these concepts into people, it should not. For they are voices, energies that move in settings of conflict and pain. They are the voices sought by individuals and groups. People in civil society organize around the energy. Victim support groups seek accountability and redress for the damage done. Families of political prisoners push for the reintegration of their sons and daughters. Peasant groups mobilize around museums and monuments to remember where their families were killed and lost. They are also the voices governments and national reconciliation programs seek to invoke and make present across the whole of an affected population. Concerned for their peoples in the aftermath of war, political initiatives and programs attempt to give this family flesh: Truth commissions, amnesty programs, war crime tribunals, national reconciliation programs, and the list goes on.

On my first visit to Belfast, Northern Ireland, I remember seeing a mural in a staunch Republican area that quoted the Irish nationalist Padric Pearse: "The fools, the fools, they have left our Fenian dead. While Ireland holds these graves, Ireland unfree shall never be at peace." And there, I remember thinking, is the paradox of reconciliation: How and in what way will the graves and the grandchildren meet? The challenge of reconciliation is not how to create the place where one can "forgive and forget." It is about the far more challenging adventure into the space where individuals and whole communities can remember and change.

The quality of practice that emerges from such a view is the capacity to see complexity, multiple energies as interconnected in a greater whole but in need of hands that keep them connected. Too often, as we work toward reconciliation, we find ourselves drawn into the energy of a given voice because each speaks with integrity. What is more difficult is to find the way to create a process and quality of space that gives voice to each energy while at the same time keeping them in connection with each other. For truth without mercy is blinding and raw; mercy without truth is a coverup and superficial. Justice without peace falls easily into cycles of bitterness and revenge; peace without justice is short-lived and benefits only the privileged or the victors. The quality of practice to which I refer is therefore best understood in a context of community that provides space for the voices, but not one at the expense of the other.

RECONCILIATION AS
A WANDERING IN A DESERT

Finally, an intriguing though disconcerting biblical metaphor for reconciliation: the desert. At numerous times in the biblical text the desert became the place of wandering and waiting, the geography of human experience located between the rush for liberation and the arrival at the promised land. The desert is referred to as the place for solace, sweat, and prayer, accompanied almost always with an internal battle to find one's way. In the greatest of these metaphors the wandering lasted at least a generation, across decades. I firmly believe such a metaphor is useful for understanding reconciliation and our timeframe for thinking about change processes in deeprooted conflict.

A wandering in the desert as a three-decade metaphor pushes us to reconsider our timeframes seriously in relationship to the healing process. In recent years we have been prone to approach reconciliation as a political exigency with a programmatic emphasis in mind, as if by some miracle a formula could be hatched by which we would harness the social energy necessary to move us expeditiously to, and through, a process of relational healing. Wandering would suggest there is no such formula. In fact, in my experience, the actual notion of wandering for the equivalent of a generation may be more literal than metaphoric if we consider the nature of contexts of protracted conflict. At a minimum, it strikes me that we have significantly misunderstood the kind of process necessary, particularly in settings where violent conflict has raged for decades if not generations. For some years I have been saying that I think it takes about as long to get out of a conflict as it took to get into it. I would not apply the formula with mathematical rigidity, but I would apply it metaphorically.

As a quality of practice wandering in the desert points us toward two ideas. First, we should take seriously the idea that there is a need for personal and community preparation, which can often take a great deal of time under less-than-ideal conditions, and which needs the space to wander across tough terrain. Second, we need to develop longer-term lenses and commitments, both programmatically and institutionally on the part of those who wish to accompany and support reconciliation. I believe we should move toward thinking in decades rather than months or a few years. We do a disservice to affected populations and, perhaps more important, to their future generations if we allow reconciliation programs to be driven by demands to move on quickly at the expense of authentic process.

CONCLUSION

If I were to highlight the most important elements of these fledging qualities of practice I would likely say the following. Focus on people and their experience. Seek a genuine and committed relationship rather than results. Be willing to set aside your notion of what works for you in order to come along side the struggle of those in the setting. Be leery of quick fixes. Respect complexity but do not be paralyzed by it. Think comprehensively about the voices you hear that seem contradictory, both within a person, between people, and across a whole community, as broad energies that make up a family. No matter how small, create spaces of connection between them. Never assume you know better or more than those you are with who are struggling with the process. You don't. Do not fear the feeling of being lost. It is part and parcel of creating safe space. Give it time. Authentic reconciliation will never be packaged and delivered at drive-through windows.

CHAPTER 11

Healing, Reconciliation, and Forgiving after Genocide and Other Collective Violence

Ervin Staub and Laurie Anne Pearlman

T̲HIS CHAPTER WILL EXPLORE the impact of collective violence on victims and, to some degree, on perpetrators as well. It will consider the role of healing, forgiveness, and reconciliation in building a better future in societies in which such violence had taken place. As a primary example, the chapter will focus on Rwanda, where the authors have been conducting a project on healing, forgiveness, and reconciliation.

Healing, reconciliation, and forgiveness are deeply interrelated. Healing and reconciliation help break cycles of violence and enhance the capacity of traumatized people for psychological well-being. Forgiving is essential for reconciliation to take place and both arise from and contribute to healing.

OVERVIEW: THE NEED TO HEAL, FORGIVE, AND RECONCILE

Victimization of one group by another that leads to great suffering by a group has intense and long-lasting impact. Members of the victim group feel diminished, vulnerable. They see the world as a dangerous place.[1] They

---

1. L. I. McCann and L. A. Pearlman, *Psychological Trauma and the Adult Survivor: Theory,*

tend to see other people, especially outside groups and their members, as hostile. Their capacity to live life well, to be happy, is diminished. When the group is in conflict with another group, when it is threatened, its members are less able to see the other's point of view, to consider the other's needs. The group is more likely to strike out, in the belief that it is defending itself. However, it may actually become a perpetrator of violence against others.[2] Alternatively, depending on the group's culture and circumstances, the group's capacity to stand up for its interests and rights may be impaired.

Healing is essential both to improve the quality of life of the group's members and to make it less likely that the group becomes a perpetrator of violence. Because of the numbers of people involved, and because the injury happened to the group as a whole, it is important for healing to take place at the group level, in the community of others. A community for healing may consist of a small number of people from the group, the whole group, or both members of the group and people from outside the group. Traumatized people require at least a rudimentary feeling of security for healing to begin. When there is continued threat from the other, depending on circumstances, healing may be difficult or even impossible.

When one group has victimized another, or when there has been mutual victimization by two groups, if the groups continue to live near each other, reconciliation is essential both to stop a potentially continuing cycle of violence and to facilitate healing. As reconciliation begins, it increases security and makes healing more possible. As healing progresses, reconciliation becomes more possible. This is a cycle in which progress in one realm fosters progress in the other.

Reconciliation is more than the coexistence of formerly hostile groups living near each other. It is more even than formerly hostile groups interacting and working together, although working together for shared goals is one important avenue to overcoming hostility and negative views of the

---

Therapy, and Transformation (New York: Brunner/Mazel, 1990); and L. A. Pearlman and K. W. Saakvitne, *Trauma and the Therapist: Countertransference and Vicarious Traumatization in Psychotherapy with Incest Survivors* (New York: W. W. Norton, 1995); J. L. Krupnick and M. J. Horowitz, "Stress Response Syndromes: Recurrent Themes," *Archives of General Psychiatry* 38 (1981): 428–35.

2. E. Staub, "Basic Human Needs and Their Role in Altruism and Aggression," manuscript, 1998, Department of Psychology, University of Massachusetts, Amherst.

other and moving toward reconciliation.[3] Reconciliation means coming to accept one another and developing mutual trust. This requires forgiving. Reconciliation requires that victims and perpetrators come to accept the past and not see it so much as defining the future as simply a continuation of the past, that they come to see the humanity of one another, accept each other, and see the possibility of a constructive relationship.

Forgiving is difficult. The very idea of it can be offensive after horrible events like the Holocaust, the genocide in Rwanda, or the genocidal violence in Tibet. Even to people outside the victim group, the idea that survivors should forgive following genocide is an affront, an anathema. It is inconceivable to them and incomprehensible how victims or anyone else would or should forgive the perpetrators. It is even difficult for many survivors to consider forgiving those members of the perpetrator group who have not personally participated in violence, either because they belong to the perpetrator group or because they were passive bystanders. Nonetheless, forgiving is necessary and desirable. It paves the way for reconciliation and furthers healing, thereby making a better future possible. And when groups live together without reconciliation following group violence, as in Bosnia and Rwanda, feelings of insecurity and the danger of violence are ever present. In addition, research with individuals has shown that in some situations forgiving benefits those who were harmed. It improves the psychological well-being of victims. It lifts the burden of anger and the desire for revenge. Conversely, people who do not forgive their transgressors have more psychological difficulties. When people forgive, a psychological and spiritual burden may be lifted from them.[4]

3. G. W. Allport, *The Nature of Prejudice* (Reading, Mass.: Addison-Wesley, 1954); T. F. Pettigrew, "Generalized Intergroup Contact Effects on Prejudice," *Personality and Social Psychology Bulletin* 23, no. 2 (1997): 173–85; and E. Staub, "The Origins and Prevention of Genocide, Mass Killing, and Other Collective Violence," in *Peace and Conflict: Journal of Peace Psychology* 5 (1999); and E. Staub, *A Brighter Future: Raising Caring and Nonviolent Children* (forthcoming).
4. R. H. Al-Mabuk, R. D. Enright, and P. A. Cardis, "Forgiveness Education with Parentally Love-Deprived Late Adolescents," *Journal of Moral Education* 24 (1995): 427–44; S. R. Freedman and R. D. Enright, "Forgiveness as an Intervention Goal with Incest Survivors," *Journal of Consulting and Clinical Psychology* 64 (1996): 983–92; M. J. Subkoviak, R. D. Enright, C. Wu, E. A. Gassin, S. Freedman, L. M. Olson, and I. Sarinopoulos, "Measuring Interpersonal Forgiveness in Late Adolescence and Middle Adulthood," *Journal of Adolescence* 18 (1995): 641–55; M. E. McCullough and E. L. Worthington, "Promoting Forgiveness: A Comparison of Two Brief Psychoeducational Group Interventions with a 'Waiting

Healing, reconciliation, and forgiving are hindered by certain conditions and facilitated by others. As we have noted, survivors are likely to feel greatly diminished as persons and as members of their group, both in general and specifically in relation to the perpetrator group. Genuine forgiveness in this state may not be possible. "Forgiving" perpetrators in this state may be more psychological and spiritual capitulation to a powerful other than real forgiveness. The perpetrator group, even if it has no more genuine power, will represent great power in the psychological experience of the survivors. Continued threat, whether real or mainly in the mind of the survivors, adds to the difficulty of healing, forgiving, and reconciliation. It is for these reasons that both some degree of real security and the beginnings of healing are important starting points.

For reconciliation to occur, perpetrators also must heal. Often there has been mutual violence between groups, so that both are victims and both are perpetrators. Even when the distinction between perpetrator and victim is clear, a group sometimes becomes the perpetrator of violence because it had previously been victimized or suffered greatly for other reasons. Even when this is not the case, perpetrators are wounded because of their violent, often horrible actions. Perpetrators must heal from the wounds they have inflicted on themselves, as they harmed others.[5] Healing can open perpetrators to face their deeds, to engage with their victims, and to enter into a process that leads to reconciliation. Members of the perpetrator group who have themselves not engaged in violence also need to heal from the impact of their own group's actions.

The common tendency for perpetrators is to continue to justify their past actions, as they tend to do while they are perpetrating them, by devaluing and dehumanizing the victims. They make their former victims into a

---

List' Control," *Counseling and Values* 40 (1995): 55–69; D. F. Greenwald and D. W. Harder, "Sustaining Fantasies and Psychopathology in a Normal Sample," *Journal of Clinical Psychology* 50, no. 5 (1994): 707–10; M. L. Zelin, S. B. Bernstein, C. Heijn, R. M. Jampel, P. G. Myerson, G. Adler, D. H. Buie Jr., and A. M. Rizzuto, "The Sustaining Fantasy Questionnaire: Measurement of Sustaining Functions of Fantasies in Psychiatric Inpatients," *Journal of Personality Assessment* 47 (1983): 427–39; J. M. Templeton, *Worldwide Laws of Life: 200 Eternal Spiritual Principles* (Philadelphia: Templeton Foundation Press, 1997).

5. E. Staub and L. A. Pearlman, "Healing, Forgiveness, and Reconciliation in Rwanda," grant proposal to the John Templeton Foundation, 1998; and Staub, "Origins and Prevention of Genocide, Mass Killing, and Other Collective Violence."

dangerous enemy bent on their own destruction, an enemy of higher values and ideals, the enemy of a vision of a better life.[6] Perpetrators can thus protect themselves from facing what they have done by blaming their victims. In this and other ways they surround themselves with a protective shell. As they begin to face their deeds, perpetrators can also begin to forgive themselves.[7] Paradoxically they may also have to "forgive" the survivors, who are living testament to their own or their group's terrible actions.

Survivors of genocide endure extreme harm and tremendous losses, including the murder of loved ones and others in the group in which survivors' identity is rooted and the attempt to eliminate their entire culture and community. For these survivors, healing, forgiving, and reconciliation seem to present an even greater psychological-spiritual demand than for survivors of other forms of victimization. Most people identify with their group, and their own identity is based to an important extent on their membership in their group.[8] Thus even people who have themselves not been harmed, or were not even present, are likely to be greatly affected. And those who suffered direct personal losses are likely to be even more affected.

GENOCIDE IN RWANDA

We will consider the case of Rwanda, where we are conducting a project on healing, forgiveness, and reconciliation. Much of what we write below seems relevant to other instances of genocide and mass killing, while some is specific to or takes special forms in Rwanda. As we will note, the material is partly from scholarly sources, partly from interviews with individuals and personal stories people told in the course of a two-week workshop that we conducted in Rwanda in September 1999.[9]

6. Staub, "Origins and Prevention of Genocide, Mass Killing, and Other Collective Violence."
7. Templeton, *Worldwide Laws of Life.*
8. H. Tajfel, "Social Categorization, Social Identity, and Social Comparison," in *Differentiation Between Social Groups,* ed. H. Tajfel (London: Academic Press, 1978), 61–76; J. C. Turner, *Rediscovering the Social Groups: A Self-Categorization Theory* (New York: Basic Blackwell, 1987); and D. Bar-Tal and E. Staub, "Introduction: The Nature of Patriotism," in *Patriotism in the Lives of Individuals and Groups,* ed. D. Bar-Tal and E. Staub (Chicago: Nelson-Hall Publishers, 1997).
9. Staub and Pearlman, "Healing, Forgiveness, and Reconciliation in Rwanda"; E. Staub, *The*

A Brief History

Rwanda was under the colonial rule of Belgium in the first part of the twentieth century. The Tutsis, who are the minority (in 1994 they were about 14% of the population of 8 million people, with Hutus about 85%), were dominant until 1959. At that point, about 50,000 of them were killed in a Hutu revolution. When the country become independent in 1962, the Hutus took power. There were large-scale massacres of Tutsis in the 1960s and '70s. Discrimination and occasional, smaller-scale killings of Tutsis continued into the 1990s.[10]

In 1990 a Tutsi group, the Rwanda Patriotic Front (RPF), invaded the country. They were stopped, with help from the French military, but fighting renewed later, partly in response to massacres of Tutsi peasants. Groups of Hutus within the country also demanded more political freedom and rights and created political parties. In 1993 the Arusha peace accord was signed. It was to lead to the creation of a government including the RPF as well as other political elements. However, while he signed the accords, President Habariyama also brought intense anti-Tutsi elements into his government.

In April 1994 the president's plane was shot down, probably by extremist Hutus. The genocide began immediately. Altogether perhaps as many as 800,000 people were killed within three months. About 50,000 of these were Hutus. They were regarded as enemies because they were politically moderate, or they came from a certain region of the country, or for other reasons. Violence usually evolves and intensifies—as did the violence against Tutsis over several decades—and in the end some Hutus were also killed by individual perpetrators for personal reasons.[11] The genocide was

Roots of Evil: The Origins of Genocide and Other Group Violence (New York: Cambridge University Press, 1989); E. Staub, L. A. Pearlman, and A. Hagengimana, "Manual for Facilitators of Healing Through Understanding and Connection Project," Project on Healing, Forgiveness and Reconciliation in Rwanda, supported by the John Templeton Foundation, manuscript in English and Kinyarwanda, Trauma Research, Education, and Training Institute, Inc., South Windsor, Conn., 1999.

10. G. Prunier, *The Rwanda Crisis: History of a Genocide* (New York: Columbia University Press, 1995); A. des Forges, *Leave None to Tell the Story: Genocide in Rwanda* (New York: Human Rights Watch, 1999); and N. S. Smith, "The Psychocultural Roots of Genocide," *American Psychologist* 53 (1998): 743–53.

11. Staub, *Roots of Evil*; Staub, "Origins and Prevention of Genocide, Mass Killing, and Other Collective Violence."

brought to a stop by the victory of the RPF over the government forces.

The genocide in Rwanda was unusual and especially gruesome in certain respects. First, a very large number of people were killed in a very short time. Second, a great deal of the killing was person to person, rather than impersonal. While guns and even grenades were used, machetes, which require close contact between perpetrator and victim, were often used. Third, while the military and paramilitary groups, the latter often made up of very young people, perpetrated much of the killing, substantial killing was also perpetrated by a segment of the population. People were killed by neighbors, and even relatives—a Tutsi married into a Hutu family, or children and adults in a family who were of mixed ethnic background.[12]

Survivors' Experiences in Rwanda: The Difficulty in Forgiving

The Tutsis we talked to in Rwanda had very varied experiences during the genocide, but all had relatives killed and were themselves in great danger. The following stories come from interviews of survivors, especially people who were helped by Hutus, from experiences people described in a workshop we conducted (see below), and from extensive conversations with individuals.

The parents and four of six siblings of one Tutsi man were killed. He himself was lying on the ground with other men who were to be killed, but for reasons he does not know he was let go.

A pregnant woman saw her husband taken away and was told soon after that he was killed. Men came for her repeatedly, but one of her former household workers, a Hutu man, sent another Hutu man to her house to protect her. This latter man repeatedly endangered his own life to stop the killers from taking her away, facing off the men who came for her.

A young woman described how her neighbors came into her house and killed her father and brothers, but then protected her, her mother and sister from other killers. They even buried the men they killed.

One man described how his sister, a Tutsi, was given to the killers by her Hutu husband and his family. The man and his wife and children were

12. Prunier, *The Rwanda Crisis*; des Forges, *Leave None to Tell the Story*; and Smith, "Psycho-cultural Roots of Genocide," 743–53.

hidden by a series of people, for a time in the house of a bishop. When remaining there became dangerous, the bishop transported them in the trunk of his car to another place, going twice through a roadblock to do this as he transported different members of the family. In contrast, other high-level Church officials in various churches betrayed their Tutsi parishioners.[13] The Church was intertwined with the government and the ruling circle, and when the genocide began many high-level Church officials became its tools.

Another Tutsi woman's Hutu husband was involved in having her mother killed. Then the husband died. Her brother would not help her children, because they were the children of the man who was responsible for the killing of his mother.

In addition to carrying the past within them, most Tutsis have constant reminders of the genocide and of what has happened to them. One woman whose husband and children were killed adopted a child who survived by staying for a long time in a pile of corpses. This child has great difficulty exercising self-control. He behaves like a very young child and wants to be taken care of like an infant. Another woman whose family was killed has no home and no money to pay tuition so her children cannot go to school (there is no publicly funded education in Rwanda, as is true in many African countries).

While the Tutsis who lived in Rwanda had very painful experiences, others returned from exile. Some, like the mother of a taxi driver with whom we became acquainted in Kigali, returned just before the genocide, when the situation had eased and the plan was to include varied parties, including Tutsis, in the government. She and other such returnees were killed.

But even those who returned after the genocide stopped have had very difficult and painful experiences. They or their parents left Rwanda after earlier massacres. They returned to a devastated country. With memories of the violence their parents experienced, with a life spent as refugees and exiles in other countries, they also found it extremely difficult to forgive and reconcile. However, many of them realize that the only hope for creating a functioning society lies in reconciliation. They dominate the current government and the policy of this government is "unity and reconciliation."

13. des Forges, *Leave None to Tell the Story.*

When we ask about forgiveness, we have to ask, forgive whom? What of different kinds of perpetrators: the planners, those who killed, others who in some ways assisted in or benefited from the killings? What of members of the perpetrator group who have not perpetrated violence but are implicated by membership in the group and many of them by their passivity? What of the outside world, which often remains passive in the face of increasing violence against a victim group?[14] The disregard of information about impending violence and then of the actual genocide was especially shocking in the case of Rwanda.[15] What about the members of the perpetrator group who actually helped Tutsis? Does their behavior in some way offer an entry point toward forgiving the others?

Even under circumstances that promote forgiveness, it is likely to take place at a different pace and to different degrees in relation to different groups of people. A first reasonable goal may be for members of a victim group to move toward, and for others to facilitate, forgiving in relation to those who have not themselves planned or directly perpetrated violence.

The injuries in Rwanda are very great, and even people who were saved by others suspect those who saved them. The woman mentioned above who was saved by the Hutu stranger who came to her house and persisted in protecting her appeared to have difficulty accepting what he did as coming from benevolent motives. She fluctuated between seeing his action as arising from goodness and suspecting him of some unidentified self-interest. This is not surprising, considering that in the course of the genocide some Hutu men "saved" Tutsi women by taking them to their house and keeping them in sexual slavery.[16] When the man who saved her came to see her for the first time since the genocide, just before our interview in September 1999, she wondered what he might want and talked about being protected from him, if necessary, by the authorities.

---

14. Staub, *Roots of Evil*.
15. Gourevich, 1998; and Staub, "Origins and Prevention of Genocide, Mass Killing, and Other Collective Violence."
16. C. Bonnet, "Le Viol des Femmes Survivantes du Genocide du Rwanda," in *Rwanda: Un Genocide du XX Siècle*, ed. R. Verdier, E. Decaux, and J. Chretien (Paris: Editions L'Harmattan, 1995); United Nations, *Report of the Special Rapporteur on Violence Against Women, Its Causes and Consequences Addendum: Report on the Mission to Rwanda on the Issues of Violence Against Women in situations of Armed Conflict*, UN document number E/CN. 4/1998/54/ADD.1.

A family—a husband, wife, and their grown children—saved another person. The husband decided to help her and was in charge, directing the others. She was hidden in a pit the family dug in a cow pasture; they handed food to her through a small hole. After a while she was moved to another such pit, with the children in the family not knowing where she was, so that they would not accidentally give her away or put themselves in danger.

Afterwards the man who helped this woman was arrested, accused of complicity in the killing of some children. In an interview with one of the man's sons, he told us that the family was hiding these children in another hole, but the children climbed out, came to the house, were seen by the killers, and taken away. His father is wrongly accused. But paraphrasing what the woman said whom the family saved: "He saved my life, and even if I knew something I would not testify against him, but some people helped one person and killed others." While interviewing the woman who was saved by the Hutu man that her worker had sent to her house, the interviewer (ES) said that two people, not one, saved her. But she said (again, in a paraphrase): "The worker was there when my husband was killed. And later he refused to tell me where my husband's body was."

An "Intervention" to Help with
Healing, Reconciliation, and Forgiveness

Theory, research, and practical experience in working with traumatized individuals suggest that prolonged avoidance of memories of painful, traumatic experiences limits healing. Engaging with such experiences under safe conditions, when others support people, is important for healing to occur. In these and in other ways reconnecting with people helps to overcome the fear and distrust that victimization and other traumatic experiences create. Other people acknowledging the pain and suffering that a particular person and a victimized group has suffered, showing empathy and caring, both people in one's own group and those in the outside world, can be important for healing after collective violence.[17]

---

17. E. Foa and B. Rothbaum, *Treating the Trauma of Rape: Cognitive Behavioral-Therapy of PTSD* (New York: Guilford, 1997); J. Herman, *Trauma and Recovery* (New York: Basic Books, 1992); McCann and Pearlman, *Psychological Trauma and the Adult Survivor*;

In our project in Rwanda we conducted a two-week seminar to promote healing, forgiveness, and reconciliation.[18] The participants in this training were Rwandese staff members of organizations from around the country which work with groups in the community. Some of the organizations try to help people heal, others try to help them reconcile, and most of them work with some form of community building, such as helping people work together in agriculture.

The training had experiential and psychoeducational elements. The experiential component included people repeatedly writing or drawing something to represent an experience they had during the genocide.[19] It soon became apparent that given Rwandese culture, with its focus on oral rather than written language, it was better for some people to simply think about their experience. This was followed by people telling each other, in small groups, what they wrote, drew, or thought about. People told about intense and painful experiences. They received strong support from other members of the group.

Before this process began, we discussed the importance of empathic responding to others' experiences. We demonstrated both lack of response and overresponse, like taking over by offering advice or immediately beginning to tell one's own story. Many of the participants responded to painful stories by simply crying with the person who told the story.

We worked with a mixed group, both Hutus and Tutsis. Given the realities in Rwanda—the genocide by Hutus against Tutsis with the Tutsis now in power—it may not be surprising that the Hutus, who participated well in the workshop in general, did not tell their "stories" of experiences during the genocide. Still, we believe that hearing the painful stories of Tutsis— stories told mostly with a focus on what happened to the victims, hardly

L. A. Pearlman, "Healing and Forgiving in Trauma Victims," paper in the symposium, Healing, Forgiving, and Reconciliation in Individuals and Groups, International Society of Political Psychology, Montreal, Quebec, 1998; E. Staub, "Breaking the Cycle of Genocidal Violence: Healing and Reconciliation," in *Perspectives on Loss: A Source Book*, ed. J. Harvey (Washington, D.C.: Taylor and Francis, 1998).

18. E. Staub, "Genocide and Mass Killing: Origins, Prevention, Healing, and Reconciliation," *Political Psychology*, 21, no. 2 (2000): 367–82; Staub and Pearlman, "Healing, Forgiveness, and Reconciliation in Rwanda"; Staub, Pearlman and Hagengimana, "Manual for Facilitators of Healing Through Understanding and Connection Project."

19. Pennebaker, 1990.

mentioning perpetrators—could promote empathy in Hutus and contribute to reconciliation.

The psychoeducational part of the training included brief lectures and discussion of various topics. One of them was about the origins of genocide, the influences leading to it. We will discuss this in the next section. Another was about the impact of trauma on individuals and communities. We expect that understanding the continuing impact of their experiences on them will help transform these experiences. A third topic was avenues toward healing: what is required for and what facilitates healing. A fourth topic was basic human needs, providing a framework for understanding psychological trauma and healing.[20]

The aim of the workshop was to provide tools that may be useful for participants in their work with community groups. An additional component of the workshop was to help participants from different organizations integrate the material from the workshop with the way they usually work with organization. Local collaborators are continuing to help participants apply material from the workshop to their work with community groups.

CONTRIBUTORS TO HEALING, RECONCILIATION, AND FORGIVENESS AFTER COLLECTIVE VIOLENCE: THE CREATION OF PEACEFUL SOCIETIES

The following discussion applies to varied "transitional societies" that are trying to rebuild after collective violence such as genocide, mass killing, or intense civil war. However, as an example, we will focus again on Rwanda.

Empowerment: Helping People Find Their Voice

The unity and reconciliation commission in Rwanda has begun in a wise manner. It gathers groups of people and asks them what they need in order to reconcile. One potential benefit of this is that people engage with the

20. Staub, *Roots of Evil*; McCann and Pearlman, *Psychological Trauma and the Adult Survivor*; K. W. Saakvitne, S. J. Gamble, L. A. Pearlman, and B. T. Lev, *Risking Connection: A*

idea of reconciliation. Another is that they can help identify what they need for reconciliation to take place. A third is that by expressing their views and then, ideally, actively engaging with each other and with the process, they are creators and actors. This is valuable since healing, forgiveness, and reconciliation can only be facilitated but not created or imposed by others.

Truth

The truth provides a base for healing, forgiving, and reconciliation. The use of truth commissions after collective violence has become a common practice, from Argentina to other South American countries, to South Africa and elsewhere.[21]

Describing what has happened acknowledges the pain and suffering of the victims. When violence has been one-sided rather than mutual, truth-telling validates the victims' innocence. It thereby helps mitigate one psychological effect of victimization, the survivors' tendency to feel that something must be wrong with them. Proclaiming the truth also tells victims that the world does not regard such behavior as acceptable, which contributes to feelings of safety and begins to restore the group's connection to the world community.

In addition, individuals and groups who harm others and then are accused of wrongdoing easily feel that they are the victims. Convincingly documenting their violent actions makes it more difficult for perpetrators to claim or feel this. It makes it more difficult for them to continue to blame the victims.

The truth is often complicated. Often harm-doing is mutual. Even when one group is clearly the perpetrator of genocide, as in Rwanda, there has often been some form of mutual victimization in the course of prior history. Acknowledging this may help perpetrators heal and open themselves to their victims.

Perpetrators acknowledging the truth can be of great value. As one

Training Curriculum for Working with Survivors of Childhood Abuse (Lutherville, Md.: Sidran Press, 2000); Pearlman and Saakvitne, *Trauma and the Therapist.*

21. Nunca Mas, *The Report of the Argentine National Commission on the Disappeared* (New York: Farrar, Straus, Giroux, 1986).

woman in Rwanda said, spontaneously introducing the idea of forgiveness: "How can I forgive them, if they don't tell me the truth, if they don't acknowledge what they did?"

Testimonies, Memorials, Group Ceremonies

When whole groups have been affected, large numbers of people must be involved in healing. Testimonials as to what has happened, memorials and ceremonies in which people grieve together can help people reexperience and acknowledge the pain and losses of traumatic events in a supportive context. Survivors and members of the perpetrator group joining together can facilitate mutual healing and reconciliation. The presence of outsiders can also be helpful; the process of bearing witness expresses acknowledgment, empathy, and support.

However, such events can be destructive as well as constructive. Rather than healing, they can maintain woundedness and build identity through enmity and nationalism.[22] This seemed to have happened with the Serb focus on their defeat by Turkey in the fourteenth century. The ceremonies created ought to offer visions of inclusive connections and a positive future.

Justice

JUSTICE AS PUNISHMENT

Even victims of simple unfair treatment often express their need for justice. People deeply resent impunity. People in Rwanda repeatedly expressed their desire that the perpetrators be punished. What kind of punishment is needed and what other avenues are open to creating the experience of justice that facilitates healing, forgiveness, and reconciliation and the creation of a peaceful society?

Individual responsibility is important. This involves identifying, to the extent possible, higher-and lower-level decisionmakers, more and less important direct perpetrators, and people who were more and less impor-

22. Staub, "Basic Human Needs and Their Role in Altruism and Aggression."

tant facilitators. When many people are involved, healing requires that punishment be limited in scope, with a focus on those especially responsible. This helps to avoid creating new wounds.

The involvement of the community in the process of punishment can be both healing and empowering. In Rwanda the government is re-creating the Gacaca to deal at least with lower-level perpetrators. Traditionally, when someone did harm to another in the community, the elders gathered to hear what happened and to decide about punishment. The punishment included bringing the perpetrator back into the community in some way. In its current form people will be elected to the Gacaca.

At the same time, international tribunals punishing important perpetrators can reduce feelings of resentment by members of the perpetrator group. They are more likely to see justice as impartial. Unfortunately, recent international tribunals, both the one dealing with Bosnia, and especially the one dealing with Rwanda, have been poorly funded, slow, and ineffective.

JUSTICE AS IMPROVEMENT
IN ECONOMIC WELL-BEING

Collective violence, in addition to everything else, usually leaves survivors impoverished. Some of those whose relatives were killed in South Africa or who were themselves victimized feel unjustly treated because changes in the government and the truth and reconciliation process have not substantially improved their economic condition.[23] At a meeting of women from Kigali with the unity and reconciliation commission in Rwanda, some women said that to experience justice they need their economic situation to improve.

Fair and just government policies are important. But to create economic justice is extremely difficult, especially in a poor society like Rwanda. If much is taken away from the Hutus, they will feel that this is revenge against them. Extensive public discussion of the conditions of the country and of what might represent justice under the circumstances might be helpful.

23. B. Hamber, "The Burdens of Truth," *American Imago* 55, no. 1 (1998): 9–28.

Economic help by the international community that immediately improves people's lives and promotes long-term development can be of great value.

RESTORATIVE JUSTICE

Restorative justice, or justice based on restitution, is an ancient concept. It stands in contrast to retributive justice, whose goal is to punish the perpetrator. In the past two decades, people have been attempting to apply restorative justice systematically in cases of victimization in an effort to provide reparations, restore community, resolve conflict, restore both perpetrators and victims into the moral and social realms (in the eyes of the larger community and one another), and provide accountability for the actions of perpetrators.[24] Restorative justice implies trying to show through actions that the perpetrators are sorry, understand the pain they have caused, and want to make amends. In Rwanda and other countries affected by genocide or collective violence, restorative justice would require the victims and the larger community to agree on reparations that the perpetrators would make to the community. In contrast to retributive justice, where reparations mean punitive sanctions, causing pain to the perpetrator, in a restorative justice model reparation means acting to benefit those whom one has harmed. The goals would be for the community to have a sense that justice has been served, that the offenders and their offenses have been denounced and held accountable, that a sense of peace and community healing have been restored, and that a process of establishing safety and trust has begun. Such a process requires the active involvement of the perpetrators, who are participants in rather than victims of the process, and could contribute to healing, forgiving, and reconciliation.

Understanding the Origins of Genocide or Collective Violence

The information we provided in our workshop in Rwanda about the origins of genocide and mass killing, exemplifying principles by reference to

24. G. Brazemore and M. Umbreit, "Rethinking the Sanctioning Function in Juvenile Court: Retributive or Restorative Responses to Youth Crime," *Crime and Delinquency* 41, no. 3 (1995): 296–316.

various cases, including the genocide in Rwanda, and the discussions that followed, had a powerful impact on participants.[25] Learning that others had similar fates and coming to understand how certain influences contribute to genocide seemed to help participants feel they were not outside history and human experience, that as terrible as it was what happened in their society is a human process. It seemed to reconnect them with humanity. One woman said, "If this happened to other people, then it doesn't mean that God abandoned the people of Rwanda."

It seemed that perpetrators were also humanized to some extent in the eyes of victims. Perhaps members of the perpetrator group were humanized in their own eyes. Perpetrators acted in response to societal, cultural, and psychological forces. Most of the influences that usually lead to genocide were present in Rwanda:[26] economic and political chaos in society and a civil war; a history of intense devaluation of and discrimination against a group; intense propaganda by leaders intensifying hostility; strong obedience to authority; a history of violence against a group (in Rwanda the Tutsis), that prepared the possibility of new and greater violence; and passivity by many bystanders (within and outside of society) and support for and hence complicity by some nations with the perpetrators. Understanding does not reduce the responsibility of perpetrators, who can choose to act differently, but may make forgiveness more possible and certainly facilitates healing. Finally, participants in our workshop seemed to feel that understanding the forces that lead to genocide might allow action to be taken to prevent genocide. One woman said, "If people created this, then people can solve it."

Exposing leaders to information about the origins of genocide may be valuable. It may promote healing and help them use the understanding they have gained for breaking the cycle of past violence. Leaders may not be open to such information, since they usually develop their own visions of the past and future. But knowledge gained from the study of collective violence around the world is likely to be useful to them in addressing cultural elements and societal processes that contribute to violence. The task is

---

25. Staub, *Roots of Evil;* Staub, Pearlman, and Hagengimana, "Manual for Facilitators of Healing Through Understanding and Connection Project."

26. Staub, *Roots of Evil;* Staub, "Origins and Prevention of Genocide, Mass Killing, and Other Collective Violence."

daunting. Since culture is deeply rooted, existing forms of it often feel comfortable and preferred and it is resistant to change. Moreover, certain elements of culture, which can contribute to genocidal violence, serve leaders well. One of these is obedience to authority, which seemed to have significantly contributed to genocide in Rwanda, as people responded to the propaganda and the orders of leaders to kill. Working to change such cultural elements requires self-sacrifice and commitment by leaders.

Perpetrators Asking for Forgiveness

Although some research suggests that forgiving does not necessarily require anything from the perpetrator, other research on forgiveness has shown that harm-doers acknowledging their responsibility for causing harm, apologizing for their actions, and asking for forgiveness contribute to victims forgiving perpetrators.[27] The latter finding is highly consistent with comments people made in Rwanda.

The explicit focus of our work in Rwanda was on healing and reconciliation. Our background research, including interviews with informants, indicated that people were not ready to talk about forgiveness. But by the time we conducted our workshop in September 1999 we found that this was not the case. Participants spontaneously talked about forgiveness. They expressed their need, in order to be able to forgive, for perpetrators to acknowledge what they had done, apologize, and ask for forgiveness.

This may have reflected in part the influence of the government, which is encouraging perpetrators who are in prison to confess and ask for forgiveness. By doing so, perpetrators can reduce their punishment. At the same time such behavior may facilitate healing, forgiveness, and reconciliation by victims. But instead of genuine remorse, perpetrators can pretend regret, without genuine change in their attitudes toward their deeds or their

27. Freedman and Enright, "Forgiveness as an Intervention Goal with Incest Survivors," 983–92; R. J. Bies and T. M. Tripp, "Beyond Distrust: Getting Even and the Need for Revenge," in *Trust in Organizations: Frontiers of Theory and Research,* ed. R. M. Kramer and T. R. Tyler (Thousand Oaks, Calif.: Sage, 1996), 246–60; and M. N. O'Malley and J. Greenberg, "Sex Differences in Restoring Justice: The Down Payment Effect," *Journal of Research in Personality* 17 (1983): 174–85; M. H. Gonzales, D. J. Manning, and J. A. Haugen, "Explaining Our Sins: Factors Influencing Offender Accounts and Anticipated Victim Responses," *Journal of Personality and Social Psychology* 62 (1992): 958–71.

former victims. Such empty apologies can inflame the rage of victims, as has indeed happened for many witnesses to the truth and reconciliation process in South Africa. Healing by perpetrators may make their request for forgiveness more genuine.

Acknowledgment of Harm Suffered by Perpetrators

Knowledge by victims of harm that perpetrators have suffered and harm inflicted on the perpetrator group by the victims' own group can contribute to reconciliation. Past victimization often contributes to perpetrators' actions. Acknowledgment of the harm perpetrators have suffered may weaken the protective shell of victim-blaming and further the process leading to reconciliation.

Under Belgian rule the Tutsi dominance over Hutus was enhanced. Hutus became more subordinate, their rights, opportunities, and well-being further diminished. In most genocides and mass killings members of the perpetrator group oppose their group's actions or try to save individual members of the victim group. In Rwanda a few Hutus publicly opposed the genocide and were killed. Others were killed because they were politically moderate, probably in part because it was assumed that they would not support the genocide.[28] Some Hutus endangered themselves to help individual Tutsis. Spreading the information about these facts would be constructive. Along the way, Tutsis' skepticism about those who helped others would have to be addressed.

Hutu civilians were also killed, after the genocide began, as the Rwanda Patriotic Front fought against the government army.[29] Such tragic, reciprocal killings almost always occur when a group perpetrates great atrocities on the other. These killings, too, must be acknowledged if healing and reconciliation are to succeed.

After the genocide was stopped, perhaps as many as two million Hutus escaped from Rwanda, including many of the perpetrators. Soon they began incursions into Rwanda, killing more Tutsis. In 1996 the government allowed Hutus to return. The returnees included many genocidaires, who

28. des Forges, *Leave None to Tell the Story;* Prunier, *The Rwanda Crisis.*
29. des Forges, *Leave None to Tell the Story.*

resumed killing Tutsis in the northwestern part of the country. In the course of trying to stop them, again Hutu civilians were killed.[30]

Before the return of the refugees from Zaire (which by that time had become the Democratic Republic of the Congo), in the course of the civil war there, the rebel army was supported by Rwandese military in its fight against the Mobutu government. An unknown but possibly large number of Hutu refugees were killed. Finally, in neighboring Burundi, which has been ruled since its independence by a Tutsi minority, there have been periodic massacres of Hutus.

It seems even more difficult for a government than for ordinary members of a group to admit to "wrongdoing" by the group, to violations of human rights by its army and people. This is especially the case when the "wrongs" committed seem minor to the group relative to the wrongs inflicted on the group. However, this is an essential part of the truth. It is essential for mutual healing, forgiveness, and reconciliation.

WORKING TOGETHER FOR SHARED GOALS

One important way for people to overcome hostility and negative views of each other is deep engagement, in the course of which they can experience each other's similarity and humanness. Working together for shared goals, which are superordinate to people's and their groups' separate and at times conflicting goals, can promote this deep engagement. The relationships that individuals develop to each other in the course of this can extend to the group as a whole. Interpersonal contact between offenders and offended after transgressions may facilitate forgiving.[31]

Governments, organizations at different levels of society, and community groups can all promote such deep engagement. These can involve cre-

30. J. Drumtra, *Life after Death: Suspicion and Reintegration in Post-Genocide Rwanda* (Washington, D.C.: U.S. Commission for Refugees, Immigration and Refugee Services of America, 1998).
31. Pettigrew, "Generalized Intergroup Contact Effects on Prejudice," 173–85; L. A. Gerber, "Experiences of Forgiveness in Physicians Whose Medical Treatment Was Not Successful," *Psychological Reports* 61 (1987): 236; and "Transformation in Self-Understanding in Surgeons Whose Treatment Efforts Were Not Successful," *American Journal of Psychotherapy* 44, no. 1 (1990): 75–84.

ating shared ceremonies and memorials, as discussed above, or building new institutions of the society. It can involve joint projects in any realm, from agriculture to business enterprise, to building new houses, to attending to children's needs. Indeed, children's needs and the desire for a better world for the next generation seems to be one likely universal meeting point for opposing groups.

Those who provide aid, like the United States Agency for International Development (USAID), are in a natural position to promote such engagement by members of hostile groups. They can offer incentives to them to join in development projects. As benevolent third parties they can help shape these projects to promote both success in development work and in the human relations required for the continued peaceful development of society.

Attention to Children

Children are deeply affected by violence in society, especially genocide and war.[32] They are directly affected, by losing parents and other relatives and suffering as well as witnessing violence. They are indirectly affected as the actions and emotions of parents and other relatives, people around them who have been deeply traumatized, impact them. We now know from work with Holocaust survivors, Vietnam veterans, and survivors of severe and early childhood abuse that trauma is transmitted through the generations.

To help children heal as well as overcome the devaluation, fear and hostility of the other implanted in them in the course of their socialization is of profound importance for breaking cycles of violence. Many avenues must be used, but their experience in school (of deep engagement with children who are members of the other group) and school programs provide a natural opportunity.[33] Watching traumatized parents commit themselves to healing and reconciliation may also be a powerful change agent for children.

32. *Peace and Conflict,* Special Issue: "The Graca Machel/UN Study on the Effects of War on Children," *Peace and Conflict: Journal of Peace Psychology* 4, no. 4 (1998).
33. N. Eisenberg, *The Caring Child* (Cambridge: Harvard University Press, 1992); E. Staub, "Altruism and Aggression in Children and Youth: Origins and Cures," in *The Psychology of Adversity,* ed. R. Feldman (Amherst: University of Massachusetts Press, 1996); Staub, "Genocide and Mass Killing," 367–82.

Finding Meaning: Working to Prevent Renewed Violence

People who have been greatly victimized need to find meaning in what seems senseless: their suffering. An aspect of healing is to make meaning of one's experience.[34] One way to find meaning after a genocide is to devote oneself to creating a world in which people will not inflict violence on each other. People who have greatly suffered, when they have healed to some extent, often devote themselves to helping other people. This is "altruism born of suffering," in contrast to the usual development of altruism through positive, growthful experiences.[35]

Participants in our workshop were eager to discuss what they might do make renewed violence, a new genocide, less likely. Working together with others to accomplish this, for example, to help people heal, to overcome antagonism and help members of the two groups work together, to enhance varied aspects of justice, to reduce unquestioning obedience to authority helps to fulfill basic needs that were deeply frustrated by the genocide. Such work contributes to a feeling of efficacy, to a positive identity, to positive connections to other people, to an understanding of the world or a world-view that is hopeful and constructive. All this enhances a sense of security. Making a contribution, serving others and the community, also helps fulfill a need for transcendence, an important aspect of spirituality.[36]

Government Policies: The Behavior of Leaders

The behavior and direction given by authorities are very important in every society—but especially in one with strong respect for authority. In Rwanda the previous leaders led the group to genocide. The current leaders can be contributors to the creation of lasting peace. It would be valuable for leaders themselves to undergo some of the processes that promote healing and open people to reconciliation. In Bosnia wounded leaders, like

34. Herman, *Trauma and Recovery;* Pearlman and Saakvitne, *Trauma and the Therapist.*
35. Pearlman and Saakvitne, *Trauma and the Therapist;* Valent 1998; Staub, "Basic Human Needs and Their Role in Altruism and Aggression"; Eisenberg, *The Caring Child;* Staub, "Altrusim and Aggression in Children and Youth."
36. Staub, *Roots of Evil;* Staub, "Basic Human Needs and Their Role in Altruism and Aggression"; Staub, "Genocide and Mass Killing," 367–82.

General Mladic whose parents were killed by Croats during World War II as part of the mass killing of hundred of thousands of Serbs, led Serbia to great violence.

As refugees or children of refugees, as members of a group that has suffered so much harm and violence, the current Tutsi leaders of Rwanda must be wounded. Depending on their personal experience and level of healing, the creation of the unity and reconciliation process may be primarily a wise, thoughtful strategy, and it may also be based on genuine desire. The more it is a combination of the two, the more likely it is to survive the difficulties and vicissitudes of the long road to a healed society.

CHAPTER 12

Hatred's End

A Christian Proposal to Peacemaking in a New Century

John Dawson

I BELIEVE IN FAITH-BASED EFFORTS toward healing. In order to know how we are mobilizing Christians as reconcilers, "listen in" as I reflect with my own constituency on the topic of forgiveness and reconciliation in a new century.

HATRED'S END

Reconciliation takes place when you and I begin to enjoy intimate fellowship with our previous enemies, people who have tempted us to bitterness by hurting us. This is a miracle made possible by the cross of Jesus Christ. At the cross mercy triumphed over justice. At the cross a mighty flood of reconciling grace was released into the earth. At the cross we ourselves were recipients of such mercy that it changed the way we viewed those who had sinned against us. Jesus healed our broken hearts through reconciling us to the Heavenly Father, but He also commissions us to the ministry of reconciliation. We begin this ministry by confessing our own story of failure and forgiveness to others.

The Gospel, Greek for "good news," is simply this. Everyone has sinned. Sin is that which violates relationships, the selfish acts that separate us from one another and from God, however an atonement for sin has been mediated through Jesus' sinless life, unjust death and triumphant resurrection. Because of Christ, we can be reconciled to our Creator and to each other.

Whom Do You Hate?

Everyone encounters the temptation to hate at some time or another. You may be a mother who has witnessed the suffering of your beloved daughter at the hands of an abusive son-in-law. You may have lost everything through betrayal in a business transaction or been fired unjustly. You may be a member of a people group who has experienced rejection and injustice for generations. It is impossible to have lived without being hurt. We know hatred is wrong, but how do we come out of it?

Paradoxically people sometimes suffer an even greater temptation to hate *after* their salvation experience. How can that be? It is because the unregenerated heart is often protected by walls of cynicism. Many people outside of Christ have lowered their expectations of their fellow man to the point where they expect to be hard done by and put upon. When injustices occur there is no shattering disappointment, it simply confirms that person's view of life. On the other hand, followers of Jesus have been flooded with hope at the moment of their new birth. They are transferred from the kingdom of darkness to the Kingdom of God's dear Son and their expectations change completely. Their standard is now love and its attributes. They begin to imitate Jesus and to anticipate Christ-like behavior from those who claim to follow Him. This is why the wounds received in a church or Christian organization cut so deeply. Disappointment comes from failed expectations, and the temptation to bitterness and alienation can be intense, particularly if it is somebody in leadership who has failed us.

What Can We Do About It?

Have you ever attempted reconciliation while the painful memories still tormented you? There will be no reconciliation with anyone until we bring our broken hearts to God first. Healing begins when we honestly confront the past. Before we can even contemplate forgiveness, we need to face what really happened and bring it to the foot of the cross.

I have a Welsh friend, Dr. Rhiannon Lloyd, who holds trauma recovery classes for both Hutu and Tutsi survivors of the Rwanda genocide. If you were in her shoes, what would you say to these devastated people? Many have experienced rape or maiming or witnessed the murder of their family members. This is what she does: In the shelter of a church house they meet for three days. Dr. Lloyd first persuades her grieving flock to write down on a piece of paper the worst experience that they had. When the awful facts have been confronted in this way, she has them come together in small groups to tell each other their stories. This is often the first trembling step toward trusting others again.

Finally the terrible atrocities are listed on a large sheet of paper for all to see and the group is asked, "What does God feel about this?" She then draws a big red cross through the list of hurts, symbolizing the cross of Christ. "This is the only place we can bring our sorrows," she tells them. "This is one of the reasons Jesus came to earth, not only to take upon Himself our sins, but also the sin of those who sinned against us. Stand and tell God of the pain in your heart," she tells them. "What you saw, what it did to you. If you're angry, tell Him. If strong emotion comes, don't hold it back, because God will be weeping with you."

At first there is silence, but sobbing and wailing soon overcome the cultural reserve of the Rwandans as people pour out their grief, anger, and hopelessness before the crucified Christ. A long time later, when quiet returns, they sing softly the old chorus, "What a friend we have in Jesus, all our sins and griefs to bear." Eventually Rhiannon brings in a big, rough wooden cross and positions it on the floor with a pile of nails. One at a time, believers begin to slip forward and taking their tear-stained piece of paper with its record of horrors, they kneel and nail it to the cross of Jesus. All afternoon the hammer pounds, echoing the agony of Golgatha, a reminder of Jesus' complete identification with our sufferings. On the third day an amazing thing happens. People begin to testify that in the midst of genocide God was at work in the darkness. They talk of heroes, Christian reconcilers, who were the first to die. Anger at God begins to turn to empathy for God as believers contemplate His heartbreak over the way we humans treat one another.

With grief resting lighter upon many, talk of forgiveness begins to
emerge. Jesus is seen not only as the innocent and suffering Lamb of God
but also as the resurrected and righteous Judge who will uncompromisingly
administer justice. Even now His hand of vengeance is stretched out toward
the wicked, the very persons haunting the memory of survivors. "If they
repent, is it all right with you if God forgives them?" Rhiannon asks. Each
person contemplates this question, weighing his or her own testimony of
cleansing against the grief, many concluding that if God forgave them, they
must eventually forgive others. Truly this is "beauty for ashes," the promise of God (Isa. 61:1–4).

Healing the Land

Finally Rhiannon tells them a personal story. "I come from a nation
where two tribes have hurt each other," she says. "One day I was in a prayer
meeting when an English Christian knelt at my feet. `We have often made
the Welsh our servants.' she said. `Please forgive us.' And she proceeded to
wash my feet. A deep healing took place in my heart that day because of the
humility of one person who chose to identify with the sins of her people
against my people."

Rhiannon's simple story contains a key, the key to the ancient gates that
isolate peoples and elements of society from one another. She has given a
wisdom gift to Hutu and Tutsi as they struggle to live together in the same
land.

You see, Jesus didn't tell us to apply the cross to the other person but to
ourselves. This is what gives us power to be reconcilers. It is a mystery
revealed in the cross of Christ. Each believer must take up the cross and
apply it to his or her own identity. Even now God is looking for people like
Rhiannon's humble English friend. He is looking for those who will express
the humility of Christ and bring healing to the nations. Rhiannon acts upon
this truth. She does one more thing. As a white person surrounded by
Africans, she takes a position of complete identification with Europeans. She
cannot represent Europeans in any official way, let alone confess the sins of
others, but she realizes that there are no "generic" Christians. We all come
from somewhere and it is obvious to the Africans that she is from one of the

European peoples that long held power in Africa. Rhiannon knows that her very appearance reminds many Africans of rejection and unjust dominance, but instead of disclaiming all association with the colonial past by such statements as "I'm not from Belgium," or "It was all in a past generation," or " My people have been oppressed, too." She volunteers to stand in the gap as an intercessor. The Bible reveals that God is looking for such people. Not just people who will stand in the gap before Him, but people who will repair the breeches in human relationships.

God does not put guilt on the intercessor. We are not individually guilty for what our group did or our parents did, but He is waiting for the "royal priesthood," which is the redeemed in Christ, to openly confess the truth of a matter before Him and before people, just as the ancient Hebrew priests once did over the sins of Israel. It is very difficult to forgive if you have never heard an open acknowledgment of the injustices that wounded you or your people. On the other hand, such grace for forgiveness is released when we are asked for forgiveness by those who identify themselves in some way with the identity of those who contributed to our suffering.

PEACEMAKING IN THE NEW CENTURY

Today we live in a wounded world. The Cold War is over. The great transnational ideologies have either failed or proved to be weak. Communism has collapsed. Even the fervor of Islamic fundamentalism has been unable to bring Islamic regions and peoples together. Into the sociopolitical vacuum has rushed the much older claims of nationality, language, religious schism, and tribal identity. The old hatreds are back with a vengeance. Ancient fault lines that were briefly covered over are once again exposed. Racial strife among the immigrants of New World cities, people group wars in the postcolonial states of Africa, ethnoreligious convulsions in east Europe: these are all symptoms of the foundational conflicts that this generation receives as a legacy of the past.

Racial conflict in particular has dramatically impacted my personal life. I am a white man. I have lived for the past twenty years in the African-American community in the United States. My neighborhood became famous

worldwide as the place where officers of the Los Angeles Police Department were caught on video mercilessly beating a black man named Rodney
King. Following their acquittal the city erupted. Fifty-nine people died in the
rioting and more than 5,000 buildings were damaged or destroyed. Mr.
King was later quoted in banner headlines around the world asking the desperate question, "Can't we all get along?" Mr. King's question hangs over
us still. The answer, of course, is no.

Unfortunately, business as usual for the human heart is envy, fear, and
contention. What an exciting time then to be a follower of Jesus, an intercessor involved in Christ's ministry of reconciliation! When we are truly
reconciled to God the Father, the "otherness" of another gender, race, or culture becomes an attraction rather than a source of insecurity and division.

Even now a wave of repentance is spreading through the world's prayer
movements, addressing the foundational sins that have hindered the
progress of the Gospel for centuries. Much has taken place in the 1990s,
starting with the issues that have wounded the New Zealand Maoris, American Indians, and other indigenous peoples. I personally have witnessed sta-
diums filled with weeping Christians where people flooded platforms to
confess not only their personal sins but also the sins of their group against
other groups. In May 1995, for example, brokenness, repentance, and reconciliation swept the almost 4,000 evangelical leaders from 186 nations
meeting in Seoul, South Korea. Leaders from Turkey and Armenia reconciled and embraced one another. Japanese leaders knelt and asked forgiveness from other Southeast Asians. Such deep repentance, I'm convinced,
not only demonstrates God's healing love but also makes the claims of the
Gospel credible to those who have rejected its message in the past. As the
Church of Jesus Christ, our goal, of course, has always been to see people
reconciled to God through the Gospel. The main hindrance to this end,
however, has been us. The world has not been able to "see" Jesus because
of the sectarian strife within the body of Christ.

For centuries this spirit of religious controversy has made us part of the
problem. But now, I believe, we are finally becoming part of the answer. The
growing wave of repentance over historic sins is leading believers of differ-
ing denominations, cultures, and movements to unprecedented affection
and respect for one another. Jesus said that when this kind of unity occurred,

the world would believe the Father sent Him (see John 17:21). Ultimately, the world will "see" Jesus when a united church carries the ministry of reconciliation beyond its own walls.

The Wounds of the World

When we study human conflict, we see that Satan's method of getting one group to abuse another is rooted in the hardheaded collision of self-righteous people within each group. Take some truth, polarize the people with different sides of that truth, tempt them to unrighteous judgment, and then watch them wound one another with rejection, harsh words, injustice . . . and so it goes on. We know that two people can hurt each other through selfish and unjust behavior. It is also possible for a wound to be sustained by a nation or people within a nation. Animosity and bitterness can fester unresolved for generations. At a Canadian conference in 1995 Christian delegates from over forty nations identified fourteen categories of deep-rooted, systemic alienation between peoples and elements of a society in which reconciliation ministry must be applied:

1. Indigenous peoples to immigrant peoples (such as the Aboriginal peoples to European-Australians)
2. Residual antagonisms, when there is justice under the law but wounds continue (e.g., between black and white Americans because of the legacy of slavery or the hearing and hearing impaired because of society's continuing insensitivity)
3. People-group conflicts (such as the Kurds vs. the Turks or the Hutus vs. the Tutsis)
4. Nation-state rivalries (e.g., disputes between Pakistan and India)
5. Independence movements (e.g., the Timorese resistance to Javanese Indonesians as a result of colonialism)
6. Civil wars (as in Nicaragua)
7. Alienation between generations (e.g., a generation returned from war dealing with the countercultures of their teenage children)
8. Societal conflicts (for example, Leftist vs. Rightist ideologies on the environment or abortion)
9. Gender-based abuses (e.g., forced prostitution of Korean, Chinese,

and Philippine women by the Japanese military during the 1940s)
10. Industry, trade, and labor disputes (such as migrant farm workers vs. agribusiness enterprises)
11. Social-class divisions (such as those caused by the Indian caste system, socialist governing elites, land and business dynasties, or aristocratic cultures)
12. Interreligious conflicts (as between Christians and Jews)
13. Inter-Christian conflicts (sectarian divisions)
14. Christianity to peoples (when elements of Christian civilization have misrepresented God's character, putting a stumbling block between those peoples and their Creator; an example is the impact of the Conquistadors on Amerindian peoples)

How do we respond to such deep, gaping, sometimes ancient wounds? The simple answer lies in the humility of Jesus expressed through His body, the Church.

A Model for Reconciliation

During the great seasons of revival in the past, the Church always placed a considerable emphasis on open acknowledgment of sin and called for changed attitudes and just actions. Likewise, today's Christians have the potential to demonstrate a model of reconciliation in the troubled world of the new century. What is that model? As Christians, we believe in confession, repentance, reconciliation, and restitution. In the context of healing the wounds of the world, this means:

Confession: Stating the truth; acknowledging the unjust or hurtful actions of myself or my people group toward other people or categories of people.

Repentance: Turning from unloving to loving actions.

Reconciliation: Expressing and receiving forgiveness and pursuing intimate fellowship with previous enemies.

Restitution: Attempting to restore that which has been damaged or destroyed and seeking justice wherever we have power to act or to influence.

Sometimes we can begin this process by organizing events and ceremonies in which representatives of offending or offended subcultures have an opportunity to express regret or extend forgiveness. An example of this occurred recently when the "Memphis Miracle" ended eighty-eight years of racial segregation among the Pentecostal movements in America. Of course, in initiating such acts we recognize that the issues involved are complex. Today's generation has inherited the task of both honoring righteous ancestors and seeking forgiveness for ancestral sins. Honesty dictates that we embrace both the guilt and the grandeur that has attached itself to our various identities.

It is also true that when we are redeemed we become part of the transcendent bride of Christ in which there is neither male nor female, Jew nor Greek (Gal. 3:28). But the Bible teaches that we become even more responsible for dealing with the implications of our identity when new life is born in us. Even though each person stands before God alone and is in no way guilty for the sins of his or her ancestors or any other group, God is looking for volunteers who will open themselves to experience godly sorrow and confess the sins of the land. This is where reconciliation begins.

God's Momentum

The reconciliation prayer movement seems to have found a God-breathed momentum far beyond human promotion. We are, I believe, in an unusual season of grace, a season of jubilee. I work with the International Reconciliation Coalition, founded in 1990 as a fellowship of Christians attempting to deal with conflict in a Christian way. The IRC has grown rapidly into a worldwide network of like-minded but culturally diverse, praying servants from all streams within God's church. There are intercessors, prophetic ministries, researchers, strategic planners, training ministries and ambassadors of reconciliation who lead the way in public confession, repentance, and reconciliation at "solemn assemblies" and other special events. The IRC has joined forces with intercessors all over the world in organizing various reconciliation initiatives. Our office in Southern California helps with research, training, and the networking of experts and materials for the growing number of events, such as the prayer journeys believers are now taking into volatile parts of the world.

A reconciliation initiative is launched when people who trust each other form an alliance around a major reconciliation issue and determine to take action together. The issue may be a perceived trend likely to result in conflict or injustice in the future, a modern group conflict or antagonism rooted in the events of the twentieth century, or a catalytic season of ancient history that still reverberates with ongoing hostility between civilizations, cultures, peoples, or institutions. The IRC helps like-minded people find each other and learn from other reconcilers in the network. At the writing of this article, there are over sixty major initiatives gaining momentum. One of the most significant is the "Reconciliation Walk," coinciding with the 900th anniversary of the Crusades. European intercessors have walked the routes of the Crusades from west to east, carrying proclamations of repentance to Muslim and Jewish communities for the slaughter done in Christ's name. The response has been very encouraging. Identificational repentance is proving to be the key to opening doors that have been closed for centuries. I don't know why we waited nine hundred years to repent for the Crusades, but I'm glad the breakthrough among Islamic peoples is coming in our lifetime. In the United States people are taking prayer journeys where American Indians were oppressed or massacred. In addition, there are prayer journeys to the historical slave ports of West Africa where black and white Americans weep together, learn together, and find an intimacy that has eluded less radical believers. Radical steps like this are needed to break through the walls of cynicism and ignorance now hedging us in and separating us along ethnic and color lines.

WALKING IT OUT

How serious are we about reconciliation? For me, reconciliation has meant moving my Anglo family into the African-American community in Los Angeles, fully identifying with its struggles and developing meaningful friendships there. Recently, I sat next to an African-American grandmother on an airplane and took the opportunity to ask forgiveness for the sins of my people. She was cool to me at first but then suddenly opened up, telling me her own great-grandmother was sold at age eight at the slave auction in

Richmond, Virginia. It was not the fact that I write books or address politicians that opened her heart; the conversation changed when she heard that I had lived for twenty years in her community. She saw an authenticity beyond my words.

Your journey as a reconciler may be very different from mine but perhaps no less radical. Abandon yourself to God's purpose, connect to the prayer movements, listen to the Holy Spirit, and then take the next step of obedience. It should be our hope that our children will not have to deal with the hatred and alienation that have marked this and previous generations because of satanic strongholds rooted in history. Let us identify the ancient and modern wounds of injustice, pride, and prejudice in our world and heal them in a biblical way, without self-righteous accusation or dishonest coverup.

Mapping the Wounds

The question confronting us is this. What does the ministry of reconciliation look like? What goals should we set? Start by doing some basic research. Some conflicts are common to nearly all societies. Look at the following list of examples from American culture and begin to think about the issues that affect your nation.

Places of Conflict and Broken Relationship

1. Race to race (e.g., Native American vs. European American)
2. Class to class (e.g., homeless person vs. holders of home equity)
3. Culture to culture (e.g., immigrant vs. native born)
4. Gender to gender (e.g., working woman vs. male hierarchy)
5. Vocation to vocation (e.g., police departments vs. civil rights advocates)
6. Institution to institution (e.g., auto industry management vs. organized labor)
7. Region to region (e.g., Westside vs. South Central L.A.)
8. Governed to government (e.g., college-age youth vs. Vietnam era government)

9. Religion to religion (e.g., Muslim vs. Christian)
10. Denomination to denomination (i.e. Protestant vs. Catholic)
11. Enterprise to enterprise (e.g., monopoly vs. small business)
12. Ideology to ideology (e.g., leftist vs. rightist political parties)
13. Nationality to nationality (e.g., Americans vs. Cubans)
14. Generation to generation (e.g., '60's youth vs. parents)
15. Family to family (e.g., neighbor vs. neighbor)

This list could be endlessly refined. However, we need something this basic as a guide in order to begin our journey toward national healing. Today's conflicts often have their roots in history so our next priority will be researching the past.

LOOKING AT HISTORY WITH DISCERNMENT

Here is a list of key questions to ask when researching your regional or national history:

1. Was there ever the imposition of a new culture or language through conquest? Were treaties made and broken?
2. What were the religious practices of ancient peoples?
3. Was there a time when a new religion emerged?
4. Under what circumstances did the Gospel first enter the region?
5. Has the national or city government ever disintegrated?
6. What has been the leadership style of past governments?
7. Have there ever been wars that affected your region or city? Wars of conquest? Wars of resistance to invasion? Civil war?
8. Was your city the site of a battle?
9. Why was your city originally settled?
10. Did your nation or city have a founder? What was his or her dream? Did these people have enemies?
11. As political, economic, and religious leaders have emerged, what did they dream for themselves and for the nation? Who were their enemies?
12. What political, economic, and religious institutions have dominated the life of the nation? Has there been conflict between them?
13. What has been the experience of immigrants to the region?

14. Have there been any traumatic events, an economic collapse, race riots, an earthquake?
15. Has there ever been religious conflict among competing religions or groups?
16. What is the history of relationships among the races?
17. What roles have been assigned to males and females in your culture?
18. Are there any common patterns of abuse within families?

GET THE FACTS

Demographics and trends are also important. Social research publications and the census can be consulted.

1. Which trends represent the greatest opportunity for the entrance of the Gospel of peace (e.g., an influx of refugees)?
2. Is there an approaching crisis that should become the focus of intense prayer and ministry (e.g., an increase of homelessness or unemployment)?
3. Is there a particular subculture that is manifesting an unusual level of satanic oppression (e.g., a sudden upsurge in teen suicide)?
4. Which subculture is experiencing the greatest degree of spiritual darkness, hopelessness, or bondage?
5. Which subculture represents the poorest of the poor, the most vulnerable and needy group in the city or region?
6. Are there sociological groups that are actually calling for help (e.g., gang-infested neighborhoods or single mothers)?
7. What is the social issue stirring the greatest community concern in each section of the your city or nation (e.g., AIDS, racial tension, or property taxes)?

When you have a working knowledge of your region, you will be able to receive revelation from God about a specific strategy for ongoing evangelism, discipleship, and peacemaking ministry.

Time for Personal Application

In order to explore your potential as a reconciler, fill in the details below:

My gender is:_____

My generation is:_____

My native language is:_____

Subcultures I identify with are:_____

My class (socioeconomic status) would be seen by others as:

_____

My religious history has been:_____

My religious affiliation now is:_____

My family name is:_____

List some of the movements, ideologies, and institutions that have touched your family line as far back as you know:

_____

My location (region/city/suburb/neighborhood) is:

_____

My vocation is:_____

To the people of my extended family I am (e.g., daughter/sister/wife/mother): _____

Referring to the list of common conflicts in society, look at what you have written and consider the opportunities for "identificational" repentance created by your unique identity. Remember, the genius of the cross is revealed when somebody who is neither the victim or the victimizer voluntarily steps into the middle and takes responsibility for an offense in the way I have described. All other methods are less powerful simply because the third party is reduced to exhorting the victim to forgive and the oppressor to cease oppressing. Jesus has shown us the most costly yet powerful form of mediation, a deeper wisdom in the cross. "For the word of the Cross is to those who are perishing foolishness, but to us who are being saved it is the power of God" (1 Cor. 1:18).

Taking Action

Initiative can be taken in two general categories.

CATALYST EVENTS

These could be prayer journeys, ceremonies, conferences, reenactments, seminars, reconciliation walks, and solemn assemblies that feature prayers of reconciliation. These intentional events occur within a time frame and are designed to educate ourselves, express repentance before God, and break through the walls of ignorance, denial, indifference, and hostility that have separated groups of people. Examples range from stadium rallies or prayer walks that involve thousands of intercessors and cover a period of years to ministries like *"Aloha Ke Akua,"* a ministry to local churches in Hawaii that dramatizes the story of the islands through song and storytelling, then gives opportunity for reconciliation in Sunday morning services.

BRIDGE-BUILDING EFFORTS

Catalyst events are important only as a beginning point for reconciliation. Bridge-building efforts will last the rest of our lives and need to be equally intentional. Most bridge-building efforts fall within the domain of individuals and their enterprises. There will be collective acts, but individual lifestyle choices are the main thing. Micah 6:8 calls us to walk in justice, kindness, and humility at all times. When millions of believers quietly act upon their values, then we will have truly demonstrated the nature of the Kingdom of God. Will you hire cross-culturally for your business not because of government policy but because of your values? Will you cultivate relationships outside your comfort zone? Will you truly listen rather than react when another element of society communicates in a less than gracious way? Will you refrain from judging everybody in a group because of the violations of some members of that group? Will you change a pattern of derogatory speech even if it has been in your family for generations? Having joined a reconciliation alliance, will you keep exploring your potential as a reconciler after the excitement of initial events is just a memory?

Learning from What Others Have Done

Reconciliation is like courtship. If you make it mechanical, you fail, but if it comes from the heart you may succeed. There are no rules except the obvious one: study the other party and respond appropriately. For this reason I cannot give you a process that applies in all circumstances, but I can give you a few examples that demonstrate humility, wisdom, and creativity. Perhaps there is a model below that fits the issue closest to your heart.

REENACTMENTS

1. In Sydney, Australia, united Christians dressed in period costume gathered near the Opera House to remember the violent mass rape of female convicts by male convicts shortly after the arrival of the first fleet. An account was read publicly, Christian men asked forgiveness of their country women and then escorted them ashore with the affection and dignity that they should have experienced the first time. Now whenever the first story is told, the action of Christians in the 1990s must be told with it, thus sowing a healing memory into the story of the land.

2. Conciliatory Giving Celebrations. In California a large suburban church bussed its members over to a struggling African-American church. They surrounded the building and surprised the Sunday morning worshipers when a delegation entered the service and presented a $25,000 gift for the building fund.

3. Solemn Assemblies. Common around the world, these events have multiplied alongside the vision for seasons of united prayer and fasting. In Hawaii 27,000 people gathered in a stadium to worship God and to seek forgiveness and reconciliation over the way elements of society had wounded one another in the story of the

islands. At the end a Japanese leader knelt before the crowd and asked forgiveness for the bombing of Pearl Harbor.

4. Commemorative Ceremonies. Significant dates related to such things as genocidal atrocities are becoming reconciliation events when believers gather to memorialize these painful memories in annual observances. German Christians have led the way.

5. Interactive Citywide Musical Events. "Heal Our Land," a contemporary musical written for united church choirs, has toured American cities. Repentance and reconciliation prayer dealing with the wounds of America is featured. Similar events using the arts have emerged in several countries.

6. Justice Action Forums. In New Zealand and Australia Christians are beginning to work with government agencies dealing with injustices in land use and the tribal claims that have been ignored. If there are unjust laws in your city that perpetuate division, Christians cannot remain silent.

7. Country to Country or Regional Student Exchanges. Christian families are using the student exchange organizations as a way to send young ambassadors or host foreign children in order to build bridges of love between cultures.

8. Appreciation Tours. Korean, Japanese, North American, and European Christians are moving beyond the traditional tours to the Holy Land and exploring the cultures of other nations in order to empathize with and appreciate the diversity of God's redemptive gifts within the peoples of the world. Reconciliation is a featured part of many of these journeys.

9. Representative Leadership Forums. Around the world Christians are acting as peacemakers by bringing together the leaders of opposing sides. Private Christians have taken surprising initiative in doing the diplomatic work required to get factional leaders or even heads of state to talk to one another.

10. Contextualized Issues Forums. In Durban, South Africa, there has been estrangement and fear between Zulu people and Asian Indians, stemming from the politically inspired violence that occurred in 1949. In 1997 Christian leaders began to call together the leadership

of both communities and healing is beginning to take place. Mapping the wounds of a city quickly leads to the need for forums in which we listen respectfully to the grievances of others.

11. Diversity in Unity Celebrations. Old wounds are eventually put behind us and unity can be celebrated as an accomplished fact. Recently a Los Angeles city councilman visited a block party put on by a neighborhood filled with believers. "If the city was like this block, LA would have no problems," said the amazed politician after observing the obvious harmony between a great diversity of cultures.

12. Receptions, Banquets, and Other Hospitality Based Gatherings. Eating together remains one of the most effective ways of bringing together elements of society, and Christians with a ministry of hospitality will always be at the forefront of the ministry of reconciliation. This is an activity that begins in the home and the church dining hall and extends all the way to the convention center.

13. Student Culture Exchange Programs. In postapartheid South Africa "African enterprise" takes students from one culture and visits another culture with a view to bringing understanding, reducing fear, and increasing admiration for the "otherness" of the other people group. In some countries Christian schools are seen as an agent of resegregation, so cross-cultural interaction programs are imperative.

14. Cross-cultural and Denominational Interchurch Hosting. It is increasingly common for pastors to exchange pulpits or for whole congregations to visit one another for combined services and fellowship. Congregations have specialty ministry gifts and the division of labor that God has created becomes evident when believers really begin to explore and "see" one another in the life of the city.

15. Joining with Feast Days and Cultural Celebrations. Chinese, Mexicans, Filipinos, and most other groups with an international diaspora have special seasons of celebration on the calendar. Events often take place in city parks and are open to all. When an invitation is given to celebrate somebody else's unique gifts and good fortune Christians should be the first to rejoice with them.

The methods above were discovered by united believers in the place of prayer. The Holy Spirit will reveal the perfect plan for you as you also seek God for wisdom.

WHERE DO I START?

Become a Worshiper

God Himself should be the focus of the reconciler's heart. Our essential motive in all this is to bring healing and joy to the broken heart of God. We seek the healing of wounds, not because people or cultures deserve healing, but because Jesus deserves to see the reward of the cross, the reconciliation of people to the Father and to each other.

Take the Opportunity of Confession, with Identification, When You Find It

Look at the circle of influence God has given you, for instance, through your job. If you have joined the Army, been elected to office, joined the police department, or become identified with any other vocation, you are an inheritor of its legacy and have become partly responsible for any unfinished business with God or offended persons. Don't miss the simple things that stem from your identity, such as being a father. A lot of people's hurts center on an absent or dysfunctional father. Sometimes a few humble words can begin a dramatic work of healing, even if there is no evidence of it at the time.

Release Forgiveness and Refrain from Judgment

We must bring our own wounded spirit to God if we are to be used by Him as reconcilers. All of us have experienced injustice. The obvious temptation of the offended person is to give in to self-pity, a feeling stemming from a deep inner vow that says, "I deserve better than this." But do we? It's one thing to champion the rights of others, but do we ourselves really deserve better, in an absolute moral sense? I have often wallowed in self-pity but the truth is, the last thing I need is justice. Justice cuts two ways. What if I really got what I deserve? I'm just another human being with my own history of selfish actions. The fact is, I continue to live and breathe by the mercy of God; and having received mercy, I should extend mercy to others. The righteousness I now live is by the power of the risen Christ, not the function of an informed intellect driven by the "milk of human kindness." When I recognize my own desperate need for mercy, the gall of bitterness is more easily removed from my own spirit. When I acknowledge how much I have been forgiven, I am suddenly more able to release forgiveness toward those who have hurt me and mine.

The Bible sets an incredible standard for us in thought and speech. "[Love] bears all things, believes all things, hopes all things, endures all things" (1 Cor. 13:7). Racism and all the other prejudicial attitudes could be eradicated from the intercessor's heart if we simply give the other person, group, or race the benefit of the doubt. Leave the judgment to God; refrain from coming to conclusions about the motives behind actions. Do not impute evil intent to any action that could be interpreted two ways. Suspicion and accusation have no place in the heart of the reconciler.

Receive God's Gifts of Friendship

God organizes and builds His Kingdom through gifts of friendship. As you follow principle and live out your particular obedience, God will call others to walk beside you from a diversity of backgrounds. Think again about the people God has put in your life; they're not just associates, God is up to something! Most of us live in cultures dominated by the ethos of trade. When we meet new people, we unconsciously calculate the advantage we can gain by the relationship. But that is not the way of the Kingdom. Jesus is ready to open our eyes to the beauty and value of the people around us. If we see with His eyes we will soon follow the natural path from attraction to covenant. Friendship is an eternal gift. All relationships are tested by difficulty from time to time, but our commitment should be to move toward one another rather than withdraw, to take up an ambition for one another's wholeness, empowerment, and release into the full purpose of God. Who is present at the edges of your life right now? I know of many white believers who long for a black friend, I know immigrant families who would throw themselves into fellowship with the native born if shown the least hospitality. Yes, there's awkwardness, yes, it takes more work than just running with your own crowd, but the rewards are great. Let's go for it!

Join United Efforts

The local church, the gathering of believers, is the place where the concepts we have explored can be lived out most dynamically. Congregational life should be the cutting edge of positive change in any society. We need sermons outlining the biblical basis for racial intermarriage. We need public confession and public reconciliation to take place in our sanctuaries on Sunday morning. We need to give place to the music of every people in our public worship. Let the performing arts flourish and give glory to God. Let the sounds of a huge, diverse world ascend from our gatherings. Our denominational diversity provides another opportunity. The united Church is beginning to flow together like an irresistible tide. Through events such as March for Jesus, the Church prophetically models the possibility of unity within a diversity on a citywide level. This also helps us, as individual believers, move beyond the tiny postage stamp of our own existence. We need to get involved in the prayer movements, missionary enterprises, and mercy ministries of the Body of Christ in our cities. Whatever God has given you to do personally, do it with all your heart.

Volunteer help where your city's pain is most evident. My sister and brother-in-law are part of the network of agencies struggling to overcome AIDS in Los Angeles County. They minister in hospitals and hospices and even nurse patients in their own home until the patients die. An army of similar heroes is already at work in the world. Find people like this, walk beside them, and help them.

Attend neighborhood prayer meetings or citywide Concerts of Prayer. If solemn assemblies or reconciliation events are sponsored, be there. You will see nation-changing power released when believers move together in praise, repentance, and intercession.

Look Around

Be an explorer. Let curiosity carry you far beyond the knowledge you now possess. Seek to understand the times and seasons as Daniel did. Seek to touch, know, and celebrate the diversity of your nation. Ignorance is a curse. It will take an informed mind and an enlarged heart to embrace the ambition of God for the people of this generation.

Discern the Body of Christ

What if I was to call you up front in a meeting and ask you a few questions? What if I threw at you the names of five or six denominations and ministries in your town and asked you to explain the redemptive purpose for each one? Could you do it? We know who is out there, but we mostly know other movements through negative caricature—what's wrong with them, how they differ from us, the biblical ones. Is there an alternative to these prejudicial stereotypes? Do you know the value of the movements and ministries in your city? How can you encourage their potential if you remain ignorant of their story? The New Testament Greek word for truth, *aletheia*, means, "That which must not be forgotten." Second Peter 3:1 says, "Stir up your pure minds by way of remembrance" (KJV). It is as though the power to remember were an ethical principle, a form of righteous behavior.

When I meet that Salvation Army officer, or that Lutheran cleric, I want to provoke them to renewal by recounting their own heritage, not calling them to imitate mine. Let us give honor to all that is honorable and avoid that contentious spirit that makes absolutes out of what the Bible does not. Every missionary knows there is a great difference between form and meaning, that the cultural interpretation of biblical truth will vary, but the bedrock remains: an understanding of the nature, character, and personality of God revealed through Jesus and His work. In addition to the foundational truths held by all the orthodox streams, there are the unique flashes of light shed by each. There is more than a division of labor in the Body of Christ. A division of emphasis also makes possible a wide view of a wide subject: God.

Hold Your Ground

We will face opposition, but God's grace is sufficient. Intense spiritual warfare has occurred during the early years of the reconciliation prayer movement, but as I pen these final pages I see victory on every side. At one point my darling wife, Julie, was told she had a brain tumor; then, after prayer and further tests, the doctor mysteriously changed his mind. On another occasion, my son David, was walking down the street near our home when he was jumped by five Latino men, forced to the ground, and beaten with baseball bats. Fighting free he narrowly escaped abduction. He had just left a barrio birthday party attended by three of his friends, gang members who had turned to Christ days before. Our van was stolen by local teens and wrecked for the second time. I was threatened by a white supremacist, my son Paul was robbed at gunpoint. And these are just the headlines.

The net result of all of this, strangely enough, is that we as a family all feel wonderfully protected. Good things keep happening. "Out of the eater came something to eat, and out of the strong came something sweet" (Judg. 14:14). It is a biblical truth that we always find provision in the midst of the enemy's attack. My son David is convinced that God delivered him from a fatal situation (many boys have died in our part of Los Angeles), and at this writing he is an inner-city youth pastor ministering to street children, obviously unintimidated by his experiences while growing up.

Go Global

Why not be a part of something big? Remember the wounds of the world discussed in chapter 3? You can be part of the answer. Shortly before the writing of this chapter I took a prayer journey. Picture the ancient throne room of Ferdinand and Isabella in the Alhambra near Grenada in Spain. The palace is buzzing with tourists coming to see where Columbus was commissioned. In walks a large crowd of Christians speaking different languages, including a contingent of Jews wearing yarmulke. The whole atmosphere changes from gaiety to grief. It was here that the expulsion of the Jews from Spain was proclaimed by these same Christian monarchs five hundred years ago. A Catholic priest and a Protestant Spanish pastor presented a statement of repentance to the Jews and the throne room is turned into a solemn place of prayer as the intercessors grieve before God over the sins of the church.

Come with me to the hilltop site of the ancient council of Elvira. Here only three hundred years after the Jewish messiah gave his life for all peoples the first anti-Semitic decrees were made by Christian leaders. One decree disallowed a Jew to even bless a field, stating that it would amount to a curse. Hear the repentance of the Spanish intercessors and the proclamation of blessing from the messianic rabbis as they look down on the twinkling lights of the cities and villages below. Night is falling, but a spiritual light is rising over Spain as the ancient Hebrew blessing is spoken over the land.

Come with me to the plaza of the great cathedral on Sunday morning. The intercessors are reading with tears the unspeakable edicts of the Inquisition. Christian leaders are repenting, repudiating, and revoking the cruel words, finally burning the paper on which they are written. The crowd parts and a small Spanish boy now stands at the center of the intercessors. He looks forlorn and his hand and arm are heavily bandaged. A Jewish boy in his teens stretches out a hand and, touching the little boy on the head, he begins to bless him in the name of *Yeshua Ha Mashiach,* the Messiah. These are some of the things I have just witnessed. All I can do is join with the Psalmist in saying, "Lift up your heads, oh gates, and be lifted up oh ancient doors, that the king of glory may come in" (Ps. 24:7).

This prayer journey was just the beginning of the "Gates of Iberia" initiative, which in turn is part of a worldwide initiative toward healing the foundational rift between Jew and Gentile in the church, stemming from 140 A.D. A reconciliation movement has been launched in Spain, which, while focused on messianic Jews, is already having a profound effect on relationships between Catholic and Protestant. There will be many more catalyst events and prayer journeys in Spain and throughout the Spanish- and Portuguese-speaking world. This will undergird Christian repentance proclamations to the general Jewish communities. You could be part of something like this.

I have described just one event in a global movement that has long since expanded beyond the possibility of human management. Get connected, join an initiative, be a part of the answer to the prayer of Jesus: "I in them and You in Me. May they be brought to complete unity to let the world know that You sent Me and have loved them even as You have loved Me" (John 17:23, NIV).

PART IV

Seeking Forgiveness after Tragedy

CHAPTER 13

Truth Commissions as Instruments of Forgiveness and Reconciliation

Audrey R. Chapman

C AN TRUTH COMMISSIONS promote forgiveness and reconciliation? Determining the answer to this question is far
more than a theoretical exercise. In the opening years of this new century,
many societies are attempting to deal with a legacy of collective violence
and severe human rights violations and to find ways to overcome the divisions and animosities of their past. To begin to do so, some fourteen countries, most recently South Africa and Guatemala, have established truth
commissions or analogous bodies.[1] Truth commissions are temporary bodies mandated by governments or international agencies to investigate and
make findings about acts and patterns of violence and gross human rights
violations that took place during a specified period of time.[2] In contrast to
tribunals or courts, truth commissions do not have prosecutorial powers
to bring cases to trial. Their role is truth-finding or, perhaps more accu-
rately, documenting and acknowledging a legacy of conflict and vicious

1. The precise number of countries and bodies depends on how strict a definition of truth commissions is applied. Truth commissions, or other mechanisms approximating a truth commission, have been set up in Uganda, Bolivia, Argentina, Zimbabwe, Germany, the
Philippines, Uruguay, Chile, El Salvador, Rwanda, Ethiopia, Haiti, and Guatemala, as well
as South Africa.
2. In a few situations, nongovernmental organizations and church agencies have also sponsored the work of unofficial truth commissions.

crimes as a step toward healing wounds and shaping a shared future.[3]

As Archbishop Desmond Tutu, the chair of South Africa's Truth and Reconciliation Commission, has observed, truth commissions offer a "third way," a compromise between the Nuremberg trials at the end of World War II or the prospective International Criminal Court and blanket amnesty or national amnesia.[4] This "third way" is significant for several reasons. Reconciliation usually requires coming to terms with the past, but doing so in a manner that will promote a new political culture and commitment to a shared future. Moreover, it is often very difficult to prosecute architects and perpetrators responsible for political violence and human rights violations, particularly when large numbers of people are involved. Even in the case of Nazi war crimes, fewer than 6,500 of the 90,000 cases brought to court resulted in convictions.[5] Given the scale of the collective violence in places like Cambodia, Bosnia, and Rwanda, it is just not feasible to prosecute all the alleged offenders, and any effort to do so is likely to have thousands of persons languishing in detention for a very long time. In addition, few transitional countries have the strong legal institutions and resources required for successful domestic prosecutions. Many of the civil servants, prosecutors, and judges serving the new government may themselves have been complicit in abuses perpetrated by the previous regime, or at least sympathetic to its philosophy. Critical evidence and records are likely to be missing or destroyed. South Africa's unsuccessful effort to convict General Magnus Malan, army chief and later defense minister, for authorizing an assassination squad responsible for the deaths of women and children, shows how very difficult it is to gather sufficiently detailed and reliable evidence to successfully prosecute alleged perpetrators.

Truth commissions potentially can provide a far more comprehensive record of past atrocities and violations than the trials of specific individuals and do so in a less divisive manner. A truth commission's purpose is to provide a narrative of a specific period and/or regime, determine the major causes of the violence, and recommend measures to undertake so as to avoid

3. Priscilla Hayner, "Fifteen Truth Commissions, 1974 to 1994: A Comparative Study," *Human Rights Quarterly* 16 (1994): 607.
4. Desmond Mpilo Tutu, *No Future Without Forgiveness* (New York: Doubleday, 1999), 30.
5. Geiko Müller-Fahrenholz, *The Art of Forgiveness: Theological Reflections on Healing and Reconciliation* (Geneva: WCC Publications, 1997), ix.

a repetition in the future. Once victims' accounts are verified, official acknowledgment of abuses can support the credibility of their suffering and help restore their dignity. Moreover, public identification of perpetrators and their offenses constitutes one form of accountability, particularly if it leads to their exclusion or ineligibility for public office, but if not, at least it imposes the punishment of shame. In addition, a truth commission can go beyond a court of law and render a moral judgment about what was wrong and unjustifiable and in that way help "to frame the events in a new national narrative of acknowledgment, accountability, and civic values."[6] If the body is considered to be impartial, fair, and competent, a truth commission's report can offer a basis on which to build a shared history.

BALANCING TRUTH AND RECONCILIATION

Two truth commissions have been given a mandate to go beyond truth finding to promote reconciliation as well. The Chilean National Commission on Truth and Reconciliation and the South African Truth and Reconciliation Commission (TRC) have at least nominally been assigned the twin objectives of establishing truth while working toward reconciliation. The Chilean commission framed its task as "a truth for reconciliation." While its focus was on investigating and determining the truth, it understood that this truth had a clear and specific purpose: "to work toward the reconciliation of all Chileans." To that end, the commission sought the advice of a broad range of groups of victims' relatives, human rights agencies, professional associations, and political parties regarding how the commission could best reach the truth and thereby aid national reconciliation.[7]

In contrast, the TRC was mandated to go beyond truth finding, "to promote national unity and reconciliation in a spirit of understanding which transcends the conflict and divisions of the past."[8] The TRC also

6. Martha Minow, *Between Vengeance and Forgiveness* (Boston: Beacon Press, 1998), 78.
7. *Report of the Chilean National Commission on Truth and Reconciliation*, vol. 1, trans. Phillip E. Berryman, published in cooperation with the Center for Civil & Human Rights, Notre Dame Law School (Notre Dame, Ind.: University of Notre Dame Press, 1993), 24–25.
8. Preamble, Promotion of National Unity and Reconciliation Act, *1995 Republic of South Africa, Government Gazette* 361, no. 16 579.

incorporated several other innovative features, the most controversial of which was its amnesty provisions. Its founding act assigned the TRC the task of reviewing amnesty applications, with the requirement that the TRC grant amnesty to all perpetrators who fully disclosed their acts and could show the violations were committed with a political motive. Unlike other truth commissions, the TRC was also empowered to provide a form of restorative justice through making recommendations about reparations for individual victims and survivors.

The influence of religious perspectives and approaches on the TRC also made the South African experience unique. In contrast with other truth commissions, whose commissioners were generally lawyers and jurists, religious thinkers and clergy played major roles in the TRC, including the chairman, deputy chairman, four other commissioners, and the director of research. Given the powerful presence of Archbishop Desmond Tutu as the chair, some of the TRC's public sessions had a decidedly religious character. Commentators have pointed out that many hearings resembled a church service more than a judicial proceeding, with a definite "liturgical character," and that the archbishop clearly operated within a religious framework.[9] The Christian atmosphere and discourse of the TRC, and particularly Archbishop Tutu's frequent framing of issues in terms of repentance and forgiveness, was applauded by some South Africans, for whom Christian ideals had served as an ethical critique of apartheid, but it was distasteful to others. The latter category included commissioners and staff of the TRC as well as some academics, victims, and victim advocates who complained about "the imposition of a Christian morality of forgiveness."[10]

Given the needs of transitional societies, assigning the TRC a dual mandate of truth finding and reconciliation seemingly makes a great deal of sense. A wide variety of religious and secular thinkers emphasize that forgiveness and reconciliation require coming to terms with the past, not attempting to forget or repress it. Establishing a shared truth that documents the causes, nature, and extent of severe and gross human rights

9. John de Gruchy, "Redeeming the Past in South Africa: The Power of Truth, Forgiveness, and Hope in the Pursuit of Justice and Reconciliation," paper presented at Deutscher Evangelischer Kirchentag, Leipzig, Germany, June 1997.
10. Lyn S. Graybill, "South Africa's Truth and Reconciliation Commission: Ethical and Theological Perspectives," unpublished paper, 1997.

abuses and/or collective violence under antecedent regimes is a prerequisite for achieving accountability, meaningful reconciliation, and a foundation for a common future. As Archbishop Tutu states in the foreword to the TRC's five-volume report, "Reconciliation is not about being cozy; it is not about pretending that things were other than they were. Reconciliation based on falsehood, on not facing up to reality, is not true reconciliation and will not last."[11]

Reconciliation and relationship building require what the German theologian Geiko Müller-Fahrenholz terms "deep remembering," a synoptic multisided vision that uncovers denial and oppression and reveals the anguish and suffering of the common person. By so doing, it encourages groups to face up to deep-seated memories of guilt and hurt, culpability and suffering as a basis for healing and working toward a united society. According to Müller-Fahrenholz, "the art of remembering is not an exercise in looking backwards but an effort to transfigure past pains in order to construct vital and forward-looking societies."[12]

That said, it is important to acknowledge that truth finding does not automatically promote forgiveness and reconciliation. While truth may be indispensable for long-term reconciliation, truth finding may be divisive in the short-term. Truth finding is a very complex task with many pitfalls, especially if both the process and outcome are to be conducive to promoting forgiveness and reconciliation. Analysts writing on truth commissions often portray truth as a single objective reality waiting to be discovered or found. But developing an official and authoritative account of a contested past, and especially doing so in an objective and careful manner consistent with strict standards of historical and/or social science research, requires far more than merely confirming widely held beliefs about what has happened and who is responsible. The documentation and interpretation of truth about the past is a more complex and ambiguous action than many analysts and proponents of truth commissions assume. Moreover, the legitimacy of a truth commission and the acceptance of its findings will depend on

11. Archbishop Desmond Tutu, Chairperson's foreword, *Truth and Reconciliation Commission of South Africa Report,* vol. 1 (Cape Town: CTP Book Printers Ltd. for the Truth and Reconciliation Commission, 1998), 17.
12. Müller-Fahrenholz, *Art of Forgiveness,* 49–59.

whether key groups—architects of the violence, victims, perpetrators, and bystanders—believe that the truth commission proceeded in an unbiased and objective manner, using appropriate methodologies and considering valid sources of evidence.

Balancing truth finding and reconciliation requires a clear conception of each task and a sense of how they interrelate. The TRC did not have consensus on either the nature of the reconciliation it was mandated to pursue or the relationship between truth funding and reconciliation. According to Charles Villa-Vicencio, the TRC's director of research, there were three positions on the TRC. The first group included commissioners who equated reconciliation with interpersonal forgiveness and believed that the commission should promote reconciliation between individuals. Archbishop Tutu was a leading proponent of this position, and he was apparently supported by several of the other clergy in high positions in the TRC. A second group considered it inappropriate for a state-sponsored commission to engage in efforts to promote interpersonal forgiveness. Instead, members of this second group, who included Villa-Vicencio, advocated that the TRC should attempt to establish a framework for national coexistence and civility. A third group had a still more limited view of the appropriate role of the TRC; they wanted to focus exclusively on truth finding, arguing that it would provide a future foundation for reconciliation.[13]

THEOLOGICAL INTERPRETATIONS OF FORGIVENESS

Despite the centrality of forgiveness in Jesus' teachings, relatively few comprehensive theological treatments of the presuppositions and implications of forgiveness or its relevance to contemporary social issues exist. Four recent books, each with a very different approach and emphasis, seek to fill this void. L. Gregory Jones's *Embodying Forgiveness: A Theological Analysis* situates the Christian account of forgiveness in the overarching context of the God who lives in trinitarian relations of peaceable, self-giving

13. Charles Villa-Vicencio, discussion with author, Washington, D.C., October 29, 1999.

communion.[14] Forgiveness for Jones is not so much a word spoken, an action performed, or a feeling felt as a commitment to a way of life and specific practices. The goal is to engage in an ever-deepening process of unlearning sin and learning to live in communion with the Triune God, with one another, and with the whole creation. He also conceptualizes forgiveness as a sign of the peace of God's original creation, as well as the promised consummation of the creation in God's Kingdom. To protect and define the theological context of forgiveness, this work contains a strong critique of the therapeutic mindset or approach and the church's psychological captivity in western culture. Taking Dietrich Bonhoeffer as his starting point, Jones rails against expectations of "cheap grace" and emphasizes the "costliness of forgiveness." Nevertheless, he also argues that repentance can contribute to but is not a prerequisite for forgiveness.[15]

Marjorie Suchocki offers a very different approach in her 1995 work entitled *The Fall to Violence*. In this book she develops an understanding of violence, "original sin," and forgiveness in the context of a relational process theology that has a social as well as personal dimension. According to Suchocki, both sin—the violence of rebellion against creation and therefore God—and forgiveness—"willing the well-being of victim(s) and violator(s) in the context of the fullest possible knowledge of the nature of the violation"—are social in nature. Forgiveness in the forms in the transcendence has three essential elements for her: memory, empathy, and imagination. The importance of memory is embedded in her very definition of forgiveness. Empathy assumes that to forgive is to accept the other, not necessarily to have warm feelings or emotions for him or her. Forgiveness for Suchocki is fundamentally a matter of intellect, an act of will and self-transcendence that accepts the violator as a subjective other in relation to the self and recognizes that the well-being of the self is interrelated with the well-being of the wider community constituted as the world. Suchocki points out that violence does not end with an act or acts; it insinuates itself into the ongoing experience of the victim to be relived time and again with

14. L. Gregory Jones, *Embodying Forgiveness: A Theological Analysis* (Grand Rapids, Mich.: Wm. B. Eerdmans, 1995). The introduction provides a good summary of Jones's views, approach, and frame of reference. See xi-xvii.
15. Ibid., 3–33, 35–70, 158–59.

the result that the violator remains psychically present to the victim. According to Suchocki the victim can break through the internal effects of violence only by willing forgiveness in the context of the fullest possible
recognition of the sin and therefore of the character of the violator. Because
Suchocki understands sin as embedded in social structures that invariably
influence the consciousness and conscience of participants, she defines social
forgiveness as "the ability of those bonded together within a subgroup not
only to examine the larger structures, but to influence the ever-fluid continuing formation of those structures." In this matrix she characterizes God
as the fullness of truth, love, and beauty, in which memory, empathy, and
imagination, the elements that make for forgiveness, merge and are carried
to maximal form.[16]

Geiko Müller-Fahrenholz's *The Art of Forgiveness: Theological Reflections on Healing and Reconciliation,* written as a reflection on the horrible
legacy of the Holocaust by a German too young to have conscious memories of the Hitler period, offers a conception of forgiveness that focuses primarily on the broader social or political level. Based on his biblical analysis,
Müller-Fahrenholz's understanding of forgiveness has at its core a mutual-
ity in which the perpetrator asks for forgiveness, the victim grants it, and
both sides are changed by this encounter. He understands forgiveness as
entailing liberation from the bondage of the past. "It corrects the distortion
which an act of evil establishes between two people or groups the distortion
of stolen power and enforced impotence" and simultaneously an act of
grace restores the dignity of both sides. To attempt to make amends through
acts of restitution is important, but he also realizes that it is not possible to
restore the status quo ante. Thus, he emphasizes that efforts not focus on
repairing the past but instead on covenanting for a better way forward.[17]

Donald Shriver's *An Ethic for Enemies: Forgiveness in Politics,* as its
subtitle announces, takes forgiveness out of its traditional exclusive association with personal religion and morality and places it within the secular
political arena. It has four elements: moral truth, forbearance, empathy,
and a commitment to repair a fractured human relationship. His views on

16. Marjorie Suchocki, *The Fall to Violence: Original Sin in Relational Theology* (New York:
    Continuum, 1994), 154, 16, 133, 147–51, 155, 158.
17. Müller-Fahrenholz, *Art of Forgiveness,* 4–5, 28, 29.

moral truth as a starting point for forgiveness, discussed above, approximate my own emphasis on the need for a shared truth about the past as a prerequisite for achieving accountability, meaningful reconciliation, and the framework for a common future. Shriver's second dimension of political forgiveness is forbearance from seeking vengeance. As he comments, forgiveness in principle does not require the abandonment of punishment of evildoers, although it may do so in practice, but it does necessitate abandonment of vengeance. His conception of empathy has many elements of similarity to that of Suchocki. According to Shriver empathy, as contrasted with sympathy, requires an element of understanding. It demands the acknowledgment of a former enemy's humanity, even in the commission of dehumanizing deeds. Forgiveness also implies some form of coexistence, some expression of willingness to repair the fractures of enmity as the basis of forming a new shared political community. Conceptualizing forgiveness as an intertwined four-strand cable, Shriver posits that each dimension assumes and depends on the others, and at any one time may have greater prominence in the construction of a new relationship.[18]

CONCEPTIONS OF NATIONAL OR POLITICAL RECONCILIATION

In Scripture, reconciliation is primarily a theological rather than a social concept, a term to describe God's supreme act of reconciling humankind and the creation to God's self.[19] National or political reconciliation may be understood as a social and political process with religious and theological dimensions. National reconciliation in a divided society perhaps most fundamentally requires that members of once-antagonistic communities develop a commitment to a shared future. Clearly reconciliation has many affinities with Shriver's concept of political forgiveness, but as conceptualized here there are also differences. It is unclear whether national reconciliation requires interpersonal forgiveness. National reconciliation among

18. Donald Shriver Jr., *An Ethic for Enemies: Forgiveness in Politics* (New York: Oxford University Press, 1995), 7–9.
19. Müller-Fahrenholz, *Art of Forgiveness*, 4.

communities and formerly antagonistic political forces may be able to go forward without interpersonal forgiveness between former victims and perpetrators.

I believe that there are six requirements for reconciliation. The discernment of the truth about the dimensions, causes, and perpetrators of the conflict, violence, and abuses in the past, preferably by a body with official status, is the first of these requirements. For a society recovering from the trauma of state violence, "Truth is medicine. Without it, a society remains infected with past evils that will inevitably break out in the future."[20]

Second, there is a need for open and shared acknowledgment of the injuries suffered and the losses experienced. "It is one thing to know, it is yet a very different social phenomenon to acknowledge. Acknowledgdment through hearing one another's stories validates experience and feelings and represents the first step toward restoration of the person and the relationship."[21] The effort to come to terms with the past further requires acknowledgment of moral responsibility by those who inflicted the harm and those who were complicit by their silence and failure to oppose the wrongdoing. Acknowledgment should also include an expression of contrition.

Like Shriver, I believe that victims' willingness to let go of the past and forbear from seeking vengeance is another important element. In addition, participants on all sides need to make a commitment to a future that is not shaped by the events of the past. As part of this process, those who suffered the harm should acknowledge the humanity of those who have committed the injury. This may entail the communication of mercy and forgiveness but more likely will involve differentiating perpetrators from their community and acknowledging that the majority of members did not personally and directly carry out harmful actions.[22]

Fourth, justice is indispensable for reconciliation. That said, it is important to recognize that there are many different forms of justice. Criminal justice involves the investigation, prosecution, and punishment of the leading

20. Walter Wink, *When the Powers Fall: Reconciliation in the Healing of Nations* (Minneapolis: Fortress Press, 1998), 53.
21. John Paul Lederach, *Building Peace: Sustainable Reconciliation in Divided Societies* (Washington, D.C.: U.S. Institute of Peace, 1997), 26.
22. Louis Kriesberg, "Paths to Varieties of Inter-Communal Reconciliation," unpublished paper, Syracuse University, 1997.

architects and executors of serious abuses, but for the reasons identified earlier it frequently is not a feasible goal in a transitional society. In contrast, restorative justice seeks to repair an injustice, to compensate for it, and to effect corrective changes in relationships and in future behavior.[23] As such, it requires providing some measure of redress for the injustices and pain endured in the form of financial compensation, direct provision of assistance, and/or more symbolic approaches to reparations. One of the TRC's innovations was to link the verification of victim status to the recommendations for financial reparations from the state. The TRC also sought collective reparations in the form of monuments named for victims and stipends for medical and therapeutic treatments. Unfortunately, the government has not acted on its recommendations to provide financial reparations for victims.

Fifth, adversaries need to make a commitment to repairing and reestablishing their relationship. This process can be facilitated by victims' willingness to forgive those responsible for harming them. It may be possible, though, to promote social healing and accommodation even in the absence of forgiveness at a personal level. At the least there needs to be a willingness to achieve some form of coexistence, and perhaps in the future coexistence can deepen into greater sharing and a more meaningful form of a relationship.[24]

Sixth, members of the communities should explicitly establish the terms of a new and common future. This requires an opportunity to look forward and establish a new social and political covenant. Many transitional societies seek to do so through the formulation of a new constitution. This is certainly an important step, but insufficient by itself to create and sustain the network of understandings and relationships necessary to shape and sustain a shared future. To do so, it is also important to make a commitment to implement the recommendations of truth commissions and other bodies seeking to rectify and overcome the tensions and problems that led to the violence and abuses in the past. A new society also requires the ability to set goals and formulate policies that are supported across social groupings and communities. In societies with a legacy of inequalities, a future that

23. Minow, *Between Vengeance and Forgiveness*, 91.
24. Shriver, *Ethic for Enemies*, 8–9.

overcomes the legacy of the past will need to begin the process of economic and social restructuring so as to achieve greater equity.

THE TRC'S ROLE IN PROMOTING FORGIVENESS

Many observers, particularly foreigners, have commented on the unusual willingness of many South Africans to forgive those responsible for perpetrating serious human rights abuses. Foreign reporting on the TRC often focused on emotional scenes at public hearings in which former victims met and forgave perpetrators. The TRC's five-volume report and memoirs subsequently written both by Archbishop Tutu and Piet Meiring, another commissioner, recount various dramatic and heartrending stories of forgiveness and reconciliation between victims and perpetrators.[25]

Many analysts have linked the TRC's unprecedented emphasis on forgiveness and restorative justice to the influence of the religious community on its process. This is certainly the view of many religious leaders, some of whom also draw the conclusion that the South African model is not exportable for this reason.[26] Yet another important factor needs to be factored into this process, the concept of *ubuntu*. As explicated by Archbishop Tutu, *ubuntu* conveys a social view of the essence of being human. It conveys a view that "my humanity is caught up, is inextricably bound up, in yours." He goes on to explain that according to the African *Weltanschauung*, "a person is a person through other persons. I am human because I belong, I participate, I share." He adds,

Social harmony is for us the *summum bonum* the greatest good. Anything that subverts, that undermines this sought-after good, is to be avoided like the plague. Anger, resentment, lust for revenge, even success through aggressive competitiveness, are corrosive of this

25. Piet Meiring, *Chronicle of the Truth Commission: A Journey through the Past and Present Into the Future of South Africa* (Vanderbijlpark, South Africa: Carpe Diem Books, 1999).
26. This is a frequent theme in a series of interviews with religious leaders conducted by Bernard Spong, a former staff member of the South African Council of Churches, for the AAAS project.

good. To forgive is not just to be altruistic. It is the best form of self-interest. What dehumanizes you inexorably dehumanizes me.[27]

It is important to note, however, that many South Africans give far less credence to these ostensible manifestations of forgiveness than do outsiders. Some of those I interviewed believed that the TRC's rhetoric of forgiveness was more a reflection of Archbishop Tutu's dominating presence than the spontaneous response of victims. A few disparaged the entire process as mere gestures. Several victim advocates criticized the TRC because the commission placed pressure on victims to forgive perpetrators but did not invest as much effort in seeking statements of repentance or contrition from perpetrators. They claimed that the TRC was more intent on restoring the human dignity of perpetrators than protecting the interests of former victims. Other members of the South African human rights community and victims' advocates argued that the entire process was faulty because victims should not have been expected, implicitly or explicitly, to forgive perpetrators. Instead they advocated for the need to recognize and legitimate the anger of victims and their family members. Rather than placing pressure on victims to forgive their perpetrators, they believe that the TRC should have provided space for people to express feelings of sadness and rage.[28]

These differences of perspective raise four separate, significant issues. The first is how to understand the role of forgiveness in a social or political context, particularly in relationship to a transitional society and a truth commission process. The second is whether it is appropriate for a truth commission to attempt to promote forgiveness between victims and perpetrators. The third is whether the TRC promoted something approximating genuine forgiveness between victims and perpetrators. And the fourth is the relationship between forgiveness and national reconciliation. This chapter can only begin to address these fundamental questions.

Whatever one's position on these issues, it is clear that public hearings of the type the TRC organized do not offer an appropriate setting for

27. Tutu, *No Future Without Forgiveness*, 31.
28. Brandon Hamber, "How Should We Remember? Issues to Consider When Establishing Commissions and Structures for Dealing with the Past," Centre for the Study of Violence and Reconciliation, Johannesburg, 1998.

effecting deep and genuine forgiveness between victims and perpetrators. Several prominent South African religious leaders have echoed this assessment. At a minimum they believe that a meaningful process of forgiveness requires an opportunity for victims to become acquainted with perpetrators and to understand their motives. Despite the TRC's emphasis on reconciliation and restoring a relationship between victims and perpetrators, there was little actual opportunity for interaction between them. The TRC's Human Rights Committee dealt with victims, the Amnesty Committee with perpetrators. The amnesty process did not allow for dialogue between them. While survivors and victims' families had the right to be present, they did not initially have time in amnesty hearings to question the applicant and comment on his testimony.[29] Nor did the TRC seek to arrange such private meetings in advance of or subsequent to the exchanges at open hearings. Instead, public hearings were usually the first and only point of contact.

What does South African data show about public attitudes toward amnesty and forgiveness? Family members of prominent slain activists argued against amnesty for perpetrators of gross human rights abuses, going so far as to challenge the constitutionality of the amnesty provisions of the National Unity and Reconciliation Act before the Constitutional Court. Nevertheless, at least in one survey done early in the TRC process (May 1996) Black African respondents were more willing to grant amnesty to perpetrators of human rights violators than were Coloured, Indian, or white respondents. Support for amnesty was strongest in provinces with predominantly rural black inhabitants. Those with the lowest incomes were the most willing to accept the TRC formula of amnesty for testimony while the wealthy were overwhelmingly opposed.[30] These data are therefore suggestive of the influence of *ubuntu* in African attitudes toward amnesty for perpetrators.

Nevertheless, amnesty was not popular among members of any community. In a subsequent survey conducted in June 1997, amnesty was regarded as appropriate only in certain circumstances, and many respon-

29. Michelle Parlevliet, "Between Facilitator and Advocate: The South African Truth and Reconciliation Commission," *Forum* 36 (December 1998): 11.
30. Gunnar Theissen, a consultant to the AAAS project, reanalyzed these data. His paper, "Common Past, Divided Truth," presented at the conference on the TRC: Commissioning the Past, University of the Witwatersrand, June 11–14, 1999, offers a preliminary analysis.

dents believed that only those perpetrators who showed remorse should be granted amnesty. In this survey only 19 percent of respondents believed that the amnesty process was necessary for reconciliation, and a considerable percentage (38%) favored criminal prosecutions over the amnesty process. In a third exercise based on ascertaining attitudes through manipulating a storyline, the willingness to forgive appeared to be less strong than the acceptance that the state grant amnesty to a perpetrator. Moreover, punishment and amnesty were not perceived as two options that rule each other out. Mercy was widely accepted, but impunity was not.[31] Thus the litany of abuse, loss, and violence uncovered by the TRC has at least in some quarters given rise to a call for prosecution of perpetrators.[32]

Widespread support for the TRC was initially contingent on commitment to a restorative approach to justice that would repair past injustices through the provision of both truth and reparations. Many former victims apparently assumed that the TRC was offering them an implied deal: "in exchange for providing the TRC with information and letting go their demands that perpetrators be punished, they would receive compensation and the truth about their victimisation would be revealed."[33] Data from community studies and focus groups conducted by the Centre for the Study of Violence and Reconciliation suggest that many of those who responded in this manner are now disappointed and perceive the TRC as reneging on this implied contract. Not as much truth was revealed as they expected, and at the close of the TRC process the award of reparations was still pending.[34] Unfortunately, while former perpetrators who qualified were granted amnesty immediately, a lack of resources has made the provision of reparations to victims much more complicated. And it seems unlikely that the Mbeki government will be motivated to implement the TRC's recommendations regarding reparations for victims. There is the danger that this situation will lead to political disillusionment, even alienation.

31. Ibid., 27–29, 34–35.
32. Parlevliet, "Between Facilitator and Advocate," 11.
33. Hugo van der Merwe, "The South African Truth and Reconciliation Commission and Community Reconciliation," The Centre for the Study of Violence and Reconciliation, Johannesburg, 1998, 10.
34. It should be noted that the van der Merwe paper from which this comment is drawn is a community study, but I think its observations apply more broadly.

ACKNOWLEDGMENT

For reconciliation to occur there is a need for open and shared acknowledgment of the injuries suffered and the losses experienced. One dimension of acknowledgment is for the perpetrators and beneficiaries of the former regime to take responsibility for inflicting harm. This is particularly relevant in South Africa given the critique of what might be termed "cheap reconciliation" in the 1986 Kairos Document written by a group of black theologians. The Kairos Document argues that "no reconciliation, no forgiveness and no negotiations are possible *without repentance.*" The Biblical teaching on reconciliation and forgiveness makes it quite clear that nobody can be forgiven and reconciled with God unless he or she repents of their sins. Nor are *we* expected to forgive the unrepentant sinner.[35]

Like the Nazi regime, apartheid in South Africa was an institutionalized form of violence and injustice that rested on the implicit, if not explicit, support of much of the white population over a long period of time. A small number of whites opposed the government, but an even greater number were directly involved as perpetrators of injustice and abuses. The vast majority of whites were silent accomplices who reaped the economic and political benefits of apartheid. Therefore, it is significant to evaluate whether the TRC proceedings prompted the white population to acknowledge their political and moral responsibility and guilt.

On one level, the TRC's strategy of holding public hearings was relatively successful in forcing all South Africans to confront the horrors of the apartheid system. The public hearings received extensive media coverage, particularly on television. The searing record of abuses that was revealed conferred credibility and dignity to scores of former victims and their relatives, finally giving them a voice to reach out to a wider public. As the process went on it became very difficult for the majority of white South Africans to deny the injustices and suffering caused by the former regime. Some analysts believe that this process of public testimony was the greatest achievement of the TRC.[36]

---

35. *Challenge to the Church: A Theological Comment on the Political Crisis in South Africa, The Kairos Document,* Theology in Global Context Program, Occasional Bulletin 1 (1986).
36. Graeme Simpson, "South Africa's Truth and Reconciliation Commission," paper presented

However, on another level the hearings were also one of the TRC's limitations. The exclusive focus on "gross violations of human rights"—killings, torture, disappearances, and severe physical injury—personalized and individualized the crimes of apartheid. Interpreting this dimension of its mandate very narrowly, the TRC did not attempt to document or assess the impact of the institutionalized racism of the apartheid system. Because the TRC chose to interpret its mandate to investigate gross human rights abuses narrowly, it dealt with the institutionalized racism of the apartheid system primarily as background. It can be argued that the profound denial of the human dignity and life opportunities of the majority of the population over the course of a half century was a far more significant affront to human rights than the gross violations on which the TRC focused.

Just as significantly, the TRC approach does not seem to have prompted the majority of white South Africans to come to terms with their own complicity in overtly or tacitly supporting the apartheid system and benefiting from its structural inequalities. The emphasis on gross human rights abuses resulted in the TRC treating violations of human rights more as the product of individuals' decisions and actions than the intended outcome of the apartheid system. This enabled the white South Africans, who as a community were the supporters and beneficiaries of apartheid, to place the burden of responsibility on individuals and not the system. Even after the painstaking TRC process,

> The increasingly familiar refrain within white South African communities, that apartheid was merely a "mistake" for which no-one was responsible, that somehow the system propelled itself impersonally, may be one of the more ironic, unintended consequences of the TRC's rendition of the past.[37]

Data from various public surveys underscore the failure of the TRC to

---

at the conference on the TRC: Commissioning the Past, University of the Witwatersrand, June 11–14, 1999.

37. Deborah Posel, "The TRC Report: What Kind of History? What Kind of Truth?" paper presented at the conference on the TRC: Commissioning the Past, University of the Witwatersrand, June 11–14, 1999.

outreach successfully to the white population.[38] From the very beginning of
the process most white South Africans were not in favor of the TRC. Less
than half (39% of white South Africans) supported the establishment of a
commission to investigate crimes that occurred under the previous government. The rejection was significantly higher among Afrikaans-speaking
whites than English speakers. While over 60 percent of African respondents
regarded the TRC as fair and unbiased, the longer the TRC process went
on, fewer and fewer white South Africans, particularly Afrikaans-speaking
whites, felt the same way.[39] Disturbingly, even after exposure to the TRC
process very few white South Africans (only 18.9%) acknowledged they
had been beneficiaries of the apartheid order. Although white South
Africans still hold the vast majority of economic resources and have been
asked to make few sacrifices, many white South Africans appear to regard
themselves as suffering under the new democratic order and consider their
lives to have been better during the apartheid period. Another troubling
tendency that the data reveals is that many white South Africans hold a
view that there is no moral difference between committing acts in the course
of a liberation struggle and crimes undertaken to suppress the black liberation movement.[40]

THE TRC'S APPROACH TO RECONCILIATION

The TRC often seemed confused about its approach to national reconciliation. Its report notes the "particular difficulty of understanding the
meaning of unity and reconciliation at a national level."[41] During its life,
the TRC slid between three basic approaches: reconciliation between political parties (ANC and National Party), reconciliation between races (blacks
and whites), and reconciliation between victims as a group and the structures

38. The data from the public surveys was reanalyzed as part of the American Association of the
　　Advancement of Science project.
39. Gunnar Theissen, "The Truth and Reconciliation Commission in South Africa: A Review of
　　Public Opinion Surveys," report prepared for the Centre for the Study of Violence and Rec-
　　onciliation and the American Association of the Advancement of Science, June 1999, 15–20,
　　43–46.
40. Theissen, "Common Past, Divided Truth."
41. *Truth and Reconciliation Commission of South Africa Report*, 1:108.

of the state. Often the commission did not distinguish clearly among these three very different relationships or consciously seek to promote any of these. And none of these dealt sufficiently with the complex dynamics of intra-community divisions and relationships, particularly the insidious role of the Inkatha Freedom Party and its role in fomenting black-on-black violence.

Too often the TRC individualized issues of reconciliation, just as it individualized its sense of responsibility for violence and abuses, and neglected the national and community dimensions. Both the TRC process and the final report focused on reconciliation between victims and perpetrators, that is, forgiveness, rather than the more complex and significant topic of national reconciliation. The section on reconciliation in volume 5 devotes most of its space to relating specific instances of reconciliation between victims/survivors and perpetrators. There is little in the way of analysis of national or community reconciliation in the report.

The TRC report notes the "potentially dangerous confusion between a religious, indeed Christian understanding of reconciliation, more typically applied to interpersonal relationships, and the more limited notions of reconciliation applicable to a democratic society."[42] Later the report observes that the religious conversion model of confession, repentance, and forgiveness is central to the dogma of religion but raises questions about its applicability and relevance to South Africa's situation.[43] This is ironic given the degree to which the TRC process was infused with religious imagery and even something approximating religious ritual. The report's defensiveness and the text that follows this statement suggests that the real issue is the acknowledged failure of the TRC to elicit confession and repentance from leaders of Afrikaner society.

CONCLUSION

So what tentative conclusions can be drawn at this point about the contributions of the TRC to truth and reconciliation in South Africa? The first is that it is difficult, perhaps impossible, to develop a new society without

42. Ibid.
43. *Truth and Reconciliation Commission of South Africa Report*, 5:442.

coming to terms with the past in a meaningful way. The TRC was a beginning, a necessary and significant effort to set the processes of truth finding and reconciliation in motion in South Africa. It made a significant contribution as a bridge between the apartheid past and a more inclusive and democratic future. Nevertheless, because reconciliation is a long-term process with many more dimensions than truth finding, no truth commission can do more than take the first steps.

Despite the TRC's inadequacies, some of which are chronicled in this chapter, and its failure to develop a coherent and consistent approach to reconciliation, many South Africans believe that the TRC contributed to peace and reconciliation in the country. However, survey data show a significant difference among black and white respondents on this point. In general, African respondents state that the TRC improved race relations, peace, and reconciliation, while many white respondents disagree.[44]

In the first volume of the TRC report, the commission both warns against expecting too much, too soon from the reconciliation process at a national level and cautions against accepting too limited a notion of reconciliation. By the fifth volume the commission seems to be tilting toward the latter approach. The report suggests that a weak or limited form of reconciliation, without apologies by those responsible or forgiveness by victims, may often be the most realistic goal toward which to strive, at least at the beginning of the process. The TRC applies this insight to relationships between former enemies within communities and to the network of relationships between communities, and between ethnic and racial groups at regional and national levels. It observes that reconciliation accepts differences among communities, cultures, value systems, and even histories, provided there is some shared history. As it states, the work and activities of the commission will certainly contribute to the development of the latter, but such a history cannot be force-fed. To the extent that the commission itself reached a final conclusion on the topic, it would be the following statements:

National unity and reconciliation calls for a commitment to share a future and for each, in his or her own way, to build towards that

44. Ibid., 53–55.

future. It calls for a commitment to respect law and the procedures and processes laid down by the Constitution. All of this already exists. It may be a fledgling, but it exists. It can only be enhanced.[45]

I would agree with this assessment. I think it validates the position of the commissioners and staff of the TRC who argued against placing an explicit emphasis on forgiveness and interpersonal reconciliation. The TRC's experience shows that it is far more appropriate for a national body like a truth commission to deal with the relationship between communities than between individuals. Had the TRC done so and developed a more intentional approach to national reconciliation, I believe that it would have made an even more effective contribution to South Africa's future.

In South Africa long-term reconciliation will depend on achieving greater economic justice between the beneficiaries and the victims of the apartheid system. And for that reason it is unfortunate that even after the TRC experience very few white South Africans (18.9%) are willing to acknowledge either their support for the apartheid system or the manner that they benefited from its operation. Because whites do not generally perceive themselves as beneficiaries of the apartheid order, very few white South Africans are committed to sharing some of their wealth. Only a small minority of white South Africans (9%) are willing to rectifying the injustices of the past through redistribution and affirmative action policies, and less than a third of all white South Africans favor compensating victims of past human rights abuses.[46] Future prospects for meaningful reconciliation will depend on going beyond the truth about the apartheid past to more equitable economic and social systems as the foundation for a new South Africa's future.

Note: This chapter is based on research collected through an ongoing project that the Science and Human Rights Program of the American Association for the Advancement of Science (AAAS) and South African collaborators are undertaking, with the support of the Templeton Foundation, to study the interrelationships between truth, forgiveness, and reconciliation in South Africa.

45. *Truth and Reconciliation Commission of South Africa Report,* 1:108; 5:400, 443.
46. Thiessen, "Truth and Reconciliation Commission in South Africa," 79.

CHAPTER 14

Implementation of
Track Two Diplomacy

Developing a Model of Forgiveness

Olga Botcharova

LIMITING CHARACTERISTICS
OF OFFICIAL DIPLOMACY

IF WE WANT TO BE MORE EFFICIENT in dealing with contemporary conflicts, it is time to recognize that the human tragedies caused by ethnic conflicts are to a significant extent the result of the international community's failure to provide political leadership that has clear vision, moral conviction, and political will. The Balkan conflict, particularly the events in Kosovo, is a clear example of such an approach. For over a dozen years numerous practitioners and experts in conflict resolution had been predicting dangerous developments in the then-existing situation in Kosovo, but the global policymakers chose first to ignore the warnings, then to close their eyes on the ethnic cleansing, and, finally, to intervene with expensive and inefficient military attacks. This "peacemaking" scenario is all too familiar, as is its outcome—a conflict unresolved.

Even when accords have been undertaken, the sad statistics are confirmed, that more than 50 percent of international initiatives and negotiations on peace fail. Why do these failures occur with frightening persistence, despite the fact that they are developed by informed experts who often offer seemingly balanced and quite rational solutions to the most complicated problems of partitioning territories and people? What is wrong with such initiatives? We may find some answers in the analyses of the nature of contemporary conflict presented from the perspective of track two diplomacy, found in the works of John Paul Lederach, Joseph Montville, Douglas Johnston and Cynthia Sampson, Donald Shriver, and others.[1] The essence of these studies and my experience in peacemaking in regions of severe conflict suggest that three major factors block the successful implementation of international peace policy: (1) a failure to attend to the deep need for healing from victimization of the parties in violent conflict, (2) strategies that impose foreign recipes for peace, and (3) strategies that appeal to the political hierarchy as the exclusive decisionmakers. Let's look at each of these factors in turn.

Failure to Attend to the Need for Healing

An inherent weakness of many official initiatives is that they are rational responses to irrational phenomena. The contemporary ethnic conflict is not rational. Warfare is directed at churches and mosques, hospitals and cemeteries, cultural and historical monuments; women, children, and old people become the planned targets of atrocities. The tools of official diplomacy and military solutions are not adequate for handling such conflicts. Who is the enemy of well-equipped, highly trained American NATO soldiers and Russian UFOR boys who are sent to the region ready for modern combat? Typically, their "combat field" is a street in a small town or village, and the "enemy" is a crowd of angry men and women, former neighbors shouting at each other, cursing each other, ready to stone or shoot each other. It may be a young widow who lost her children under the ruins of her family home and who turned herself into a sniper. It may be a Palestinian child who witnessed how his brother bled to death, shot by an Israeli soldier, a boy who then grabbed a stone and became a "freedom fighter." Drawn into the war by the

---

1. John Paul Lederach, *Building Peace: Sustainable Reconciliation in Divided Societies* (Washington, D.C.: U.S. Institute of Peace Press, 1997); Joseph Montville, *The Arrow and the Olive Branch: A Case for Track Two Diplomacy. The Psychodynamics of International Relationships* (Lexington, Mass.: Lexington Books, 1990), and *The Healing Function in Political Conflict Resolution: Conflict Resolution Theory and Practice* (Manchester: Manchester University Press, 1993); Douglas Johnston and Cynthia Sampson, eds., *Religion: The Missing Dimension of Statecraft* (New York: Oxford University Press, 1994); and Donald W. Shriver, *An Ethic for Enemies: Forgiveness in Politics* (New York: Oxford University Press, 1997).

manipulations of ambitious nationalists, the people are unable to break the cycle of revenge. Considering the extent of suffering and the losses they have experienced, it should not be surprising. How is it possible to ignore pain and forget the hurts committed against one's family or ethnic group?

Even though one may realize that partnership in a solution (the idea vigorously promoted by outsiders and often perceived as insulting by deeply victimized groups and individuals) is the only way to stop further tragedies, one may still not be able to disconnect from one's emotions and to betray those principles and values fundamental to life itself. People forced by their leaders to fight with each other only yesterday cannot readily shake hands today just because their leaders finally draw lines on maps and put their signatures on important papers prepared in America, Paris, or Geneva. Alas! Only a paper peace can be reached on paper. Appeals to develop partnership and cooperation based on a policy of "carrots and sticks" do not deal with the wounds, feelings, and deeply rooted perceptions of the victimized sides. This is the reason that we see little change in behavior even after peace agreements are imposed. It is next to impossible for victims to look to their enemy or abuser as a partner in search of a solution to conflict unless they undergo dramatic and painful inner changes. This transformation is possible only after the individual's, and group's, sense of victimhood is understood, respected, and properly addressed—hardly a task for foreign boys with guns in military uniforms. Although international troops can successfully suppress military activities and introduce a ceasefire—and these are undeniably necessary conditions to begin any work on true peace—they are not able, not prepared, not equipped, and not trained to deal with matters of healing trauma, addressing existing stereotypes, and other challenges that must be met if we hope to achieve sustainable peace and future reconciliation.

Official diplomacy (known as track one in conflict-resolution terminology) is oriented to a "carrot and stick" policy and to the short-term results achieved through military pressure. It does not take into consideration the nature of conflict, where perceptual, social-psychological, and spiritual dimensions are core, rather than peripheral, concerns. As Lederach observes,

> The immediacy of hatred and prejudice, of racism and xenophobia,
> as primary factors and motivators of the conflict require approaches

to its transformation that are rooted in social-psychological and spiritual dimensions that traditionally have been seen as either irrelevant to or outside the competency of international diplomacy.[2]

Strategies Imposing Foreign Recipes for Peace

The second critical factor that blocks progress in international efforts is that the international community often sees people in the regions of conflict as passive recipients, rather than active resources, in peace building, although it is these people who are an instrumental and integral element to sustainable change. "We in the international community have too easily approached these settings as if they were devoid of resources for peacemaking." Bosnia in particular, with its multinational, pluralistic traditions, provides us with numerous examples of how its people are able to successfully implement those resources. Crimea, a small peninsula at the Black Sea that Ukraine received after difficult negotiations with Russia, is another example of the tremendous efforts of dozens of local communities struggling, thus far successfully, to resist tremendous tension and massive ethnic violence. The desired changes will be sustainable only if the indigenous people develop a sense of ownership over the peace initiatives. When we the outsiders leave, the local people will stay and will have to implement those changes and live with them. Besides, only they have enough "here and now" knowledge and experience to address the true reasons for the conflict. Therefore, from the very beginning, everything that outsiders attempt to do in the region should be done in conjunction with the people living there. Eliciting ideas, cherishing the seeds of grassroots reconciliation, and providing all necessary support for their implementation involves a slow and delicate process that requires great trust, network development, and long-term commitment. This approach is based on faith, discipline, and patience. It does not provide quick sensational results and cannot be measured with the traditional tools designed to evaluate a "fix the problem" approach. Instead, following the concept of sustainable transformation, we move away from approaching a given setting with a single set of tools for peacemaking

2. John Paul Lederach, "Pacifism in Contemporary Conflict: A Christian Perspective," paper commissioned by the U.S. Institute of Peace, 1993, p. 12

and place emphasis on discoverig and empowering resources, modalities, and mechanisms that emerge naturally from the setting of the conflict.[3] Only with these conditions do the peace initiatives become an essential part of the people's lives. Then we may hope that the first fragile efforts will be rooted into people's hearts and minds and will lead to powerful changes grown from inside, thus building a long-term commitment to peacemaking.

Strategies Appealing Exclusively to the Political Hierarchy

The third factor preventing the successful implementation of global initiatives is related to the second. It is connected with existing diplomatic biases, which, as Lederach notes, deal primarily with hierarchies of political and military structures, short-term results, especially in terms of ceasefires, and media attention given to eminent figures.[4] Political leaders have a very limited ability to work patiently on subtle issues of nonviolent conflict resolution, even if they may choose to do so. They are seen, above all, as the stewards of people's defense and strength.[5] Although peacemaking is seen as trickling down from the top to other levels of the population, sustainable transformation of conflict calls for more than that. It goes beyond traditional concepts of ceasefire, and beyond top-level negotiations and highly visible efforts, toward the most delicate, challenging, and painful issues of relational transformation—through reconciliation among common people. When a critical mass of medium-level and top grassroots enthusiasts manages to heal its traumas, process its sense of victimhood, and come to forgiveness, there will be hope that the war mentality in the society will gradually be changed. These respected people, who possess great initiative, are in the best position both to promote a new shift in grassroots perceptions and to influence the attitudes of top-level decisionmakers. Without a safe, supportive environment, there is a little hope that political leaders will risk changing the positions with which they are strongly identified. Sustainable peace is more about relationships than about reconstruction work and suppressing gunfire, thus it is possible only through the trans-

3. Ibid.
4. Lederach, *Building Peace*.
5. Montville, *Arrow and the Olive Branch*.

formation of people and relationships from below. The transformed people would then be able to change their relationships and build adequate new structures to support them, including changing the leaders if required. For the necessary infrastructure to be in place, the processes and solutions for a lasting peace must provide space for input and implementation across all levels of the affected society.

THE ROLE OF TRACK TWO DIPLOMACY: FILLING THE VOID

Consistent with the shortcomings described above, official diplomacy has generally failed to consider social-psychological and spiritual approaches in peace building. Track two diplomacy has emerged to fill this void. Montville describes track two diplomacy as an unofficial interaction between members of adversarial groups or nations to develop strategies, influence public opinion, and organize human and material resources in ways that might help resolve their conflict. He notes that track two diplomacy is in no way a substitute for official, formal track one government-to-government or leader-to-leader relationships. Rather, it is designed to assist official leaders by compensating for the constraints imposed upon them by the understandable need for leaders to be strong in the face of the enemy. He observes further that track two diplomacy seeks political formulas or scenarios that might satisfy the basic security and esteem needs of the parties to a particular dispute. "On a more general level, it seeks to promote an environment in a political community, through the education of public opinion, that would make it safer for political leaders to take risks for peace."[6] Promoted by political psychology track two concepts are being recognized increasingly by some decisionmakers in politics. The civil peace accords mentioned in the Dayton agreement are a recent example of this.

In practice, however, track two has not yet been supported as a vital and strategic component of peacemaking, and its cost effectiveness has not yet been evaluated and fully realized. The failure of the international community

6. Ibid., 163.

to implement the aforementioned Dayton Accords might serve as an example of this. Specific activities of track two diplomacy may vary from a one-step action to long-term projects, and include observation, riot control, conciliation and negotiation, joint reexamination of historical events, ecumenical prayers, establishing interfaith peace centers, rebuilding clinics, and creating new school curricula on ethnic tolerance or aid distribution, depending on the needs of the specific place, time, and cultural impact.

The most powerful tool of a track two strategy has proven to be a series of facilitated workshops that bring together representatives of groups in conflict for dialogues that target relational transformation and the integration of the society. Such workshops, as Montville observes, make it possible to undermine negative stereotypes and rehumanize relationships between the parties. "Dialogue, the engine of relationships, promotes mutual confirmation and thereby serves a fundamental need of parties to a conflict to be recognized as individuals with values and unique (and valued) identities."[7] Three projects that I have been involved in during recent years—Conflict Resolution Training for Religious People and Community Leaders from Bosnia and Herzegovina, Croatia, and Yugoslavia (Center for Strategic and International Studies), International Youth Camp for Israelis and Arabs, and for Turkish and Greek Cypriots (Seeds of Peace), and Crimea Dialogue (Search for Common Ground and Ukraine Mediation Group)—are typical and, at the same time, unique illustrations of this type of reconciliation effort. In the section that follows I will use the first project as an exemplar to more fully describe the implementation of a track two strategy. This project is of particular interest since its initial development and implementation took place when military actions between the parties were still active and hence made the dialogue particularly intense.

An Exemplar for Track Two Projects: A Focus on Religion

In 1994 the Center for Strategic and International Studies (CSIS, a Washington-based independent research institute focusing on international affairs) founded a project on conflict resolution training for representatives

7. Montville, *Healing Function in Political Conflict Resolution,* 115.

of religious communities from Bosnia and Herzegovina, Croatia, and Yugoslavia (Serbia and Montenegro) as a part of the Center's program on preventive diplomacy. Why religious communities? What does the conflict in the Balkans have to do with religion? Was this a religious war? These questions are often asked concerning contemporary conflicts (e.g., Northern Ireland) in which ethnicity and religious affiliation are intertwined. In my judgment, in its beginnings this conflict had nothing to do with differences in faith. It was mostly about dividing a pie of economic, territorial, and political power. When the conflict escalated, however, religion became part and parcel by virtue of its association with geographical location, organizational or denominational affiliation, or ethnicity. And although we may argue about the different roles that Orthodox, Catholic, or Muslim leadership played in the conflict's development, the fact is that the people came to perceive each other as threats and as enemies because of their religious affiliation and sometimes killed each other thinking that they were defending their cultural and religious heritage.

It was also evident in the Balkan conflict that right after peace was declared religious institutions and communities, by and large, found themselves in the midst of a most dramatic struggle, appealing for forgiveness in their general statements but not being able to stop blaming and judging each other. It is a long journey from pointing fingers to sharing responsibilities, to confession and repentance, perceived as an integral part of true reconciliation. In spite of these contradictions, only natural in this postwar period, the primary arena of religious activity is still the spiritual, emotional, and relational well being of people, issues that lie at the heart of the contemporary Balkan conflict. Therefore, as extensive evaluation has suggested, any sensitive efforts aimed at helping religious people deal with these questions are highly appreciated by those truly willing to contribute to the peace process. Besides, it is religion that possesses the most powerful traditions and tools, not to mention doctrines for peace building and reconciliation.

A seven-year study by CSIS scholars and practitioners that culminated in the book, *Religion: The Missing Dimension of Statecraft,* analyzes the role that religious activists from seven different parts of the world played in the constructive resolution of conflict within their respective societies.[8] The

8. Johnston and Sampson, eds., *Religion.*

book identifies situations where the potential exists for interventions by religious and spiritually motivated laypersons and speaks to political leaders, foreign policy communities, and religious institutions. Pointing to tremendously underutilized resources in church communities that could be applied to peacemaking, the book set forth the base for our work with religious communities in Bosnia, Croatia, and Serbia. In our work we tried to implement the concepts at the center of this research by assisting the religious people and communities of the region in planting the seeds of long-term reconciliation.

Our project was designed to help the various religious communities to become empowered to pursue a variety of peace-building initiatives during postwar reconstruction. Our purpose was to develop a critical mass of support for such activities among religious and community leaders, and to get them to work together to overcome the stranglehold of ethnic division on both the individual and collective spirit of their people. We did this by identifying middle-level clergy and laity who had already shown leadership in areas of peace and justice and working with them to help them become more effective as agents for conflict resolution.

The project sponsored a series of three- to four-day seminars in community-building and conflict-resolution training, many of which had to be conducted in locations of violent confrontation and extreme suffering. The seminars were designed to promote interethnic trust, assist people to move beyond victimization, and provide tools for indigenous people to resolve their own internal and cross-cultural disputes.

An Exemplar for Track Two Projects:
The Structure of Workshops

Seminars were structured around an experiential approach using group exercises, role-playing, presentations, and discussions. A working manual on conflict resolution, revised and distributed at each seminar, helped provide concrete resources. Furthermore, each seminar concluded with a session on future planning, out of which arose a variety of interfaith project initiatives for implementation locally. Examples include a mediation program in a Croatian church, a seminar in conflict resolution for young people in Serbia, a scholarly book on conflict resolution, and lectures given to Bosnian political parties by one of our workshop participants. All of these activities were done with materials developed in our seminars.

The seminars were organized on three levels, offered in sequence. First-level seminars served local constituencies and were focused primarily around community building. They were designed to help people face issues of grief and loss, heal grievances, share the contributions of their religious traditions to the task of peacemaking, build relations across ethno-religious lines, and examine the role of confession and forgiveness in reconciliation. With the entire spectrum of religious communities present (Muslim, Catholic, Orthodox, and others), the seminars succeeded in eliciting remarkably open dialogue relating to bias awareness, identity formation, and fears of the future.

Second-level seminars extended this work by bringing the alumni from the first-level workshops to a central location and providing them with the opportunity to help each other out of their isolation. These workshops, held within one country or region, focused on attitudinal change and skills development. In addition to reestablishing contacts within the larger community torn apart by war, the seminars helped people to clarify perspectives, assess their own style of handling conflict, and practice conflict-resolution skills (such as communication and mediation).

Third-level seminars further extended the work by helping the participants to identify specific creative roles for their religious communities in fostering social change, to understand where and how to motivate the individuals or structures, and to build competence in community organizing skills. The seminars were designed to help religious communities develop self-generating local programming. Examples include organizing ecumenical peace centers, interfaith counseling teams, mediation training teams, efforts for interethnic cooperation in community reconstruction, human rights advocacy, and interfaith programs for refugee resettlement.

In addition, we offered single confessional seminars to respond to the specific needs within any one particular religious community (with such a high degree of tension in the region at that time, each group faced very complicated issues regarding its self-identity and its role in society), and we organized international seminars in Hungary, which brought together past workshop participants to create stronger ties between participants from Serbia, Croatia, and Bosnia, as well as to promote trust and coordination across republic lines. Finally, at the request of the participants, we held annual international seminars for a group of influential alumni to further facilitate dialogue and cooperation regarding future peace-building efforts, and we planned seminars to help prepare our alumni to interact with officials of greater influence regarding a variety of peacemaking issues.

Overall, our efforts were directed to local program development, with the intention of gradually turning over responsibility for this project to indigenous people and institutions. We began a cooperative relationship with the Center for Peace, Nonviolence, and Human Rights in Croatia, whereby our project became a part of their center, and investigated a similar arrangement in Serbia with MOST ("Bridge"), a Belgrade Center for Peace. We also sponsored the establishment of the Institute for Interfaith Dialogue in Sarajevo headed by one of our most active alumni. Notably, it quickly achieved a trustworthy reputation among multiple religious confessions in the area. In each country we helped develop an institutional framework and train a corps of people so that CSIS personnel could function only as initial consultants to the indigenous organizations in each country.

MOVING TOWARD RECONCILIATION: THE CENTRAL ROLE OF FORGIVENESS

Over six years of its operation, the Conflict Resolution Training for Religious People and Community Leaders from Bosnia and Herzegovina, Croatia, and Yugoslavia project was successful on several major fronts. First, we helped to develop workable relationships among leaders and laypersons of various denominations within the areas affected by violent conflict and across the new borders. Second, we helped people to better understand the conflict and its dimensions from the perspective of their adversary. Third, we developed strategies for dealing with conflict as a shared problem, whose solution resided in cooperative initiatives. And finally, from the many days we spent as active observers, trainers, and facilitators, we learned a great deal about the process of peace building.

The most significant lessons were:

✦ No skill training for problem solving was possible until the feelings of trauma were addressed and some basic healing from victimhood was achieved.

✦ Achieving forgiveness, as the culmination of the healing process, made it possible for the parties to move forward to reconciliation.

✦ Forgiveness cannot be taught, preached, pointed out, or in any other way imposed by outsiders. However, a framework revealing its evolving, sometimes mysterious, nature was identified and proved to be very effective in facilitating dialogue.

✦ The most powerful tool of the workshops was the sharing of stories by individuals from opposite sides of conflict, stories that served as an initial bond of empathy in rebuilding trust.

It had become evident quite early in our workshops that we faced a serious challenge in helping the participants to take yet another step toward resolving the conflict and achieving reconciliation. Before that step could be taken, the victims needed to understand that their sufferings were not to be dismissed but instead fully recognized, and that their anger and passion for justice were not wrong, inadequate, or illegitimate. The participants of our first seminar in Serbia were, for a long time, not able to speak from the bottom of their hearts and to get into meaningful dialogue with each other. The fears of being judged for feeling victimized were so strong that no one dared to take the risk of speaking from the heart. The room was filled with "nice" small talk and sophisticated theological discussions. That was not what we wanted to facilitate at the seminar, having spent two years in the most persistent efforts to include the Serbian Orthodoxy in the interfaith dialogue. By the end of the first day it became clear that unless the people could better understand victimization and what it does to all living beings they would not be able to choose freely between continuing to live as victims and beginning a journey toward healing.

Cycle 1: Seven Steps Toward Revenge

To address this unspoken need, I developed a diagram that assimilates the psychological stages of the dynamics between victimhood and aggression. It demonstrates, in other words, how natural human responses to harm and injustices may move people from being victims to becoming aggressors. This cycle (see fig. 14.1), gives full recognition to the victim's suffering, on one hand, but also to the logical and dangerous progression to escalating violence, on the other. What follows is a brief description of the process illustrated through the diagram.[9]

The cycle recognizes that victims of aggression experience tremendous pain as a result of serious physical, psychological, or moral injury (step 1). The pain is often accompanied by shock, denial, and, eventually, panic. Victims initially experience a state of paralysis, an inability to comprehend the

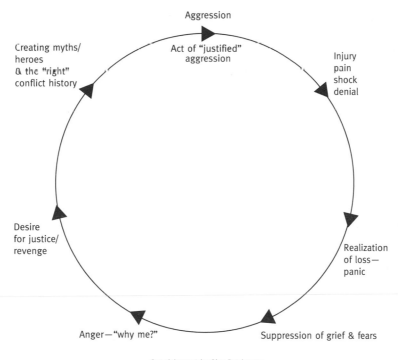

Figure 14.1. Seven steps toward revenge

9. The more explicit text may be found in the CSIS workshop manuals. It was published later as speaking notes for Woodstock Colloquium on Forgiveness In Conflict Resolution: Reality and Utility by Woodstock Theological Center, Georgetown University, 1996.

reality and respond to it, followed by denial, as an attempt to avoid facing the ugly gaping wound caused by severe loss.

Eventually, as victims begin to realize their loss, they can be overwhelmed by a profound fear of seeing the immediate horrible truth—loss of limbs and vital organs, of lifelong possessions, of loved ones—and the future it implies (step 2). Hence, as victims begin to realize their loss, what was a denial of the reality is supplanted by a denial, or suppression, of their grief and fears.

The denial grows in a "snowball effect" as emotions caused by loss become so closely associated with the loss itself that they come to be perceived as its source, and as such they evoke increasing fear and avoidance (step 3). Suppression of grief also serves as a way of hiding from shame, the most damaging factor in undermining self-esteem and sense of identity. The reasons for the suppression are, indeed, many and justifiable—there may be no time to attend to grief, as the victim's survival or the well-being of loved ones may demand demonstrated strength and immediate action. But, however justifiable the suppression, the grief and fears will not disappear.

Rather, the suppression serves to heighten feelings of anger directed toward the perpetrator, and often toward anything associated with the perpetrator—family, friends, neighbors, or members of the same political, national or religious group, or gender (step 4). Sometimes the anger is directed toward outsiders who were unable to prevent the loss, or even toward others who did not experience a similar loss. The whole world may be seen as hostile. Moreover, this anger may be "directed against innocent victims rather than the original object of the anger."[10] At this stage, victims often find themselves totally isolated in their anger and tormented by their victimhood. This state is typically expressed in the question, "Why me?"

Growing anger leads to the belief that healing will occur only if the perpetrator, perceived as the source of the pain, is destroyed. From the victim's perspective—dominated by confusion about the true source of the pain—revenge, justice, healing, punishment, and even problem solving, all become

10. G. R. Williams, "Negotiation as a Healing Process," *Journal of Dispute Resolution,* no. 1 (1996): 1-66 (Center for Dispute Resolution, University of Missouri-Columbia School of Law).

one and the same (step 5). The need to destroy the source of pain drives victims to seek uncompromising justice.

What often happens at this stage is that victims find themselves feeling even more abused, as in many cases, particularly in the presence of open conflict, no justice is achieved. Even when justice is achieved, it never seems adequate to the degree of the victim's suffering. The reason that executed justice seldom satisfies victims lies in the fact that it fails to provide the desired healing from the pain of loss. Enraged by the absence of justice, the victim becomes open to an act of justified aggression (step 6). Hence, a quest for justice becomes transformed into a crusade for revenge, though striking back does not take place immediately.

A pause here is needed to eliminate any doubts about the legitimacy or the evil nature of a vengeful response. These doubts, often weak and unclear, are hidden deep within the victim's initial confusion. If victims allow these doubts to emerge, the act of revenge may never take place. If victims choose to turn away from them, they will create an environment where it will be safe to carry out the planned action. The image of the perpetrator is deprived of any possible signs of human goodness; self-pity, blame, and demands for justice are reinforced; a history of conflict, with its myths, legends, and heroes is created, and the history of genuinely complex relationships is seen and presented as a chain of violent actions committed by the other side (step 7). Such a black-and-white mentality excludes the possibility of hearing any other voice. This mobilization of emotions and perceptions is fashioned to appeal to semirepressed fears and anger, and requires rather manipulative behavior on the part of the victim, though he or she is often not fully aware of it.

Finally, when the victim performs the act of "justified" aggression, the cycle of violence is completed, with the roles now reversed. The former perpetrator now feels victimized, seeks revenge, and, finally, strikes again when an opportunity occurs.

Although the above pattern reflects typical tendencies in the development of victimhood, not all victims are doomed to become aggressors and not all conflicts turn into wars or violence. (The history of those conflict outcomes is yet to be written.) We, as a human race, would have ceased our existence on this planet long ago if the rationale of the vicious spiral had constantly prevailed. Thus, the challenge for the participants of the work-shops was to identify the mechanisms that resist the logic of conflict escala-tion and help to break the cycle of revenge. Before addressing these issues and before sharing their stories, the participants were encouraged to reflect silently on the choices that they had made as victims in conflict, whether those choices were related to individuals or their identity groups. (It seems sometimes too embarrassing to admit to the confusion and weakness behind such choices in the presence of the other side. Initial sharing may take place within the safety of their own group.) I believe that these quiet moments are very important as true transformation takes place in the setting of deep intimacy.

After examining the logic of revenge, some of the participants of our first seminar in Serbia, who had strongly avoided addressing the conflict, finally began to share the most powerful stories of their struggle with victimhood, including giving recognition to certain manipulative aspects of their behav-ior as an ethnic group. Some of the stories told by our participants of dif-ferent workshops, typical for a violent ethnic conflict, had a shared nontypical continuation.

The story of Ivo, a Franciscan brother whose old parents were killed in front of him in their home in Sarajevo by Muslim soldiers, or of Dragomir, a Serbian Orthodox priest pulled out of his house at night and shot by Croatians who then left him to die, or of Bojo, a Protestant layperson who together with his sixteen-year-old daughter was humiliated, tortured, and sent to walk through a minefield by Serbian gunmen.

All these individuals who survived atrocities, who faced death, and who seemed to have a legitimate right to hatred and revenge, instead dedicated their lives to peacemaking. Moreover, some of them tried to reach the other side and communicate their forgiveness and at least one succeeded in restor-ing a relationship with his direct abusers. Such stories became turning points at our seminars. Having heard them other participants who had been unable to let their hatred go felt challenged and inspired to take the risk and tell their own stories of suffering, thus beginning their healing. The process was often accompanied with immense inner struggles for overcoming fears, pain, shame, and helplessness of victimhood. Not everyone was able to come to forgiveness within a few days of the seminar, but most began their journeys with the first steps toward healing.

HUMAN NATURE:
THE PHYSICAL AND SPIRITUAL

The continuing dialogue focused primarily on the psychological and spiritual aspects of forgiveness, identified as a force that breaks the cycle of revenge. The early stage of the discussion often began with remembering small secret doubts that, in spite of the evident rightness of the victims, prevented them from striking back. The origin of such doubts does not seem clear, as they do not belong to either reason or mind, or to our emotions. They are articulated by an inner voice, of which there is no objective proof, the voice that comes from the very depth of a soul (a word that in Slav languages indicates a place for spirit in a human being, "*dusha*"). Mihailo Mihailov, a contemporary Russian philosopher who completed most of his work while locked in Yugoslav prisons during Tito's regime, wrote explicitly about the meaning of the soul and faith from the perspective of achieving individual liberation and gaining social political freedom.[11]

By exploring a side of human nature that "in spite of threat of physical destruction and against all the dictates of reason" sometimes resists a vengeful response the workshop participants were reunited in their rediscovery of spirituality. Similar to the experiences of many political prisoners, as described by Mihailov, exposed to all possible physical and moral humiliation, the participants who survived atrocities of ethnic cleansing came to the conclusion that turning away from the inner voice, in other words, betraying the soul, was the worst evil.[12] However, by obeying the voice of the soul, they reconnected with the source of the spiritual power that releases them from all fears and, thus, from anger.

In the story of Bojo, even knowing that he and his daughter were to be killed at any moment, he experienced relief and, in a way, joy, because, unlike their abusers, though given the opportunity, he had not committed an act of evil. He had chosen not to run his vehicle over the three gunmen when they had been trying to stop his car. Now, in the face of certain death, he felt great moral strength and a freedom from fear that could not be taken from him by any outside force including death. Mihailov writes, "To obey

11. M. Mihailov, *Underground Notes* (New Rochelle, N.Y.: Caratzas Brothers, 1982).
12. Ibid., 23.

the inner voice means nothing less than to define actions in time in terms of eternity," meaning that belief in the immortality of the spiritual power with which a person comes to associate himself, removes the basic fear of death, which is the source of all other earthly fears. In other words, the spiritual takes over and overcomes the major natural human reactions that are rooted in our fears and in the instinct of survival. As a result of the struggle at moments of severe suffering, a struggle that "demands separation from everything except the soul," the most tragic human calamities are viewed through a different lens, from the perspective of an achieved freedom (salvation) and new wisdom.[13] The most dramatic events are seen rather as challenging life experiences, lessons to be learned and problems to be solved. Moreover, the victims who trust their inner voice and act upon that faith, as their stories record, often experience not only spiritual salvation but also miraculous rescue from physical dangers. (It is interesting to note that similar discussions also occurred with groups of people who did not identify themselves as believers, but who reported strong empirical experiences of a mysterious spiritual strength following an inner voice that made them recognize its empowering presence in situations where they had made tremendous sacrifices.)

The discussions concerning physical and spiritual identities of people had important implications for the continuing development of the dialogue between the parties in conflict. First, the participants began to realize the existence of a unifying connection, which, in the context of conflict, with its stereotypes and "black-and-white" thinking, allowed inclusion of the other and "rehumanizing of the enemy." Second, forgiveness was seen as a complex phenomenon, an intimate spiritual dialogue with one's own soul, a blessing from God and relief from pain. As such, it could not be guaranteed, traded, or demanded. Suzanne R. Freeman and Robert D. Enright noted that the success of the interveners working with victims of abuse applying forgiveness therapy was to a great degree due to the fact that the word *forgiveness* was not even mentioned in the process.[14] Thus every victim had an opportunity to walk towards forgiveness at his or her own pace

13. Ibid., 25.
14. Suzanne R. Freeman and Robert D. Enright, "Forgiveness as an Intervention Goal with Incest Survivors," *Journal of Consulting and Clinical Psychology* 64, no. 5 (1996): 983–92.

and experience the act of forgiving in his or her unique fashion with no pressure. At the same time, there is a required condition of being attuned to the inner voice, the voice of faith. Third, the stories of the victims who were transformed as a result of the most severe suffering served as powerful examples of how inner faith can be strengthened, as suffering was the path to the very depth of the soul.

From the perspective of psychology we cannot ignore or suppress suffering if we want to develop our sense of selves, our identities, and become happier and stronger. Demanding recognition for their suffering from the others, the victims have to learn to respect their own suffering themselves—instead of ignoring or suppressing it. It is with addressing the pain of loss and developing a different attitude toward suffering that breaking the cycle of victimhood begins.

SEVEN STEPS TOWARD RECONCILIATION

In this section I will illustrate and discuss the second cycle, Seven Steps Toward Reconciliation (see fig. 14.2), which captures the stages of transformation from being victimized, through processing of suffering, toward healing, forgiveness, and future reconciliation. The model was developed based on many days of observation, training, and facilitation with the religious leaders and laity from the full spectrum of religious communities (Muslim, Catholic, Orthodox, and others). The description that follows represents my interpretation, analysis, and assimilation of the extensive dialogue engaged in during the workshops.

While the victims' immediate experience of aggression or abuse does not leave room for any reaction or processing, it is possible to begin to process the suffering as soon as initial realization of loss occurs (step 1).

The victims have to allow themselves to feel the pain, to stay with it in order to be able to leave it later (step 2). They have to learn how to cry instead of hide their tears. By mourning, they are saying goodbye to the past, and to whom they were in that past. By expressing feelings of sadness and grief, they are, in a way, beginning to separate from their pain. The more they release, the more they will be free from it. (Participants were

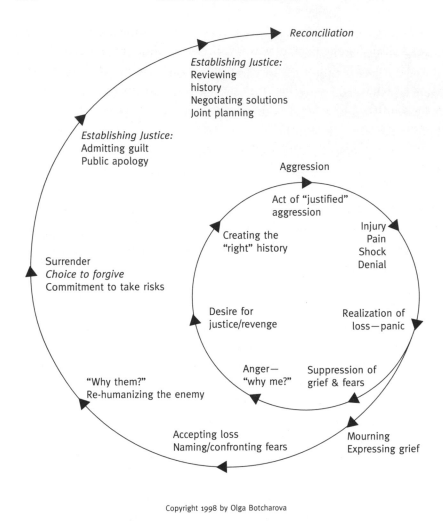

Copyright 1998 by Olga Botcharova

Figure 14.2. Seven steps toward forgiveness

encouraged to explore the tremendous resources that their cultures and religions offer in dealing with grief.)

The first steps in healing require restoring love to oneself. Forgiveness begins for the victims when they make themselves look at the "ugly gaping wound" caused by loss and confront the secret shame and guilt that accompany the damage to their sense of self-identity (step 3). The process of

attending and overcoming the shame is as painful as the process of opening and cleansing the wound, which is needed in order to give it a chance
to heal. Confronting the fears of their new reality requires identifying and
naming each fear, recognizing them one by one. Only by pulling them out
of the darkness, admitting them, sorting them out, do we deprive them of
the power that they have over us. As victims we are usually more fearful of
the emotions that accompany our fears than of the fears themselves. Recognizing and expressing these emotions may help victims not to turn these
emotions into anger. This process takes time and courage, but victims are
rewarded with the ability to think of fears as challenges of life rather than
as fatal tragedies.

Continuously questioning themselves with "Why me?" fails to provide
an acceptable answer (no one deserves to be treated unfairly, moreover, to
become a victim of aggression or abuse) and prevents victims from further
accepting their reality. If they want to restore their sanity, their ability to
think rationally, and if they can yet realize that they were in no way at fault
for what happened, they need to reframe the question to "Why them?"
("what made them, these particular people, do it to us?"). The reframing
may be approached gradually, beginning with the question "Why not me?"
(or "If not me, who then?"). The search for an answer evokes tremendous
resistance, as victims are used to thinking of the other side as "nonhuman"
(it is easier to destroy someone who is not as human or as good as we are).
All of the victims' stereotypes get mobilized, blocking the search that might
reveal any similarity between the victims and the aggressors. Hence the
answer, "They are just crazy," sometimes prevents the further journey. Victims are left, then, in even greater panic, confronted with the possibility of
an unpredictable attack, as craziness is not a subject to any rational control.
If the evil is senseless, they will never know how to resist it. On the other
hand, if victims allow themselves to continue the search, they may discover
that however brutal or criminal the actions of the aggressor may have been,
the basic needs that drive such actions are usually very human and are usually related to fear and hopelessness, feelings that are so familiar to the victims. (I want to again emphasize the importance of direct emotional
interaction between the people from opposite sides of the conflict. Nothing
seems as important as the sharing of personal experiences through their

stories.) In fact, victims may discover that they and the aggressors have very similar, if not common, concerns and beliefs. Thus, in trying to get away from their own pain and fears, victims begin to feel the hidden pain and fears of their enemy/aggresor. Rejection and then confusion gradually give way to a sense of affinity and even compassion. At this stage, the enemy becomes rehumanized (step 4). Moreover, from the perspective of a believer, if the one who performed the act of evil is human, then the aggressor is a child of God and as such must have a soul and love of God. Although the act of aggression continues to be perceived as evil, the perpetrator is now seen more as a person who had become disconnected from his own spiritual self by the power of his fears. At this point the victim begins to separate the evil act from the one who committed it. He is perceived as a sinner, a lost soul, overwhelmed by his fears, who perhaps needs love and help in order to understand his sinfulness and restore the connection with the source of the spiritual strength—the only guarantee that the evil will not be committed again.

Feeling the other's pain and restoring the inner connectedness lessens the strength of the quest for revenge. The victim discovers that they are all connected through their fears and basic needs, and their human inability to assert these needs in open, constructive ways. After initial confusion and unwillingness to let the anger go (anger may have served as the only source of energy for a victim), a deep inner transformation takes place that leads to complete surrender to a new openness. In this way, victims find a tranquility in which they feel much more united with their spiritual center. Inclusion of the "other" culminates in forgiveness. Forgiveness relieves the victims from the desperate desire to change the past; it evolves into an acceptance of the present and openness to an unknown future. Forgiveness is the culmination of healing, the most vital need of a victim, and a way to freedom from victimhood. As such, it creates solid ground for developing a new identity. The past cannot be restored, but the transformed person is no longer the person who needs that past. Forgiveness reveals the true meaning of suffering, as a reuniting with the spiritual strength on a deeper level. It transforms suffering from a curse into a blessing. This is the time when the spiritual core of human nature is celebrated. The spiritual power of forgiveness allows the victims to risk vulnerability. The forgiving one is vulnerable to rejection—the aggressor may not care about being forgiven, may avoid communication out of a fear of revenge, and moreover, may even return to strike again, blinded by his fears. However, at this stage, the former victim's newly found strength allows him to take those risks. The commitment to forgiveness and the intensification of the inner dialogue with God are motivated by a personal need for complete healing, which now becomes focused on communicating the forgiveness to the perpetrator. The act of injustice is experienced as an extreme form of rejection of love, the love that all human beings so muh crave and without which we cannot exist. For this need, we are sometimes prepared to sacrifice our physical survival.

Having rediscovered love through a most challenging journey, the former victim believes that there is some hope that the perpetrator might be encouraged to step along a similar path. Thus, the forgiving victim offers a safe embrace for the perpetrator to respond to the call of forgiveness (step 5). Yet an even greater labor of love may be required to open the former aggressor's heart and remove his fears of the future.

Since forgiveness is a culmination of healing, and a primary need of the victim, it is unconditional in nature. Reconciliation, however, is based on two key conditions, forgiveness and justice. Forgiveness provides a different imperative for seeking justice—reintegration of the relationship between former victims and aggressors in a new, safe surrounding designed and built by both sides. And this justice, oriented to the future, presumes a leading role for the former victim in its formulation and focuses on the perpetrator's admitting guilt (step 6). The idea of punishment resides in the exposure of the perpetrator to the shame of the wrongdoing. The suffering that accompanies the process of repentance serves as "purification" and a guarantee of inner transformation. (This interpretation of justice has a rich tradition in the works of Dostoyevskij and other spiritual writers.)

The second major component of establishing justice implies coming to terms with the past. It requires a "walk through history," examining the wounds on all sides and recognizing mutual responsibilities.[15] We cannot build a future if we remain afraid to know our past. Painful memories must be examined and a joint history written, free from the biases of national

15. Montville, *Arrow and the Olive Branch*.

mythologies (step 7). Continued conflicts are directly related to unhealed wounds. (Ex-Yugoslavia is a typical example. After World War II, during the Tito era, Serbs and Croats went back to living side by side, but discussion of the atrocities of war was practically forbidden.) Silence serves as a continuing suppression of fears. "Re-writing" history opens the way to a cooperative approach, based on newly gained recognition and respect for each other's suffering. Only then can negotiations on the practical issues of preserving restored relationships and changing the structures of the sociopolitical environment lead to true reconciliation.

The following are excerpts from the comments of the participants of our workshops in the former Yugoslavia. These reflect their experiences and the growth that manifested from their being able to confront their victimhood. These passages are indicative of how their viewpoints had been affected:

> During those three days that the seminar was taking place, I have learned more in some areas then during my entire life (62 years).

> I was not aware of the value of grieving before.

> We need awareness of our potential power to change the present situation.

> I felt stimulated when we were talking about overcoming the fear.

> I learned about a need for the healing of the collective spirit.

> I have discovered much new about myself. We are both victims and aggressors to each other.

> I discovered the feelings of refugees. . . . I became aware of the benefit of gradual steps in conflict resolution (it is the "little people" that form a base for reconciliation). I have experienced my own feeling of being a victim. I have my peace of heart now and I have more strength to help others come along a similar path I am better able to listen to other people.

SUMMARY AND CONCLUSIONS

In this chapter I argue for the critical role of track two diplomacy in dealing with contemporary conflicts, filling the void left by the often rationalized, politicized and militarized approaches of official (track one) diplomatic initiatives. The shortcomings of track one diplomacy lie in its failure to attend, in any meaningful way, to the many people who have fallen victim to conflict. While we stop the hostilities and impose an immediate "peace," we fail to address the victims' suffering or healing, and we seldom invite them as partners, or even as contributors, in developing and implementing peace processes.

I presented and discussed a particular approach to crafting and implementing peace-building initiatives from a track two perspective, which derives from an explicit recognition of the importance of perceptual, social-psychological, and spiritual dimensions of peace building. More concretely, this approach recognizes that attending to the relationships among the people ravaged by conflict is essential to achieving a peace that is sustainable. Further, religious leaders and laity are identified as having to play a central role in resolving conflicts in many parts of the world.

I derived the model from the training and facilitation workshops that I engaged in with the leaders of ethnic and religious communities in Bosnia, Serbia, and Croatia, and other professionals in conflict resolution and I have since used it in various parts of the world. The concept of forgiveness is at the core of the model and is seen as the culmination of a healing process that makes it possible for the parties in conflict to move forward to reconciliation. Without it there is little hope for a sustainable peace, but achieving it is a formidable challenge. Forgiveness is seen as evolving and mysterious and as something that cannot be simply taught, indoctrinated, or imposed. It can, however, be fostered through thoughtful, sensitive, facilitated dialogue among the parties to a conflict. In the chapter I present a framework for dialogue that reveals the nature of forgiveness and describes the stages and processes through which it may be achieved.

Because of its centrality to achieving a sustainable peace and reconciliation, forgiveness must be considered as a practical and strategically important issue in the policy of peace building. Within this framework, "outsiders" must be willing to go beyond "fixing the problem" and to reach beyond the traditional political hierarchies, to create an environment that allows those hurt by conflict to find and nurture their capacity for forgiveness.

CHAPTER 15

Through Nonviolence to Truth

Gandhi's Vision of Reconciliation

Anthony da Silva, S.J.

WHILE MUCH IS HAPPENING in the world today that may bespeak of despair and hopelessness, one cannot overlook the extraordinary scenes enacted time and again on the world's stage that also bespeak of peace, and reconciliation. One such recent example is the astonishing and moving visit to North Korea by the president of South Korea. This highly visible act of reconciliation between two warring nations populated by the same peoples not only caught the imagination of the world but also filled the hearts of millions of Koreans with a craving for peace and unity. Fifty years in a state of war has neither crushed the human yearning for reconciliation nor silenced the cry for peace.

A little less than a hundred years ago, Mahatma Gandhi of India strode onto the world's stage and challenged the people of India to fight British colonial power and regain the country's independence. However, his fight was no call to armed militancy; rather, it was a call to militancy based on the twin principles of truth and nonviolence. Gandhi lived this philosophy and demonstrated its success. Nevertheless, since his death, nonviolence has been practiced only sporadically and in isolated pockets in India and elsewhere. Ironically, violence and armed militancy are perceived as more attractive alternatives than nonviolence to resolve some of India's political and social problems.

As this new millennium dawns, it might well be that the vision and voice of Gandhi will find greater resonance in the world of today. His message of reconciliation through nonviolence may be the message for our times as powerful reconciliation movements gain ground from South Africa to Chile and from Kashmir to Kosovo.

The purpose then of this chapter is, first, to present the two key Gandhian concepts of Truth and Nonviolence with their Eastern moorings; second, to study the relevance and relationship of these concepts to the current discussion on forgiveness and reconciliation as articulated mostly from a Western perspective; and, finally, to illustrate through three case studies from India that though reconciliation may be embedded and expressed through a variety of cultural hues, it still remains a universal human yearning.

KEY GANDHIAN CONCEPTS IN RECONCILIATION

Satya (Truth)

For M. K. Gandhi there was no concept more dear than *satya* or "truth." Without getting into the metaphysical Gandhi used the concept of truth to galvanize his followers into action. In other words, truth became a motivator for both social and political action. As Gandhi himself explains,

> The word "Satya" (Truth) is derived from "Sat" which means being. And nothing is or exists in reality except Truth. That is why "Sat" or Truth is perhaps the most important name of God. In fact, it is more correct to say that Truth is God, than to say that God is Truth"[1]

Gandhi's truth is, therefore, not about the accuracy or falsehood of a statement but about striving to achieve a sense of God-realization in one's life. In any case, according to Gandhi no human is capable of knowing the absolute truth. Humans are limited in the way they perceive reality. This makes them vulnerable to error and therefore in need of change. Hence humans have no

---

1. *Young India,* July 30, 1931, 196, as quoted in Joan Bondurant, *Conquest of Violence: The Gandhian Philosophy of Conflict* (Princeton, N.J.: Princeton University Press, 1958), 17.

right to punish others or do violence to them because humans are constantly seeking as well as interpreting truth from their own perspectives. Gandhi used this human relativity to advance his thesis "that [the] pursuit of Truth did not admit of violence being inflicted on one's opponent but that he [the opponent] must be weaned from error by patience and sympathy."[2]

Satyagraha (Truth Force)

Truth not only excludes violence, according to Gandhi, but has a built-in "force" (*graha*) or power; it can drive individuals as well as masses of peoples to fight for a truthful cause or to prevent evil. *Satyagraha*, which is commonly associated with Gandhi's sociopolitical protests and noncooperation movements against the British rulers of India, is deeply rooted in God and religion. It is translated variously as "soul force" or "truth force," in contrast to physical and violent force. Raghavan Iyer quotes Gandhi as saying,

> *Satyagraha* is not physical force. A *satyagrahi* (person involved in nonviolent resistance) does not inflict pain on the adversary; he does not seek his destruction. A *satyagrahi* never resorts to firearms. In the use of *satyagraha*, there is no ill-will whatever. . . . *Satyagraha* is pure soul-force. Truth is the very substance of the soul. That is why this force is called *satyagraha*.[3]

Furthermore, in a speech Gandhi delivered in 1946, he insisted that "the root of *satyagraha* is in prayer. A *satyagrahi* relies upon God for protection against the tyranny of brute force."[4]

Bhikhu Parekh, a Gandhian scholar, elaborates further on the concept of *satyagraha*. He says,

> For Gandhi *satyagraha*, meaning civil insistence on or tenacity in the pursuit of truth, aimed to penetrate the barriers of prejudice, ill-will,

2. Jag Parvesh Chander, ed., *Teachings of Mahatma Gandhi* (Lahore: Indian Printing Works, 1945), 494, as quoted in Bondurant, *Conquest of Violence*, 16–17.
3. Raghavan Iyer, ed., *The Essential Writings of Mahatma Gandhi* (Delhi: Oxford University Press, 1994), 309.
4. M. K. Gandhi, *Non-violence in Peace and War* (Ahmedabad: Navajivan Publishing House, 1949), 2:62.

dogmatism, self-righteousness, and selfishness and to reach out to and activate the soul of the opponent. . . . *Satyagraha* was a "surgery of the soul," a way of activating "soul-force."[5]

When questioned as to how "soul-force" operated, Gandhi strongly emphasized the value of *tapasya,* which translates roughly to mean self-suffering or self-sacrificing. He was convinced that through self-suffering a *satyagrahi*'s heart as well as that of the opponent is moved. Gandhi had "an implicit belief that the sight of suffering on the part of the multitudes of people will melt the heart of the aggressor and induce him to desist from his course of violence."[6] Gandhi never advocated suffering for its own sake. But when suffering is undertaken out of love, then it has the power to move and transform the opponent. For, as Gandhi rightly points out, "Love never claims, it ever gives. Love ever suffers, never resents, never revenges itself."[7] In a leaflet he published in 1919, Gandhi further emphasized the relationship between love and truth. He says,

> We shall find too on further reflection that conduct based on truth is impossible without love. Truth-force then is love-force. We cannot remedy evil by harbouring ill will against the evil-doer. . . . In thousands of our acts the propelling power is truth or love.[8]

How then would a Gandhian *satyagrahi* be described? At a *satyagraha* training camp in 1918 Gandhi gave these instructions to the young trainees: they should utter no harsh word about anyone, neither should they have rancor in their hearts; they should maintain the highest type of nonviolence and be ready for voluntary suffering. In a later publication in 1930, under the heading "Rules for *satyagrahis,*" Gandhi once again emphasized that a *satyagrahi* will harbor no anger; in fact, he will suffer the anger of the opponent. Moreover, a *satyagrahi* is never to retaliate.[9]

---

5. Bhikhu Parekh, *Gandhi* (Oxford: Oxford University Press, 1997), 54.
6. Iyer, ed., *Essential Writings of Mahatma Gandhi,* 323.
7. *Young India,* July 9, 1925, as quoted in Chander, ed., *Teachings of Mahatma Gandhi,* 352.
8. *Harijan,* October 22, 1938, as quoted in Iyer, ed., *Essential Writings of Mahatma Gandhi,* 316.
9. Iyer, ed., *Essential Writings of Mahatma Gandhi,* 315, 319–22.

The concept of *satyagraha* can never be fully understood unless the complementary concept of *ahimsa* (nonviolence) is also understood. *Ahimsa,* which has sometimes been poorly rendered as "passive resistance," is actually quite active; it initiates nonviolent "action" in pursuit of truth.

Ahimsa (Nonviolence)

The word *ahimsa,* with its negative prefix *a,* has usually been translated to mean nonviolence. This, however, does not fully bring out the rich fabric of meaning of what is implied in *ahimsa.* As Joan Bondurant rightly states, the full force of *ahimsa* means "action based on the refusal to do harm."[10] Implied is that *ahimsa* is more than merely passive resistance; it is a proactive decision to do no harm to anyone. To quote Gandhi:

> [N]onviolence that merely offers civil resistance to the authorities and goes no further scarcely deserves the name *ahimsa.* You may if you like, call it unarmed resistance. . . . Nonviolence is the greatest and most active force in the world. One cannot be passively nonviolent.[11]

Elsewhere, to the readers of his newspaper, *Harijan,* Gandhi reiterated the same point when he wrote,

> Passive resistance is a misnomer for nonviolent resistance. It is much more active than violent resistance. It is direct, ceaseless but three-fourths invisible and only one-fourth visible. . . . In its visibility it appears ineffective, but it is really intensely active and most effective in ultimate result.[12]

Much as *satyagraha* has been described as "truth force," *ahimsa* could be described somewhat paradoxically as "nonviolent force."

---

10. Bondurant, *Conquest of Violence,* 23.
11. Thomas Merton, *Gandhi on Non-violence* (New York: New Directions Paperback, 1965), 23, 44.
12. Gandhi, *Non-Violence in Peace and War,* 1:128–29.

Cynics have sometimes parodied the philosophy of *ahimsa* as being too sentimental or as emanating from a position of weakness and cowardice. In fact, Gandhi referred to *ahimsa* as an attribute of the brave:

> Cowardice and *ahimsa* do not go together any more than water and fire. . . . Nonviolence is not a cover for cowardice, but it is the supreme virtue of the brave. Exercise of nonviolence requires far greater bravery than that of swordsmanship. Cowardice is wholly inconsistent with nonviolence. . . . It (nonviolence) is a conscious deliberate restraint put upon one's desire for vengeance.[13]

In other words, Gandhi is promoting forbearance through nonviolence.

Ahimsa and Interdependence of Humans

One of the more important assumptions underlying the Gandhian principle of *ahimsa* was his strong belief in the interdependence of humans. Parekh summarizes Gandhi's views on this subject: "That human beings were necessarily interdependent and formed an organic whole was another 'basic' truth about them according to Gandhi." Furthermore,

> since human beings were necessarily interdependent, every human action was both self- and other-regarding. It affected others and shaped the agent's own character and way of life, and necessarily influenced his relations with others and with himself. . . . Human beings could not degrade or brutalize others without also degrading and brutalizing themselves, or inflict psychic and moral damage on others without inflicting it on themselves as well.

Finally, Gandhi is quoted as saying,

> [N]o man takes another down a pit without descending into it himself and sinning in the bargain. Since humanity was indivisible, every

13. Ibid., 243, 59–60.

human being was responsible to and for others and should be deeply concerned about how they lived.[14]

Gandhi's emphasis on societal interdependence and coresponsibility enabled him to draw out the value of *ahimsa* in human society. In his vision of a nonviolent society, Gandhi argued,

> [S]ince human beings were interdependent, the good society should discourage all forms of exploitation, domination, injustice and inequality, which necessarily coarsen human sensibilities . . . and find ways of institutionalizing and nurturing the spirit of love, truthfulness, social service, cooperation and solidarity.[15]

Truth and Nonviolence

Gandhi was deeply aware that truth and nonviolence are inseparable, and in fact, are intricately intertwined. In the ultimate analysis truth is the goal and nonviolence the means to arrive at it. At the same time, nonviolence divorced from truth is a totally meaningless course of action. Gandhi, in reply to a friend's question about this relationship, said,

> *Ahimsa* is not the goal. Truth is the goal. But we have no means of realizing Truth in human relationships except through the practice of *ahimsa*. A steadfast pursuit of *ahimsa* is inevitably bound to Truth—not so violence. That is why I swear by *ahimsa*.[16]

Along similar lines, when writing about the spirit of nonviolence in 1926, Gandhi says, "Nonviolence is the greatest force man has been endowed with. Truth is the only goal he has. For God is none other than Truth. But Truth cannot be, never will be, reached except through nonviolence."[17]

14. Parekh, *Gandhi*, 39–41.
15. Ibid., 75.
16. Gandhi, *Non-Violence in Peace and War*, 2:104.
17. Iyer, ed., *Essential Writings of Mahatma Gandhi*, 240.

For Gandhi the glue that holds truth and *ahimsa* together is faith in the God of love. He says,

> *Ahimsa* is impossible without charity [love]—one needs to be saturated with charity. It is only he who feels one with his opponent that can receive his blows as though they were so many flowers. Even one such man, if God favours him, can do the work of a thousand. It requires soul-force [truth force]—moral courage—of the highest type.

Further, "where there is *ahimsa* there is Truth and Truth is God. How He manifests Himself I cannot say. All I know is that He is all-pervading and where He is all is well."[18]

Ultimately, the enterprise of *ahimsa* is a spiritual one, where God-realization (truth) is the goal. Hence the faith of the practitioner of *ahimsa* is a *sine qua non* for the success of every nonviolent action. Gandhi, writing in the *Harijan* of 1936 about the conditions for the success of nonviolence, remarked,

> [I]n the last resort it [nonviolence] does not avail to those who do not possess a living faith in the God of love. . . . Nonviolence is a power which can be wielded equally by all—children, young men and women or grown-up people, provided they have a living faith in the God of Love and have therefore equal love for all mankind. It is a profound error to suppose that whilst the law is good enough for individuals it is not for masses of mankind.[19]

This final observation removes any elitist misgivings some may have associated with his doctrines and practices. *Ahimsa* and *satyagraha* are ideals that challenge the human spirit universally and thus hold the promise of reconciliation for a broken society.

18. Merton, *Gandhi on Non-violence*, 66, 33.
19. Gandhi, *Non-Violence in Peace and War*, 1:119.

KEY CONCEPTS IN THE
CURRENT DISCOURSE ON RECONCILIATION

Forgiveness

Forgiveness is most often associated with religion, which in turn tends to cast it in the realm of individual sinners making their peace with God. However, in the present-day discourse, forgiveness is also viewed as a societal event, whereby whole peoples or nations forgive others or receive forgiveness from others. Hence forgiveness has presently moved from the private to the public domain.

Donald Shriver, in his *An Ethic for Enemies*, has an elaborate discussion on forgiveness. He suggests four dimensions that bring out the richness of the concept of forgiveness. His multidimensional description suggests than an act of forgiveness begins first with "memory suffused with moral judgment"; secondly, it abandons vengeance and subscribes to forbearance; thirdly it elicits empathy for the enemy's humanity; and finally it aims at repairing a broken human relationship.[20]

The role of memory has to be given prime location in the forgiveness process. For it is only in remembering that we can call up courage to forgive. Traditionally, forgiveness has tended to be associated with forgetting. Hence the familiar adage "forgive and forget." But now having witnessed and heard countless forgiveness stories from South Africa to Latin America, "forgive and remember" seems like a wiser safeguard; it ensures that we remain alert to not repeating similar painful and unjust actions in the future.

Memory makes the past available to us so that we can work through events and traumas without trivializing or denying them; in fact, memory makes it possible to reclaim and reinterpret past events in the light of the present and the future. This can be a freeing and liberating experience; we do not have to be held prisoner or become merely obsessed by the narrative of past misdeeds and injustice. Such a liberating process of remembering also tends to generate a variety of emotions; empathy for the "enemy's humanity" is one among them. Of course, a concrete manifestation of such empathy is the foregoing of vengeance and making room for forbearance.

20. Donald Shriver Jr., *An Ethic for Enemies: Forgiveness in Politics* (New York: Oxford University Press, 1995), 6–9.

Forbearance becomes actualized in reconciliation behaviors, when one reaches out to the other in order to repair or rebuild relationships.

Reconciliation

Reconciliation, which broadly means "to restore harmony" is a concept closely related to forgiveness. It is generally viewed as being consequent to forgiveness.[21] However, its exact location, whether consequent or prior to forgiveness, is sometimes disputed. In social reconciliation one would have little problem agreeing with the sequence: repentance, forgiveness, reconciliation. However, Robert Schreiter, in his *The Ministry of Reconciliation*, makes the case that in individual reconciliation the sequence may differ slightly: reconciliation, forgiveness, repentance.[22] In any case, since all individuals are social beings the two reconciliation paradigms are to be viewed as interdependent. For our purposes we shall focus principally on social reconciliation, a process of reconstructing societal relationships by reconstructing the moral order.

One of the more important implications of societal reconciliation is its emphasis on restorative justice rather than retributive justice. The latter tends to focus more on the perpetrators and how they should make retribution to society for their wrongdoings. As Howard Zehr says, "[Retributive justice] determines blame and administers pain in a contest between the offender and the state directed by systematic rules." Restorative justice, on the other hand, tends to focus on the perpetrators, the victims, and the community; while it seeks justice for the victim it also explores ways to restore harmony between the three parties. Once again, to quote Zehr, "[Restorative justice] involves the victim, the offender and the community in a search for solutions which promote repair, reconciliation and reassurance."[23] Restorative justice, therefore, has the added quality of opening channels of communication between perpetrators and victims. Such a dialogue tends to create an enabling climate for forgiveness and reconciliation

21. Ibid., 8–9.
22. Robert J. Schreiter, *The Ministry of Reconciliation* (New York: Orbis Books, 1999), 63–64, 111–16.
23. Howard Zehr, *Changing Lenses* (Scottsdale, Pa.: Herald Press, 1995), 181.

while at the same time holding the perpetrators accountable for their unjust actions. It seems that restorative justice is a more inclusive and wholistic process for bringing about reconciliation in society.

In the ultimate analysis, as Schreiter rightly points out, reconciliation is the work of God.[24] It is a manifestation of God's love for a broken humanity, struggling to forgive and begin anew. In Schreiter's words, "Divine forgiveness has to be seen from the vantage point of God's love. . . . God's constant proffering of love is at once the offer of forgiveness and the opportunity to renew a broken union or to deepen that union. When humans accept God's love, they are able to experience this greater union and also come to see the extent of their wrongdoing."[25] Though Schreiter is writing from a Christian perspective, his views are rather similar to those of the Eastern Gandhi, who also strongly subscribed to divine assistance to promote the mission of nonviolence and reconciliation.

Reconciliation East and West: Some Common Threads

Though the term "reconciliation" has a strong Christian religiocultural rootedness, it is reassuring that the Gandhian concepts of *satyagraha* and *ahimsa* share some remarkable similarities. This is perhaps indicative of a common psychological need all humans share, which is to want to live in harmony with fellow humans while minimizing the stresses and strains of conflict. Since it is also part of the human experience that relationships break down and are in constant need of repair, reconciliation becomes a prized currency across cultures and religions in human society.

The following are some of the more striking similarities that surface when we take a closer look at Gandhian concepts of *satyagraha* and *ahimsa* and a Western view of reconciliation:

1. Nonviolence (*ahimsa*) and reconciliation are deeply rooted in God. They derive their dynamism and transforming power in the belief that the love of God demands that we repair broken human relationships, that we forgive or adhere to *ahimsa*.

24. Robert J. Schreiter, *Reconciliation: Mission and Ministry in a Changing Social Order* (New York: Orbis Books, 1992), 42.
25. Schreiter, *Ministry of Reconciliation*, 57.

2. Gandhi's *satyagraha* (truth force) is an Eastern articulation of reconciliation. "Truth force" sustains and drives nonviolent behaviors, which are expressions of forgiveness and reaching out to the other. Nonviolence is implied in forgiveness, since we cannot be violent and promote reconciliation at the same time.

3. Reconciliation through nonviolence has much in common with the four dimensions of forgiveness mentioned earlier by Shriver, namely, moral judgment, forbearance, empathy, and repairing of broken relationships.

4. Finally, the assumption of human interdependence that underlies *ahimsa* is also an important part of the reconciliation process that seeks to bring together the perpetrator, the victim, and the community through restorative justice.

As R. Scott Appleby so rightly points out in his *The Ambivalence of the Sacred*, ultimately each society and culture will have to shape its own form of reconciliation. He says,

> Some will choose to forego "forgiveness" and opt instead for what they judge in their situation to be a more realistic goal of "nonviolent tolerance." No general pattern will obtain; no uniform model need or should be proposed for peoples hoping to live together peacefully after extended periods of bloodshed between them. What is needed for each and every case, rather, is local cultural analysis wedded to political insight.[26]

It is hoped that the case studies presented below will enrich the concept and process of reconciliation since these come from a different cultural perspective. Though played out in conflict situations typical of India, the similarities as well as differences are highly instructive for understanding the process of reconciliation.

26. R. Scott Appleby, *The Ambivalence of the Sacred* (Lanham, Md.: Rowman and Littlefield, 2000), 168.

THREE CASE STUDIES

The three case studies give us an opportunity to observe reconciliation in action; the cultural contexts are obviously located in India and as such are different from most of the reconciliation paradigms discussed in this book.

At the end of each case study a few reflections are offered within the framework of the Gandhian principles of reconciliation, namely, *satyagraha,* and *ahimsa*. These should highlight the dynamics of the reconciliation process. Finally, readers are presented with a reflective question related to the case study; this may help when mulling over the complexity of the reconciliation process and possibly act as a springboard for further discussions.

Case Study 1: The Darshana Salt March and Gandhian Nonviolence and Reconciliation

In the history of the struggle for the independence of India from the British, the salt march to the Darshana salt depots by the followers of Gandhi is an epic "battle" of nonviolence. Gandhi's unshakeable belief in *"satyagraha"* (truth force) and *"ahimsa"* (nonviolent force) came into direct confrontation with British belief in the use of violent force to suppress dissent. The date was May 21, 1930. Gandhi was imprisoned by the British at this point, ostensibly to maintain the peace. This, of course, fired up his followers to challenge oppressive British laws by using Gandhi's twin strategies of *satyagraha* and *ahimsa*.

The Darshana salt depots served as the ideal spot for a nonviolent confrontation. The British had recently imposed a series of restrictive measures as well as taxes on the use and distribution of salt. Hence on the morning of May 21 the *satyagrahis* (nonviolent marchers) approached the salt depots in order to demonstrate the unfairness of the British laws. The depots were heavily guarded by Indian soldiers under the command of British officers.

Webb Miller, an American correspondent for the United Press and an eyewitness, has given a most graphic description of the confrontation between violence and nonviolence.[27] He wrote:

27. Quoted in Asha Rani, *Gandhian Non-violence and India's Freedom* (Delhi: Shree Publishing House, 1989), 197–202.

Slowly and in silence the throng commenced the half mile march to the salt-deposits. . . . The police carried lathis (five footclubs tipped with steel). . . . In complete silence the Gandhi men drew up and halted a hundred yards from the stockade. . . . Suddenly, at a word of command scores of native police rushed upon the advancing marchers and rained blows on their heads with their steel-shod lathis. Not one of the marchers raised an arm to fend off the blows. They went down like ten pins. From where I stood I heard the sickening whacks of the clubs on unprotected skulls. The waiting crowd of watchers groaned and sucked in their breath in sympathetic pain at every blow.

. . . Those struck down fell sprawling, unconscious or writhing in pain with fractured skulls or broken shoulders. In two or three minutes the ground was quilted with bodies. . . . Then another column formed while the leaders pleaded with them to retain self-control. They marched slowly towards the police. . . . The police rushed out and methodically and mechanically beat down the second column. There was no fight, no struggle; the marchers simply walked forward until struck down.

. . . At times the spectacle of unresisting men being methodically bashed into a bloody pulp sickened me so much, that I had to turn away. . . . I felt an indefinable sense of helpless rage and loathing, almost as much against the men who were submitting unresistingly to being beaten as against the police wielding clubs. . . . Finally, the police became enraged by the nonresistance, sharing, I suppose, the helpless rage I had already felt at the demonstrators for not fighting back. They commenced savagely kicking the seated men in the abdomen and testicles. . . . Hour after hour stretcher-bearers carried back a stream of inert, bleeding bodies.[28]

Miller concludes his report by indicating the activities of the demonstrators and police eventually subsided around noontime.

The outcome of this nonviolent confrontation was the withdrawal by the British government of the punitive measure they had taken. Also, an invi-

28. Ibid., 198–201.

tation was extended to Indian leaders to start a dialogue with the British Viceroy in India and eventually with the authorities in London. All of this led to several years of peaceful negotiations between the British and the Indians and finally to the peaceful handover of power by the British to the Indians.

REFLECTIONS ON CASE STUDY I

The Background

This case study is very meaningful because the event occurred during the time Gandhi was training the first *satyagrahis* to confront the British colonialists in a nonviolent manner. It was 1930, a time when the Indian subcontinent was gripped in the fever for independence. Gandhi was convinced that the only way to independence was through nonviolent agitation and ongoing dialogue with the British.

Satyagraha

The unfairness of the British salt laws in particular, and the general climate of colonial repression, sparked within Gandhi and a large numbers of his followers the thirst for "Truth" in the arena of political freedom and human rights. Gandhi successfully evoked and harnessed this "truth force" among his followers so that they would challenge the British nonviolently and get them to leave India after granting her political independence.

Ahimsa

The path to nonviolence chosen by Gandhi stood in remarkable contrast to the physical and military might of the British described in the case study. Moreover, it showed up the moral weakness of the colonial machinery while highlighting the commitment of the *satyagrahis* to suffer brutal force and pain; seeking vengeance or harboring anger against the British was completely out of the purview of the *satyagrahis*. The very size of the nonviolent agitation and its public manifestation served to inspire the whole nation and reinforce its belief in the effectiveness of nonviolence as taught by Gandhi.

Reconciliation

One of the outcomes of this large-scale nonviolent agitation was that it reinforced mutual attitudes of respect and tolerance between the British and the Indians. These in turn created a climate for negotiations that, though difficult, were always civil; hence, negotiations were carried out in an atmosphere of openness and sincerity. Disagreements were not glossed over but neither did they become occasions for violence. It is remarkable that independence was won without a war or any other violent military operation. An atmosphere of reconciliation prevailed and this permitted Gandhi and the British to negotiate over several years until freedom could be achieved in a nonviolent settlement.

Reflective Question

In the much more fast-moving world of today, how could one sustain belief in *satyagraha* and *ahimsa* over an extended conflict? Furthermore, how could one get a whole nation to subscribe to such a creed?

Case Study 2: *Dalits* (Untouchables), Nonviolence, and Reconciliation

Arthur Bonner in his book, *Averting the Apocalypse,* documents an interesting example of reconciliation between the Dalit caste people in a village and their landlord.

K. Prasad is a social activist who now wears the long orange robes of a *swami* (religious teacher). He had been working for several years with the *Dalits* (the untouchables) in the south Indian state of Andhra Pradesh. The following case study focuses on the unjust denial of property rights to a *Dalit* family; simultaneously, it is illustrative of a commitment to the teaching and practice of nonviolence in the field.

A *Dalit* man had been awarded 2.2 acres of surplus and unused land by the government, according to a new law called the Land Ceiling Act. However, he could not take possession of it due to the cunning and machinations of the previous landlord. The landlord hastily dug a well and installed a diesel pump to show the land was his and prevented the *Dalit* man from using the land. However, since the land now legally belonged to the *Dalit* man, he encouraged the other *Dalit* families to gather the deadwood on the plot and use it for fuel. This upset the higher caste people. Prasad says, "They came to the *Dalits* with knives and *lathis* [steel-tipped clubs] and told the men of all the sixty *Dalit* families in the village to go away."[29]

In the midst of this tension Prasad intervened and convinced the *Dalits* that they needed to dialogue and start a reconciliation process with the caste people. He also urged the caste people to enter into a direct dialogue with the *Dalits* and work things out. As it turned out, the landlord at first refused to listen to any talk of nonviolence. In fact, attempts were made to intimidate the *Dalits* by a show of violence. After all, the landlord and his people were of the upper castes, and as far as they were concerned the *Dalits* had no choice but to obey their landlords. This was tradition and it had to be maintained. It was only after many meetings and the acceptance of the rights of the *Dalits* that the landlord was persuaded to change his mind; he finally gave up the land to the *Dalit* family in accordance with the law. When asked why he had changed his mind, he said, "[B]ecause the *Dalits* did not use any violence, even though they were shown *lathis* and knives by the landlords" (292).

"A year after the settlement there was a ceremony for presentation of gifts. The *Dalits* went to the surrounding villages and brought representatives to a meeting with the landlord and all the important people. It was the first time *Dalit* families had crossed into the upper caste part of the village and first time they had gone to a landlord's house to eat food" (292).

REFLECTIONS ON CASE STUDY 2

Background

Within the Indian caste system, the *Dalits* (the untouchables or outcastes) are at the bottom of the social hierarchy. As such, they are the objects of intense discrimination, exploitation, and inhuman treatment. In spite of the government's affirmative action programs, large numbers continue to suffer at the hands of the upper-caste landlords and others.

29. Arthur Bonner, *Averting the Apocalypse* (Durham, N.C.: Duke University Press, 1990), 291–92. Subsequent page references appear in the text.

Satyagraha

In this case, "truth force" originates in the realization that the *Dalits* have as much a right to property as do the upper-caste people. The continual denial of this right and the oppressive tactics of the landlord became an affront to the *Dalits;* the "truth force" spurred the *Dalits* to militate against the landlord but in a nonviolent manner.

Ahimsa

A violent confrontation would have suited the landlord much better. He would then have relished the excuse for a violent counterattack, ostensibly in self-defense. Generally, the *Dalits* come out the losers in such violent encounters. However, in this case the *Dalits* refused to get provoked and in fact mounted a nonviolent counteroffensive. By not responding violently to the "knives and *lathis*" of the landlords, the *Dalits* set in motion an introspective process of healing and reconciliation in the hearts of the upper-caste people. As explained earlier, Gandhi's insights in the transformative power of truth and nonviolence are clearly visible here.

Reconciliation

The reconciling outcome of this nonviolent confrontation seems to have climaxed a year later at a "presentation of gifts" ceremony and a community meal. In the Indian context this is unheard of. For caste people to "deign" to eat with untouchables is the ultimate signal of the acceptance of and equality with the *Dalits*. Normally strict social ostracism and discrimination would have prevailed against the caste people for violation of the food taboos. Also, permitting *Dalits* to enter the upper-caste part of the village at the risk of "polluting" the upper castes is a profound symbol of reconciliation and forgiveness.

Reflective Question

How does one arouse the latent power of *satyagraha* and *ahimsa* from within the broken psyche of an abused and exploited people?

Case Study 3: Caste, Water, and Reconciliation

In addition to discrimination against the *Dalits*, there is also widespread intercaste discrimination. Indian society is hierarchically structured and the hundreds of castes that make it up are rank ordered. Intercaste discrimination is a vicious and pervasive form of prejudice present to this day in India.

Once again Arthur Bonner documents an enlightening example of reconciliation in a multicaste village near the city of Patna, in India.

Father Philip, the local Catholic priest and social activist, was surprised one hot summer's day to find no water in a village he was visiting. On inquiring about the reasons, he discovered that apathy and a lack of initiative on the part of the people stopped them from tackling such a life-and-death issue.

As it turned out, underlying much of the apathy were intercaste rivalries, hostility, and discrimination, which prevented any concerted efforts at solving the water problem. In other words, a lack of unity and harmony in their relationships acted as the greatest obstacle toward working for the common good. Father Philip promptly realized that unless the villagers were first reconciled among themselves a solution to the water problem would never be forthcoming.

Father Philip, therefore, initiated a series of dialogue sessions that brought the villagers together around the theme of the water problem. He thrust upon them the responsibility to draw up action plans and strategies for problem solving. In effect, he started a process of reconciliation among the villagers, since they were forced to set aside their caste discrimination, accept each other's strengths and weaknesses, and basically stay focused on solving the water problem. A sense of community belonging started to come about, enabling the villagers to set aside earlier prejudices and caste differences.

The next step was for the villagers to confront the government bureaucracy with their just demand for a water pump. The villagers encountered rudeness, manipulation, and greed from the officials. This strengthened their resolve to remain united as a community, since they needed each others' talents to beat the corrupt officials at their game.

Finally, as Father Philip says, "after waiting months and months they got water through their efforts, without bribing. This was their first experience of the whole village getting together for what we call animation work among themselves" (243–44). As is clear, "animation" here is only another word for reconciliation. It is only because the villagers learned through a process of dialogue and reflection to accept each other's caste differences in a spirit of forgiveness and reconciliation that they were able to fight for the common needs of the community.

As for some of the more practical results from this process of reconciliation, Father Philip said,

> [N]ow no outsiders disturb them, and they have much fewer quarrels and fights. They have a lot more enthusiasm for life. . . . There is also social integration. . . . There are about ten caste groups in the village. . . . Some felt they were better than someone else and would have no social interaction with them, like eating, being together, and marriages. Now, with our help and the consensus of the people, they're developing new economic opportunities that also provide new ways for social interaction. . . . It has given them confidence and a feeling of togetherness: they say they belong to the *samiti* (society). (244)

With regard to the reconciliation and the meetings between the various castes, Father Philip said,

> [The meetings] are full of people, with very low caste people sitting with others. It was not that way in the beginning: the very low caste people would sit just outside the door. But now, if a little higher caste (person) tries to assert himself in the village, the lower caste man will say, "You can't feel more superior than me. You're only as good a member as I am: You paid eleven rupees and I paid eleven rupees." That's the primary membership fee [to belong to the *samiti*]." (244)

REFLECTIONS ON CASE STUDY 3

Background

Generally, it is extremely difficult to initiate a process of reconciliation in intercaste situations. Thanks to the history of at least two millennia of rigid caste rules and social sanctions, loyalty to these rules is almost sacrosanct. This is especially true in the State of Bihar in North India, where caste warfare engineered by private militias is not uncommon.

Satyagraha

As the water problem grew more acute and no solution seemed in sight, Father Philip brought the villagers to realize that they were their own worst enemy. Unless they were ready to accept each other and build a sense of community they would end up hurting themselves. He used the water problem as a catalyst to arouse the "truth force" from within each individual first, and then the group as a whole. Father Philip carefully harnessed and directed this awakened "truth force." He mobilized the community for action.

Ahimsa

The villagers were carefully schooled in the code of conduct of nonviolence while pursuing their goal of acquiring water for the village. Dialogue, cooperation, and forbearance were the attitudes and behaviors they acquired in order to be able to work together as a community as well as vis-à-vis the government officials. *Ahimsa* was followed even in the face of aggression, rudeness, or manipulation by the officials. Above all, they learned to face the odds together, in a spirit of intercaste equality and camaraderie.

Reconciliation

These nonviolent behaviors spurred by "truth force" set in motion a reconciliation process among the villagers. Villagers who were erstwhile enemies and discriminated against each other started to repair relationships and rebuild the community. A further truth became reality for them, when in action they realized they needed each other and shared equal status, as humans. They were able to build a partnership for the future through this reconciliation.

Reflective Question

What are the blocks that tend to prevent reconciliation in the first place? Are some of these culturally universal?

CONCLUDING REMARKS

Gandhi's vision of a "truth-force" that motivates one to nonviolence is as much a challenge today as it was in the early part of the twentieth century. Gandhi demonstrated that it was possible and desirable to handle issues of confrontation in ways that bring peoples together, in ways that build rather than destroy communities. Fittingly, we recall the example of Dr. Martin Luther King Jr. a disciple of Gandhi and a fervent believer in nonviolence, who also demonstrated the power of nonviolence in uniting the African American community in its struggle for civil liberties.

Furthermore, irrespective of cultural differences or religious roots, reconciliation through nonviolence is the healing balm available universally to all humans. In a world where confrontation and violence seem to show up with great regularity, reconciliation via nonviolence seems not only a less expensive proposition in monetary terms but also in terms of human lives saved. Peace-making and peace-keeping have blossomed into multi-billion-dollar enterprises; in contrast, could Gandhi's more human though technologically less sophisticated vision for peace become more accessible to more nations?

It is indeed felicitous that the nation of South Africa, where Gandhi first practiced nonviolence against a dehumanizing apartheid policy, finally claimed its victory in 1994 over this evil system. Its armory consisted of forgiveness, reconciliation, and nonviolence. Giants of forgiveness like Nelson Mandela and Archbishop Desmond Tutu and scores of other ordinary South Africans have taught the world there is hope even in the most desperate situations of conflict. The archbishop in his *No Future Without Forgiveness* says, "No problem anywhere can ever again be considered to be

intractable. There is hope for you too. . . . Our experiment is going to succeed because God wants us to succeed. . . . God wants to show that there
is life after conflict and repression—that because of forgiveness there is a
future."[30]

30. Desmond Mpilo Tutu, *No Future Without Forgiveness* (New York: Doubleday, 1999), 282.

CHAPTER 16

Brokenness, Forgiveness, Healing, and Peace in Ireland,

Geraldine Smyth, O.P.

IN THE QUEST FOR PEACE in Ireland there is a strange dialectic of innocence and betrayal, sin and forgiveness, memory and the reconciling of memories. In Christian terms we confront once more the shocking interconnections between sin and grace as the ground where the human heart encounters divine mystery and where human ways—more often than not—part company from the ways of God.

Recently, a stark and significant book was published in Belfast under the title *Lost Lives*.[1] It recorded the names of the men, women, and children who died as a result of the Northern Ireland Troubles and gave a short synopsis of their lives and the circumstances of their deaths. In its 1,630 pages we are presented with the most comprehensive overview ever of the death of every person who died in the Troubles, constructed from media reportage and interviews. Between the covers of one book was the stark record of names, page upon page of them, 1,630 pages of human suffering distilled from 3,637 lost lives and from the pain of 3,637 families bereaved of loved ones. On taking up the book, I turned to the entry for July 28, 1972, and read the short account of the death of Philip Maguire, my

1. David McKittrick, Seamus Kelters, Brian Feeney and Chris Thornton, eds., *Lost Lives: The Stories of the Men, Women, and Children Who Died as a Result of the Northern Ireland Troubles* (Edinburgh: Mainstream Publishing, 1999).

cousin's husband, and the brief references to his widow, Sheila, and to their five children. I found myself recalling forgotten details of the summer evening in their home in Belfast, the part of the room where I had sat with Sheila, unable to find words, hearing her insisting that there must be no retaliation; the family rallying around, the disbelief in the young eyes, and the word "forgive" spoken in whispers. And then, the funeral and heartbreak, the years of unseen grieving, and the effort to stitch life back together again "for the sake of the children."

Last year, not long after the publication of *Lost Lives,* Sheila Maguire died after a sudden illness. At her funeral I listened to the parish priest as he made the links in his homily between the Gospel reading from the Beatitudes announced by Jesus and the story of Sheila's life. "Blessed are those who mourn, for they will be comforted. . . . Blessed are the merciful for they will receive mercy. . . . Blessed are the peacemakers, for they will be called children of God" (Matt. 5:4ff). He went on to highlight the Christian witness of a woman who had followed in the way of Jesus as a woman of peace. He told of that July day in 1972 when her world was horribly shattered by the murder of her husband by a Loyalist gunman as he went about his day's work. Sheila had struggled to cope with her terrible loss. To those who looked on, the idea of forgiving the killer seemed an act beyond human possibility. For Sheila, the impossible was a necessity. The act of forgiving expressed her will to overcome evil with good and to protect her children from the anonymous sectarian hatred that had fired the bullets into Phil's head. Forgiveness was the only way she knew to disarm that hatred and prevent it from wreaking further destruction on her family. The message of the preaching was simple and direct. It bore witness to a Christian woman and man who had lived and died in faithfulness to Christ's example. In the ritual of remembering Sheila and Phil were reunited in the bond of life beyond death, at one with the Risen Christ.

The preached word brought comfort to those who mourned. Through it, the congregation could sense the simple power of personal suffering related to the death and resurrection of Jesus Christ. They could also grasp the connection between that bond of suffering and the contemporary public efforts on all sides to hold together the fragile peace. A few hours later I commented separately to a son and a daughter on how truly the priest had portrayed Sheila as the great Christian woman she was, and particularly her courage in forgiving. Each of the two agreed—the priest's words had been a comfort—but with a reservation: "I wish he hadn't said it was a Loyalist who killed my Father. None of us in the family told him that it was a Loyalist." One of them added, "That doesn't add anything to Dad's death, and somebody might make it an excuse to be bitter." They were also concerned in case some of their mother's Protestant bowling friends who had come to the funeral would be embarrassed by the reference to a "Loyalist gunman." Their mother would not have wanted that. How well the lesson of forgiveness had been taught, how well learned. In the convictions of these adult children the mother's gift of forgivingness was being relived with a passion and grace that was all their own. In the midst of death and sin, forgiveness was once more finding a space. The quality of mercy was not strained.

More than nine out of ten of those killed in the Troubles were men. It was mostly women who watched and waited and were left behind. Ulster poet W.R. Rodger's words are painfully apt:

> It is always the women who are the Watchers
> And keepers of life: they guard our exits
> And our entrances. They are both womb and tomb,
> End and beginning. Bitterly they bring forth
> And bitterly take back the light they gave.
> The last to leave and still the first to come,
> They circle us like sleep or like the grave
> It is always the women who are the Watchers
> And Wakeners.[2]

It has been observed that one reason why violence was not much greater during the years of the Troubles was "the way that Christians and their Churches have chosen consistently to seek to cut cycles of vengeance by calling for and practising non-retaliation and forgiveness" and the fact that the Gospel message of forgiveness "has significantly penetrated Irish life, and its practice—particularly by many victims and their families—has had social and political effects." But it has also been asserted, "The victims of

2. W. R. Rodgers, "Resurrection: An Easter Sequence," *W. R. Rodgers: Poems,* edited and with an introduction by Michael Longley (Oldcastle, Ireland: Gallery Books, 1993), 66–75, 74.

violence and their families cannot be burdened with the demand that they forgive those who have perpetrated crimes against them."[3] So, too, those who have suffered deeply through violence have their own particular needs: "for justice, for the seriousness of the harm to be acknowledged, for compensation, for apology and repentance from those who have done them wrong, for their stories to be heard."[4] In this there is also recognition that forgiveness should not be approached in an atomized way, but rather as part of a wider process of reconciliation and peace building.

It would seem that in geopolitical situations of transition out of protracted conflict characterized by ethnic, political, and religious intransigence, the negotiation of new relationships must be conducted along different tracks, on multiple levels and drawing in protagonists from the widest possible range of sectoral interests and competencies. John Paul Lederach's work sheds much light on the field of conflict transformation and its processes. Conflicts, he tells us, characteristically take as long to wind down as they do to escalate. We must recognize the need for dedicated painstaking work rather than look for the quick fix. In this sense, he speaks of the need for "decade-thinking."[5] Such a recognition has been borne home with sobering insistence, from the first flush of euphoria over the Good Friday Agreement, through the revoking and reconvoking of ceasefires, the establishing, decomposing, and reconstituting of the Northern Ireland Assembly, all against the drumbeat of continuing low-intensity conflict and civil disruption over the "right to march" or over the contested scope of police reform, and the intermittent high-profile crisis points where David Trimble negotiates his survival as leader of the Ulster Unionist Party on the knife-edge of a deeply split party and bitterly divided loyalties.

It is becoming increasingly evident that while politicians and leaders of state broker the nature and scope of new power relationships and interests, any new political and judicial arrangements must be embedded in their

3. Interchurch Group on Faith and Politics, *Forgive Us Our Trespasses: Reconciliation and Political Healing in Northern Ireland* (1996), 8 (see n. 14 below).
4. Ibid.
5. John Paul Lederach, *Building Peace: Sustainable Reconciliation in Divided Societies* (Washington, D.C.: U.S. Institute of Peace, Washington, 1997), 77. Lederach sees reconciliation as a social space where people and paradoxes are brought together in an integrative "process-structure" approach to peace building, with a range of time-frame-related strategies. Relationships are seen as key (73–85).

acceptance by local communities, and that the political strategies will succeed only if some counterbalancing weight and vitality is allowed to the role of groups and movements in civil society—officially through the second chamber or Civic Forum (to be established before the end of 2000) and in the unofficial networks of relationship within and between communities. More will be said of this later, but it is apposite at this point to situate the quest for reconciliation and peace within this complex and precarious sociopolitical context. So, too, any theological attempt to raise questions about forgiveness or about the role that churches might exercise in encouraging reconciliation must reckon with this complexity while refusing to let it paralyze or overwhelm.

For Christians the metaphor of a pilgrim journey suggests itself as a way of moving forward in faith.[6] Rooted deeply in the Judeo-Christian self-understanding and tapping, albeit by different roots, into both the Catholic and Reformed traditions, the pilgrim journey motif underscores the invitation to be converted in mind and heart, restates the promise of forgiveness, and invites communities to be reconciled through sharing with strangers the bread of suffering and hope.

W.R. Rodgers speaks of such a journey beyond narrow identifications with one's own place as the way to discover more fully the strange richness of one's own plural identity:

Strange that, in lands, and countries quite unknown,
We find, not other's strangeness but our own;
That is one use of journeys; if one delves,
Differently, one's sure to find one's selves.
O in what wildernesses of one another
We wander looking for ourselves![7]

This journey into self-discovery is somehow shaped by discovery of the other. Rodgers portrays this journey into the wilderness as a passaging out of alienation into an encounter with strangeness—and paradoxically—toward the possibility of relationship. We shall look more closely at the

6. Cf., e.g., Robin Boyd, *Ireland: Christianity Discredited or Pilgrim's Progress*, Risk Book Series (Geneva: WCC Publications, 1988).
7. W. R. Rodgers, "The Journey of the Magi," in *W.R. Rodgers: Poems*, ed. Longley, 59–63.

nature and dynamics of this "journey" now in relation to the search for peace in Ireland.

BECOMING AWARE
OF THE BROKENNESS AND ALIENATION

Brokenness, division, and *separation* are words that come to mind when we reflect on the civic and Christian reality of Ireland. At the most obvious level, in Northern Ireland, we are a people divided, culturally and historically, in politics and in religious understanding. Before attending to this reality, however, other divisions should not be overlooked. There are deep structural divisions between insiders and outsiders, people whose dignity has been undermined by social and economic exclusion. The increasing numbers of young people who are homeless and who, because they fall below the statutory age, are left untitled to normal state provision come to mind; so, too, do the majority whose human rights are protected by the law, and the minority groups such as travelers, or asylum seekers whose claims carry no weight. Some exclusions, determined by a long history of gender bias, are at last being challenged within political life, not least with the advent and impact of the Women's Coalition, and in church life. That women are largely rendered invisible in these contexts is compounded by the media's systematic disregard of the contribution of women's ideas and activities.[8] Such gendered exclusions betoken a construal of politics, too narrowly conceived, whether structured along the axis of traditional or liberal interests.[9] Such socially constructed exclusions have a bearing upon our political and religious experience and the patterns of alienation within them. In turning attention to these, it is important to keep an eye to such root injustices that structure and determine them.

8. To verify this, one need only do a random check of journalistic coverage of public events here. In one Belfast journal of quality—*Fortnight*—there has been a monthly "Chronology" feature, where on average only two or three out of the thirty to fifty diary entries on events of social, cultural, or political significance relate to women's contributions to civic life as worthy of mention.
9. Cf. R. Miller, R. Wilford, and F. Donoghue, *Women and Political Participation in Northern Ireland*, (Aldershot: Avebury Press, 1996), a published research survey that underlines similar conclusions.

Looking more focally now at the first movement in the journey into self-discovery, change, and relationship, we need to recognize the importance of self-knowledge and self-questioning in regard to one's particular religious and political identity. Self-knowledge is the beginning of wisdom. It calls us to a conversion in thinking and to an awareness of the levels of alienation within and between different traditions. Here we need to be on guard against temptations to self-absorption. Paradoxically, one will forfeit any real integrity to the extent that one thinks wholeness is possible without reference to the other. Those who would see reality truthfully are called to admit that our histories and identities are neither as simple nor as single as we have protested, with most or all righteousness on our side, and most or all wrong, or indeed evil, on the other. As Christians who profess to live by faith, we are called to probe the illusions of our own righteousness and scrutinize the interests and ideologies that we use to categorize or separate ourselves—Protestant from Catholic, Unionist from Nationalist. Our identities are reflected in mindsets that mirror one another in rivalry and blame, claim and counterclaim. It is as if within every Catholic there is something of a repressed Protestant, and within every Protestant a crypto-Catholic.

This is not a clever idea, but a simple insight. Psychologically expressed it suggests that in our difference and likeness, we constitute one another and mould one another. Putting that in historical terms, in our histories, doctrines, and political aspirations we have defined ourselves over against each other, thus mutually sculpting each other's identity to a remarkable degree.[10] It can be seen in the dates that divide us, the events we separately commemorate, our different understandings of each other's Eucharist or Church structures. Later, we will look more explicitly at some of the theological dimensions of aspects of such rivalry in identity.

John F. Kennedy once lamented that so often humanity prefers the comfort of opinion to the discomfort of thought. To engage in open-minded dialogue with another is to be willing to undergo a self-critical appraisal of one's own worldview. It is not a common pursuit. But for those who undertake it, such reflective self-critique will reveal the ease with which we can

10. Cf. Frank Wright, *Northern Ireland: A Comparative Analysis* (Dublin: Gill and Macmillan, 1987), in which the author applies the perspectives of René Girard's mimetic rivalry to Northern Ireland's ethnic and political "system of mutual deterrence" (141–60).

succumb to propaganda, to bolster our particular bias. Propaganda operates by stereotyping one's opponents, by exaggerating *their* stupidity, bitterness, and blindness in direct proportion to *our* intelligence, generosity,
and objectivity. As evidenced in traditional party politics, propaganda often
posits the cure for our political ills in terms that admit no shades of grey and
posit only one solution. Alternatively, propaganda manipulates ambiguity
into duplicity, distorting the reality in front of us. Political discourse and
refusal of discourse here are driven more by the inertia of ideology than by
open exchange. This stage of the journey to peace requires a "decommis-
sioning" of the old mindset with its citadel of clichés that keep a politics of
prejudice in place. Scottish poet Iain Crichton Smith asserts that "Dogma
is a measure of our inability to live," a false and unsafe refuge against life
and true vision:

> It is time to pull down the walls,
> it is time to capture the dogmas
> and bury them in the wilderness.
> It is time to live in the accidents of the everyday. . . .

We need faith to uncover the belief-systems that keep each group "unto
itself" and to see more deeply into the heart of life disclosed in "the acci-
dents of the everyday."

It should be recognized, too, that there can be no liberation of the mind
without liberation of memory. Ireland has many folk memories and songs
that turn upon themes of siege and victimhood, upon the treachery of the
other group, and on the heroism of the martyrs and heroes of one's own.
Such folk memory tends to close out more than it discloses. Slogans and
doggerel serve to shutter one's vision and horizon. One's own group grievances are more fondly nursed than the dying, and the wrongs of the other
side are carved in stone, in short, a memory cut adrift from imagination and
hope. Here, each side has remembered separately, fragmentarily, and with
partiality.[11] The challenge is to transcend selective memory. Vamik Volkan's

---

11. Cf. Alan Falconer and Joseph Liechty, eds., *Reconciling Memories,* 2nd ed. (Dublin:
    Columba Press, 1998). This, and the first edition, edited by Alan D. Falconer (Dublin:
    Columba Press, 1988), represent an initiative of the Irish School of Ecumenics. For relevant
    Jewish biblical insights on the need for a double-edged approach to remembering correlated

observations about the recycling of the "chosen trauma" or conversely of the "chosen glory" finds echo chambers in Irish minds[12]—the Cromwellian persecution of Catholics, the 1641 drowning of Protestants in the River Bann, the Easter Rising of 1916, the Republican Hunger Strikes of 1981. These events are felt on the pulses as contemporary. At this moment, the Orange Order and its supporters continue the five-year standoff at Drumcree Hill near Portadown. Despite annual outbreaks of deaths and violence arising from their protests, they do so in the unreconstructed conviction that they are reenacting the seventeenth-century Siege of Derry, in the same cause of civil and religious liberty, and with a mythic confidence that perseverance will bring relief and victory.

In recent years there have emerged, despite such selective cherishing of traumas and glories, significant individuals and groups who seek to reconcile memories and to remember some fragments of a common story with its interplay of darkness and light. There is a slow-growing but real willingness within each ethnic or religious group to remember more inclusively and tell history "against the grain" of their own tradition. This is indeed a necessary move in loosening the grip of historical materialism.[13] Stories and memories, if they are to hold some hope of redemption, must be allowed to interrupt, modify, and even find echoes in the stories of the other. So also this process of telling and listening is drawing in people from all sections of the community—children, women and men, activists and scholars, church people and political people, voluntary and community activists, educators and chambers of commerce. These people incline toward the healing of memories. One can note here the contribution of such bodies as the Interchurch Group on Faith and Politics who meet regularly with politicians or church leaders and promote new understanding, through dialogue and written analyses of contested topics, including the ambiguous role of memory in the

---

to the Irish context, see Geraldine Smyth, "Sabbath and Jubilee," in *The Jubilee Challenge: Utopia or Possibility—Jewish and Christian Insights*, ed. Hans Ucko (Geneva: WCC Publications, 1997), 59–76, 72.

12. Vamik Volkan, *Bloodlines: From Ethnic Pride to Ethnic Terrorism* (Boulder, Colo.: Westview Press, 1997), 48–49; for a theological reflection on the phenomenon of collective memories, cf. Geiko Müller-Fahrenholz, *The Art of Forgiveness: Theological Reflections on Healing and Reconciliation* (Geneva: WCC Publications, 1997), 49–59.

13. Cf. Walter Benjamin, *Theses on the Philosophy of History, Illuminations* (1955, 1968; London: Fontana Press, 1992), 245–55.

reassessment of history.[14] The Irish School of Ecumenics provides another setting for ecumenical encounter and exchange of memories. Currently it offers programs in twenty towns and cities in Northern Ireland and in a number of locations in the Republic of Ireland. To these come adults of different perspectives and denominations, who are seeking to understand themselves and one another more fully through study and dialogue. At such encounters often a prophetic word is uttered as people risk telling their stories, wrestle with painful questions, or show willingness to stand in the gap and read the signs of the times. By such willingness to reevaluate their inherited belief systems and go against the grain of the received wisdom, they discover their own power to be authors of new stories and coauthors of new visions. It is in coming together to name the brokenness that people recover the capacity to see more widely and deeply than before. It is a movement of faith in the possibility of greater wholeness, without the pressure to eliminate difference.

Much that has been observed above is posited at the level of the mind although stressing the importance of stretching the limits of inherited opinions and worldviews. For Christians seeking some way of structuring the search for truth according to some guiding Christian vision, the Gospels offer both challenge and resource. In his own life and ministry Jesus confronted absolutism wherever he met it and taught that literalizing or narrowing of the Torah message was a betrayal of that law which God intended as a truth that set people free.[15] Jesus was not motivated solely by compassion when he sat at table with poor and rich, or spoke to friend and enemy

14. Cf. some recent pamphlets published by the Interchurch Group on Faith and Politics include: *Remembering Our Past: 1690 and 1916* (1991); *Forgive Us Our Trespasses: Reconciliation and Political Healing in Northern Ireland* (1996); *New Pathways: Developing a Peace Process in Northern Ireland* (1997); *Doing Unto Others: Parity of Esteem in a Contested Space* (1997); *Remembrance and Forgetting: Building a Future in Northern Ireland* (1998); *Self-righteous Collective Superiority as a Cause of Conflict* (1999). These and earlier publications going back to 1981 are obtainable from 48 Elmwood Avenue, Belfast 9.

15. One is aware of the need for hermeneutical integrity here in not harnessing to one's own ideological project. Facilely drawn oppositions between law and Gospel, law and freedom, law and grace as a means of contrasting in-group/out-group identity are unfaithful to the deeper integrity of Torah and to be particularly eschewed. Cf. Frank Crüsemann, *The Torah: Theology and Social History of Old Testament Law* (Minneapolis: Fortress Press, 1996). With a focus on the Hebrew Scriptures, the central thesis of the book challenges, on the basis of the unity of God and the unity of Torah and in respect of the constantly changing sociopolitical context, any simplistic dichotomy between law and prophecy, cult and ethics, law

alike, but by the need to subvert narrow applications of Torah rooted in a theology of scarcity and ethics of striving. Rather, Jesus spoke of God in terms of abundance and of salvation in terms of God's free gift. The weary preacher who sat by a well and spoke with the Samaritan woman was challenged to reassess his inherited economy of salvation. Through his dialogue with her, his mind caught a glimpse of a new horizon of mission *beyond* his own people and a changing understanding of who his own people were.

In Jesus, shocking though it seems, sin and grace meet. Jesus the innocent one is portrayed dipping into the same dish as Judas. He does not stop acknowledging Peter after he had three times denied Jesus. So, too, Jesus challenges our sense of justice by valuing equally the worker who came at the eleventh hour as those laboring from sunrise. Paul tells us that "Christ died for us *while we were yet sinners*. . . . When we were God's enemies we were reconciled to him through the death of his Son" (Rom. 5:8, 10). All have sinned. All stand in need of grace. In the new meaning-world of the Kingdom, followers of Jesus are called to move beyond human logic—what Paul Ricoeur describes as the logic of strict equivalence, merit and law, into God's logic of superabundance, grace, and love.[16] In becoming aware of our alienation and sin we draw down on ourselves not the law of punishment but the economy of grace.[17] There is no innocent place to start. Aware of our small-minded arrogance, alienation, and loss of meaning, we begin the journey where we are, in faith.

LETTING GO TO FORGIVENESS: THE PAIN AND THE HOPE

The journey of reconciliation will take us beyond the moment of new awareness, critique, and questioning, into the place where suffering is

---

and love. The author also makes useful new extrapolations for a more nuanced hermeneutical approach to New Testament texts that center upon these tensions and that are often subjected to a hermeneutics of crude oppositionalism between law and faith. See 1–6, 23–24, 115–30, 230, 322–25 and passim.

16. Paul Ricoeur, "The Logic of Jesus, the Logic of God," in *Figuring the Sacred: Religion Narrative and Imagination* (Minneapolis: Augsburg-Fortress, 1995), 279–83.

17. Ibid., 282–83.

acknowledged and there is a letting go of the grief or anger that new awareness may evoke. As we begin to *accept* our actual feelings of bitterness at the
lost lives, shame at our own apathy, disillusionment with our leaders, resentment at the injustice, the sense of inevitability and of paralysis begins to
shift. It is perhaps at this stage that the churches can offer the most oppor-
tune ways of accompanying the suffering and disillusioned. Returning to
the sources of worship, they can revitalize communities in prayer and resistance in the same manner that Moses aroused the Israelites from their
enslavement in Egypt. Until the moment when "they cried out," it was as if
they were paralyzed and, in a manner of speaking, prevented God from
meeting them in their pain. It is in such crying out that oppressed hearts
awaken and begin to imagine the radically new alternative of living in freedom and security. We witnessed something of that crying out in protest after
the series of tit-for-tat killings in October 1993 on the Shankill Road,
Belfast, and the village of Greysteel. So also, after the bomb that killed thirty
children, women, and men in the town of Omagh in 1998 there was a
crescendo of protest that cried, "Enough." Many thousands gathered at city
halls and town squares throughout Ireland. In rituals of shared silence people protested for a peace and committed to seeking and finding peace. That
cry continues to rise with the Psalmist's. It is a cry from the pit of suffering:

> Will your wonders be told in the grave
> Or your faithfulness among the dead?
> Will your wonders be known in the dark?
> Why do you hide your face? (Psalm 87)

It is in the willingness to embrace the pain of betraying and being
betrayed that our hearts begin to let go of the desire to control. In this place
of desolation we admit our need to receive and offer forgiveness. Such letting go to the suffering within our community is the condition of transformation. Dorothée Soelle claims the need for suffering to go beyond "mute
pain," to find its voice in "a language of lament, of crying, of pain, a language that at least says what the situation is."[18] We need to recover such
psalm language in our liturgies and recreate shared rituals in which anger

---

18. Dorothée Soelle, *Suffering* (Philadelphia: Fortress, 1975), 70–71.

and lament draw forth God's grace and forgiveness. As we allow the anger or suffering of the other into our hearts, the Spirit may hover over our past failures and bring forgiveness to birth. It is in so being vulnerable that we once more become capable of hope.

Such a sense of forgiveness in the midst of loss was evoked in the ecumenical "Counting the Cost" ritual, televised throughout Ireland on Good Friday 1995. In this ritual Christians from North and South gathered to remember all who had died as a result of the Troubles.[19] This public mourning rite drew even television viewers to face into the darkness of loss. But it also opened to another level of meaning, for there were hints of redemption in the simple naming of names and the tender carrying of the names written on small, white crosses to the stark Good Friday cross. In a ritual such as this, debate about the "whether" and "when" of forgiveness finds a different starting point. For through such rituals we find ourselves accepting the commonality of pain, a coming to know Christ and the fellowship of his suffering and an opening to the future which comes to meet us out of the past. It is perhaps above all in this spirit of hope that the courage for forgiveness emerges as a reconciling grace between divided Christian communities mired in ancient conflict and enmity. While not possible here to examine the complex interplay of religion and politics in Northern Ireland's Troubles, some discussion of forgiveness within this complexity may be helpful at this point, not least because Christianity (the primary religious tradition there) is a religion of incarnation and mission. So also, as with

19. Ricoeur's maxim, "The symbol gives rise to thought," springs to mind here. Out of the process of this ritual were sown the seeds of other ideas, including a memorial exhibition that toured educational establishments throughout Ireland. Research projects issuing in publications such as Marie-Thérèse Fay, Mike Morrissey, and Marie Smyth, eds., *Northern Ireland's Troubles: The Human Costs* (London: Pluto Press, 1999), represent other related outcomes. The latter presents some useful profiling analysis of data along various lines of research enquiry, for example, demography, social and economic aspects, and patterns of violence. Most significantly, it both attempts a comprehensive audit of damage done and makes a significant contribution to creating a "common account of the Troubles which includes all accounts in a larger, complex and perhaps contradictory picture." So too it recognizes that in the building of a peaceful society, "the hurts of the past cannot be swept under the carpet. If we are to have society based on justice, then those who have suffered must be a central concern. If we are to have a society based on humanitarianism, then we must go out of our way to comfort, support and listen to those who have lost most. If we are to move beyond the divisions of the present, then we must learn to listen to those who have been hurt in the name of politics or causes we support. And when we are listening, we must learn to allow our hearts to soften in compassion. . . . People have suffered enough" (4–6).

ethnic conflicts elsewhere, religion and politics mutually permeate and influence each other's fields of discourse, ethical values, norms, and praxis.

Christian communities are called to embody the values of the reign of God in the world: The embodiment of values of truth and justice, love and peace can bring theology and politics into fruitful dialogue. Forgiveness has both a political and a religious face. It is no accident that words with primarily a religious meaning like *sin, victim, reconciliation,* and *forgiveness* are sometimes heard in the vocabulary of politicians. Kenneth Kaunda, for example, suggested that forgiveness is not so much an isolated act but "a constant willingness to live in a new day without looking back and ransacking the memory for occasions of bitterness and resentment."[20] At root that is a central goal of politics—how to move beyond hostility to cooperation in justice and peace. From ancient times politics had to take up where war left off, by endeavouring to interrupt the cycle of revenge with processes of justice. Writing theologically Dorothée Soelle makes fruitful comments on the interplay between Christian life and secular politics, articulating a hermeneutical interconnection between political injustices like war or racism and the pain of God. To force them into separate boxes, she asserts, is to "take away from God the possibility of drawing our pain into God's pain; [and] make ourselves incapable of participating in God's pain."[21] In Ireland the witness of people like Gordon Wilson and Sheila Maguire testifies that suffering borne in relationship with others opens up the capacity for self-transcendence. It points to forgiveness as a mysterious process wherein God's pain embraces human pain. In this process a politics of peace is created and redeemed.

Gordon Wilson's daughter Marie died in the Enniskillen bomb on Remembrance Sunday 1986. He spoke often of Christ's forgiveness as the source of the power within him to forgive those who had mercilessly planted

---

20. Cited in Interchurch Group on Faith and Politics, *Forgive Us Our Trespasses,* 9. For a much wider-ranging examination of this reality, cf. Donald W. Shriver Jr., *An Ethic for Enemies: Forgiveness in Politics* (New York: Oxford University Press, 1995). See his chapter on "Forgiveness in Politics in the Christian Tradition," 33–62.
21. Dorothée Soelle, *Theology for Sceptics* (London: Mowbray, 1995), 80. Soelle explores how the pain of the world connects to God's pain and demonstrates the relationship between the pains of the poor as the pains of God. She describes some concrete experiences of entering into another's pain, especially the pain of the poor, and of the strength that grows out of grief. She asserts: "I believe it is our task to change the `sorrow of the world' into God's pain" (78), which by some *coincidentia oppositorum* is alive with joy as well as pain in a depth experience of which perhaps birth is an profound metaphor (79).

the bomb. I have witnessed people shaking their heads at this, commenting that his stance was "unreal" or that he was "in denial." A core reality in his narrative, however, usually goes unnoticed by those who listen to his testimony. In point of fact, Gordon Wilson never spoke of forgiveness in a disembodied way. Rather, he described and depicted those final moments and the ultimate expressions of love that passed between Marie and himself as she lay dying, trapped behind the devastation of buildings and masonry: In response to his calling her name and asking her if she was all right, she whispered with all her fading strength, "Daddy, I love you very much." It seems to me that this dialogue was alive with the mystery of love at the core of the suffering, and it was this love that was the matrix of Gordon Wilson's forgiveness. Marie died, but not before he several times called out her name and not before she called back to him, "Daddy, I love you very much!" Gordon Wilson's forgiveness of his enemies was far from unreal. It was distilled to the extremist purity of both pain and love. It was out of the actual relationship with his daughter as she lay dying that Gordon Wilson found the transcending courage to forgive and to overpower evil with good. Second, though not secondarily, Gordon Wilson's forgiving arose—as he so often affirmed by his own "confession of faith"—out of his profound faith in a merciful God. This way of reading the "text" of Gordon Wilson's willingness to forgive raises the question of *who* is in denial and whether it is perhaps a dulled capacity for the transcendent that makes if difficult to see to the heart of Gordon Wilson's capacity to forgive—arising as it did out of an ultimate "I-Thou" encounter, a wholly "Other" experience of love beyond the power of death to destroy.

The Hebrew Scriptures contain insights into human forgiveness expressed in the public sphere exemplified by Joseph who forgave the brothers who abandoned him to slavery (Gen. 37:45). But the prominence is given to divine forgiveness as a manifestation of God's faithful covenant. Jesus in his own ministry stressed an ethics of forgiveness ("till seventy times seven") and the practice of love as the defining quality of his disciples. It can also be argued that early Christian communities understood themselves as called to exercise forgiveness in public life.[22]

22. Cf. Shriver, *Ethic for Enemies*, and, particularly, his noting and accounting for the appearances and disappearances of forgiveness in the "Christian: political order, including what he terms the "sacramental captivity of forgiveness 500–1500" (49–52).

Hannah Arendt, although avowing no religious belief herself, claims that the "discoverer of the role of forgiveness in the realm of human affairs was Jesus of Nazareth" and the fact "that he made this discovery in a religious context and articulated it in religious language is no reason to take it any less seriously in a strictly secular sense."[23] Even while exercizing a hermeneutical reserve against the ideological misuse of biblical texts, within the life of Jesus, we do indeed find approaches to forgiveness that are a resource for political and religious transformation.

From the Gospels we see that forgiveness is not a simple matter, for it involves both sinned against and sinner. Neither is forgiveness a once-off act followed by reserved coexistence. Forgiveness is costly, sometimes painful, and implies a new orientation to relationship between those formerly at enmity. Usually, in biblical narratives, sinners who seek forgiveness experience emotions of contrition expressed in lament and pleading for mercy:

> Out of the depths I cry to you, O Lord,
> Lord, hear my voice!
> O let your ears be attentive to the voice of my pleading.
> If you, O Lord should mark our guilt,
> Lord, who would survive?
> But with you is found forgiveness.
> For this we revere you. (Psalm 129)

There are texts in which the command is to repent or perish (Luke 13:1–5), though this is immediately followed by the parable of the barren fig tree that was given another chance to bear fruit (vv. 6–9). On other occasions, forgiveness is given without either request or repenting, as in the case of the paralytic whose sins were forgiven by Jesus. In Jesus' teaching on prayer he includes a petition on release from trespasses (debts) in words that conjoin divine and human forgiveness. And in the parable of the unforgiving servant the king condemns the man who was himself forgiven but refused to forgive a fellow servant (Matt. 18:21–35). It is neither possible nor desirable to rationalize these into a univocal approach to forgiveness, but there is enough to suggest the complexity of process underlying the

23. Hannah Arendt, *The Human Condition: A Study of the Central Conditions Facing Modern Man* (Chicago: University of Chicago Press, 1958, 1959), 238–39.

imperative that we "forgive till seventy times seven," in tension with the utter freedom to forgive even when there is no obvious sign of repentance in advance.[24]

Auschwitz has taught us that we cannot forgive on behalf of the victims. Where such lived relationship is not possible because one party refuses or is already dead, perhaps all we can do or need do is to ask the Father to forgive the offenders. This is what Jesus did as he hung on the cross. Deprived of the possibility of coming face to face with his persecutors, Jesus brought them under his Father's gaze and prayed, "Father, forgive them." In the economy of salvation, grace is not cheap but it is not scarce either. There is hope for wholeness flowing from the heart of God.

In theological terms Roman Catholics and Protestants have developed different emphases in their understanding of forgiveness. The Catholic tradition in the West has centered largely on forgiveness and reconciliation in sacramental terms. Here the person confesses sin to God with repentance and firm purpose of amendment, in the presence of a priest who absolves the penitent in the name of Christ. Catholic practice has at times distorted the meaning of forgiveness by a forensic yet routine-like approach that runs the risk of cheapening forgiveness. Since the Second Vatican Council, more prominence has been given to the communal dimension of sin and forgiveness and with renewed stress on the mercy of Christ.

The Protestant tradition has tended to concentrate on the inner experience of God's forgiveness, insisting that justification by grace through faith happens in the inner domain of personal conscience. This approach, too, can slip into a largely privatized approach to sin and forgiveness, but it also sounds salutary warnings against "cheap grace." It points to the cross and insists on the costliness of forgiveness. Ironically, as the practice of "going to confession" regularly has lessened among Roman Catholics, its practice in various nonsacramental forms is increasing in some Protestant contexts. Perhaps each tradition with its particular and partial emphases can correct and enhance the other. There could be a real benefit in discovering and sharing

---

24. On the moot point of whether repentance is a prior requirement, see L. Gregory Jones, *Embodying Forgiveness: A Theological Analysis* (Grand Rapids, Mich.: Eerdmans, 1996), 135–62. I find Jones's case against Swinburne's insistence on prior repentance more theologically consistent and more congruent with the inner logic of the Gospels. See above.

of our various understandings of forgiveness—a mutual valuing of what Paul Tillich has described as "Protestant principle" and "Catholic substance."[25]

In Protestant and Roman Catholic theologies alike, the forgiveness of sin is seen as God's gracious initiative. Forgiveness is indeed an attribute of the divine, an expression of God's freedom and grace made visible in the life, death, and resurrection of Jesus Christ. Even though we often pray the words that Christ taught us—"Forgive us our trespasses as we forgive those who trespass against us"—anyone I have ever asked has expressed a discomfort about taking on him- or herself the idea of offering forgiveness to another. Typically in our personal relationships when we hurt another, the words, "I am sorry," may be voiced. But to say, "I forgive you," seems to sit uneasily with most. Is it that we fear being thought self-righteous or that we will be rejected? Or perhaps, in subjectively pronouncing, "I forgive you," we would make ourselves vulnerable to the grace given and responsible for a new and free way of relating in the future. To actually say to someone, "I forgive you," is an experience of transcendent awe and responsibility from which we would shelter ourselves. The Little Prince's words about the fox might be adapted without slight to the original—"You are responsible forever for what you have forgiven."

If there is such "diffidence" at a personal level, it is no wonder that people do not know how to relate to forgiveness as communities.[26] Yet there is a fundamentally relational dynamic to forgiveness. And so, forgiveness is not straightforward for us, well adjusted as we are to "the logic of strict exchange rather than God's logic of superabundance." But just as forgiveness is not something a person can merit, neither, as we have intimated already, can forgiveness be demanded from people who may be too wounded still to let go of their pain or let go to the implied responsibility of forgiveness. It may be all that they can do to forbear. The forgiveness that Christ practiced and enjoined on his followers was unconditional. It

---

25. Paul Tillich, *The Protestant Era*, abridged ed. (Chicago: University of Chicago Press, 1957), 94, and 109–10. For an imaginative analysis of Tillich's insight and a critical extension of it in terms of the need for ecumenism rooted in truth and love, see Gabriel Daly OSA, "One Church: Two Indispensable Values—Protestant Principle and Catholic Substance," Occasional Paper, Irish School of Ecumenics, 1998.
26. Cf. Gabriel Daly, "Forgiveness and Community," in *Reconciling Memories*, ed. Falconer, 99–115.

demanded no apology or guarantee in advance. He offered forgiveness first and opened a way for the sinner to go in peace. It is within a community of forgiveness that those who sin and are forgiven can find the freedom or courage to repent and open toward a new way of living. Forgiveness and repentance posit the continuing struggle to relate to one another in a new way.[27] In postconflict settings, where traumas are still raw, it is this move to reconciled relations with one's enemies that puts a stumbling block in the way of forgiveness. This is a current dilemma within the peace process in Ireland, and it is this third move in the journey that we will now explore.

LIFE AFTER VIOLENCE: HEALING COMMUNITIES AND LIVING RECONCILED RELATIONS

To experience healing is to know that we have been made whole, but that we are still wounded people. In the Gospel stories of Christ's post-resurrection appearances Christ still showed the wounds of his passion. The kind of integrity that we seek after we become aware of the brokenness and acknowledge the need for forgiveness is radically different from a state of first innocence. The embracing of the pain in some public way can and does bring healing, and motivates the engendering of new actions of solidarity and reconciliation. In this third stage we are invited to take on the responsibility of living toward one another in love.

The Latin salus can be related to healing, blessing, or wholeness. It is also the word for salvation. Thus, "salvation" is not only a saving act or event (soteria) but also a condition of blessedness (salus), distinguishing God's work of deliverance and God's creative and continuing blessing.[28]

---

27. Arendt also sets before us the baleful consequences of forgiveness refused: "Without being forgiven, released from the consequences of what we have done we would remain the victims of its consequences forever" (The Human Condition, 237). "Without being bound to the fulfillment of promises, we would never be able to keep our identities . . . for no one can forgive himself and no one can feel bound by a promise made only to himself; forgiving and promising enacted in solitude or isolation remain without reality and can signify no more than a role played before one's self" (213).

28. Claus Westermann, Blessing in the Bible and the Life of the Church, trans. Keith Crim (Philadelphia: Fortress Press, 1978), 1–14 and passim.

The cognate Hebrew word *shalom* is grounded in God's peace and evokes blessing within the whole of creation living at peace with itself. Shalom is both God's gift and the human calling, grace and practice. Shalom originates in God and is expressed in the relationship of God's covenant. It signifies fullness of life and flourishing for all, whether friend or stranger, and reaches out to embrace all nations and generations. Notions of power and of promise are thus inherent in this understanding of blessing: "Blessing is also the power of fruitfulness."[29] And too, "[t]he act of blessing, *berekh,* means imparting vital power to another person: The one who gives the other person the blessing gives the other person something of his own soul. . . . Interpersonal relations are not possible without blessing."[30]

Where there is injustice or violence toward the weak, God's peace is driven into exile. Shalom brings justice, and it is this justice that ensures that shalom reigns rather than human interests or false peace.[31] In the post–Good Friday Agreement situation the imperatives of justice and the need for peace often seem to be at odds in practice. But it is within this gap that the work of reconciliation must be worked out as a vision of shalom.[32] Ceasefires are but the absence of the worst atrocities for most people in most neighborhoods. Even with ceasefires, many are still being forced to flee from their homes; others are victims of "punishment beatings." Internal feuding and turf wars continue. Controlled violence is viewed as inevitable by some paramilitaries during a ceasefire, a necessary "penultimate" aspect in the peace process. It is necessary to keep resisting this claim, for there will not be healing as long as talk of a "peace process" is coded language for violence as a way to peace, or of violence as "redemptive" in the longer term.[33]

Peace and violent war are mutually exclusive, no matter how much of a "process" peace may be. Few have escaped some wounding experiences

29. Ibid., 18.
30. Ibid., 19.
31. Jürgen Moltmann, "Justice Creates Peace," unpublished paper delivered at Conference of Peace Groups, Budapest, 1987, 5.
32. Geraldine Smyth, "Sabbath and Jubilee," in *The Jubilee Challenge: Utopia or Possibility— Jewish and Christian Insights,* ed. Hans Ucko (Geneva: WCC Publications, 1997), 59–76, esp. 66ff.
33. Cf. Walter Wink, *Engaging the Powers: Discernment and Resistance in a World of Domination* (Minneapolis: Fortress Press, 1992). Adducing Girardian theories of violence and the sacred in relation both to biblical narratives and the emerging discourse of active non-violent conflict resolution, Wink exposes the lies beneath the myth that "violence saves."

of injustice and violence, but this cycle of violence must nevertheless be interrupted so that the process of healing and the reconciling of relationships can be encouraged, especially for those most deeply wounded—the widowed and orphaned and parents whose children have been killed, those denied even the last dignity of burying their dead, prisoners and prisoners on parole—many of whom were drawn while still in their teens into a war they did not understand, many of them endeavoring now to make some atonement through lives and actions that strengthen the social fabric of their local communities.[34] It is interesting that the current development in Northern Ireland of "restorative justice schemes" has emerged, by and large, as community-development initiatives in liaison with community-based policing. Here social offenders and their victims engage in a concrete process of trying to restore what has been "stolen." There is an essentially relational dimension to the process, insofar as the perpetrator is willing to give the offender a chance of amending the loss and insofar as the perpetrator meets his or her victim and undertakes some agreed work of restoration. Thus, there is the possibility not only of reciprocal healing and atonement toward the one offended against. But also the perpetrator is able to be an agent in restoring the victim's capacity to trust, and even risk relationship with whomever it was that caused pain and loss. One would suppose that the churches might have something to contribute to this process through a radical retrieval and reimagining of the atonement tradition in relation to this praxis of social healing and the reconciling of Christian communities.[35]

As this book goes to press, eighty-six political prisoners—all but the last few are walking free from the Maze Prison under the early release terms of the Good Friday Agreement. In the glare of publicity and media debate on the rights and wrongs of this fact, some relatives of murder victims voiced their outrage and sense of betrayal. They seemed trapped on a relentless wheel of no release either for themselves or the perpetrators. There was no

---

34. In the contemporary context of early prisoner-release schemes, relatives of victims need some sense that the suffering inflicted on them or their families is atoned at least in symbolic terms, and that their deaths might be suffused with some meaning and transformative value in the building of peace.

35. The *locus classicus* for a survey of classic atonement theology is Gustaf Aulén, *Christus Victor: An Historical Survey of the Three Main Types of the Idea of Atonement* (1931; London: SPCK, 1980). From this point of departure, see also F. W. Dillistone, *The Christian Understanding of Atonement* (London: SCM, 1984).

end in view, either possible or desired. Other relatives, on seeing the convicted killers of their loved ones released, expressed deep distress ("a bitter pill to swallow" was a phrase used by several) but who also saw the releases as something, no matter how hard, that was necessary to accept "because of the greater good of peace" or, "for the sake of my grand-children and the life my children missed out." To the reporter's questions, "Is this necessary? Do you forgive?" one widow replied, "It is painful, but it is necessary. Forgive?" She hesitated, "I haven't crossed that bridge yet."[36] These observations remind us again that we are dealing with a still-emerging process wherein people find themselves at different stages and at times experiencing ambiguity in different levels within themselves. Some seem powerless to move on. Some have been able to make the supreme act of letting go to forgiveness. Others acknowledge that they are not yet there.

Forgiveness is perhaps the key redemptive step on the journey into reconciliation. In this journey one step may beget another and where neither forgiveness nor reconciliation can be demanded or forced. The Presbyterian Peace and Peace-Making Committee some years ago made a helpful intervention in a public statement. Drawing on the Christian and Reformed symbol of pilgrimage, they urged their people to acknowledge the need for everyone to move on in the journey into a more just and peaceful society. But there was a recognizing that everyone was at a different stage of the journey and that this needed to be respected, given different insights, experiences, and capacities. But it urged everyone to move, to make a step from where they were. This touches upon the role of the churches in Northern Ireland. People there (and not just Christians) have in the past looked to the churches for pastoral support in the face of intolerable human suffering. But many also need release from what binds them. Others are actively seeking ethical and theological guidance for taking on themselves more fully than in the past the Gospel call to live in peace. They have a right to expect Christian leadership in their search to find resources in their tradition for healing on the way to salvation. In the immediate instance, there is a role for pastors in showing compassion to those who are feeling the suffering of the past reinscribed in their lives, as they see the murderers of their children,

36. Cf. *Irish Times*, Dublin, July 28, 2000, 1, 8, and 9.

siblings, or parents walk free. But it is also necessary for Christian pastors and leaders to accompany those seeking ways to let go and move on.

In instances where people cannot yet find it in themselves to forgive or to receive forgiveness, a different approach to the theology of atonement and the creating of authentic symbols and moral patterns of atonement can help open the way toward release and healing, and some sense that the life, death, and love of their departed ones have not been in vain, that their own lives can be inscribed with some hope of transformation. The work of atonement can be seen as the action of the Spirit sustaining those actively cooperating to reweave the torn fabric of communities. It is visible in the small circles and quiet processes of keeping alive memory and hope among bereaved families or generating training and employment opportunities for young people, or persevering with cross-community schemes of trust building and learning to value difference.[37] Where forgiveness is still too difficult to envisage, atonement may offer the needed bridge

But it belongs to the Christian leaders and teachers to keep the gift and call of forgiveness before the eyes of their community. Dietrich Bonhoeffer puts this starkly:

For the Church and for the individual believer there can only be a complete breach with guilt and a new beginning which is granted through the forgiveness of sin, but in the historical life of nations there can always be only the gradual process of healing. . . . It is recognized that what is past cannot be restored by any human might, and that the wheel of history cannot be turned back. Not all the wounds inflicted can be healed, but what matters is that there shall

---

37. Hannah Arendt's words come to mind again on the desperate need to break out of the felt "irreversibility" of the experience and break free from the pressure toward revenge and relentless retribution. "In this respect, forgiveness is the exact opposite of vengeance, which act in the form of re-acting against an original trespassing, whereby far from putting an end to the consequences of the first misdeed, everybody remains bound to the process, permitting the chain reaction contained in every action to take its unhindered course. In contrast to revenge, which is the natural, automatic re-action to transgression and which can be expected and even calculated, the act of forgiving can never be predicted. . . . Forgiving, in other words, is the only reaction which does not merely re-act, but acts anew and unexpectedly, unconditioned by the act which provoked it and therefore freeing from its consequences both the one who forgives and the one who is forgiven" (240–41).

be no more wounds. . . . This forgiveness within history can come only when the wound of guilt is healed, when violence has become justice, lawlessness has become order, and war has become peace.[38]

Here Bonhoeffer affords some indulgence to the world as the secular city, though contrary to what one might expect of someone in the Lutheran tradition of the Two Kingdoms, with different laws governing church and state. (He does in fact see a place for forgiveness in secular history.) But in addressing the church, Bonhoeffer expects "a complete breach with guilt and a new beginning which is granted through the forgiveness of sin."

If churches remain complacent with the status quo of their divisions they may secure some cohesiveness in the short term but risk compromising their deeper identity in Christ—to live and share as a forgiven community of new creation, called to share in Christ's work of reconciling the world to God's love, through the forgiveness of sins (2 Cor. 5:16–21). Churches, no less than individual Christians, are called to conversion—not ministering within closed denominational groups as "chaplains to their tribes."[39] Research has shown that the institutional churches in their separated structures and practice both reflect and reinforce prevailing political and community divisions and that the theological attention of clergy is harnessed to maintaining the status quo rather than in guiding change toward reconciled communities. The pattern revealed was of expecting the other church to change first. Cross-community encounter was generally acceptable, but there was still a reserve about interchurch relationships and even more of ecumenism.[40]

One must concede that such a movement would be a risk to churches that are caught up in the need to preserve identity by turning inward theologically and pastorally. If such an inward focus was understandable during

---

38. Dietrich Bonhoeffer, *Ethics,* ed. Eberhard Bethge (London: SCM, 1955), 53–54.

39. This term has passed into common parlance in the North of Ireland. I trace its original coinage to Robin Boyd and John Morrow, two Presbyterian ecumenists, and erstwhile directors of the Irish School of Ecumenics and the Corrymeela Community, respectively. See Boyd, *Ireland,* 50–51.

40. Duncan Morrow, *The Churches and Inter-Community Relationships* (Coleraine: University of Ulster, 1991), 8, 121. Although the research is ten years old, there is little evidence of significant change.

the worst years of the Troubles, when people felt insecure and under threat, the time has come for something quite other. From a sociological perspective, conflict can act as a cohesive force, and this has been so of churches in Ireland. The churches were perhaps more prepared for war than ready for peace. But now, increasingly, conscientious Christians are ready for something more proactive. The oft-quoted excuse made by minister/priests— that they cannot afford to go too far ahead in interchurch relations for fear of alienating members of the congregation does not hold water. I know of churches where members are seeking to take part in ecumenical initiatives without the support of—and even despite—their ministers. Conscientious difficulty is another oft-presented rationalization for noninvolvement. But conscience too needs to be situated vis-à-vis the needs of the wider community. Such ecclesiological provisos as are posed should be questioned in terms of putting the narcissism of small differences into the context of dialogue and mutual accountability. Terence McCaughey helpfully situates "conscience" in terms of "consciousness of the other."[41] Theologically interpreted, our willingness to encounter the other church in its otherness may open us to the possibility of encounter with the divine Other, who questions and transcends every claim to religious or institutional belonging. Even if churches cannot yet see themselves giving an unambiguous leading witness to forgiveness and reconciliation, perhaps they can act in the role of midwife to the peace, assisting and supporting those in their congregations who feel ready to take further steps in their relationship with other Christian groups, risking their denominational identity for the sake of Christ and his church.

The report on Sectarianism commissioned by the Irish Interchurch Group on Faith an Politics poses a strong challenge to the churches to tackle the mutual ignorance and prejudice in their relations with one another. The churches have contributed to the building and cementing of sectarianism; now they need to collaborate in deconstructing it.[42] Sectarian disunity between the churches is an obstacle to the love that Christ gave to his

41. Terence McCaughey, *Memory and Redemption: Church, Politics and Prophetic Theology in Ireland* (Dublin: Gill and Macmillan, 1993), 87ff.
42. "Sectarianism: A Discussion Document," presented to the Irish Inter-Church Meeting, Belfast, 1993.

followers and which he willed to the church. Churches are called to mutual healing of relationships, solidarity with the outsider, and to risk forgiveness as a people redeemed. The times demand that Christian leaders bear witness to the wide horizon of Christ's church as a community of freedom and love. In opening with the wider community to this new moment, churches too are called upon to acknowledge their failure to witness to Christ's Gospel of reconciliation and peace. As we find shared ways of confessing that failure, we will find Christ's grace revealed in the faces and in needs of strangers. Whatever blessings we have are to be given away, shared with others. To live otherwise is to live out of our own striving and scarcity as if all depended on ourselves. Christ calls his Church to live out of the abundance which is his gift and blessing to us.

LOOKING TO THE FUTURE: THE WAY OF JESUS AS ABUNDANT LIFE AND GRACE

As the people of Ireland look toward an era of peace, the challenge is to move out from the "narrow ground," as one local historian entitles his book on the modern history of Ulster.[43] Developing the earlier image of reconciliation as a journey, and linking that with A.T.Q. Stewart's image of "the narrow ground," this can be epitomized as a journey out of scarcity to abundant life. The Gospels present models and metaphors for this journey and indeed the very structure of the synoptics embodies this. Perhaps one of the greatest services that the churches can render in the current situation is *together* to create some ecumenical spaces where the word of Scripture can be broken and shared as food for the journey. With this in mind, we shall conclude by reflecting on the parable of the Prodigal Son—or if one prefers, of the Lost Son and the Prodigal Father—in correlation to the insights of Reformed theologian Paul Ricoeur and vis-à-vis this new moment in Ireland. For in this parable the tensions between the logic of scarcity and the logic of abundance is writ large as the very paradigm of the reign of God (Cf. Luke 15:11–32).

43. A.T.Q. Stewart, *The Narrow Ground: Patterns of Ulster History* (Belfast: Pretani Press, 1986).

At the outset, the son's grasping for his inheritance meets with the father's willingness to give it out ahead of time. In a way, the son's squandering of his inheritance on dissolute living is the parody of the father's generosity and a travesty of real freedom. Jesus tells this parable to demonstrate that in God there is no scarcity and that those who follow him are called to live not in misery but with faith in a God whose grace will never be wanting. God's grace is never spent. God's house is always open to those who would return there.

When the younger son comes to a true awareness of his own alienation, starving and cast out, we are told, "He came to himself." We can relate this moment to that outlined above as becoming aware of our brokenness. For those who know there is no further to fall, there can arise a new consciousness of need and a readiness to name the brokenness within and around. "How many of my father's hired hands have bread enough and to spare, but here am I dying of hunger?" (again the abundance scarcity contrast). He has a hunch that there is a way of ending his isolation and obsession with autonomy. There is a way back to his father's house and to living with the economy of the gift rather than with assertions of entitlement. From the perspective of this son's insight and self-knowledge we can agree with Ricoeur that there is no innocent place to start. Rather, grace over and above that of first innocence is to be found on the far side of betrayal. The journey out of isolation leads back home to the father's house with and the rather meager intention of stating some of the wrong done and of gaining a half-measure relationship with those who live there.

In the second stage of the story, as in the second stage of the journey to reconciliation described above, comes the invitation to acceptance and forgiveness. In Luke the father's compassion is shown: the embrace and the outpouring of emotion are the structuring impulses of the narrative at this point rather than recriminations or calculations of loss. The son speaks out his rehearsed words but they are swept aside in the father's embrace. The sense of excess is expressed in the symbols and gestures of honor, reinstatement, and celebration: robe, sandals and ring, the fatted calf and preparations for the feast to ritualize the homecoming.[44] Significantly, for

44. Cf. Robert J. Karris, O.F.M., "The Gospel According to Luke," no. 147, in *The New Jerome*

346 GERALDINE SMYTH, O.P.

our purpose, the pain of loss is not glossed over but acknowledged. But this, too, is the very reason for celebrating extravagantly: "for this son of mine was dead and is alive again; he was lost and is found. And they began to celebrate" (v. 24). The forgiveness is disclosed with unobtrusive grace, without drawing attention to itself.

In the final turn in the parable we can see further possibilities of making some correlation with the peace process in Ireland and the third stage of the journey—of healing communities and living toward reconciliation. The emphasis in the parable at this point is only partly the rivalry of the elder son toward the younger. It relies also on undertones from other stories in the Hebrew Scriptures where the claims of the elder son's entitlement were subverted through guile, chance, or God's free gift.[45] The jealousy of the older son in the face of the royal treatment lavished on his brother culminates in his refusal of relationship with the other, whom he calls "this son of yours." He is angry, and his resentment shows in the lurid detailing to the father of the corruption of his erstwhile brother and the comparative self-righteous narrative of his own virtues. From his perspective there can be no second chance, no mercy shown. Because his demand for strict equivalence is not met, he refuses to join in the feasting. To him the feast is gratuitous and unfair. But, addressing him too as "Son," the father repeats the logic of mercy: "Son, you are always with me and all that is mine is yours. But we had to celebrate and rejoice, because this brother of yours was dead and has come to life; he was lost and is found" (vv. 31–32). Read from the perspective of the contemporary task in Ireland of the healing of communities and the reconciling communities divided by historic cycles of resentment and blame, this parable challenges Christians and churches in Ireland to break free of the self-perpetuating game of winners and losers, sinners and sinned against.

Again Ricoeur's insights go to the heart of the matter when he addresses

---

Biblical Commentary, ed. Raymond E. Brown, S.S., Joseph A. Fitzmyer, S.J., and Roland E. Murphy, O.Carm. (London: Chapman, 1991), 70–77,

45. For example, Esau and Jacob (Gen. 25:27–34, 27:1–36), and Joseph and his brothers (Gen. 37:1–4). But there is a double subversion of the tradition in that parable of Jesus, for here the prodigal son is a parody of the successful younger brother and the elder is not decided against but is also invited to the feast.

the need to *reconcile* the logic of equivalence based on the rule of retribution and the logic of superabundance. He questions whether Jesus's example of love of enemies and doing good with no expectation of return does not in effect retract the golden rule of equivalence. His conclusion, however, is that Jesus reinterprets the rule in terms of generosity. Thus, it is not a question of overriding the ethical by the gratuitous but of allowing the "hyper moral" to pass through the principle of morality and its formalizations in the rule of justice.[46] But Ricoeur also presses home the counterposition:

> In this living tension between the logic of superabundance and the logic of equivalence, the latter receives from its confrontation with the former, the capacity to raise itself above its perverse interpretations.[47]

The new twist is a move from a position of "interest"—of giving or showing mercy *in order that* you will obtain mercy—to a stance of disinterest—of giving, or showing mercy *because* you have received mercy.[48] This argument apposite vis-à-vis the clashing interpretations of the different parties within Northern Ireland, Ireland, and Britain in respect of the compromises on traditional interests that every party and partner is obliged to make, in the process of peace building and risking the responsibilities of new and interdependent relationships. It is apposite not because of the beauty and appeal of his dialectic between "the poetics of love" and the "prose of justice" (p. 324). Ricoeur's construal is intellectually sinewy in its refusal to deny "the secret discordance between the logic of superabundance and the logic of equivalence beneath the "compromise formulas"; it also asserts a role for theology and philosophy in the task of ongoing moral

---

46. Paul Ricoeur, "Love and Justice," in *Figuring the Sacred*, 326–28.
47. Ibid., 328.
48. Ibid. Ricoeur indicates a great variety of expression in the New Testament of the logic of superabundance. Thus it "governs the extravagant twist of many of Jesus' parables." But he also adduces Paul who "interprets the whole history of salvation following the same law of superabundance: 'If because of one man's trespass, death reigned through that one man, much more will those who receive the abundance of grace and the free gift of righteousness reign in life through the one man Jesus Christ' (Rom. 5:17)" (326 n. 14).

discernment within particular situations, to ensure that the "unstable equilibrium can be assured and protected."

For Ricoeur it is eminently practicable in everyday life "in good faith and with a good conscience—on the individual, judicial, social and political planes." In terms of the peace process—particularly in relation to the discourse on parity of esteem (which is at times pursued with an obsessive single edge in favour of one's own tradition), or in relation to the search for some equilibrium between justice and mercy—his call for "a supplementary degree of compassion and generosity in all of our codes" could not be more fitting.

Moving on in the journey of reconciliation will require a capacity to recognize that the logic of the gift invites us to give because we have abundantly received, to forgive because we have been prodigally forgiven, and to live by grace in return for the grace received. Grace may come to us through awareness of brokenness and alienation, or in experiences of betrayal, forgiveness, or gestures of atonement. Reconciliation may catch us unawares, for God's Spirit blows where it will.

In *Four Quartets,* T. S. Eliot imagines himself meeting the ghost of a dead poet (thought by some to be W. B. Yeats).[49] They look back on the barrenness of old rivalry and on their respective attempts to "purify the dialect of the tribe." For us they can stand in some way as a symbol of those in Ireland who wish for forgiveness but cannot let go of the hungry ghosts of the past. In the words of this ghost, something different stirs:

> . . . I am not eager to rehearse
> My thoughts and theory which you have forgotten.
> These things which have served their purpose: let them be.
> So with your own, and pray they be forgiven
> By others, as I pray you to forgive
> Both bad and good. Last season's fruit is eaten
> And the fulfilled beast shall kick the empty pail.
> For last year's words belong to last year's language
> And next year's words await another voice.

49. T. S. Eliot, "Little Gidding," in *T. S. Eliot: The Complete Poems and Plays* (London: Faber and Faber, 1969), 194.

Echoes are here of our own embattled ghosts and of the clashing dialects of the tribe. But there emerge, too, shades of the Spirit, encouraging a new language of forgiveness and hope.

CHAPTER 17

Forgiveness and Reconciliation in the Mozambique Peace Process

Andrea Bartoli

M OZAMBIQUE IS A COUNTRY AT PEACE.[1] After more than four hundred years of colonial rule by Portugal and armed struggles that lasted more than thirty years, the country is now at peace.[2] Remarkably, it does not experience the same level of internal violence so prevalent in its neighboring South Africa.

Did forgiveness and reconciliation play a role during the long peace process that led to the new political arrangement? Are they playing a role now? Can the Mozambique model be exported and replicated? What was the role of the religious actors?[3]

While the mechanisms of forgiveness and reconciliation played a role during the peace process and in the aftermath of the signing of the agreement on October 4, 1992, analysis and understanding of their input have not yet been completed.[4] This chapter will argue that the religious leaders,

1. For a recent evaluation of the peace process see Richard Synge, *Mozambique: UN Peacekeeping in Action, 1992–94* (Washington, D.C.: USIP Press, 1997), and *The United Nations and Mozambique, 1992–95,* Department of Public Information, United Nations, 1995.
2. William Finnegan, *A Complicated War: The Harrowing of Mozambique* (Berkeley: University of California Press, 1992).
3. Andrea Bartoli, "Mediating Peace in Mozambique," in *Herding Cats: Multiparty Mediation in a Complex World,* ed. Chester Crocker, Fen Hampson, and Pamela Aall (Washington, D.C.: USIP Press, 1999).
4. Some references to the overall issue of religion and peacemaking and the case of the

actors, and entities played a crucially active and indispensable role in the peace process both locally and internationally.

However, while the religious actors contributed significantly to the resolution of the conflict in Mozambique, a more careful evaluation of how religious those actions were needs to be undertaken. I will argue that religion played a role in the motivation of prominent actors, in the availability of resources through the religious networks, and in the overall vision and style of the peace process, especially during its two and a half years at the headquarters of the Community of Sant'Egidio.[5] The undertaking succeeded because these elements were brought together harmoniously in the design and implementation of peace as a political process. In other words, the political character of the peace process was not transformed by the presence of religious elements, but simply enriched by them.[6] A religious contribution made the political discourse more flexible and able to respond to the increased complexity of the process.

In particular, the nongovernmental character of three out of the four mediators allowed the Mozambican parties to express and resolve the problem of legitimacy that would have been overwhelming in a more rigid and formal environment. Therefore, a religious contribution to peace-making, as in this instance, needs to cooperate with all the other actors, especially in the formal sectors both locally and internationally, in order to be successful.[7] Religious peace-making needs to be conceived as a contribution to a larger political process to which both religious and nonreligious elements contribute.[8] Significantly, the main facilitator of the Mozambican process, the Community of Sant'Egidio, was able after the positive con-

Community of Sant'Egidio's role may be found in R. Scott Appleby, *The Ambivalence of the Sacred: Religion, Violence, and Reconciliation* (Lanham, Md.: Rowman and Littlefield, 2000) and in Douglas Johnston and Cynthia Sampson, eds., *Religion: The Missing Dimension of Statecraft* (New York: Oxford University Press, 1994).

5. Roberto Morozzo della Rocca, *Mozambico, dalla guerra alla pace: Storia di una mediazione insolita* (Milan: Edizioni San Paolo, 1994).

6. Andrea Bartoli, "Providing Space for Change in Mozambique," in *Transforming Violence: Linking Local and Global Peacemaking*, ed. Robert Herr and Judy Zimmerman Herr (Scottdale, Pa.: Herald Press, 1998), 190–202.

7. John Paul Lederach, *Building Peace: Sustainable Reconciliation in Divided Societies* (Washington, D.C.: USIP Press, 1997), especially on "Coordination," 99–106.

8. Harold H. Saunders, *A Public Peace Process: Sustained Dialogue to Transform Racial and Ethnic Conflicts* (New York: St. Martin's Press, 1999), 5–17.

clusion of the Mozambique peace process to contribute positively to the resolution of other deadly international conflicts, such as in Albania, Burundi, Kosovo, Guatemala, Algeria, and the Democratic Republic of the Congo.[9]

A BRIEF HISTORY OF THE CONFLICT

The case of Mozambique demonstrates that conflicts do experience cycles and transformations, especially when they are prolonged.[10]

Mozambique gained independence from Portugal in 1975 and hoped to end its history of colonialism, imposed too long ago by the Portuguese presence since 1498. The Frente da Libertacao de Mozambique (FRELIMO) was founded in June 1963 when three major nationalist groups joined forces, electing Eduardo Mondlane, an anthropologist with a Ph.D. from an American university, as the first president.[11] FRELIMO found a more militant tone under the leadership of Samora Machel, who succeeded Mondlane after his death. While making some gains in the control of territory in the northern part of the country, FRELIMO was not in a position to overcome the Portuguese military presence.[12] Eventual independence resulted, therefore, partially because of the armed struggle and partially as the result of a Portuguese decision to abandon its colonial rule.

Unfortunately, the transition period between the recognition of independence and the establishment of the legitimate and recognized Mozambique government was disrupted by regional interests, first of Rhodesia and later of South Africa. Fearful of an independent, native-led Mozambique, Rhodesia exploited the tensions internal to the newly independent state and encouraged a guerrilla movement to challenge the authority of the central

9. Mario Giro, "The Community of Saint Egidio and Its Peace-Making Activities," *The International Spectator,* no. 3 (July–September 1998).

10. Michael Lund, *Preventing Violent Conflicts: A Strategy for Preventive Diplomacy* (Washington, D.C.: USIP Press, 1996), 38–39.

11. Eduardo Mondlane, *The Struggle for Mozambique* (New York: Penguin, 1996).

12. For a comprehensive overview of Mozambique's history, see Allen Issacman and Barbara Issacman, *Mozambique: From Colonialism to Revolution, 1900–1982* (Boulder, Colo.: Westview Press, 1983), and Malyn Newitt, *A History of Mozambique* (Bloomington: Indiana University Press, 1995).

government in Maputo.[13] The guerrilla movement took the name of Resistencia Nationial Mozambiqana (RENAMO) and soon became well known to the local population and to the international community as a synonym for violence and disruption. RENAMO's military tactics, aimed to prevent the central government from asserting control over the whole country, was designed to impede regular cultivation of the land and a stable social life.[14] State infrastructure, such as bridges and roads, were not the only military targets. Services, such as schools and health centers, were also targeted. RENAMO attacked everything that was a sign of a healthy central government.[15]

In terms of human costs in the war, the results were astonishing.[16] The government was unable exert real control in many areas, yet RENAMO systematically avoided generating a new political and social civil structure. Its tactics seemed to be aimed more toward making it impossible for the central government to function properly than to establish its own control over the territory. Additionally, the recruitment strategy used by both parties, especially by RENAMO, made a mark on the population. While some people joined military forces voluntarily, the kidnapping of young males, even those very young, was not uncommon. Sometimes these young recruits were

13. William Minter, *Apartheid's Contras: An Inquiry Into the Roots of War in Angola and Mozambique* (London: Zed Books, 1994).
14. As a way to acknowledge an independent evaluation of an anthropologist living in the country at the time of the war I share the following quote: "The extent of the violence in Mozambique can be captured in a few statistics. Over one million people, the vast majority noncombatants, have lost their lives to the war. Over two hundred thousand children have been orphaned by the war (some estimates are much higher). Adequate assistance is more hope than reality in a country where one-third of all schools and hospitals were closed or destroyed by RENAMO and where a single orphanage operates. Nearly one-fourth of the entire population of 15 million people has been displaced from their homes by the war, and an additional one-fourth of the population has been directly affected by the war. In a country where 90 percent of the population lives in poverty and 60 percent in extreme poverty, the toll has been devastating"; Carolyn Nordstrom, "Creativity and Chaos: War on the Front Lines," in *Fieldwork under Fire: Contemporary Studies of Violence and Survival,* ed. Carolyn Nordstrom and Antonious C.G.M. Robben (Berkeley: University of California Press, 1995), 133.
15. Robert Gersony, *Summary of Mozambican Refugee Accounts of Principally Conflict-Related Experience in Mozambique: Report Submitted to Ambassador Jonathan Moore, Director, Bureau for Refugee Programs; Dr. Chester A. Crocker, Assistant Secretary of African Affairs* (Washington, D.C.: Department of State, 1988).
16. James Ciment, *Angola and Mozambique: Postcolonial Wars in Southern Africa* (New York: Facts on File, 1997).

asked to perform violent acts in their own villages in order to sever the ties with their relatives and friends. The war was therefore a systematic chaos, a powerful experience of disruption that affected everything from the ability to survive to the possibility of inhabiting the territory of the ancestors.[17] Millions of Mozambicans were forced out of their homes, away from their lands, and confined in refugee or internally displaced people's compounds. The very social structure of the whole country was devastated by a war that lasted more than fourteen years.

Regional ramifications of the war were a central preoccupation of national and international leadership for a long time.[18] Rhodesia, a few years after Mozambican independence, was no longer a white supremacist state, but an independent, native-led, proud African country. Robert Mugabe, the new leader of Zimbabwe, was certainly grateful to the Mozambican allies who had supported him during his armed struggle with the old regime in Harare.[19] Mozambique was, in fact, actively involved in the successful military and political attempts to obtain real independence for Zimbabwe. The positive conclusion of that process strengthened its own desire for a solution to its internal struggle.

Mozambique's leadership was also aware that South Africa played a major role in their internal struggle. In order to prevent South Africa from justifying its operation in Mozambique as due to security concerns, Mozambican president Samora Machel negotiated with South Africa and signed a cooperation agreement that would prevent the two countries from unduly interfering in each other's territory. The Nkomati Agreement, named after the city in which it was signed, took away from South Africa any justification for interfering in any Mozambican affairs because of its support for RENAMO. Consequently, Mozambican leadership promised not to allow military action against South Africa to take place from Mozambican territory. Some commentators felt that the agreement was unfair to the African

---

17. Africa Watch, *Conspicuous Destruction: War, Famine, and the Reform Process in Mozambique* (New York: Human Rights Watch, 1992).

18. Robert H. Davies, *South African Strategy Towards Mozambique in the "Accord Phase" from March 1984 to September 1985: Destabilization and Regional Security Concerns in Southern Africa* (Roma, Lesotho: Institute of Southern African Studies, 1991).

19. M. Tamarkin, *The Making of Zimbabwe: Decolonisation in Regional and International Politics* (London: F. Cass, 1990).

National Congress (ANC), which was still struggling against the South African apartheid regime by political and military means. However, Mozambique's action was based on the assumption that the ANC was a genuine, widespread, popular movement in South Africa and that ANC military action in Mozambique was insignificant in a struggle that was led and implemented by South Africa itself.[20]

The regional elements of the confrontation in Mozambique, namely the interest first of Rhodesia and later of South Africa in destabilizing independent Mozambique, also had ideological overtones. FRELIMO was, in fact, a Marxist/Leninist party. The single party regime and the Cold War still provided the framework of the first years of Mozambique's independence. However, while it is clear that FRELIMO leadership sought support from the Soviet bloc to deal with the country's reconstruction after its independence, it is remarkable that RENAMO never succeeded in rallying the anti-communist support that comparable movements in Africa did.[21]

For many years, RENAMO was able to prevent the FRELIMO government from functioning properly, but was unable or unwilling to assert itself as a serious viable alternative.[22] Therefore, in the late 1980s, after the death of President Samora Machel, the new president of Mozambique, Joaquim Chissano, started seeking ways to resolve the conflict with RENAMO. He faced several challenges. The first one was to establish credible contact with RENAMO and elaborate an interpretation of this movement as a political force beyond its military disruptive tactics. This challenge was exacerbated by the relentless FRELIMO policy of demonizing the enemy, which made the transformation of RENAMO into a political party almost impossible to conceive. Then, President Chissano had to overcome the rigidity created by the mono-party system he inherited from the early days of the FRELIMO regime. Communication, political and institutional problems were there-

---

20. Cameron Hume, *Ending Mozambique's War: The Role of Mediation and Good Offices* (Washington, D.C.: USIP Press, 1994), 11–14.
21. In particular, the most striking difference lies between RENAMO and UNITA that, in Angola, RENAMO was not only perceived as supported militarily by Western forces and regimes, but also politically able to connect with powerful political and economical anti-communist forces in Washington and elsewhere: D. Hoile, *Mozambique: A Nation in Crisis* (London: Claridge Press, 1989), and D. Haile, *Mozambique, Resistance, and Freedom: A Case for Assessment* (London: Mozambique Institute, 1994).
22. H. Andersson, *Mozambique: A War against the People* (London: Macmillan, 1992).

fore high priorities on the agenda of President Chissano at a time when neither party had the chance to win the war militarily.

THE ROLE OF RELIGIOUS ACTORS

Significantly, Chissano decided to explore channels of communication, political frameworks and institutional settings that were not traditional in Mozambican national history. The president, showing his ability as a diplomat, extended an invitation to religious leaders from Mozambique to facilitate the establishment of direct channels of communications with RENAMO.[23] While the ideological stand of FRELIMO was distant from an appreciation of the religious actors' role, Chissano perceived in a pragmatic way the usefulness of including them in a long-term strategy of unification and pacification of the country. While the great majority of Mozambicans was and still remains animist, many political leaders were educated in missionary schools and were therefore attuned to Christian teachings.[24] This familiarity clearly left them ambivalent about a greater political role for religious leaders, especially those of Christian background. On one hand was a perception of collusion with the colonial legacy. On the other was a recognition of the positive contribution of missionary work in crucial sectors, especially education and health.

On another front, Muslim minorities in Mozambique were politically active and respected. President Chissano also established direct links with representatives of Eastern religions devoted to meditation and nonviolent transformation. Moreover, the role of local traditional leadership in the whole peace process in Mozambique is not to be underestimated. In fact, even if the more internationally recognized Christian leadership of the country (mainly Catholic and Anglican bishops)[25] played a role in facilitating the establishment of contacts with RENAMO, the traditional leadership

23. Catholic Institute for International Relations, ed., *The Road to Peace in Mozambique, 1982–1992* (London: Catholic Institute for International Relations, 1994).
24. M. Venancio, "Mediation by the Roman Catholic Church in Mozambique, 1988–1991," in *Mediation in Southern Africa* (London: Macmillan, 1993).
25. Cynthia Sampson, "Religion and Peacebuilding," paper prepared for *Handbook on International Conflict Resolution* (Washington, D.C.: USIP 1995).

also strongly encouraged the local population to support peace.[26] More-over, it is noticeable that, at a time when it was illegal to establish any con-tact with RENAMO and the FRELIMO-controlled press was filled with negative rhetoric against the "Banditos Armados," religious leaders were able to play a role in keeping the very idea of peace alive. The Mozambique Catholic Bishop Conference on several occasions published official docu-ments calling for and advocating peace. This action was somehow prob-lematic, as it was perceived as indirect support for the rebels. However, when Chissano determined that regional and ideological concerns had diminished the justification of international support for RENAMO, and was thus able to engage RENAMO in some form of direct dialogue, the reli-gious leaders were in a position to claim the moral high ground, as those who had called for peace while secular forces were embroiled in the logic of a violent confrontation.

Monsignor Jaime Gonçalves, a native of the region of Beira, the second largest and most central city of Mozambique, played the most significant role.[27] Monsignor Gonçalves had been appointed to that diocese by the Vat-ican shortly after Mozambican independence. Reversing a long-standing policy that had allowed only white and Portuguese bishops to be appointed by the Vatican in Portuguese colonies, the Holy See appointed Monsignor Gonçalves as bishop of Beira while he was still studying abroad. Prior to his appointment Monsignor Gonçalves had established fruitful contact with the Community of Sant'Egidio, a lay Catholic association founded in Rome in 1968 by the initiative of a young high-school student, Andrea Riccardi. When Monsignor Gonçalves returned to Rome for his visit *Ad Limina* a few years after his appointment as bishop, he shared with the members of the Community of Sant'Egidio his concern for the somehow intolerant and antireligious climate imposed by the new regime of Mozambique.

The FRELIMO government, in fact, was trying to build a nation out of many ethnic groups while absorbing a legacy of more than four hundred years of colonization. The missionary presence in the country, especially if Catholic, was not favorably perceived. Religious groups were considered to

---

26. Carolyn Nordstrom, *A Different Kind of War Story* (Philadelphia: University of Pennsylva-nia Press, 1997), 142–51.
27. Morozzo della Rocca, *Mozambico, dalla guerra alla pace,* 61–63.

be too close to the former colonial powers and not easily usable in the effort of nation building that was the priority of the FRELIMO leadership.[28] The Community of Sant'Egidio responded to the challenges of the young bishop by facilitating contacts with the leadership of the Italian Communist Party, which at that time was a strong supporter of FRELIMO. The Italian communist leader, Enrico Berlinguer, accepted an invitation to meet Monsignor Gonçalves in Sant'Egidio's headquarters to discuss the issue of religious freedom in Mozambique. Berlinguer was interested in establishing direct contacts with Catholic groups as part of an overall strategy to gain support for a leftist government in Italy.[29] The community was therefore able to use an Italian political calculation to serve the interest of a church that was quite removed from its headquarters, culturally and geographically. This intervention marked the beginning of a long-standing relationship between the Community of Sant'Egidio and Mozambique through both the Catholic Church and FRELIMO representatives.

That this relationship was established through ecclesiastical channels is significant for understanding the religious contribution to the Mozambique peace process. Although the community's members are laypeople who do not take any vows and are requested to work professionally in a secular environment, Sant'Egidio has many elements of a religious organization, more than simply through the recognition of its status by the Holy See. The community's main goals are related to its religious identity and take the character of prayer, service to the poor, and friendship.[30] Members all over the world are asked to pray, serve, and be friendly every day. This highly religious configuration distinguished Sant'Egidio from any other conflict-resolution agency, even in the nongovernmental world.[31]

Sant'Egidio did not seek to establish itself as a mediator in the peace process in Mozambique. It was more the serendipitous sequence of an unexpected series of events that led certain community members to play that role. It is important to note that the first religious aspect that played a role in the Mozambique peace process was Sant'Egidio's capacity for international

28. Hume, *Ending Mozambique's War*, 9.
29. Ibid., 17–18.
30. Andrea Riccardi, *Sant'Egidio, Rome and the World* (St. Paul's, 1999), 81–82.
31. Sampson, "Religion and Peacebuilding."

religious networking.[32] Significantly, the contact between the community and Mozambique was established in Rome and not elsewhere. It is true, especially for Catholics who have a global point of reference in Rome, that their access to international networks is one of the greatest assets available to religious leaders who may be allowed to contribute to conflict resolution in their country. Religious leaders are able to create change through the help of resources not available to others. In the example of Mozambique, Monsignor Gonçalves, during his first visit to Rome as a bishop, did not have a specific request to make. However, through the interactive process of sharing and considering alternatives to meet the problem described by the archbishop, the idea of involving Berlinguer and, through him, the Italian Communist Party emerged.

The Community of Sant'Egidio therefore offered a forum for alternatives to be conceived, evaluated, and implemented. Beyond simply offering an opportunity for discussion, the community was able to execute the necessary actions for a successful strategy: the contact with Berlinguer, issuing of invitations, organization of the meeting, and follow-up. They were able to do so immediately after the identification of possible responses to the problem of religious freedom in Mozambique.[33] That is to say the availability of some professional expertise and logistics were essential in transforming a generic idea into a plan of action.

Additionally, the community's offer was viewed as being more credible than official channels because all members of Sant'Egidio are volunteers and are not paid for their efforts, but rather contribute their own resources to the community's activities. While the community was not a conflict-resolution center, it proved able to address serious problems positively, with satisfaction from all parties involved. Significantly, after almost ten years of quiet work, the community was instrumental in facilitating the visit of President Samora Machel to the Holy Father Pope John Paul II, which led to the reestablishment of diplomatic relationships between Mozambique and the Holy See. This ability to produce results, together with the trust built in

32. Andrea Riccardi, "Promoting Democracy, Peace, and Solidarity," *Journal of Democracy* 9, no. 4 (October 1998): 157–67.
33. Andrea Bartoli, "Somalia and Rwanda vs. Mozambique: Notes for Comparison on Peace Processes," in *Somalia, Rwanda, and Beyond*, ed. Edward Girardet et al. (Boston: Crosslines, 1995), 195–202.

long relationships, was the basis for the Community of Sant'Egidio's involvement in the peace process for Mozambique.[34]

After President Chissano made overtures to the religious leaders to establish contact with RENAMO, the community helped Monsignor Gonçalves meet directly with the leader of RENAMO, Alfonso Dklakama. The encounter was significant in many respects because it established the crucial role of Monsignor Gonçalves in allowing a more precise evaluation of RENAMO's intentions and perceptions. Also significant was the fact that both Monsignor Gonçalves and Dklakama discovered themselves as Ndau, an ethnic group present in Central Mozambique and some areas of Zimbabwe. The recognition of common language and ancestry certainly helped the trust-building process necessary to start the peace process. While RENAMO claimed some generic references to Catholic values,[35] it is clear that Monsignor Gonçalves was able to play a role in the peace process because all parties perceived him as genuinely Mozambican, fair, committed to peace, and able to communicate with all.[36]

While his ecclesial role and affiliation certainly helped him play the pivotal role of observer and eventual mediator in the formal negotiation process that took place at Sant'Egidio's headquarters from July 10, 1990, until October 4, 1992, the personality and interpretation of that role and affiliation seem to be more relevant. This observation is indispensable in order to avoid the misleading hope that in the period of transition from war to peace religious leadership may necessarily be able to facilitate the transition by playing a positive role.[37] Unfortunately, that is not the case. Religious leadership may be biased, may be perceived to be unfairly supporting one side, or may be so politically insignificant as not to be recognized as a viable channel of communication. In order to play a significant role in a process of transition from war to peace, religious leadership needs to be recognized by all parties involved, be able to perform the requested role, and be willing to take the risk of such an involvement.[38]

34. Morozzo della Rocca, *Mozambico, dalla guerra alla pace,* 20.
35. Alex Vines and K. Wilson, "The Churches and the Peace Process in Mozambique," in *The Christian Churches and Africa's Democratization,* ed. P. Gifford (Leiden: Brill, 1995).
36. Venancio, "Mediation by the Roman Catholic Church in Mozambique."
37. Appleby, *Ambivalence of the Sacred,* 10–13.
38. Sampson, "Religion and Peacebuilding."

While religious motivations can certainly help this decisionmaking process (in terms of nurturing the vision and the goals of the religious actors) they may also be perceived as a threat by one or more parties. Religious affiliation does not authorize a simplistic assumption that a fair judgment will be observed. Actually, there are many cases in which religious affiliation is the basis for sectarian and intolerant intervention and discourse.[39] The case of Monsignor Gonçalves is remarkable because of his ability to use religious discourse to express the feelings of a large portion of the Mozambican population, while at the same time maintaining a connection with religiously affiliated international entities, specifically the Holy See, the Community of Sant'Egidio, missionary congregations, and the large Catholic effort in support of humanitarian aid. His most precious ability vis-à-vis the peace process was to play a political role respectful at once of the government, RENAMO, and all other international and local actors, including other religious leaders.

FORGIVENESS AND RECONCILIATION

President Chissano's primary goal of establishing direct channels of communication with RENAMO succeeded through the help of religious leaders. However, the president was also using representatives of the business community. For example, Tiny Rawlands, the British-based multimillionaire with wide interest in Southern Africa, positively helped to frame the effort toward a resolution of the conflict in Mozambique. This use of a multiplicity of channels is indicative of the commitment of the FRELIMO leadership to design and implement an inclusive peace process.[40] After the first steps were taken, more traditional diplomatic efforts were made involving mainly Kenyan diplomats and Zimbabwean leadership.

Unfortunately, the formal setting, which consisted of a few meetings among leaders, proved to be unsuccessful in providing the necessary con-

39. David Little, "Religious Militancy," in *Managing Global Chaos,* ed. Chester Crocker, Fen Hampson, and Pamela Aall (Washington, D.C.: USIP Press, 1996), 79–89.
40. Paul Rich, ed., *The Dynamics of Change in Southern Africa* (New York: St. Martin's Press, 1994).

tinuation to the process of conflict resolution. Hence, the Community of Sant'Egidio was chosen as the place where direct negotiation between the Mozambique government and RENAMO would take place.[41] Four people were identified as observers: Mario Raffaelli, a representative to the Italian parliament who was asked to act as chairman, Monsignor Jaime Gonçalves, archbishop of Beira, Don Matteo Zuppi, and Professor Andrea Riccardi, both of the Community of Sant'Egidio. While the religious affiliation and practice of the Community of Sant'Egidio and of Monsignor Gonçalves were clearly stated and understood by all parties, no attempt was made to impose any form of religious discourse on the participants themselves. The religious dimension offered a space where the exploration of alternatives was possible.[42] It also provided a setting in which the two parties could talk directly with one another, tackling the issue of legitimacy of a government that acknowledged a guerrilla movement.

Both parties were satisfied with Sant'Egidio's setting, even though they each saw different elements of this religious community. On one hand, RENAMO felt that Sant'Egidio was international, substantial, and credible enough to offer guarantees necessary for RENAMO's participation in the peace process. On the other hand, the government felt that Sant'Egidio was not going to infringe on the prerogatives of the legitimate government. Therefore, the Roman forum was formal enough for RENAMO but informal enough for the government.[43] The community, therefore, was put in a position of influencing without having any direct power. However, by merely providing space for direct communication to take place, its contribution to the peace process was noteworthy.

As previously noted, the goal of the Community of Sant'Egidio was not to impose solutions but to facilitate direct communication between the parties. Beyond the traditional services offered by international diplomacy, the community was also able to offer an analytic framework mediated through a consistent and reliable web of human relations.[44] The understanding that arose between the parties on their positions and interests was not a mere

41. Hume, *Ending Mozambique's War,* 25–32.
42. Roger Fisher and William Ury, *Getting to Yes* (New York: Penguin, 1981), 56–80.
43. Bartoli, "Mediating Peace in Mozambique."
44. Giro, "Community of Saint Egidio and Its Peace-Making Activities."

result of cold, official dialogue, but rather a more continuous, direct, informal network, which involved many members of the community. An observer spoke about this process as a form of "pastoral diplomacy."[45]

The participants in the negotiations in Rome were certainly accompanied and supported by members of the Community of Sant'Egidio, both in their human and personal needs, as well as in the political and cultural ones. This went well beyond the traditional diplomacy format. The community, however, never interfered in the talks with religious language or imposed on the participants useless religious images. While daily prayer continued at the adjacent church from which the community takes its name, participants were not asked to participate in religious services, nor was religious discourse used otherwise. Although religion did not directly affect the format or the content of the talks, it played a role as a motivating factor and as a contributor to the originality of the process while offering an overall vision of the possible peace to the mediators.

The blend of formality and informality was certainly key to the success of the Mozambique peace process. Formal meetings between the two delegations were carefully planned and prepared from both ceremonial and substantive points of view.[46] In this sense, it may be said that the liturgical tradition of the community also played an indirect role in stressing the importance of symbols and rituals. These traditions could be observed on numerous occasions from the welcoming of the participants and officials, to the meeting place, to the setting of the tables, to the ways in which meals were conducted. A clear awareness of the importance of symbols and rituals emerged.[47] At the same time, the informality of a nongovernmental organization allowed for some flexibility that would not otherwise be possible in the formal sector. For example, delays and rudeness were somehow absorbed in a general climate of friendliness.

One function that religious leadership consistently played during the peace process was to represent the deep desires of the Mozambican population beyond the established institutional political framework. The participation of Monsignor Jaime Gonçalves at the negotiating table as a

45. Sampson, "Religion and Peacebuilding."
46. Morozzo della Rocca, *Mozambico, dalla guerra alla pace,* 101–21.
47. Riccardi, *Sant'Egidio,* 81–82.

mediator assured a connection with established religious circles in Mozambique. This connection with the religious structures was very significant because it allowed an understanding of the underlying current in Mozambican society.

Credit must be given to the leadership of the government under President Joaquim Chissano and of RENAMO under Alfonso Dklakama for seriously understanding the necessity of popular support for a successful peace agreement. Religious entities, through prominent individuals as well as through grassroots entities, were able to play this magnifying role in assuring that the desire and commitment to peace would emerge and strengthen throughout the peace process.

While international and regional changes allowed a level of political compromise that would have been unthinkable just a few years before, the odds that the peace process might unravel, due to the disintegration of Mozambican society as a direct result of more than four hundred years of colonization and thirty years of war, before and after independence, were high.[48] Many observers were convinced that RENAMO leadership was actually unable to rein in its forces and that the conflict would continue through widespread banditry for many years to come. Small weapons were easily available. Resources, including food and water, were scarce. A major heat wave that hit the country in the early 1990s had brought about a serious drought. All this led many analysts to think that it would be difficult to stabilize such a country, which had never been independent, unified, or at peace simultaneously.[49]

Peace processes are political processes that transform military confrontation into nonviolent exchanges. The ultimate credit for the success of the Mozambique peace process goes to the Mozambicans themselves and to their political leadership, who created a framework for all elements of society to contribute positively to the peace process.[50] Credit must be given, in particular, to the government and RENAMO leadership for having

48. Thomas Ohlson and Stephen John Stedman, *The New Is Not Yet Born: Conflict Resolution in Southern Africa* (Washington, D.C.: Brookings Institution, 1994).
49. U.S. Institute of Peace. *A Conference Report: Discussions from Dialogues on Conflict Resolution: Bridging Theory and Practice, July 13–15, 1992* (Washington, D.C.: U.S. Institute of Peace Press, 1992).
50. Bartoli, "Mediating Peace in Mozambique."

requested and obtained support from religious leadership and groups that were able to service the peace process creatively. Fortunately for Mozambique, religious groups did not have hegemonic claims over the structure of the state or was ethnic secession ever considered. This framework of a legitimate government, ruling a unified country that needed to have credible political processes, able to absorb a military challenge into renewed political and institutional structures, allowed for a peace process to be conceived as a synergy of local, international, and religious forces.

The lengthy documents that constituted the general agreement for Mozambique were made possible by more than two years of negotiations in Rome through the participation of the Mozambican government and RENAMO, along with the contribution of many countries, especially the United States and Italy, as well as international organization such as the United Nations.[51] Essential, nonbiased, and competent information was made available to the participants, allowing issues as diverse as ceasefires, recognition of political parties, unitary questions, and electoral acts to be addressed properly. It is fair to say that religious actors and entities facilitated the emergence of a secular, tolerant, nonbiased setting where germane political issues were handled cooperatively by the parties.

The experience of Rome created a political framework of mutual respect and recognition that is very auspiciously captured by the first Joint Communiqué of July 10, 1990. According to that document,

> Taking into account the higher interest of the Mozambican nation, the two parties agreed that they must set aside what divides them and focus, as a matter of priority, on what unites them, in order to establish a common working basis so that, in a spirit of mutual understanding, they can engage in a dialogue in which they discuss the different points of view.[52]

In other words, the Joint Communiqué states that the parties did not necessarily agree on specific content first but rather agreed on a process

51. Hume, *Ending Mozambique's War,* 138.
52. United Nations, *The United Nations and Mozambique 1992–95,* Department of Public Information, United Nations, 1995, 124.

that would possibly lead to a shared solution to problems that were perceived as common.

Some may argue that this shift from enmity to partnership was influ-
enced or made possible by the intervention of religious actors.[53] Others,
however, may also argue that religious actors simply played a traditional
third-party role, facilitating direct contact between two factions that were
ready, due to the political situation, to make the shift from an adversarial
mode to a cooperative one.

Religious conclusions to political realities are always possible, as well as
the reverse, the reduction of religious discourse to its political dimension.[54]
However, a respectful look at both of these factors may offer us a fairer
and more promising line of research. It is, in fact, not unusual to find religious leaders playing a role in transitional societies at the time in which distribution of power is unclear and stability is far from being established.
Often religious leaders do have some characteristics that facilitate this
process. Among them we can identify:

Knowledge of language and culture

Access to firsthand information

Political expertise

Long-term vision

These four characteristics may help religious leaders to bridge the gap
that is frequently the most relevant obstacle to a peace process: the
hermeneutical gap.[55]

Conflicts need to be "seen" and "read" properly, especially those that
have major cultural, ethnic, and religious components. External actors may
find it difficult to have access to knowledge unique to the situation that
enables them to use their analytical framework properly. Religious leaders,
because of their training and their role, can be better positioned in interpreting the conflict "correctly." Because they are closer to the scene of
events, at ease with many actors, and familiar with the language and the
issues at stake, religious leaders may offer important interpretative frameworks.[56] This was certainly the case in Mozambique. Religious actors were

53. Sampson, "Religion and Peacebuilding."
54. Appleby, *Ambivalence of the Sacred*, 281–82.
55. Andrea Bartoli, ed., *Reflections on Religious Peacemaking* (forthcoming).
56. Ibid.

consistently able to contribute to the peace process through their interpretation of events, issues, and possibilities, and to orient the debate toward a positive solution.[57]

However, these positive contributions are one of many possibilities. It cannot be possible to draw simplistic connections between religious identities and positive contributions to peace processes. This is to say, religious leaders in other cases and circumstances may have played a much more negative role in using their knowledge of language and culture, their access to firsthand information, and their expertise to foster a long-term vision of hatred and intolerance.[58] In the Mozambique case religious groups, a minority in the country, were actually able to play a much more significant role in the peace process inasmuch as they were connected with both the local civil society and the international community. In this vein, it may be said that one aspect of the Mozambican peace process was this dual representation of local and international concerns to the negotiating parties.[59]

The Mozambican peace process did not have any reference to religious language as was present in the subsequent South African experience.[60] Forgiveness and reconciliation do not appear in the text of the agreement.[61] Not only was a truth and reconciliation commission not established, but a more traditional amnesty was granted to allow combatants of both sides to return to civilian life without fear of punishment.

The Mozambican negotiators' attitude, putting the war and its tragic consequences behind them, has been criticized by human rights activists, who felt that the agreement was insufficiently precise on the issue of human rights. These criticisms were based on the argument that the very attempt to contact and communicate with groups that perpetrated horrifying action during the war was morally wrong and politically unsustainable.[62] This

57. Morozzo della Rocca, *Mozambico, dalla guerra alla pace*, 117.
58. Appleby, *Ambivalence of the Sacred*, 57–120.
59. Bartoli, "Mediating Peace in Mozambique."
60. On the notion of forgiveness and its relevance in the context of the anti-apartheid struggle in South Africa see Desmond Mpilo Tutu, *No Future Without Forgiveness* (New York: Doubleday, 1999).
61. The full text of the agreement is available in the United Nations, *The United Nations and Mozambique, 1992–95*, Department of Public Information, United Nations, 1995, 93–145.
62. Kathi Austin, *Invisible Crimes: U.S. Private Intervention in the War in Mozambique*, ed. William Minter (Washington, D.C.: Africa Policy Information Center, c. 1994).

chapter cannot address the existing conflict between those who are devoted
to making peace and those who are devoted to pursuing injustice. Tensions
may at times occur when people focus on these crucial dilemmas while trying to design and implement political processes that may transform a society's experience from war to peace.[63] However, it must be noted that
religious actors in the specific case of Mozambique supported the notion of
amnesty and the general trend of integration without individual punishment for acts perpetrated during the war.

The basis for this support was both political and religious.[64] Politically,
the emphasis on reintegration created conditions for the newly established,
self-sustainable political processes in which former enemies participated
freely. Religiously, two main approaches supported the amnesty and integration effort. On the one hand, Christians stress the value of redemption
in the transformative power of spiritual experiences, which could allow
even for a criminal to be reintegrated into a society in the spirit of forgiveness and reconciliation. On the other hand, a more traditional animist
approach stresses the power of war as a force at work that has overwhelmed
individuals and communities. Hence, it was war and not specific individuals or parties such as FREMILO and RENAMO per se that was to be
blamed for the massacres, destruction, and suffering. Therefore, when war
ends, so does the need for revenge. If the people were freed from submis-
sion to the power of war, then they would be free from the very power of
violence. The challenge was to reconstruct "a world no longer human."[65]
Significantly, both approaches matched a widespread and much more secular effort by the government to promote reintegration, both nationally
and locally.

All the institutions of FRELIMO were involved in "selling" the peace
process, allowing several phenomena to occur at the same time. Traditional
rights were performed to welcome back to the community combatants who
had been tainted by horrific experiences, such as cleansing and purification
rituals. At the same time, Christian communities expressed their joy and

63. Pauline Baker, "Conflict Resolution versus Democratic Governance: Divergent Paths to
    Peace?," in *Managing Global Chaos,* ed. Crocker, Hampson, and Aall, 563–72.
64. Appleby, *Ambivalence of the Sacred,* 163–64.
65. Nordstrom, "Creativity and Chaos," 165.

support of the peace process through liturgical and solidarity acts. Considering the overall success of the experiment, the experience in Mozambique, therefore, seems to indicate that success lies in the ability of traditional societies to formulate their own strategies, consistent with local costume and international norms, rather than the imposition of abstract international standards to local positions. The success of the Mozambique case seems therefore to lie more on the resilience of creativity of the population as a whole.[66]

There is no doubt that reconciliation and forgiveness actually took place in Mozambique after the signature of the agreement on October 4, 1992. The signing of the agreement and its ceremony was broadcast live throughout the whole country. People expressed joy and exultation when they realized that the war was finally over. This jubilation replaced the silence and wonderment in the moments before the signing. Therefore, many Mozambicans remember that day as one of both silence and jubilee. People celebrated in the streets, symbolizing in many ways the immediate unification of the country.

The following year was naturally marked by great difficulties and volatile periods of hardships. Thus far, however, the commitment of Mozambicans to a peace process that profoundly reshaped the political landscape of the country is remarkable.[67] Religious leaders and communities participated actively before, during, and after the negotiation took place, adding to the newly established democratic experience in Mozambique accomplishments that would otherwise be unimaginable. However, this contribution was made possible by a respectful attitude toward the need for a secular space where interests could be mediated independent of religious affiliation.

Citizenship, not religious identity, is the basis upon which Mozambique determined to define its character. Yet the social contract was negotiated with the active involvement of religious leaders, who were committed to

66. In this sense I find extremely rich the reflections of Carolyn Nordstrom as in the following quote: "But if war, especially terror warfare, strives to destroy meaning and sense, people strive to create it. . . . No matter how brute the force applied to subjugate the people, local level behaviors arise to subvert the hold violence exerts on a population. . . . Traditional Western approaches to violent conflict do not often recognize the creative strategies people on the front lines employ to survive the war": Nordstrom, "Creativity and Chaos," 143.
67. Synge, Mozambique, 169–76.

peace and undertook the necessary search to embed it in an institutional framework. Religious leaders, while still concerned with the general welfare of the Mozambican experiment, are now focusing on their respective religious communities.

As the Joint Communiqué of July 10, 1990, signed in Rome at the headquarters of the Community of Sant'Egidio stated, "The necessary political, economic and social conditions for building a lasting peace and normalizing the life of all Mozambican citizens" has been designed. The contribution of religious leaders, actors, and entities to the process has been momentous. Its success lay in a respectful attitude toward the warring parties and the possibilities created by a political environment in which it has been possible to acknowledge all citizens as "compatriots and members of the great Mozambican family."[68]

ACKNOWLEDGMENTS

I would like to thank Anita Matta for her priceless research and editorial work, and Ray Helmick, S.J., for his careful editing and warm support.

---

68. United Nations, *The United Nations and Mozambique, 1992–95*, Department of Public Information, United Nations, 1995, 124.

CHAPTER 18

Conversion as a Way of Life in Cultures of Violence

Ofelia Ortega

The days are prolonged, and every vision
comes to nothing. —Ezekiel 12:22

INTRODUCTION

A SERIES OF BIBLE STUDIES in which I was involved in collaboration with Lynda Katsuno in a meeting at the Canada
Council of Churches always comes to my mind when I think of the violence experienced by so many in our world today. On that occasion I based
the studies on the Book of Judith, which is the only Deutero-canonical book
having a woman as the protagonist, that is, as a heroine. I cannot help feeling fascinated by this book. It is a permanent cry that breaks with narrow-
minded nationalist patterns. It goes beyond them, reaching all times and
places, and inviting everyone, whether big or little, strong or weak, male or
female, to join hands with Yahweh—the God of the slaves—and with
Jesus—the servant of the lost and the oppressed—in order to improve the
lot of the marginalized.

However, in that presentation, as we were just carrying out the analysis and discussion of the text, a woman leader who was a member of the
Society of Friends (Quakers), lifted up her voice and said, "For me it is
hard to accept that it is necessary to cut somebody's head off [the reference
was to Holofernes] to build justice and peace." I must confess my surprise
when hearing her remark. Then I immediately remembered the passage,
"Blessed are the peacemakers for they shall be called children of God"
(Matt. 5:9), and started to call my own presentation into question, in

which I had presented the beheading of the Tyrant Holofernes in very positive terms. This also brought to my mind a discussion that took place
not long ago at the National Assembly of the People's Power in Cuba
(which is our Congress) about the sentence of death pronounced against
some Centro-American terrorists who placed bombs at several hotels in
Havana, causing the death of an Italian tourist. During the debate, Rev.
Raúl Suárez, a congressman, member of our National Assembly, and pastor of the Baptist Church, lifted up his voice and in opposition to the opinion generalized in the assembly stated that as a Christian and as a Baptist
pastor he could not agree with the death penalty for any human being.
That is, the construction of peace in every one of our societies is always
closely linked to ethical as well as decisionmaking issues. This includes the
values of the Gospels as the basis of all our struggles and all our everyday
tasks.

These ethical judgments are also associated with the way we perceive the
"other," whether it is a man or woman. Robert J. Schreiter points out seven
ways to distinguish "the other."[1]

1. We can *demonize* the other, treating the other as someone to be
   feared and eliminated if possible.
2. We can, on the other hand, *romanticize* the other, treating the other
   as far superior to ourselves.
3. We can *colonize* the other, treating the other as inferior. In situations
   of violence, this is one of the attitudes commonly taken by oppres-
   sors. The assumption is that the victims are not on the same level
   of humanity as the oppressor.
4. We can *generalize* the other, treating the others as non-individual.
   This happened in the case of the "disappearances" in Argentina,
   Chile and other Latin American countries.
5. We can *trivialize* the other by ignoring what makes the other disturbingly different.
6. We can *homogenize* the other by claiming that there is no difference.
7. We can *vaporize* the other by refusing to acknowledge the presence
   of the other at all.

1. Roberto J. Shreiter, *Reconciliation: Mission and Ministry in a Changing Social Order* (Maryknoll, N.Y.: Orbis Books, 1992), 51–53.

Thus, this ministry of peace and reconciliation will always lead us to the acceptance of the *otherness* and the *difference* as an essential basis for the "healing" and reconstruction of our communities.

VIOLENCE NEVER GOES ALONE— IT GOES ALWAYS IN COMPANY

Some anthropologists consider violence a normal component of the relationships between people. That is to say, they believe that violence exists in all cultures in every period of time or historical era. The erroneously labeled "civilizations" have integrated violence into their societies, exerting it as defense for survival. For example, the death of Jewish men and women in Central Europe was a fact. It was a sacrifice on the altar of technology in the times of Nazism. It is a common occurrence that technological advances are associated with the suppression of life. The death of the indigenous people did not take place out of a kind of "spontaneous generation," as it were, it was a part of the merchandise transactions of free commerce.

We, the people from Cuba, have suffered for five months a kind of violence against the life of the boy Elián González. Violence against this child is linked to the hatred and grudges that part of the Cuban community in the exile holds against the leaders of my country and the socialist regime. This hate, which has accumulated for more than four decades, has turned a case that was open for easy solution into a nationwide problem, bringing two governments and two countries into a situation of endless legal struggles. Many involved in this crisis appeared to remain indifferent to the demands of psychologists and the leaders of the civil society and the church, who demanded the liberation of a child chained to a kind of hate that he had never before experienced.

On January 1, 1994, an insurrection of the indigenous people from Chiapas, Mexico, took place. This armed upheaval is associated with December 31, 1993, when Mexico was involved in the process and promise of entering the world of the wealthy nations "via NAFTA" (Free Commerce Treaty of North Atlantic), a treaty that challenges and may contribute to the elimination of all national production and which sacrifices the national identity or dignity associated with such goods and merchandise.

The great economic crisis did not take long. In January 1995 the Mexican crisis broke out, causing incredible poverty. However, instead of investigating the real causes that produced the upheaval of the Chiapas aboriginals, Mexican executives and businessmen declared that "the Mexican crisis had a concrete name and this name is Commander Marcos [the leader of Chiapas indigenous people]." This was an easy way to excuse a much more complex reality that needs to be seen in light of the violence often done to the marginalized and poor for the sake of larger economic interests, a situation that calls to mind the efforts on the part of the churches to call the world to a season of Jubilee, in which forgiveness and reconciliation promote a meaningful restorative justice.

As it is stated in the introduction to the Program to Overcome Violence, sponsored by the World Council of Churches,

> The culture of violence is extremely complex. Militarism, oppression, exploitation and the marginalization of the poor are among its expressions. The misuse and manipulation of ideology, nationalism, ethnicity, religion, gender, the media and the global economic system are among its causes. A serious analysis is required in each area in order to develop strategies to overcome violence and promote forgiveness and reconciliation. Those strategies have to contribute to the creation of societies with a non violent character.[2]

WHY MUST THE AFFIRMATION OF LIFE PRODUCE DEATH?

We constantly ask ourselves why does all that has been created to produce life turn back against it? Why, together with the cultivation of life, must there always be a culture of death threatening around? How hard to face this reality! Sow life and harvest death!

2. *Programme to Overcome Violence: An Introduction,* World Council of Churches, Geneva, 35.

One of our most outstanding Cuban storytellers wrote a story with the title "Francisca and Death." Death arrives on a train at a small town to pick up Francisca, goes to Francisca's home, but does not find her. People tell Death that Francisca is busy trying to heal a child that is ill. Death then decides to walk to the house of the sick child and, in a hurry and in a sweat since the countryside in Cuba is quite warm, arrives exhausted from the walk and knocks at the door. But Francisca was not in. She had gone to help in the potato crop. Death goes on walking and searching, searching and walking, but does not succeed in finding Francisca, who is always somewhere else lending a helpful hand. So finally Death has to go back without getting the old lady. In the meantime, Francisca walks with light steps back home when the day is over, and on her way home she comes across a fellow farmer on horseback. The man happens to ask her, kiddingly, "Francisca, when will you die?" And she answers, "Never, there is always something to do!"

A True Culture of Life

And here are we then, confronted with the challenge of analyzing and finding what is to be done, so that the cultivation of life results in a true culture of life. And this needs to be done as we are reminded by Desmond Tutu that there will be no future without forgiveness and the life changes that occur when forgiveness is genuine and reconciliation restorative.[3]

The writers of the Bible had this same feeling of perplexity about a pervasive culture of death despite our best efforts. It is fascinating the way in which Habakkuk talks with God. The Prophet does not accept the solution that God seems to give him to resolve the problem of injustice at the hands of the ruling empire. God makes him see a future that is coming. The end of the aggressor and tyrannical empire is coming near, because an even more powerful empire is taking over its place. Is that then a way out of the problem or just a vicious circle?

Habakkuk evaluates the solution of the problem and finds it is not acceptable for him. The words of the Prophet are conclusive: "They all

3. Desmond Tutu, *No Future Without Forgiveness* (New York: Doubleday Press, 1999).

come for violence, with faces pressing forward. They gather captives like sand. [T]heir own might is their god!" (Habakkuk 1:9, 11).

Habakkuk was right—an empire that makes the use of force into its God can overcome an unjust empire but cannot bring about peace with justice.

This dialogue between Habakkuk and Yahweh leads us to affirm in the words of Margot Kässmann:

> Rather than being troubled or repelled time and again by the legitimization of violence within the Hebrew part of the Bible, we should point to texts like the story of Shiphrah and Puah, an account of courageous civil disobedience—to put it in contemporary terms (Exod. 1:15–22). We can think of Micah 4:32–34, where swords become ploughshares—or many other visionary texts of the prophets.[4]

A Symbol of Death: The Rusty Pot

One of these visionary texts is found in chapter 24 of the Book of Ezekiel. In our societies, where greatness has become a basic criterion for happiness and smallness is seen as a misfortune, this parable of the Prophet leads us to observe him not from the perspective of the great oracles but from the perspective of the pots, the fire, the timber, the tears, and the moans.

There are two pots in the parable. One contains tasty slices for a feast, whereas the other is rusty. Ezekiel, no doubt, had literary talent. He was also a good musician and an excellent declaimer. The symbols and images he resorts to are amazing, which is why the text sounds like the working song of a cook on the day of the great feast, when the special guests will be (ironically) the soldiers of Babylon. A similar image is to be found in Micah 3:2–3. The context for the prophetic vision is the violence and crime that had become so common in Jerusalem that even the inhabitants did not care

---

4. Margot Kässman, *Overcoming Violence*, Risk Book Series (Geneva: WCC Publications, 1998), 26.

to hide this, "throwing earth on the facts." Such an acceptance of violence is the greatest sin. Dealing with injustice and finding the way to forgiveness is serious business. God sees to it that the criminals do not hide the blood, so that the blood cries out to heaven and God can answer this cry. Allow me here to remind you of the text in Genesis 4:9–10:

> Then the Lord said to Cain, "Where is your brother Abel?" He said, "I don't know; am I my brother's keeper?" And the Lord said, "What have you done? Listen; your brother's blood is crying out to me from the ground, which has opened its mouth to receive your brother's blood from your hand.

Therefore, in the parable Jerusalem is the pot. The blood of the city is the rust in the pot. The people in the city do not care any longer to remove the rust from the pot. The pot adheres to the rust and the rust to the pot. Nobody cares to clean it. So, to the festive song of the cook with the pot of the feast, there will be a tragic lament of God before the rusty pot. Purification will only be possible when we get rid of the violence that is marking the city in a way that cannot be effaced. And this rusty pot can be your city or my city. There is violence in our homes, in our interpersonal relationships, in our schools, in our churches, in each one of our societies, in the relations between our countries. Kässmann reminds us that "the weakest members of a community are the most vulnerable to violence, and in a time of rising violence it is women, youth and children who suffer the most." She refers to a horrifying mass rape of schoolgirls that took place at a residential college in Kenya in 1992. Several of the victims were killed. When asked later why the staff had not come to rescue the girls, the headmistress said, "We did not think it was anything, only the boys raping the girls."[5] Such violence, borne out of insensitivity or brutal carelessness, adds to the weight of trauma and to the cycles of violence noted elsewhere in this volume. The rusty pot that was not cleaned in time! Without a lament and recognition that change is in order, the cycle of oppressor and victim will continue and destroy us as a people.

5. Ibid., 46.

Nonviolence as a Way of Life

Nonviolence is a way of life and a system of personal, social, and international change based on the force of truth and the power of love to overcome evil and obtain justice and reconciliation. It is a way of life that seeks to avoid the cycle of violence into which we are easily drawn. It was striking to read the report of visits to the churches during the Ecumenical Decade—Churches in Solidarity with Women. In this report of the "living letters," we learned that

> during our time with the churches, we note with sadness and anger that violence is an experience that binds women together across every region and tradition. The phenomenon is so pervasive that many women expect violence to be a part of their lives and are surprised if it is not. Often, girls are brought up to expect violence, perhaps at the hands of a loved one. Almost everywhere we went, this reality was acknowledged.[6]

It is necessary to add that as against the unjust and irreversible logic of the present violent systems, that which Elsa Támez called "the logic of death,"[7] women opposed consistently and persistently a "logic of life." We determined that this logic consists of the following elements: resistance, creativity, solidarity, freedom, and hope. This "logic of life" is what Rosemary Radford Ruether called "covenantal ethics" and "sacramental cosmology."[8] Covenantal ethics gives us a vision of an integrated community of humans, animals, and land, which seeks to live a spirituality and code of continual rest, renewal, and restoration of just, sustainable relations between humans and the land, in one covenant under a caretaking God.

Covenant ethics can be completed by the Jewish and Christian heritages

6. *Living Letters: A Report of Visits to the Churches During the Ecumenical Decade—Churches in Solidarity with Women* (Geneva: WCC Publications, 1997), 25.
7. See Dr. Elsa Támez, *Contra toda Condena, la justificación por la Fe desde los Excluidos* (San Jose, Costa Rica: Editorial DE, 1991).
8. Mary John Mananzan, Mercy Amba Oduyoye, Elsa Támez, J. Shannon Clarkson, Mary C. Grey, and Letty M. Russell, eds., *Women Resisting Violence: Spirituality for Life* (Maryknoll, N.Y.: Orbis Books, 1996), 34.

of sacramental cosmology. Here we have a sense of the whole cosmos come alive, as the bodying forth of the Holy Spirit, the word and wisdom of God, which is its source and renewal of life.

IS IT POSSIBLE TO WORK FOR A "CULTURE OF PEACE" FOR OUR PEOPLES?

At this point we would like to mention several ecumenical and community endeavors.

Peace Plan of the Latin American Council of Churches: Peace Promoters

One of the mandates of the Fourth Assembly of the Latin American Council of Churches (CLAI) held in Concepción, Chile, from January to February 1995, reads as follows: "To carry out actions and initiatives oriented to the promotion and education for a culture for peace, in a biblical and pastoral perspective." This peace plan is based on three basic principles:

1. The search for a culture of peace that is capable of bringing about consensus and offering alternatives.
2. Peace culture must be deeply pervaded by an ethics. We are experiencing the phenomenon of an extremely violent globalization, where there prevails not the one who is just, but the one who is stronger, and conflicts find their resolution in terms of power. Hence the importance of a kind of ethics that creates a spirit of community and solidarity.
3. Thirdly, we find reconciliation as a basic element. The existence of a system of peace means that there cannot be people excluded.

These principles are based in the need to seek and offer forgiveness. They lead us to two basic initiatives: first, a project of education for peace, at a continental scale that should focus on activities for training and supervision in human rights, mediation, conciliation, conflict resolution, and ecumenical dialogues about ethics and peace; And second, the Peace Plan, the action of which covers three countries—Colombia, Guatemala and Peru—that is, countries where old armed internal conflicts call for special attention.

CHURCHES SEEKING RECONCILIATION AND PEACE: THE DECADE TO OVERCOME VIOLENCE

The inspiration for this decade comes from a text in Psalms 34:14. "Seek peace and pursue it." The Central Committee of the World Council of Churches writes as follows: "In response to a call by the Eighth Assembly of the World Council of Churches, we embark on a Decade to overcome violence in the years 2001–2010 and invite churches, ecumenical groups, individual Christians and people of good will to contribute to it." What will this mean? And what will be required of us in light of the themes taken up in this book?

Prior to the assembly in Harare, the WCC Programme to Overcome Violence and the Peace to the City Campaign have shown the following: peace can be practiced, it grows at grassroots levels and is nurtured by the creativity of people. People can cooperate locally with each other and create a healthy civil society. They can engage in dialogue and common action with people of other faiths. Again, we can notice how a certain ethics is associated with this culture of peace: Insofar as the central aim is to work for a peace-based culture, this must be grounded in just and sustainable communities.

In her book *Peace in Troubled Cities*,[9] Plou Dafne, an Argentinean journalist, presents creative models of civil societies that have worked intensively to build peace communities in the middle of violent situations. In this book Dafne shares with us stories of the Peace to the City Campaign of the World Council of Churches. In those stories we can discover some important clues to respond to situations of extreme violence with nonviolent efforts. Dialogue, advocacy for civil rights, community development, analysis, action, and reconciliation all helped to prevent further tragedy

9. Plou Dafne, *Peace in Troubled Cities*, Risk Book Series (Geneva: WCC Publications, 1998), 131–33.

and build communities of peace with justice. The experience of working for peace in the seven cities selected by the program also shows that people need symbolic acts through which to express peace. For example, in Rio de Janeiro, the two minutes of silence by a population dressed in white on a Friday in December dynamized a great movement for inclusiveness and social peace.

It has become manifest throughout this campaign that problems gradually found solution as the communities started to work together.

> The experience common to all these seven cities is that wherever and whenever people from different backgrounds and from different decision levels are willing to work together they can find solutions to growing violence. To do so requires a sense of vocation and considerable courage, but also an open mind, adequate training and the conviction that working for peace cannot be separated from working for justice and equal opportunities. When a community adopts these values and puts them into practice, it is possible to build the foundations for a culture of peace.[10]

CONCLUSION: A CULTURE OF SOLIDARITY VIS-À-VIS A CULTURE OF ANTI-LIFE

The year 2001 begins the Decade to Overcome Violence with a similar emphasis coming from the United Nations. We will have personal and social stories to tell. The coordination of all the forces of the civil society struggling against violence is a necessary condition. We will have to develop a kind of spirituality that enables us to be receptive to the needs of those who live together in our environment, while acknowledging that today we are living in pluralist societies, where receiving the "stranger" is practically a command of the Gospel that is now even a necessity in our contemporary societies. Offering and receiving forgiveness and taking the meaningful steps

10. Ibid., 133

that give substance to reconciliation will be necessary in order to overcome violence and produce a culture of life.

We need to develop a culture of solidarity vis-à-vis a culture of anti-life. To do so, we need to foster basic human education, which consists of teaching that which is useful for life. We need to instill the value of human relationships, the value of common life. Without the feeling of such value, building an ethic becomes impossible. For this reason, as Konrad Raiser states in his book *Challenges and Hopes for a New Millennium to Be the Church*, "It seems urgent to return to basic forms of conciliarity by strengthening the capacity for reciprocity, solidarity, dialogue and non-violent resolution of conflicts and reinforcing the process of sharing. The main emphasis should be on contributing to transformation on the level of systems by changing the cultural consciousness. The concept of *metanoia*—in the sense of conversion or change of heart—moves in this direction. Such conversion is not a momentary act of moral decision, but a process of learning and a new way of living!"[11] We need to be a people committed to forgiveness and meaningful patterns of reconciliation for a culture of life to take root.

---

11. Konrad Raiser, *Challenges and Hopes for a New Millennium to be the Church*, Risk Book Series (Geneva: WCC Publications, 1997), 36.

Afterword

Exploring the Unique Role of Forgiveness

George F. R. Ellis

ORGIVENESS IS NOT AN ABSTRACT CONCEPT. Together with its counterpart of revenge, it is a real force in family, social, and political life. It has enormous practical effects in the world. If it were not for the leadership in forgiveness offered by our two great leaders, Nelson Mandela and Desmond Tutu, it is virtually certain that my country would have ended in a bloodbath like that in Rwanda or Bosnia or New Guinea. Indeed it is Bishop Tutu who best makes this case about forgiveness in a broad South African context. He has written a great book called *No Future Without Forgiveness* that reflects on his years as chairman of the Truth and Reconciliation Commission (TRC).[1]

Forgiveness is not easy in the face of both the ordinary banal incident that is undermining of the dignity and value of an individual's live and the specific horrific things that have happened in individual or group contexts. The nature of both in my country's recent history have been detailed in Bishop Tutu's book and also in a more narrative style in Antjie Krog's book *Country of My Skull*.[2] Faced with such appalling acts, hate and revenge are much easier. It is easier to feel righteous and demand punitive justice rather than following the road of forgiveness and reconciliation. What is the

1. Desmond Tutu, *No Future Without Forgiveness* (New York: Doubleday, 1999).
2. Antjie Krog, *Country of My Skull* (New York: Random House, 1998).

385

purpose of doing so? Why pursue the issue? These concerns will be considered around four headings.

WHY IS FORGIVENESS IMPORTANT IN THE MODERN WORLD AND FOR ITS FUTURE?

Forgiveness can make a fundamental difference and have a transforming influence in four different areas of human life: personal life, regional and national life, international life, and spiritual and religious life.

Personal Life

The point here is the difficulty of forgiveness and the pleasure of resentment. But giving in to that pleasure does not take into account the fact that the effect of resentment is character destruction. This is made very clear in the training courses offered by the Life Training Kairos Foundation,[3] which includes a resentment process where specific incidents leading to resentment are remembered and examined in detail, including an accounting of the payoffs and costs from resentment or revenge. On closer examination it happens that every feature that may have been taken to be a positive reason for indulging in resentment is, in fact, a cost: there are almost always no real positive payoffs. Who suffers from your resentment? You do! As stated by Dr. Charlotte Witvliet, you have two choices, forgiveness or bitterness, and bitterness is a cancer that will destroy you (as shown in almost all the tragedies from the Greeks to Shakespeare).[4] Furthermore, there is a second major aspect: If I don't forgive people, who will forgive me? We must all remember: "There but for the grace of God go I."[5]

> If we hope to be forgiven, we must also forgive one another. He who yields to a suspicious and unforgiving spirit is led on to imagine things against his brother that are exaggerated, or even false. How

3. For information regarding the Life Training Kairos Foundation, see http://www.lifetraining.org/.
4. Dr. Charlotte Witvliet, quoted in *Newsday,* Monday, September 14, 1998, B6.
5. Tutu, *No Future Without Forgiveness,* 76, 110, 151, and 155.

can they, whose only hope is in the Lord's mercy, indulge in hard and unforgiving thoughts towards a brother or sister? (322, Yearly Meeting 1870)[6]

By contrast, the positive question is how to transform people's lives, our own and others.

Ethics is ultimately about character building. From this perspective the challenge to us is to develop a character that has a transforming quality—and this demands that it has a forgiving character. According to Paul Coleman, "Forgiveness is more than a moral imperative or theological dictum. It is the only means, given our humanness and imperfections, to overcome hate and condemnation and proceed with the business of growing and loving."[7] This is true in all personal life. It is particularly important in married life, which is still the foundation of a stable and healthy society.

Our life is love, and peace, and tenderness; and bearing one with another, and not laying accusations against another; but praying for one another, and helping another up with a tender hand. (404, Isaac Pennington, 1667)[8]

Regional and National Life

Similar issues arise in regional and national life. We have, of course, to prevent any major abuses occurring or continuing, and this may sometimes call for stern action that is of a judicial nature and requires severe enforcement. But we also need to lay the foundations that will remove the causes of those abuses. This cannot be achieved unless we include reconciliation and forgiveness in our aims and actions. Consider the consequences of not forgiving: What is gained by revenge? As a specific example, consider the death penalty. It is natural to want the death of those who have mindfully

---

6. *Christian Faith and Practice in the Experience of the Society of Friends* (London Yearly Meeting, 1960). Numbers are the reference number in the volume, together with the number of the author of the given contribution and its date.
7. Paul Coleman, quoted in *Christian Science Monitor,* January 28, 1999, p. 14.
8. *Christian Faith and Practice in the Experience of the Society of Friends* (London Yearly Meeting, 1960). Numbers are the reference number in the volume, together with the number of the author of the given contribution and its date.

caused the death of others. But consider the case of Aba Gayle, mother of murdered Catherine. After visiting her daughter's condemned killer in jail she joined an organization called Murder Victims' Families for Reconciliation. She now does not want the death penalty for her daughter's killer. Why? "It is the way I honor Catherine . . . to murder someone in her name and say we are doing it for her is horrible."[9]

The further point is a simple one in a community context: If we don't forgive other people, where will we end up? We have seen the consequences of a culture of hate and revenge in many large-scale examples: Northern Ireland, Rwanda, Yugoslavia, and East Timor. The bombs and knives take their vengeance, and community hate feeds on itself without any prospect of resolution. Eventually one has to seek reconciliation, or genocide will feed genocide in mounting horror. The question, then, is how to transform national and community life.

The goal is to break the cycle of violence by helping both victims and perpetrators heal. A strategy of reconciliation, involving forgiveness and a commitment to nonviolence, is the only hope. Gandhi said:

> It is the acid test of non-violence that in a non-violent conflict there is no rancor left behind, and in the end, the enemies are converted to friends. That was my experience in South Africa with General Smuts. He started with being my bitterest opponent and critic. Today he is my warmest friend.[10]

The essential insight is that expressed so eloquently by Ruby Bridges Hall: instead of hating those who perpetrate these hateful deeds, realize they are the people who are in desperate need. In her famous words, "Don't you think they need forgiveness?"[11] I salute her for the courage and generosity of that insight. That is the basis of a transformed life. Without forgiveness we are lost: there is no future, as emphasized by Desmond Tutu.[12] The essential element is that you deserve to hold on to the resentment, yet

9. "Should All Be Forgiven?" *Time Magazine,* March 22, 1999.
10. Mahatma Gandhi, as selected by Richard Attenborough, *The Words of Gandhi* (Newmarket Press, 1982), 45.
11. Ruby Bridges Hall, as cited by Robert Coles, *The Story of Ruby Bridges* (New York: Scholastic Trade, 1995).
12. Tutu, *No Future Without Forgiveness.*

you voluntarily give it up and thereby open the way to transformation.

That decision changes everything. So the need is to develop an ethic and national character of forgiveness rather than retribution—as happened in South Africa under the leadership of Nelson Mandela and Desmond Tutu, but of course also made possible by the agreement and support of many others in the country. And the same spirit inspires the development of systems of restorative justice that apply at other levels in society.

International Life

Again, we have to prevent the continuation of any major abuses. This may sometimes call for stern action. But we also need to lay the foundations that will remove the causes of violent conflict and war. This cannot be achieved unless we include reconciliation and forgiveness in our aims and actions.

Consider this on a large scale: However we justify a just war, in the end it almost inevitably ends up with unjust acts. I cite specifically the case of the city of Dresden in the last world war, where at least 45,000 people, mainly civilians and mostly refugees from other areas, were burned to death by systematic firebombing in an act of vengeance that had no military significance whatever. Nancey Murphy and I used a picture of the results on the cover of our book, *On the Moral Nature of the Universe,* to emphasize where the road of vengeance leads.[13] The picture shows a carved angel on the old City Hall building looking down in pity on row after row after row of totally devastated houses—just burned-out shells amid the rubble. This is the effect that hate has on us: through a desire for revenge we respond to the Holocaust with Dresden. And then where are we? We have become similar to those we are opposing.

We might consider the evolutionary imperative on the largest scale of all: In this century we have finally developed the ability to destroy the entire human race. Furthermore, this technology is becoming more and more accessible to all. If we don't develop an international culture of working in a broadly peace-based and reconciliatory way, it is inevitable—in the cosmological perspective, looking at the evolution and development of life and

13. Nancey Murphy and George Ellis, *On the Moral Nature of the Universe* (Minneapolis: Fortress Press, 1996).

consciousness over thousands of millions of years—that we will destroy all human life, not necessarily in the next millennium but in the course of the next 10,000 years or so. The entire world will look like Dresden in 1945 if we do not succeed in an ethical transformation at an international level. The human race will succeed in bringing to an end the highest order of development that evolutionary development has been able to create.

Spiritual and Religious Life

The final reason for moving toward reconciliation and forgiveness is that it is the way of Christ, not just as an isolated incident on the cross, but as a central theme of his life. Forgiving is a central theme in the life of God.

For the Christian this is indeed expressed most powerfully in Jesus' words on the cross: "Father forgive them for they know not what they do" (Luke 23:34). His call to us is take up the challenge of loving one's enemy in various ways, as we are enjoined in the Sermon on the Mount and the Lord's Prayer. And this is not just a Christian insight: it is implied in eight major world religions, that each embodies to varying degrees the idea of *agape* love, as explained by Sir John Templeton in his book, *Agape Love: A Tradition found in Eight World Religions.* Sir John emphasizes in that book that *agape* love means, "Feeling and expressing pure, unlimited love for every human being with no exception."[14]

And that includes one's enemies, or those who have hurt or otherwise offended you. That is seen as one of the major religious goals we should aspire to in our lives. It necessarily implies an attitude and practice of forgiveness.

These perspectives can be bound together in a unifying view of the nature of the universe and of moral action as put forward in *On the Moral Nature of the Universe,* and as experienced in the lives of some faith communities. For example, it has been expressed as follows in my own tradition, the Quakers:

> The Quaker testimony concerning war does not set up as its standard
> of value the attainment of individual or national safety, neither is it

---

14. John Templeton, *Agape Love: A Tradition Found in Eight World Religions* (Philadelphia: Templeton Foundation Press, 1999), 1.

based primarily on the iniquity of taking human life, profoundly important as that aspect of the question is. It is based ultimately on the conception of "that of God in every man" to which the Christian in the presence of evil is called on to make appeal, following out a line of thought and conduct which, involving suffering as it may do, is, in the long run, the most likely to reach to the inward witness and so change the evil mind into the right mind. This result is not achieved by war. ("Christian Faith and Practice no. 606, A. Neave Brayshaw [1921])[15]

It is thus seen that this is the most fundamental way to fight evil, with the most noble and spiritual end as its purpose: the transformation of evil intentions to good, and the redeeming of those who do evil into what God intended them to be. The fundamental questions here might be put as follows:

What is it to be human?

What is the purpose of life?

What is worth doing?

The answer to each of the above questions is to be loving and forgiving and reconciling, in the image of God.

HOW HAS FORGIVENESS BEEN IMPORTANT IN RECONCILIATIVE PEACEMAKING IN THE PAST?

There are major examples of the power of this approach on a national level. For example, in India Gandhi used these methods to great effect through his practice of *ahimsa* in the fight for the independence of India. In the United States Martin Luther King Jr. fought his battle for the freedom of his people on these principles. In South Africa the recent political transition was made possible by leaders who worked so hard for it in this spirit, but also based on the one hand on a reconciling spirit in the African peoples of our land, the spirit of *ubuntu* written about by Desmond Tutu, so that

15. *Christian Faith and Practice in the Experience of the Society of Friends* (London Yearly Meeting, 1960). Numbers are the reference number in the volume, together with the number of the author of the given contribution and its date.

they were willing to accept a path of reconciliation rather than that of vengeance, and also on a small but important group of white people who continually worked for change and helped provide hope to the black people that peaceful change was indeed possible. It was explicit in the South African case that the majority were giving up retributive justice in exchange for peace and reconciliation. This worked at the first election, and again at the second. In my view a peaceful second election would not have been possible without the work of the TRC.

There are many other smaller-scale examples. I would particularly like to refer to Amy Biehl and her family: an inspiring U.S.–South Africa link.[16] Amy Biehl was an American girl who was killed by militant black youth in a black township of Cape Town because she was white, although she had gone there to help their cause and was working with the African National Congress. Four black youths were tried and convicted for her murder. Linda and Peter Biehl contacted their families and set up a relationship with them, acknowledging thereby that both sets of parents were powerfully hurt by what had happened and making reconciliatory moves to the others in this way. The youths then applied for and were given amnesty by the TRC and so were released from jail. The Biehl family did not oppose amnesty. Rather they set up the Amy Biehl Foundation to improve life in the black townships where the youths came from who had killed their daughter. This foundation is currently running programs

✦ in the environment (the Gugulethu Community Policing Forum, and Mural workshops),

✦ in education (support for educationally challenged adolescents after school, weekend tutorial programs, afterschool-care program, family literacy program),

✦ in health (safe sex education and AIDS prevention, first aid training),

✦ in employment (job skills for male adolescents, a community bakery), and

✦ recreation (developing sports fields, a golf driving range, and a music program).

Two of the convicted youths approached them for assistance with the

16. For information regarding the Amy Biehl Foundation, see http://amybiehl.org/whoare we.htm.

Thosanang Youth Club that they wished to set up. On Saturday, July 10, 1999, this club started with support from the Biehl Foundation, which was thus supporting the attempts of two of Amy's killers to better life in their community. Here is surely an inspiring example of the power of this reconciling and forgiving approach to make something positive and constructive come out of horror and despair.

This goal of reconciliation is the broad aim of the Restorative Justice movement, tried and developed, for example in New Zealand, as an extension of the traditional Maori system. Offenders and victims are brought into contact with each other and work out a practical program of reparation, allowing a move toward reconciliation. This led to a 27 percent reduction in reoffenders among young men in New Zealand.[17] In this same tradition a very successful Community Peace Program operates in the Zwelethemba township in the Paarl area near Cape Town. It is a young but very promising development in our violence-wracked townships.[18]

The same kinds of moves can be seen internationally. Returning to Dresden, the international effort to assist in the restoration of the Frauenkirch, the major symbolic church in the center of Dresden that has lain in ruins for forty-five years since the burning of Dresden, is an attempt to offer reconciliation for the deeds of the past. International figures such as Yehudi Menuhin played a major role in this project. I am delighted that my son Andrew and particularly his wife, Ute, are playing a part in this reconstruction.

On a larger scale there is a fundamentally important difference between the attitudes and programs adopted by the victors at the end of the First World War and at the end of the Second World War. The Treaty of Versailles at the end of the First World War was a vengeful treaty that humiliated the German people and gave them no path to the future. It set the stage for the rise of Hitler and the Second World War. But the lesson was learned. At the end of the Second World War, the Marshall Plan was set in place as part of a process of reconstruction that offered hope and a path to the future. Comparing Germany after the First and Second World Wars, there is no

17. Jim Consadine, *Restorative Justice: Healing the Effects of Crime* (Lyttelton, New Zealand: Ploughshare Publications, 1995); see also the interview in *Weekly Mail and Guardian* (South Africa), June 30, 1995, 16.
18. Community Peace Foundation, Barrington Road, Observatory, Cape Town 7925; email: cpfound@wn.ap.org.

GEORGE F.R. ELLIS

comparison. The generous settlement in 1945 paid off handsomely. It is a fundamentally important example, with a similar process in Japan, that is perhaps not recognized enough. If any example is needed of the fundamental importance of an essentially forgiving approach to international affairs, this is it.

WHAT HAS SYSTEMATIC STUDY GOT TO DO WITH IT?

Why would it be useful to invest in research on forgiveness and reconciliation?

The answers and methods are not obvious. We have to search to understand the hidden nature of reality and in particular the moral nature of the universe. Learning is the way to understanding, and research is systematic learning. Our goal should be life-long learning in all important matters. Therefore, we should clearly aim at life-long learning on forgiveness.

We need research into the nature of forgiveness, where issues of importance arise, and how to make it work effectively in practice—how to make the idea effective in the real-world context. The need is for experiential research with analysis as to how one can employ forgiveness effectively and work to reconciliation. A variety of specific issues arise.

What Is the Nature of Forgiveness?

It can be suggested that the central feature is giving up resentment, letting go of hate (which is part of the broader theme of self-sacrifice as embodied in the idea of *kenosis*).[19] This specifically involves acknowledging the humanity and value of the opponent, a direct counter to the fundamentally important poisoning role of dehumanization of the opponent that is so often the aim of political movements. This also involves a reality and reciprocity check: considering and acknowledging one's own possible role in any offenses that may have taken place. All these are active choices to be

---

19. See Murphy and Ellis, *On the Moral Nature of the Universe.*

made. As Robert D. Enright has said in *Exploring Forgiveness,* "Forgiveness is a matter of a willed change of the heart, the successful result of an active endeavor to replace bad thoughts with good, bitterness and anger with compassion and affection."[20] It does not involve demanding a return or remorse from the other person: neither is it tolerating, exonerating, or condoning that person's actions. Indeed you can't demand remorse—to do so would be an invitation for play-acting, for how can you judge true remorse? This also frees us from the ability of the opponent to deny us the ability to forgive by refusing to acknowledge what they have done, or by refusing to express any regret over it.

✦   We can always give forgiveness, and by so doing offer reconciliation.

✦   We cannot force people to accept that offer, but we can free ourselves from their ability to refuse us the option of forgiveness.

Implicit in this approach is the understanding that while the facts of the past cannot be changed, their meaning and implications can. We can be hostage to the past, letting it hold us in bondage, or we can transform it by an active choice of how to react to it and interpret it.

Research is needed into all of this, in particular issues such as the following:

✦   the difference between soft forgiveness, which does not take the seriousness of the offense fully into account, and hard forgiveness, which does;

✦   the roles of acknowledgment, repentance, contrition, and how to act so as to encourage them;

✦   how to deal with the other withholding recognition, or not acknowledging their error, and how to act so as to tend to change that situation.

From a social science viewpoint, there is a need for models that make clear this is not a completely irrational option. Specifically, the need is for well-developed dual models to the game-theory models such as the Prisoner's Dilemma. That is, we need the same game-theory models but with the signs of the "rewards" inverted. Suitable social settings of such models should be explicated. A good name is important; it could perhaps be called "The *Agape* Alternatives."

20. Robert D. Enright and Joanna North, eds., *Exploring Forgiveness* (Madison: University of Wisconsin Press, 1998).

What Are the Effects of Forgiveness?

There are a whole series of issues to be examined here, for example, as in the present programmed:

Does it affect health?

Does it improve personal and community life?

What if it is *not* present, what, then, are the effects of its absence?

Helping Forgiveness Happen and Making It Easier

The theory is all very well; the issue here is how to make this kind of thing work in practice, often in very difficult conditions where it is not the "natural" thing to do. How does one counter the enemy image and dehumanization and promote reconciliation and forgiveness? What are good ways to spread the idea of forgiveness, to provide role models, and to give training in the individual social and political context in which forgiveness might occur? There are specific items to bear in mind:

We can make it clear that forgiveness is a choice that we can make. It is in your and my power to do so. If we do so habitually it becomes part of our character and we have become a transformed person who then has the capacity to transform the lives of those around us. This is in contrast to the situation depicted by C. S. Lewis in *The Great Divorce*—where a person just fades away into nothing because his life has become nothing but a litany of complaint.[21]

We might begin by visualizing the other: realizing that I am capable of the same and that had I had his or her background I would probably have done the same. There but for the grace of God go I. This is true both in the American South and the South African context; given how horrific things were that were done, we need to learn to acknowledge that we all have that same evil capacity and darkness in us. If we recognize this, we can start to recognize the position of the person who has caused distress or harm, or who is an evildoer. Forgiveness requires focusing on understanding the other person as well as seeing oneself as capable of hurting other people, too. This capacity can be developed.

21. C. S. Lewis, *The Great Divorce* (1945).

We can provide community support for this kind of action, building a community that believes in it and assists it .

We can provide for the practical needs of reconciliation for those who have suffered hurt and harm—giving support, counseling, and friendship, providing for material needs and health concerns. This involves recognizing the reality of the desperate lonely lives of poverty and destitution, or long-term physical suffering—the pain encountered every day until death, which can make it much harder to bear evil done than if one has material and social resources at one's disposal. In the South African context this is the contrast between Bishop Retief and his congregation at St. James Church, victims of a PAC attack that left many dead and injured, as compared with the lonely lives of many destitute country folk who lost their livelihood through the actions of the security police and are living out a desperate life of suffering without support and resources.

Fitting the Context and the Time for Forgiveness

Each situation is different: there will be times and places when this approach will work, and others when it will not.[22] When is the time when it is possible? When are conditions right? Each individual situation is different; each act has to be individual and personal if it is to be meaningful, even though the same broad underlying principles apply. In the case of South Africa, a bargain was made for attaining peace and truth in exchange for giving up retributive justice and also enabling a hope for the measure of reconciliation that was sometimes achieved. This kind of option may or may not be appropriate in other cases.

Finding the Limits of Forgiveness

What are the limits of this approach—when, if ever, is it not applicable? Can all be forgiven? What cannot be forgiven? Should there be any boundaries? All this needs exploration but only while bearing in mind the fundamental point: one is not necessarily giving up justice as such through these

22. Desmond Tutu, *In South Africa, The Time Was Right* (London: Collins/Fontana, 1977), 99–109.

moves, but only one particular vision of justice. Justice does not have to be retributive, based on revenge: it can be restorative, based on forgiveness and restoration.[23]

Extending the Limits of Forgiveness

How can one develop effective analysis attitudes and methods that can extend the boundaries of forgiveness, making it work where it has not been successful so far? To put this on a sound footing one needs to develop an analysis of the factors affecting the ability to forgive. For example, these include:

The nature and degrees of hurt

The nature of context and its influence on possible options

The nature and types of forgiveness and associated strategies

This leads to the idea of different levels of forgiveness, and the identification of methods that work in different circumstances.

Developing a Religious Understanding in an Interfaith Perspective

Finally, an important issue is how does this relate to theology and to faiths of all kinds? How does one get religious communities to develop the moral force or "soul power" that takes this all seriously and can then transform the social communities in which they live?

Ultimately, applying forgiveness cannot be a science but rather is a reflective art that can be improved by continuing analysis and improved understanding. An important example here is Martin Luther King. In his book, *Martin Luther King: The Making of a Mind,* John J. Ansbro points out how King's life's work was based on deep study of these ideas in a theological context—decades of reflection combined with action. This is the proper practice of action research, which is the foundation of real understanding.[24]

23. See Murphy and Ellis, *On the Moral Nature of the Universe,* for details and references.
24. John J. Ansbro, *Martin Luther King, Jr.: The Making of a Mind* (Maryknoll, N.Y.: Orbis Books, 1982).

WHY WOULD VISIONARY PEOPLE WANT TO JOIN TOGETHER FOR THIS CAUSE?

It is special, important, honorable, and visionary to support the work of forgiveness. It will make an important difference to the future. There is great value in supporting such a venture, where one is joining a pioneering community of extraordinary vision: A community of those who care and want to make it work.

The work drawn together by this book represents such a community. It is good life practice and finds its analogy in good business practice. Consider the following points of reference from John Marks Templeton's *Discovering the Laws of Life*:

"Invest for maximum total real return." We need to evaluate the essential aspects of all situations, taking a panoramic view of the whole, not just what is easiest to deal with. Make sounds choices, not allow ourselves to be led down the easiest way simply to avoid challenges or fear. Such is the choice for forgiveness rather than retribution.

"Buy low—at the point of maximum pessimism." People who seem to be at their lowest point have innate goodness and potential that may go unrecognized. Seeing that value and investing time, trust, and attention in those who hit the bottom can bring rich rewards. It is an investment that will likely bring high personal and spiritual dividends for those we help and ourselves.

"An investor who has all the answers doesn't even understand the questions." If we think we know all the answers, we are in a very sad state. Such a perception comes from a closed mind, which will not allow an influx of new inspiration and discoveries. Being humble is the first step to attaining wisdom.[25]

And that is why the search for understanding is needed. Research is not an academic way of avoiding the real world. It is the true way to understand the real world in an effective way. This applies as much to the issues of forgiveness and reconciliation as it does to everything else.

25. John Marks Templeton, *Discovering the Laws of Life* (Radnor, Pa.: Templeton Foundation Press, 1995), 17, 38, 96.

CONCLUSION

The Templeton Foundation has done an innovative and important piece of pioneering through its program in the study of forgiveness which has already explored many of these areas. A continuation and expansion of this program, linked to an educational and developmental arm, will be a great contribution to the future for all of us.

Worldwide Organizations Promoting Forgiveness and Reconciliation

Those who forgive and reconcile are the healers of humanity.

NORTH AMERICA

Agenda for Reconciliation
See under Europe.

Americans and Palestinians for Peace
P.O. Box 113
Muscatine, IA 52761
Phone: (319)263-8145
Fax: (319)288-6074
Email: Info@ampal.net
Web site: www.ampal.net

Americans and Palestinians for Peace (AMPAL) is a national not-for-profit organization working for peace in the Middle East. AMPAL was created to fill the need of informing the American public about the Palestinian dream of self-determination. Relying on facts and statistics concerning the peace process, AMPAL is the counterbalance of what is shown in the media and the propaganda from which most individuals receive their information.

Amnesty International
322 Eighth Avenue
New York, NY 10001
Phone: (212)807-8400
Fax: (212)627-1451
Email: admin-us@aiusa.org
Web site: www.aiusa.org

Amnesty International is a worldwide campaigning movement that works to promote all the human rights enshrined in the Universal Declaration of Human Rights and other international standards. In particular, Amnesty International campaigns to free all prisoners of conscience; to ensure fair and prompt trials for political prisoners; to abolish the death penalty, torture, and other cruel treatment of prisoners; to end political killings and "disappearances"; and to end human rights abuses by opposition groups. Amnesty International has nearly one million members and supporters in 162 countries and territories.

Campaign for Forgiveness Research

P.O. Box 842018
Richmond, VA 23284-2018
Phone: (804)828-1193
Fax: (804)828-1193
Email: glodek@templeton.org
Web site: www.forgiving.org

Campaign for Forgiveness Research is a nonprofit organization that seeks to deepen the meaning of forgiveness and build roads toward reconciliation. With support received from a variety of sponsors, Campaign for Forgiveness Research sponsors research projects that help to heal individuals, families, communities, and nations by offering a place for sharing personal stories.

Catherine Blount Foundation: "A Journey of Light"

P.O. Box 4952
Santa Rosa, CA 95402
Email: abagayle@pacbell.net
Web site:www.catherineblountfdn.org

The mission of the Catherine Blount Foundation is to facilitate the demonstration and teaching of the healing power of forgiveness so that individuals, groups, and governments can attain the change of perception that will allow them to heal old hurts and injustices and find peace. Aba Gayle's teenage daughter was brutally murdered, but Aba has miraculously found her faith and begun her journey toward forgiveness, which included developing a relationship with her daughter's murderer.

Center for International Policy

1755 Massachusetts Avenue NW, Ste. 312
Washington, DC 20036

Phone: (202)232-3317
Fax (202)232-3440
Email: cip@ciponline.org
Web site: www.ciponline.org

The Center for International Policy was founded in 1975 to promote a U.S. foreign policy that reflects democratic values. Through research, education, and direct public advocacy, CIP works to define and put into practice a more sympathetic, reconciliatory, farsighted, and nonmilitaristic approach to the developing world.

Centre for Peace in the Balkans

P.O. Box 1500-1292
Toronto, Ontario M9C 4V5
Canada
Phone: (416)201-9729
Fax: (416)201-7397
Email: scontact@balkanpeace.org
Web site: www.balkanpeace.org

Centre for Peace in the Balkans is a nonprofit Toronto-based corporation whose members are actively engaged in the collection of information and materials related to the region. Its goal is to scrutinize the cultural and geopolitical assumptions behind the West's flawed Balkan strategy and provide support and alternative solutions to the conflict management process in the Balkans. The Centre is also working toward eliminating the discriminatory practices that currently exist in Canada for individuals from the Balkan region.

Christian Peacemaker Teams

P.O. Box 6508
Chicago, IL 60680-6508
Phone: (312)455-1199
Fax: (312)432-1213
Email: cpt@igc.apc.org

Web site: www.prairienet.org/cpt

Christian Peacemaker Teams (CPT) is an organization committed to reducing violence by challenging systems of domination and exploitation. The Christian Peacemaker Teams are working closely with the Mennonite Churches, Church of the Brethren and Friends United Meeting, as well as other Christians. CPT has worked in Haiti, the Middle East, Bosnia, Chechnya, Colombia, Mexico, Canada, and the United States. In all locations, CPT responds to invitations from grassroots movements seeking to rectify injustice in nonviolent ways.

**Clergy Coalition
to End Executions**
The Rev. Melodee A. Smith
Gables One Tower, Suite 450
1320 South Dixie Highway
Miami, FL 33146
Email: msmith@clergycoalition.org
Web site: www.clergycoalition.org

The Clergy Coalition to End Executions is an international interfaith coalition that fosters new alternatives in dealing with the death penalty and advocates for the end of execution. The CCEE receives moral support from the World Council of Churches and the National Council of Churches.

Coexistence Initiative
477 Madison Avenue, 4th fl.
New York, NY 10022
Phone: (212)303-9445
Fax: (212)980-4027
Email: info@coexistence.net
Web site: www.coexistence.net

Coexistence Initiative is a nonprofit organization that provides resources

for those working in community rebuilding, reconciliation, conflict resolution, multiculturalism, and war studies. The Coexistence Initiative seeks to catalyze a global awareness of and commitment to creating a world safe for difference. To achieve this mission, the Initiative develops and promotes programs for positive coexistence among people who are different.

Dallas Peace Center
4301 Bryan Street, Ste. 202
Dallas, TX 75204
Phone: (214)823-7793
Fax: (214)823-8356
Email: admin@dallaspeacecenter.org
Web site: www.dallaspeacecenter.org

Dallas Peace Center is a dynamic nonprofit organization that believes wholeheartedly in grassroots activism, progressive democracy, and reconciliation. The mission of the Dallas Peace Center is to promote peace through action, education, dialogue, and research for peace and justice. All our active campaigns are volunteer-driven and each project is constantly changing to meet current world situations.

East Timor Action Network
ETAN Washington Office
1101 Pennsylvania Avenue SE
Washington, DC 20003
Phone: (202)544-6911
Fax: (202)544-6118
Email: karen@etan.org
(Karen Orenstein)
Web site: www.etan.org

The East Timor Action Network was founded in November 1991 to support self-determination and human rights for the people of East Timor in accordance with the Universal Declaration of Human Rights, the 1960 United Nations General Assembly Resolution on Decolonization and Security Council and General Assembly resolutions on East Timor. Our primary focus has been to change U.S. foreign policy and raise public awareness to support self-determination and now genuine independence for East Timor.

End Violence Project
P.O. Box 41948
Philadelphia, PA 19101
Phone: (610)527-2821;
(800)732-0999
Email: MBEVP@aol.com
Web site: www.endviolence.org

End Violence Project is a nonprofit organization created by Mahin Bina and others with the shared vision of ending violence without violence. The Project provides educational programs, seminars, and symposium and support-group discussions. The most important program trains and equips inmates and ex-offenders to live a nonviolent life and possibly become End Violence spokespersons. The End Violence Project has received national recognition for focusing on ending the cycle of violence and including the inmates and ex-offenders as an inherent part of the process.

Fellowship of Reconciliation
P.O. Box 271
Nyack, NY 10960
Phone: (845)358-4601
Fax: (845)358-4924
Email: for@forusa.org
Web site: www.forusa.org

Fellowship of Reconciliation (FOR) is a nonviolent, interfaith, tax-exempt organization, which promotes nonviolence and seeks to replace violence, war, racism, and economic injustice with nonviolence, peace, and justice. FOR has members from many religious and ethnic traditions and is within the framework of the International Fellowship of Reconciliation (IFOR), with over forty countries affiliated. Since 1915 the Fellowship of Reconciliation has carried on programs and educational projects concerned with domestic and international peace and justice, nonviolent alternatives to conflict, and the rights of conscience.

Foundation for Middle East Peace
1763 N Street NW
Washington, DC 20036
Phone: (202)835-3650
Fax: (202)835-3651
Email: info@fmep.org
Web site: www.fmep.org

The Foundation for Middle East Peace (FMEP) is a nonprofit organization dedicated to provide information on Israeli-Palestinian conflict and assist in the process of reaching peaceful solutions for the future security of Israelis and Palestinians. FMEP publishes bimonthly a Report on Israeli Settlement in the Occupied Territories that provides up-to-date information on Israel's settlement policies as well as the ongoing negotiations with the Palestinians over the future of the West Bank, Gaza Strip, and Jerusalem.

Fund for Reconciliation and Development
475 Riverside Drive, Ste. 727
New York, NY 10115
Phone: (212)367-4220

Fax: (212)367-4366
Email: usindo@igc.org
Web site: www.usirp.org

The Fund for Reconciliation and Development is a nonprofit organization that has worked for more than fifteen years to bring about normal diplomatic, cultural, and economic relations with Cambodia, Laos, and Vietnam. FRD was the first and it remained as the only American nongovernmental organization specializing in mutual understanding and cooperation with these three countries. FRD began similar work with Cuba in 1998.

Healing Center for Survivors of Political Torture
9 Peter Yorke Way
San Francisco, CA 94109
Phone: (415)241-1562
Fax: (415)703-7222
Email: terrilynz@aol.com
Web site: www.pacinfo.com/
eugene/tsnet/DSPCenterh.html

Affiliated with the California Institute of Integral Studies, the Healing Center for Survivors of Political Torture is an accredited institute of higher learning in San Francisco, which provides mental health and social services free of charge to survivors of political torture. Survivors of political torture need to be coached in a specialized process of healing because remembering and confronting the trauma can have severely deleterious effects, including re-traumatization.

International Forgiveness Institute
Communications Center
6313 Landfall Drive

Madison, WI 53705
Phone: (608)231-9117
Fax: (608)262-9407
Email: webmaster@forgiveness-institute.org
Web site:
www.forgiveness-institute.org

Established in 1994 as a private, non-profit organization, the International Forgiveness Institute was an outgrowth of the social scientific research done at the University of Wisconsin-Madison. For the first few years the IFI primarily answered scholars' inquiries about setting up research programs on forgiveness. The IFI's action-oriented programs will be accelerated as individuals, families, and communities learn to explore and implement forgiveness for the purpose of restoring healthy emotions, rebuilding relationships, and establishing more peaceful communities.

International Reconciliation Coalition
P.O. Box 3278
Ventura, CA 93006-3278
Phone: (805)642-5327
Fax: (805)642-2588
Email: ircio@pacbell.net
Web site: www.reconcile.org

The International Reconciliation Coalition (IRC) informs and strengthens the rapidly growing worldwide network of Christians who are applying the biblical principals of confession, repentance, reconciliation, and restitution to conflicts both corporate and personal. Individuals, churches, and organizations support the IRC and as a network the IRC is sensitive to the needs of the 700-plus members.

Jewish Peace Fellowship

P.O. Box 271
Nyack, NY 10960
Phone: (845)348-4601
Fax: (845)358-4924
Email: jpf@forusa.org
Web site: www.jewishpeacefellow
ship.org

Jewish Peace Fellowship is a Jewish
voice in the peace community and a
peace voice in the Jewish community.
A nondenominational Jewish organization committed to active nonviolence as a means of resolving conflict,
the Jewish Peace Fellowship draws on
Jewish traditional sources within the
Torah, the Talmud, and contemporary
peacemaking sages like Martin Buber,
Judah Magnes, and Abraham Joshua
Heschel.

Journey of Hope . . .
From Violence to Healing

P.O. Box 210390
Anchorage, AK 99521-0390
Phone: (877)924-4483 (toll-free)
Email: Bill@journeyofhope.org
Web site: www.journeyofhope.org

The Journey of Hope . . . From Violence to Healing is a nonprofit organization led by murder victims' family
members who support alternatives to
the death penalty. The purpose of the
Journey is to spotlight murder victims'
family members who do not seek revenge and have chosen the path of love
and compassion for all of humanity.
Forgiveness is seen as strength and as
a way of healing.

Middlesex Community College

Economic and Community
Development
591 Springs Road

Bedford, MA 01730
Phone: (781)275-3534
Fax: (781)275-0741
Email: falcettaf@middlesex.cc.ma.us
Web site: www.middlesex.cc.ma.us

Since 1996 the Middlesex Community College has developed a program to assist the Phnom Penh
community of Cambodia in dealing
with issues on conflict resolution.

Murder Victims' Families
for Reconciliation

2161 Massachusetts Avenue
Cambridge, MA 02140
Phone: (617)868-0007
Fax: (617)354-2832
Email: mvfrliz@yahoo.com
Web site: www.mvfr.org

Members of Murder Victims' Families
for Reconciliation (MVFR) is a nonprofit organization defined by a common experience: the murder of a loved
one. MVFR members share values in
response to homicide, the core of
which is opposition to the death penalty. They honor the lives of their lost
loved ones not by supporting more
killing, but by working to fashion a
criminal justice system that holds murderers accountable for their actions,
protects the public, reduces violence,
and helps both individuals and society heal in the aftermath of homicide.

National Coalition to Abolish
the Death Penalty

1436 U Street NW, Ste. 104
Washington, DC 20009
Phones: (202)387-3890;
(888)286-2237
Fax: (202)387-3890
Email: info@ncadp.org
Web site: www.ncadp.org

National Coalition to Abolish the Death Penalty is a coalition of organizations and individuals committed to abolish capital punishment by informing, mobilizing, and advocating for a public policy that will reject the state's use of homicide as an instrument of social policy.

Nazareth Project
12-B South Seventh Street
Akron, PA 17501-1331
Phone: (717)859-1389
Fax: (717)859-1437
Email: nazproj@redrose.net
Web site: www.nazarethproject.org

Nazareth Project, Inc., promotes a Christian ministry of healing, peace, and reconciliation in the Middle East through support of health-care services. By providing medical care to all individuals in the spirit of Christ without regard to religious or ethnic background, the organization bears witness that wholeness and healing for humanity is most completely found in Jesus of Nazareth.

Pax Cristi International
See under Europe.

Project Hearts and Minds
P.O. Box 252
Thornwood, NY 10594
Phone: (973)328-5311
Fax: (973)887-7644
Email: kelsey@email.njim.net
Web site: www.illyria.com/pham.html

Project Hearts and Minds, Inc., is a volunteer, nonprofit, nongovernmental organization. Many members are war veterans and all seek to put a human face on the tragedy of war. Since 1992 Project Hearts and Minds has worked, in a nonpartisan way, to establish on a person-to-person basis an evolving and healing relationship of friendship and reconciliation with countries where the United States has been at war. The Project's present focus is Vietnam.

Reconciliation Ministries Network
5608 Bradford Avenue
Chattanooga, TN 37409-2211
Phone: (423)822-1091
Fax: (423)822-1091
Email:
Info@ReconciliationNetwork.org
Web site: www.reconciliation network.org

The Reconciliation Ministries Network is an evangelical Christian, tax-exempt mission that puts its efforts in advocating the reconciliation of humanity divided by race and poverty. Its vision is to perform cross-cultural ministry, especially in the African American church, and to develop strong relationships with their pastors.

Reconciliation Mission
P.O. Box 1986
Indianapolis, IN 46206-1986
Phone: (317)713-2445
Fax: (317)635-3700
Email: chaskett@cfc.disciples.org
Web site: www.disciples.org/cfc/reconcil.htm

Reconciliation Mission is a nonprofit organization that seeks to dissect the concept of race and to deconstruct its convergence with the concept of colonial expansion, assigning human worth and social status by using a race as a model for humanity. Its task is to offer training for local disciple teams for the purpose of instructing their members to promote an antiracist policy and develop a pro-reconciliation ministry.

Reconciliation Networks of Our World

2839 Whippoorwill Court
Tucker, GA 30084-3085
Phone: (770)934-7955
Fax: (770)414-8610
Email melanielatham@hotmail.com
Web site: www.reconciliation
networks.org

Reconciliation Networks of Our World (RNOW) is a global, international, transdenominational and grassroots fellowship of Christians networking as ambassadors of reconciliation. Out of this bonding an international team is forming to facilitate the vision of reconciliation and unity of the worldwide Body of Christ. Christians of diverse backgrounds come together in reconciliation events and activities, where spiritual bonding often occurs.

Reconciliation Walk
See under Europe

Religious Organizing Against the Death Penalty Project

c/o Criminal Justice Program
American Friends
Service Committee
1501 Cherry Street
Philadelphia, PA 19102
Phone: (215)241-7130

Fax: (215)241-7119
Email: information@
deathpenaltyreligious.org
Web site: www.deathpenalty
religious.org

Religious Organizing Against the Death Penalty Project seeks to build a powerful coalition of faith-based activists. Nationally, it works with official religious bodies to develop strategies and to promote antideath-penalty activism within each faith tradition. At the grassroots level, the project links with individuals and faith communities, establishing "covenant" relationships to foster local abolition efforts.

Resource Center for Non-Violence

515 Broadway
Santa Cruz, CA 95060
Phone: (831)423-1626
Fax: (831)423-8716
Email: bookstore@rcnv.org
Web site: www.rcnv.org

The Resource Center for Non-Violence is a twenty-five-year-old peace and social justice organization dedicated to promoting the principles of nonviolent social change and enhancing the quality of life and human dignity. It offers a wide range of educational programs in the history, theory, methodology, and current practice of nonviolence as a force for personal and social change. The Resource Center has an international focus, with interns coming from Bosnia, Herzegovnia, as well as from California. Their programs focus on places as far as the Middle East and as near as Southern Mexico.

Restitution Incorporated

106-E Melrose Place
Chapel Hill, NC 27516
Phone: (919)932-7680
Fax: (919)932-7680
Email: comments@restitution
inc.org
Web site: www.restitutioninc.org

Restitution Incorporated is a nonprofit organization dedicated to promoting healing between offenders and victims by helping offenders make restitution for their crimes. The organization believes that every offender has a gift that can be used to give back to the victim or to the community that has been harmed. Rather than returning offense or harm, rather than dreaming of revenge, they stop the evil at themselves, they exhaust its venom.

Society of Professionals in Dispute Resolution

1527 New Hampshire Avenue NW, 3rd fl.
Washington, DC 20036
Phone: (202)667-9700
Fax: (202)265-1968
Email: spidr@spidr.org
Web site: www.spidr.org

Society of Professionals in Dispute Resolution (SPIDR) was organized in 1972, growing out of the labor-management mediation and arbitration movement. SPIDR performs three primary functions. It guards the standards and ethics of the field of dispute resolution and collaborative decisionmaking. It seeks to develop the intellectual and professional roots of the field to educate the public about various dispute resolution procedures that were available in order to clarify the expanding role of the conflict resolver;

and it supports its members and provides them with tangible and intangible membership benefits.

Trauma Research, Education, and Training Institute

22 Morgan Farms Drive
South Windsor, CT 06074
Phone: (860)644-2541
Email: info@tsicaap.com
Web site: www.tsicaap.com

Trauma Research, Education, and Training Institute is a nonprofit organization dedicated to increasing psychotherapists' and other trauma workers' abilities to provide effective ethical treatment for survivors of traumatic life experiences. The Institute's mission is to pursue work through programs as professional training, community education and research on the psychological impact of trauma on survivors, the impact of this work on both therapists and clients, and effective interventions with therapists and clients.

U.S. International Committee for Peace in the Middle East

16020 94th Avenue
Stanwood, WA 98290
Tel/Fax: (360) 652-4285
email: USICPME@aol.com
Web site: www.usicpme.org

The U.S. Interreligious Committee for Peace in the Middle East is a national organization for Jews, Christians, and Muslims dedicated to dialogue, education, and advocacy for peace based on the deepest teachings of the three religious teachings. Founded in 1987, the Committee organizes and supports national and local programs of dialogue, education, and advocacy for peace, while at the same time challenging the persistent prejudices and stereotypes members of one tradition may have of the other two. The Committee works to generate public interreligious support for U.S. efforts to help Israel, the Palestinian Authority, and the Arab states achieve a negotiated, comprehensive, and reconciliatory peace.

**Veterans Vietnam
Restoration Project**
P.O. Box 369
Garberville, CA 95542
Phone: (707)923-3357
Fax: (906)483-3183
Email: srutherford@patsy.com
Web site: www.vvrp.org

The VVRP is a small nongovernmental organization (NGO), whose primary mission is to provide American veterans and others with opportunities to return to Vietnam for humanitarian service. The VVRP operates under the premise that returning to Vietnam, working directly on community projects, and returning to places where they served helps veterans heal the legacy of their war.

**Victim Offender
Reconciliation Program
of the Central Valley, Inc.**
2529 Willow Avenue
Clovis, CA 93612
Phone: (559)291-1120
Fax: (559)291-8214
Email: vorp@fresno.edu
Web site: www.vorp.org

The Victim Offender Reconciliation Program of the Central Valley, Inc. (VORP), advocates to offer an alternative process to judges, police, and pro-

bation officers in dealing with criminal offenses. Meetings are arranged between offenders and their victims, providing the opportunity for communication, responsibility, restitution, and reconciliation. VORP offers a very practical total or partial substitute for jail or prison incarceration.

**Visions of Peace with Justice
in Israel/Palestine**
44 Cypress Street
Brookline, MA 02445
Phone: (617)984-0532
Email: info@vopj.org
Web site: www.vopj.org

Visions of Peace with Justice in Israel/Palestine is an organization that works to promote a lasting peace between Israelis and Palestinians based on mutual respect, justice, and equality. The peace envisioned is one in which Jews and Palestinians share the land of Israel/Palestine and its resources, acknowledging and respecting each other's rights as equal citizens and neighbors, free from violence and able to develop their own futures with full respect for human and civil rights.

**Western Washington
Fellowship of Reconciliation**
225 North 70th Street
Seattle, WA 98103
Phone: (206)789-5565
Fax: (206)789-5565
(telephone first)
Email: wwfor@connectexpress.com
Web site: www.scn.org/wwfor

WWFOR is a faith-based pacifist organization, which works on a variety of peace and justice issues. WWFOR is affiliated with local chapters, the national Fellowship of Reconciliation, and the International Fellowship of Reconciliation.

Worldwide Forgiveness Alliance

International Forgiveness Day
20 Sunnyside Avenue, Ste. A268
Mill Valley, CA 94941
Phone: (415)381-3372
Fax: (415)381-3372
Email woodyk@mediaone.net
Web site: www.forgivenessday.org

The Worldwide Forgiveness Alliance is a nonprofit, tax-exempt educational foundation. The mission of the Worldwide Forgiveness Alliance is to celebrate the healing power of forgiveness worldwide through the establishment of the first global holiday, International Forgiveness Day, to be celebrated annually by every country on the first Sunday of August, in or before the year 2005. As a grassroots networking organization, the Alliance is committed to generating increased interest and support for various programs from national leaders, mayors, community church organizations, and individuals.

World Relief Corporation

P.O. Box WRC
Wheaton, IL 60189
Phone: (630)665-0235
Fax: (630)665-4473
Email: pbaarendse@wr.org
Web site: www.ccih.org/op-wrc.htm

World Relief Corporation is a nonprofit organization that works with the church in alleviating human suffering worldwide in the name of Christ. World Relief Corporation's mission is accomplished by the way in which collective values are shaped; by response to the hungry, refugees, other homeless persons, and victims of war and disaster; and by empathy with those who live with little hope or under oppression.

World Vision International

800 West Chestnut Avenue
Monrovia, CA 91016
Phone: (626)303-8811
Fax: (626)301-7786
Email: info@wvi.org
Web site: www.wvi.org

World Vision International is a global partnership of Christians whose mission is to follow Jesus Christ in working with the poor and oppressed to promote human transformation, seek reconciliation and justice, and bear witness to the good news of the Kingdom of God.

EUROPE

Action for Peoples in Conflict

Silverbirch House
Longworth, Abingdon
Oxon OX13 5EJ
United Kingdom
Phone: 01235 519393
Email: afpicuk@gn.apc.org
Web site: www.
oneworld.org/afpic/index.html

Action for Peoples in Conflict (AfPiC) is a registered charity organization that helps to break cycles of violence, hatred, and despair by providing psychological and emotional support in conflict situations. AfPiC is initially focusing its activities on children and young people, who have the greatest capacity to transcend the conflicts of their communities and to bring about change in the future. There is also an ongoing need for willing volunteers to help construct play areas in Kosovo, refurbish the Enterprise in Southampton, help at the refuge in Kenya, and to help with the fundraising and administration associated with AfPiC's projects.

AfPiC supports projects that, with varying degrees of support, are thought to be likely to be self-sustaining in the longer term and capable of reproducing themselves as other people take up the same ideas.

Agenda for Reconciliation
International Secretariat
24 Greencoat Place
London SW1P 1RD
United Kingdom
Phone: 44 171 798 6000
Fax: 44 171 798 6001
Email: afr@mra.org.uk
Web site: www.caux.ch/afr

International Conference Centre
Mountain House
CH-1824 Caux
Switzerland
Phone: 41 21 962 91 11
Fax: 41 21 962 93 55
Email: admin@caux.ch
Web site: www.caux.ch/afr

U.S. Office
40 Dana Street
Cambridge, MA 02138
Phone: (617)547-0761
Fax: (617)547-4301
Email: 102367.2373@
compuserve.com
Web site: www.caux.ch/afr

Agenda for Reconciliation seeks to create an environment where individuals can find liberation from hatred, greed, and indifference. In its development, the Agenda for Reconciliation has experienced that healing,

which starts in individuals and small communities and can ripple out far beyond any boundaries. Agenda for Reconciliation supports individuals and groups involved in peacemaking through meetings, exchanges, and connections.

Centre for the Study of Conflict
Faculty of Humanities
University of Ulster
Cromore Road Room L014
Coleraine BT52 1SA
Ireland
Phone: (028)7032 4666
Fax: (028)7032 4917
Email: ja.dunn@ulst.ac.uk
(Prof. Seamus Dunn)
Web site: www.cain.ulst.ac.uk/csc

The Centre for the Study of Conflict is a research center based in the University of Ulster. The Centre was founded in 1977 as an interdisciplinary research unit within the framework of the University. Its central aim is to carry out research on the conflict in Ireland, and to encourage the growth of an academic community involved in conflict research and to support this process through seminars, publications, visiting scholars, and liaison with other institutions.

Center for the Study of Forgiveness and Reconciliation
Coventry University
Priory Street
Coventry CV1 5FB
United Kingdom
Phone: 024 7688 8247
Fax: 024 7688 8679
Email: a.rigby@coventry.ac.uk
Web site:
www.coventry-isl.org.uk/forgive

Center for the Study of Forgiveness and Reconciliation fosters research, teaching, and related activities for the benefit of a deeper understanding and promotion of the reconciliation process and forgiveness throughout the world. It is intended that the fruits of the work carried out at the Center will empower those at the grassroots, national, and international levels who are striving to transform violent conflict situations by nonviolent means and lay the foundations for peace and reconciliation between the parties to conflict.

Community of Sant'Egidio

Piazza S.Egidio
3/A Roma
Italy
Phone: 39 06 585661
Fax: 39 06 5800197
Email: m2000@santegidio.org
Web site: www.santegidio.org

Community of Sant'Egidio is a movement of laypeople with over 30,000 members, dedicated to evangelize and perform charity in Rome, Italy, and in over thirty-five countries worldwide. The Community of Sant'Egidio functions as a "public association of lay people of the Church."

European Centre for Conflict Prevention

P.O. Box 14069
NL-3508 SC Utrecht
The Netherlands
Tel: 31 (30) 253 7528
Fax: 31 (30) 253 7529
Email: euconflict@euconflict.org
Website: http://www.euconflict.org

The European Centre for Conflict Prevention is a Dutch foundation hosting the Secretariat of the European Platform. It has also a role in fostering activities on conflict prevention in the Netherlands by facilitating, initiating, and coordinating activities of the European Platform through regular consultations with the Steering Group.

European Special Support Program for Peace and Reconciliation in Northern Ireland and the Border Counties of Ireland

DHFETE
39-49 Adelaide Street
Belfast BT2 8FD
Ireland
Phone: 02890 257668
Web site:
www.eu-peace.org/contacts.htm

The strategic aim of the Peace Program is to reinforce progress toward a peaceful and stable society and to promote reconciliation. The five priority areas for action include employment, urban and rural regeneration, cross-border development, social inclusion, and industrial development.

Glencree Centre for Reconciliation

Enniskerry
County Wicklow
Ireland
Phone: 353 (0)1 282 9711
Fax: 353 (0)1 276 6085
Email: info@glencree-cfr.ie
Web site: www.glencree-cfr.ie

Glencree Centre for Reconciliation is a membership-based association of individuals who foster mutual respect, tolerance, and understanding between individuals and groups in conflict, for building peace and reconciliation in

Ireland, between Ireland and Great Britain, and beyond. It is an autonomous organization that seeks to work together with all those trying to build peace, in whatever area of society.

Initiative on Conflict Resolution and Ethnicity
Aberfoyle House
Northland Road
Londonderry BT48 7JA
Northern Ireland
Phone: 44 (0) 28 7137 5500
Fax: 44 (0) 28 7137 5510
Email: incore@incore.ulst.ac.uk
Web site: www.incore.ulst.ac.uk

The Initiative on Conflict Resolution and Ethnicity (InCoRE) was established in 1993 by the University of Ulster in conjunction with the United Nations University in order to perform research and policy work on ethnic conflict resolution, as well as finding strategies for solving political and religious conflicts. Currently, InCoRE's research focuses on postconflict issues, issues of diversity governance, and research methodology in violent societies. InCoRE also produces a web-based Conflict Data Service that provides current and historical information on all major on-going conflicts, theme sites on a variety of issues relevant to conflict, and information on conflict-resolution institutions throughout the world.

International Fellowship of Reconciliation
Spoorstraat 38
1815 BK Alkmaar
The Netherlands
Phone: 31 72 512-3014

Fax: 31 72 515-1102
Email: office@ifor.org
Web site: www.ifor.org

International Fellowship of Reconciliation (IFOR) is an international, spiritually based movement of people who share the belief in the power of love and truth. Through its worldwide network of groups and its international secretariat, IFOR acts to promote a global culture of nonviolence. Some of its strategies include education and training in active nonviolence, with special attention to world religions. It brings awareness by informing a wider public about nonviolence, and it serves as a resource center and maintains active relations with UN and other similar institutions and organizations.

International Rehabilitation Council for Torture Victims
Borgergade 13
P.O. Box 2107
DK-1014 Copenhagen K
Denmark
Phone: 45 33 76 06 00
Fax: 45 33 76 05 00
Email: irct@irct.org
Web site: www.irct.org

The IRCT is an independent, international health-professional organization that promotes and supports the rehabilitation of torture victims and works for the prevention of torture worldwide. The global vision of the IRCT is a world that values and accepts shared responsibility for the eradication of torture. In support of the organization's global vision, the IRCT seeks to promote and support new and existing rehabilitation centers and prevention programs and to initiate emergency intervention projects, as a result of a strategic and cohesive advocacy program to secure and increase the necessary political will and sustainable funding.

Orthodox Peace Fellowship
Kanisstraat 5
1811 GJ Alkmaar
The Netherlands
Phone: (31-72) 511-2545
Fax: (31-72) 515-4180
Email: incommunion@cs.com
Web site: www.incommunion.org

The Orthodox Peace Fellowship of the Protection of the Mother of God is an association of Orthodox believers trying to apply the principles of the Gospel to situations of division and conflict, whether in the home, the parish, the community, the workplace, within a particular nation, and between nations. The Fellowship works for the conservation of God's creation and especially of human life. The Fellowship is not a political association and supports no political parties or candidates.

Pax Cristi International
U.S. Office
532 West Eighth Street
Erie, PA 16502-1343
Phone: (814)453-4955
Fax: (814)452-4784
Email: info@paxchristiusa.org
Web site:www.nonviolence.org
/pcusa

Pax Christi Wallonia-Brussels
(EU Office)
216, Chaussée de Wavre
B-1050 Bruxelles
Belgium
Phone: 32 2 646-6800
Fax: 32 2 646-9441

Email: pax.christi@skynet.be
Web site: www.paxchristi.nl

Pax Christi Switzerland
Chemin du Cardinal-Journet 3
CH-1752 Villars-sur-Glâne
Switzerland
Phone: 41 26 426-3475
Fax: 41 26 426-3476
Email: pxch@com.mcnet.ch

Pax Christi International is a nonprofit, nongovernmental, Catholic peace movement working on a global scale on a wide variety of issues in the fields of human rights, reconciliation, disarmament, economic justice, and ecology. Pax Christi International includes autonomous national sections, local groups, and affiliated organizations spread over thirty countries and five continents with over 60,000 members worldwide. Most of the regular work at the international level is done through commissions, thematic and regional working groups, and consultations. It is recognized and has representation status at the United Nations in New York and Vienna, the UN Human Rights Commission and Subcommission in Geneva, UNESCO in Paris, UNICEF in New York, and the Council of Europe in Strasbourg, France.

Peace Brigades International
International Office
5 Caledonian Road
London N1 9DX
United Kingdom
Phone: 44 (0) 20-7713-0392
Fax: 44 (0) 20-7837-2290
Email: pbiio@gn.apc.org
Web site:www.igc.org/pbi
/index.html

Peace Brigades International (PBI) is a

grassroots organization that explores and promotes nonviolent peace-keeping and support for human rights. When invited, PBI sends teams of volunteers in areas of political repression and conflict. The volunteers accompany human rights defenders, their organizations and others threatened by political violence. Currently, Peace Brigades International has long-term projects in Colombia, Indonesia/East Timor, and Mexico, as well as joint projects with other organizations in the Balkans and Chiapas, Mexico.

Reconciliation Walk
P.O. Box 61
Harpenden
Herts AL5 4JJ
United Kingdom
Phone: 44 1582 766 019
Fax: 44 1582 766 019
Email: info@reconciliationwalk.org
Web site: www.reconciliation
walk.org

USA Coordination Office
Phone: (877)925-5872
Email: recwalkusa@yahoo.com
Web site:
www.reconciliationwalk.org

Reconciliation Walk is dedicated to overcoming the bitter legacies of the past by fostering friendship and mutual understanding across civilizations. From 1996 to 1999 over 2,500 Western Christians from over twenty-five different nations came to visit the Middle East carrying a message of forgiveness for the Crusades of 900 years ago. The RW hopes to continue fostering understanding and friendship between East and West by continuing to undo the bitter legacies of the past. Three and one-half years of groups traveling

in the region showed the RW how stereotypes are broken when people meet face to face.

Redress
6 Queen Square
London WC1N 3AT
United Kingdom
Phone: 44 (0) 20 7278 9502
Fax: 44 (0) 20 7278 9410
Email: redresstrust@gn.apc.org; redress@gn.apc.org
Web site: www.redress.org

Redress is a London-based, internationally focused, nonprofit legal/human rights organization. Founded on Human Rights Day, December 10, 1992, Redress helps torture survivors use available legal remedies to obtain reparation and to campaign for effective remedies where they do not exist. Reparation (including compensation and rehabilitation) plays an important part in healing and restoring the lives of those who have been tortured. Seeking legal redress also helps to combat the practice of torture and deter repressive regimes.

Special Support Program for Peace and Reconciliation
Department of Finance
Ballaugh House
73 Lower Mount Street
Dublin 2
Ireland
Phone: 003531 6045743
Email: Euro.div@dfpni.gov.uk
Web site: www.nics.gov.uk/eu/eusspr/progsumm/intro.htm

Special Support Program for Peace and Reconciliation (SSPPR) was established by the Department of Finance of Ireland in order to reinforce progress toward a peaceful and more stable society and to promote reconciliation by increasing economic development and employment, promoting urban and rural regeneration, developing cross-border cooperation, and extending social inclusion. SSPPR promotes the social inclusion of those who are at the margins of social and economic life; it exploits new opportunities and addresses the needs arising from the peace process in order to boost economic growth and advance social and economic regeneration.

Transnational Foundation for Peace and Future Research
Vegagatan 25
s-224 57 Lund
Sweden
Phone: 46 46 145909
Fax: 46 46 144512
Email: tff@transnational.org
Web site: www.transnational.org

Transnational Foundation for Peace and Future Research is an independent, small, innovative peace force, networking seventy-one associates worldwide. It expresses its vision on reconciliation, thus representing an experiment in applied peace research and global networking. Its focus is on conflict-mitigation, peace research, and education to improve conflict understanding at all levels and to promote alternative security and global development.

War Resisters' International
5 Caledonian Road
London N1 9DX
United Kingdom
Phone: 44 171 278 4040
Fax: 44 171 278 0444

Email: warresisters@gn.apc.org
Web site: www.gn.apc.org/war resisters/index.html

War Resisters' International (WRI) is an extensive network that brings together peace researchers and nonviolence trainers from over forty countries, participating through national sections and Associate organizations, ranging from Gandhian teachers in India to antiwar campaigners in former Yugoslavia. While many WRI members take an activist role in campaigns, others may carry out their war resistance in quieter ways in the decisions they make in their daily lives.

World Council of Churches
P.O. Box 2100
1211 Geneva 2
Switzerland
Phone: 41 22 791 6111
Fax: 41 22 791 0361
Email: info@wcc-coe.org
Web site: www.wcc-coe.org

The World Council of Churches (WCC) is an international fellowship of Christian churches, built upon the foundation of encounter, dialogue, and collaboration. The WCC was formed to serve and advance the ecumenical movement—the quest for restoring the unity of the church—by encouraging in its members a common commitment to follow the Gospel. The WCC's mission is to pray for and pursue the visible unity of Christ's church "in one faith and in one eucharistic fellowship, expressed in worship and common life in Christ, through witness and service to the world."

AFRICA

African Centre for the Constructive Resolution of Disputes
ACCORD House
2 Golf Course Drive
Mount Edgecombe
Durban
South Africa

ACCORD
Private Bag x018
Umhlanga Rocks 4320
South Africa
Phone: 27 (31) 5023908
Fax: 27 (31) 5024160
South Africa: (031)5024160
Email: info@accord.org.za
Web site: www.accord.org.za

The African Centre for the Constructive Resolution of Disputes (AC-CORD) was established in 1992 as an educational trust and associated with South Africa's five historically black universities: Western Cape, Fort Hare, Transkei, the North, and Durban-Westville. The primary objective for the establishment of ACCORD was to provide a mechanism to deal with conflict arising out of South Africa's transition from apartheid to democratic governance. There was an urgent need for people to be better informed about the negotiation process and to be trained in negotiation strategies in order to engage in negotiations at local levels and to popularize negotiation as a way to deal with disputes.

Centre for Conflict Resolution
UCT, Private Bag
Rondebosch 7701
South Africa
Phone: 27 21 4222512
Fax: 27 21 4222622

Email: mailbox@ccr.uct.ac.za
Web site: www.ccrweb.ccr.uct.ac.za

Founded in 1968, the Centre for Conflict Resolution (formerly the Centre for Intergroup Studies) is an independent institute that seeks to contribute toward a just peace in South Africa and elsewhere in Africa by promoting constructive, creative, and cooperative approaches to the resolution of conflict and the reduction of violence. Associated with the University of Cape Town, the Centre is based in the Western Cape but works nationally and internationally to fulfill its mission. Mediation, facilitation, training, education, and research comprise the Centre's main activities, with an emphasis on capacity building.

Centre for the Study of Violence and Reconciliation
Braamfontein Centre, 4th fl.
23 Jorissen Street
Braamfontein, Johannesburg
South Africa

P.O. Box 30778
Braamfontein, JHB, 2017
South Africa
Phone: 27 (11) 403-5650
Fax: 27 (11) 339-6785
Email: info@csvr.org.za
Web site: www.wits.ac.za/csvr

The Centre for the Study of Violence and Reconciliation (CSVR) is a multidisciplinary South African nongovernmental organization. Since its inception in 1989 the CSVR has been dedicated to making a meaningful contribution to peaceful and fundamental transformation in South Africa and in the Southern African region.

Institute for Justice and Reconciliation

P.O. Box 205
Rondebosch
7701 Cape Town
South Africa
Phone: 021-686-5070
Fax: 021-689-7465
Email: ijr@grove.uct.ac.za
Web site: www.ijr.org.za

The Institute for Justice and Reconcil-iation, based in Cape Town, draws on expertise provided by the law faculties and other disciplines at the University of Cape Town, University of Stellen-bosch, and University of Western Cape, as well as broader structures of civil society. It seeks to cooperate with all organizations and individuals in-terested in the promotion of its ideals on reconciliation. The Institute for Jus-tice and Reconciliation seeks also to grapple with this legacy, promoting justice and reconciliation in the after-math of the Truth and Reconciliation Commission (TRC) and into the new century.The Institute is open to col-laborate with educational institutions worldwide.

Truth and Reconciliation

Old Mutual Building, 9th fl.
106 Adderley Street
Cape Town 8001
South Africa

P.O. Box 3162
Cape Town 8000
South Africa
Phone: 27 21 424-5161
Fax: 27 21 424-5225
Email: trcctn@iafrica.com
Web site: www.truth.org.za

In a move toward uncovering past events without further polarizing the society, the government of South Africa created the Truth and Recon-ciliation Commission on April 15, 1996, presided over by Archbishop Desmond Tutu. The purpose of the commission is to collect and investi-gate victims' accounts from 1960 through 1994, to consider amnesty for those who confess their participation in atrocities, and to make recommen-dations for reparations. The commis-sion was established in the hope that it would foster healing and prevent such crimes from happening again.

AUSTRALIA

Australians for Native Title and Reconciliation

P.O. Box 1176
Rozelle, NSW 2039
Australia
Phone: 02 9555 6138
Fax: 02 9555 6991
Email: antar@antar.org.au;
davidc@antar.org.au
(national coordinator:
David Cooper)
Web site: www.antar.org.au

Australians for Native Title and Reconciliation (ANTaR) is an inde-pendent national network of non-indigenous organizations and individuals working in support of jus-tice for Aboriginal and Torres Strait Is-lander peoples in Australia. ANTaR has a close and unique working rela-tionship with indigenous leaderships. ANTaR's purpose is to support in-digenous people speaking for them-selves rather than to speak for indigenous people. ANTaR receives no grants from federal or state govern-ments and is non-party-political.

Council for Aboriginal Reconciliation
Pryor Knowledge (ACT) Pty Ltd
29 Urambi Village
Kambah ACT 2902
Australia
Phone: 02 6231 6423
Fax: 02 6231 6423
Email: car@dpmc.gov.au; gefpryor@ozemail.com.au
Web site: www.reconciliation.org.au

The Council for Aboriginal Reconciliation is a broad network of Australians interested in advocating reconciliation in their community or within organizations to which they belong. The council's vision is to create a united Australia to promote respect for the aboriginal values, and heritage, and to provide justice and equity for all. This network is called Australians for Reconciliation and has coordinators for each state and territory.

Journey of Healing
South Australian Sorry Day/
Journey of Healing
ANTaR
5 Hutt Street
Adelaide SA 5000
Australia
Phone: 08-8227 0170
Fax: 08-8223 3039
Email: dhollins@camtech.net.au
Web site: www.alphalink.com.au/~rez/Journey

The Journey of Healing program is focused on bringing home the stolen generations of Aboriginal Australians, offering every local community the chance to come together across the racial divides, listen to each other's experiences, and plan for healing. It has organized study circles and daylong seminars throughout the country, bringing together members of the Aboriginal community in each locality with police, civic officials, and others. Through ten years of steady work, the program has done much to create a greater awareness of Aboriginal perceptions among the wider community.

World Institute for Non-violence and Reconciliation
P.O. Box 352
Kingston 7050
Tasmania
Australia
Phone: 03 6227 1494
Fax: 03 6227 1520
Email: aalomes@institute-for-nonviolence.com.au
Web site: www.institute-for-nonviolence.com.au

The World Institute for Nonviolence and Reconciliation is a nonprofit organization that contributes to the reduction of violence by promoting a strategic protocol for peace building. It also seeks to empower individuals, communities, and institutions to solve disputes through negotiation, reconciliation, and peace-building initiatives. The Institute is deliberately secular but openly welcomes all members of the interfaith community.

CENTRAL AMERICA

Center for Peace and Reconciliation
Fundación Arias para la Paz
y el Progreso Humano
Apartado 8-6410-1000
San José
Costa Rica

Phone: 506 255-2955
Fax: 506 255-2244
Emails: cpr@arias.or.cr;
info@arias.or.cr
Web site: www.arias.or.cr

Focusing its work on Central America, the Center for Peace and Reconciliation seeks to promote pluralistic participation in search for strategies to achieve lasting peace and security. Based on principles and norms of international law, the Center for Peace and Reconciliation aims to develop efficient mechanisms by supporting methods and spaces for dialogue aimed at the prevention and peaceful resolution of conflicts. It also defines approaches and strategies that contribute to the construction of democratic governance and that guarantee sustainable and equitable human development in societies affected by internal armed conflict.

Central American Dialogue
(El Diálogo Centroamericano)
Apartado 8-6410-1000
San José
Costa Rica
Phone: 506 255-2955;
506 255-2885
Fax: 506 255-2244
Email: dialogo@arias.or.cr
Web site: www.ciponline.org/
dialogue

Founded in 1995, the Central American Dialogue for Security and Demilitarization seeks to address regional security issues. Its membership includes individuals and institutions from throughout Central America which share a desire for a greater civilian role in questions of security.
The Dialogue recognizes that the peoples of each Central American state face different security threats, which include not only external military threats but extreme poverty, malnutrition, illiteracy, environmental degradation, crime, drug-trafficking, and state-sponsored repression and intimidation. Members of each of the Dialogue's national chapters collaborate to design and promote nonmilitary solutions to their countries' specific problems.

MIDDLE EAST
Americans and Palestinians
for Peace
See under North America.

Gush Shalom
P.O. Box 3322
Tel Aviv 61033
Israel
Phone: 03 5565804
Fax: 03 5271108
Email: info@gush-shalom.org
Web site: www.gush-shalom.org

Gush Shalom (The Peace Bloc) is a nonpartisan and extraparliamentary grassroots movement whose aim is to influence public opinion and advocate peace in the Middle East.

Contributors

Andrea Bartoli is founding director of the International Conflict Resolution Program at Columbia University and vice-president of the lay Catholic Community of Sant'Egidio based in Rome (which played an instrumental role in the peace process in Mozambique). Professor Bartoli also chairs the Columbia University Seminar on Conflict Resolution and the Role of Religion and is associate director of the Italian Academy for Advanced Studies in America. As a vice-president of the Community of Sant'Egidio, Dr. Bartoli has been actively involved in conflict resolution and preventive diplomacy since the early 1980s. He has authored or coedited several books, including *Somalia, Rwanda, and Beyond: The Role of the International Media Wars and Humanitarian Crises* (New York: Crosslines, 1995), *Conflict Resolution and the Role of Religions* (forthcoming); and *Migrations and Multiculturalism: Africa, Europe and the Americas* (forthcoming).

Olga Botcharova is an adjunct and visiting fellow with the Preventive Diplomacy and Conflict Resolution Program, Center for Strategic and International Studies (CSIS), Washington, D.C. She is a conflict resolution expert who has designed and conducted numerous workshops on conflict resolution and reconciliation (community, ethnic, interpersonal, family), conflict management (organization/ workplace) and cross-cultural communications, working with over eighteen countries and having focused for a number of years on Bosnia, Serbia, and Croatia. Fluent in Russian, Serbo-Croatian, and French as well as English, she has also served as a consultant and facilitator in cross-cultural communications for the International Action Commission for St. Petersburg cochaired by Dr.

H. Kissinger and Mayor Sobchak. Published widely in the field, Olga Botcharova holds degrees in liberal arts and social psychology from universities in St. Petersburg, Russia.

Audrey R. Chapman serves as the director of the Science and Human Rights Program of the American Association for the Advancement of Science (AAAS) and directs the AAAS Program of Dialogue Between Science and Religion. She received a Ph.D. in public law and government from Columbia University and graduate degrees in theology and ethics from New York Theological Seminary and Union Theological Seminary. Ordained by the United Church of Christ, Dr. Chapman has been on the faculty of Barnard College, the University of Ghana, and the University of Nairobi. She served as a consultant for the Ford Foundation in Lebanon and Kenya and as an advisor in social statistics for the Kenya Central Bureau of Statistics. She is the author, coauthor, or editor of numerous books and articles related to human rights and religious ethics, including *Unprecedented Choices: Religious Ethics on the Frontiers of Genetic Science* (Minneapolis: Fortress Press, 1999), *Consumption, Population, and Sustainability: Perspectives from Science and Religion* (Washington, D.C.: Island Press, 1999), and *Perspectives on Gene Patenting: Science, Religion, Industry, and Law in Dialogue* (AAAS, 1999). She is currently working on a book assessing the ability of the South African Truth and Reconciliation Commission to balance truth-finding with forgiveness, and reconciliation.

John Dawson is founder and director of the International Reconciliation Coalition, USA. A native of New Zealand, Dawson lives with his wife and family in Southern California, working as international director of Urban Missions for Youth with a Mission (YWAM). The International Reconciliation Coalition is an organization dedicated to healing wounds between people groups and elements of society. He is the author of such highly acclaimed books as *Taking Our Cities for God: How to Break Spiritual Strongholds* (Altamonte Springs, Fla.: Creation House, 1990) and *Healing America's Wounds* (Ventura, Calif.: Regal Books, 1994), and more recently has written a booklet entitled *What Christians Should Know about Reconciliation* (Ventura, Calif.: Gospel Light, 1998).

George F. R. Ellis is professor of applied mathematics at the University of Cape Town, South Africa, working on relativity theory and cosmology. After completing a Ph.D. at the University of Cape Town, he studied at Cambridge University, where he coauthored the book *The Large Scale Structure of Space-Time*

(Cambridge: Cambridge University Press, 1975) with Stephen Hawking, and has written over 200 technical papers and a number of books in the area. He has been visiting professor at universities in the United States, Canada, Germany, Italy, and the United Kingdom. He is past president of the International Society of General Relativity and Gravitation, and of the Royal Society of South Africa; in the latter capacity, he was an adviser to the new government on the development of South Africa's new science policy. As a Quaker, Ellis has been involved in developmental and peace projects in South Africa, including being chairman of the Quaker Service Fund and of the Quaker Peace Centre. He has also been actively involved in the science-religion debate, in particular taking part in the Vatican Observatory/CTNS (Centre for Theology and the Natural Sciences) systematic series of meetings on this issue. He is coauthor with Nancey Murphy of the book *On the Moral Nature of the Universe: Cosmology, Theology, and Ethics* (Minneapolis: Fortress Press, 1996). Ellis is the recipient of various prizes and honorary degrees, and was awarded the Star of South Africa medal by President Nelson Mandela in 1999.

Stanley S. Harakas taught Orthodox Christian Ethics for twenty-nine years at Holy Cross Greek Orthodox School of Theology, Brookline, Massachusetts, retiring in 1995. He served as acting dean and dean of Hellenic College (1969-75) and dean of Holy Cross School of Theology (1970-80) and has been active in the ecumenical movement, having given a plenary address at the World Council of Churches Assembly in Canberra. Rev. Dr. Harakas has authored twelve books, the most recent, *Wholeness of Faith and Life: Orthodox Christian Ethics* (Holy Cross Orthodox Press, 1999) in three volumes: 1, *Patristic Ethics*; 2, *Church Life Ethics*; and 3, *Orthodox Social Ethics*. In 1986 he was the inaugural appointee to the Archbishop Iakovos Endowed Professorship of Orthodox Theology. He continues to write and publish and assists Tampa Bay, Florida, parishes as supply priest, preacher and lecturer.

Raymond G. Helmick, S.J., teaches conflict resolution in the Department of Theology at Boston College. He has mediated over the years in a number of conflicts: Northern Ireland, the Israelis and Palestinians, Lebanese, Kurdish conflicts in Iraq and Turkey, East Timor, the liberation of Zimbabwe, the countries of the former Yugoslavia, and so on. Founding member and executive board member of the U.S. Interreligious Committee for Peace in the Middle East, he is also a senior associate of the Center for Strategic and International Studies. In addition to his numerous monographs and articles, Helmick is coproducer of the video documentary "Unexpected Openings: Northern Ireland Prisoners," and has been actively engaged as coproducer of a series of films on religion and conflict resolution.

Donna Hicks is the deputy director of the Program on International Conflict Analysis and Resolution (PICAR) at the Center for International Affairs, Harvard University. PICAR is devoted to advancing the understanding of international and interethnic conflicts, and to developing interactive, problem-solving processes that can be effective in managing or resolving such conflicts. Dr. Hicks has been involved in numerous unofficial diplomatic conflict resolution efforts including projects in the Middle East, Sri Lanka, Colombia, and Cuba. Her research interests focus generally on issues of reconciliation and specifically on examining ways in which the conflict resolution, international development, and human rights communities can work together to develop an integrated approach to sustainable conflict transformation. In addition to teaching conflict resolution at Harvard and Clark Universities, Dr. Hicks conducts training seminars in the PICAR methodology in the United States and abroad.

Douglas M. Johnston Jr., has served in a number of senior positions in the public and private sectors, including deputy assistant secretary of the Navy and director of policy planning and management in the Office of the Secretary of Defense. He taught courses in international affairs at Harvard and was the founder and first director of the university's Executive Program in National and International Security. A veteran of the Navy's nuclear submarine service, Johnston chairs the center's programs on maritime studies and preventive diplomacy. He is the editor and principal author of *Religion: The Missing Dimension of Statecraft* (New York: Oxford University Press, 1994) and *Foreign Policy into the 21st Century: The U.S. Leadership Challenge* (Washington, D.C.: CSIS, 1996). Johnston is a distinguished graduate of the U.S. Navel Academy and holds an M.A. in public administration and a Ph.D. in political science from Harvard University.

John Paul Lederach, a professor in the Conflict Transformation Program, Eastern Mennonite University, has served as director of International Conciliation Services for the Mennonite Central Committee, and continues as a consultant for MCC's work in international conciliation. He has done training in conflict resolution and worked at mediating conflicts around the world, including Nicaragua, Somalia, the Philippines, and Northern Ireland. Among his recent publications are *Preparing for Peace: Conflict Transformation Across Cultures* and *Building Peace: Sustainable Reconciliation in Divided Societies* (Washington, D.C.: U.S. Institute of Peace Press, 1997).

Joseph V. Montville is director of the Preventive Diplomacy Program at the Center for Strategic and International Studies, Washington, D.C. A former career diplomat who served in the Middle East, North Africa, and the Department of State, Montville is also a founding member of the International Society of Political Psychology. He is author/editor of *Conflict and Peacemaking in Multiethnic Societies* (Lexington, 1990) and coeditor of *The Psychodynamics of International Relationships* (Lexington 1990 and 1991). He did his graduate work at Harvard and Columbia.

Ofelia Ortega has been the president of the Evangelical Theological Seminary in Matanzas, Cuba, since 1997. She serves as vice-president of the Cuban Council of Churches and as vice-president of CETELA (Community of the Ecumenical Theological Seminaries in Latin America and the Caribbean). Having received degrees from schools in Cuba, Switzerland, and the United States, Ortega does writing and research in the areas of ministerial formation and leadership, and on topics of popular religion in the Caribbean. She has served as professor at Union Theological Seminary, Cuba (1960-85), as director of the Ecumenical Study Center, Cuba (1968-69), and as general secretary of the Program Agency of the Presbyterian Church in Cuba (1962-85). From 1985 to 1993 she was professor at the Ecumenical Institute of the World Council of Churches, Bossey, Switzerland, and worked extensively in areas of women's studies. From 1988 to 1997 she served as director of the Program on Theological Education for Latin America and the Caribbean of the WCC. She has served in WCC in a variety of other capacities throughout her long ministry. Author of articles and books in French, German, Spanish, and English, Ortega served as coeditor of *Ministerial Formation,* and has contributed to a number of other journals and books published by the World Council of Churches. She edited *Women in Church Leadership* (1986) and wrote *Confessing Jesus Christ in Dialogue* (1986).

Laurie Anne Pearlman is a clinical psychologist, research director of the Traumatic Stress Institute/Center for Adult and Adolescent Psychotherapy LLC, and president of Trauma Research, Education, and Training Institute, Inc., in South Windsor, Connecticut. She is currently chair of the public education committee of the International Society for Traumatic Stress Studies and a member of its board of directors. Dr. Pearlman has authored and coauthored numerous books and papers on psychological trauma and vicarious traumatization. She has received awards for clinical excellence and for distinguished contributions to the science and the practice of psychology. She has taught therapists and other trauma workers around the globe and is an internationally known teacher and dynamic speaker.

Rodney L. Petersen is executive director of the Boston Theological Institute (BTI), the consortium of Orthodox, Roman Catholic, and Protestant theological schools, in the Greater Boston area. He teaches in areas of history and ethics, currently focusing on issues of religion and violence. Together with Professor Helmick, their courses in Comparative Christianity take students to various regions of the world in order to understand and film ways in which faith communities are implicated in regional violence and how they can be avenues of reconciliation. An ordained minister in the Presbyterian Church, USA, Dr. Petersen has taught at the Trinity Evangelical Divinity School (Illinois), Webster University (Switzerland), and for the Fédération des Institutions ètablies à Genève (FIIG). A graduate of Harvard University and Princeton Theological Seminary, Dr. Petersen did further work at the University of Geneva and at the World Council of Churches. He is author or editor and contributor of several articles and scholarly works, including the books, *Preaching in the Last Days* (New York: Oxford University Press, 1993); *Christianity and Civil Society: Theological Education for Public Life* (Maryknoll, N.Y.: Orbis, 1995); *Consumption, Population, and Sustainability* (Washington, D.C.: Island Press, 2000), and *Earth at Risk*: An Environmental Dialogue between Science and Religion (New York: Prometheus Press, 2000).

Donald W. Shriver Jr., a graduate of Davidson College, Union Theological Seminary-Virginia, Yale Divinity School, and Harvard University, is an ordained Presbyterian minister and has held teaching positions at North Carolina State University, Emory University, and Union Theological Seminary in New York. At Union he was president of the faculty (1975–91) and William E. Dodge Professor of Practical Christianity (1975-96). He is author of twelve books, the most recent of which is *An Ethic for Enemies: Forgiveness in Politics* (New York: Oxford University Press, 1997). He has traveled in fifty-five countries, is a member of the Council on Foreign Relations, and was president of the Society of Christian Ethics in 1980.

Anthony da Silva, S.J., is associate professor of social psychology at Jnana Deepa Vidyapeeth, Pontifical Institute of Philosophy and Religion, Pune, India. He is a Jesuit priest and holds a doctorate in personality and social psychology from the University of Michigan and other degrees in philosophy and theology. He has been teaching for several years in Pune and has focused his research on the interreligious conflict between Hindus, Moslems, and Christians in India. He also teaches courses on the psychology of religion, and the social psychology of prejudice and conflict. He was rector and president of the Pune Institute from 1993 to 1999. He is also a visiting lecturer at the State run University of Pune. He is now involved in the forgiveness and reconciliation research literature and intends to relate it to indigenous traditions and conflicts in India.

Geraldine Smyth, O.P., is from Belfast and a Dominican theologian and ecumenist. With a background in education and psychotherapy, she is currently prioress of her Dominican congregation, and senior lecturer at the Irish School of Ecumenics where she completed her term as director in 1999. Dr. Smyth holds a Ph.D. from Trinity College, Dublin, and is the author of *A Way of Transformation: A Theological Evaluation of the Conciliar Process of Mutual Commitment to Justice, Peace and the Integrity of Creation, WCC, 1983-1991* (Peter Lang, 1995). She is committed to doing theology at the crossroads where encounters with politics, philosophy, literature, and social theory make it particularly significant and lively. She contributes to conferences nationally and internationally on ecumenical topics and on issues where theology, peace, gender psychology, and ecology come into play.

Ervin Staub is professor of psychology at the University of Massachusetts at Amherst. Dr. Staub has studied the origins of altruism, as well as of genocide and mass killing, published as *The Roots of Evil: The Origins of Genocide and Other Group Violence* (New York: Cambridge University Press, 1992) and their prevention. He has been conducting a project, together with Dr. Laurie Pearlman, on "Healing, Forgiveness, and Reconciliation in Rwanda," supported by the John Templeton Foundation.

Miroslav Volf is the Henry B. Wright Professor of Theology, Yale Divinity School. Educated at Fuller Theological Seminary and the University of Tübingen, Germany, Dr. Volf spent the 1998-99 academic year as a Pew Fellow at the Center for Theological Inquiry. An internationally recognized human rights advocate, Volf has been an outspoken advocate for peace in the Serbian-Croatian conflict.

He has worked extensively in nineteenth- and twentieth-century European theology and philosophy, as well as seventeenth- and eighteenth-century Protestantism, patristics, contemporary Eastern Orthodoxy, and evangelicalism. His books in English include *Exclusion and Embrace: a Theological Exploration of Identity, Otherness and Reconciliation* (Nashville: Abingdon, 1996). With his wife, Judith Gundry Volf, he wrote *A Spacious Heart: Essays on Identity and Belonging* (Valley Forge, Pa.: Trinity Press International, 1997) He is currently working on another book entitled *Western Values—Public Theology*. A pastor for several years in his Croatian homeland, Professor Volf served on the Evangelical Theological Faculty in Osijek, Croatia, and on the faculty of Fuller Theological Seminary in Pasadena, California.

Everett L. Worthington Jr., is professor and chair of psychology at Virginia Commonwealth University. He directs the nonprofit organization, A Campaign for Forgiveness Research. Dr. Worthington conducts basic research in unforgiveness, forgiveness, and reconciliation and applied research on the Pyramid Model to REACH Forgiveness, a five-step psychoeducational and psychotherapeutic intervention to help people forgive. He also conducts intervention research on a nine-hour couple-enrichment program entitled FREE (Forgiveness and Reconciliation through Experiencing Empathy). Author of numerous monographs and articles, Dr. Worthington has written and edited books on forgiveness, including *Dimensions of Forgiveness: Psychological Research and Theological Speculations* (Philadelphia: Templeton Foundation Press, 1998), and with M. E. McCullough and S. J. Sandage, *To Forgive Is Human: How to Put Your Past in the Past* (InterVarsity Press, 1997). See the website for the forgiveness campaign at *http://www.forgiveandreconcile.org/*.

Index